Kant and the Feeling of Life

SUNY series in Contemporary Continental Philosophy

Dennis J. Schmidt, editor

Kant and the Feeling of Life

Beauty and Nature in the *Critique of Judgment*

Edited and with an introduction by

JENNIFER MENSCH

Published by State University of New York Press, Albany

Printed in the United States of America

For information, contact State University of New York Press, Albany, NY
www.sunypress.edu

Library of Congress Cataloging-in-Publication Data

Name: Mensch, Jennifer, editor.
Title: Kant and the feeling of life : beauty and nature in the Critique of judgment / Jennifer Mensch.
Description: Albany : State University of New York Press, [2024] | Series: SUNY series in contemporary continental philosophy | Includes bibliographical references and index.
Identifiers: LCCN 2023055142 | ISBN 9781438498638 (hardcover : alk. paper) | ISBN 9781438498652 (ebook)
Subjects: LCSH: Kant, Immanuel, 1724–1804. Kritik der Urteilskraft. | Life. | Judgment (Aesthetics) | Philosophy of nature.
Classification: LCC B2784 .K35 2024 | DDC 121—dc23/eng/20240506
LC record available at https://lccn.loc.gov/2023055142

Dedicated to Rudolf Makkreel (1939–2021),
scholar, teacher, mentor, and friend

Contents

Acknowledgments ix

Preface xi

Introduction: *Lebensgefühl* and *Geistesgefühl* in Kant's *Critique of Judgment* 1
Jennifer Mensch

1. From the Beginning: Kant on the Feeling of Life Itself 19
Dennis J. Schmidt

2. The Furtherance of Life as the Bridge between Nature and Freedom in Kant's Critical Philosophy 41
James Risser

3. Pure Aesthetic Judging as a Form of Life 57
Courtney D. Fugate

4. The Aesthetic Perfection of Life in Baumgarten, Meier, and Kant 83
J. Colin McQuillan

5. The Ideal of Beauty and the Meaning of "Life" in Kant's Philosophy 107
Kristi Sweet

6. The Momentary Inhibition and Outpouring of the Vital Powers: Kant on the Dynamic Sublime 129
Rachel Zuckert

7. Imagination, Life, and Self-Consciousness in the Kantian Sublime 153
Robert R. Clewis

8. A Matter of Life and Death, or The Anthropological Deduction of the Sublime 179
Dilek Huseyinzadegan

9. On the *Sensus Communis* as a Feeling of Life 197
Rodolphe Gasché

10. Kant, the Feeling of Life, and the Reflective Comprehension of Teleological Purposiveness 215
Rudolf A. Makkreel

11. Organizing the State: Mechanism and Organism in Kant's Political Writings of the 1780s and 1790s 239
Susan Meld Shell

12. Kant on the Feeling of Health 271
Michael J. Olson

13. Kant and Organic Life 293
Joan Steigerwald

14. Personality: The Life of the Finite, Moral-Rational Being 319
G. Felicitas Munzel

List of Contributors 343

Works by Kant 349

Bibliography 357

Index 373

Acknowledgments

This book took many years to come together, and I want to thank the contributors for their patience, good humor, and continued support for the volume despite the various interruptions and delays encountered along the way. This work would also not be in the shape it is without the research support I have had from Antje Kühnast. Antje's enthusiasm for bibliographic niceties, her tenacity in tracking down errant references, and her good-natured intelligence and wit did much to keep the project moving over the years, and I will be forever grateful to her for this steady support. Finally, I want to acknowledge the financing provided by the Australian Research Council for research assistance, Discovery Project DP190103769 (2019–2024).

Preface

The idea for this volume grew out of conversations with Rudolf Makkreel in 2016. Rudi Makkreel was a meticulous and original scholar and philosopher, as well as a devoted teacher and mentor, who did much to call attention to the radicality and reach of Kant's *Critique of Judgment*. As this volume came together, Makkreel's presence and importance for the topic was undeniable; a number of the contributors to this volume were Rudi's students, friends, and colleagues, and all of us knew him through professional circles as well. He was especially delighted by the idea of the volume's focus on the concept of life, having devoted a chapter to the issue in his book *Imagination and Interpretation in Kant: The Hermeneutical Import of the "Critique of Judgment"* (1990). This volume demonstrates that his insights have contributed to many of the most compelling interpretations of Kant's third *Critique*, and this is felt throughout the text.

Sadly, Rudolf Makkreel passed away after a relatively brief illness in the fall of 2021, and I am sorry that he missed not just this book's publication, but that of his own book as well, *Kant's Worldview: How Judgment Shapes Human Contribution* (2021). The North American Kant Society hosted a memorial session to him in 2022 and, as it was a virtual event, many of us were able to speak for a few minutes, sharing favorite memories and our gratitude toward him as a mentor and friend. Rudolf Makkreel is perhaps best known as a Dilthey scholar, having translated and edited, with Frithjof Rodi, Wilhelm Dilthey's selected works for an English-speaking audience. He was, however, broadly interested in hermeneutics and taught and published on each of the major figures associated with that tradition. It was in this way that Makkreel had a foot also in continental philosophy discussions, and a memorial session was held in honor of him at the meeting of the Society for Phenomenology and Existential Philosophy in 2022. People who knew Rudi appreciated his patience and generosity of spirit, the twinkle in his eyes at a good story or funny joke, his sweet tooth, and his love of Renée Fleming and the transporting beauty of her voice. We will miss him, and this volume is dedicated to him on behalf of all his students and friends.

Introduction

Lebensgefühl and *Geistesgefühl* in Kant's *Critique of Judgment*

Jennifer Mensch

It might come as something of a surprise for today's readers to learn that of the three critical investigations undertaken by Immanuel Kant during the 1780s it was the *Critique of Judgment* that would have the broadest readership and the largest impact in Kant's own lifetime. Virtually all of the leading lights of German idealism and Romanticism—Schelling, Schiller, Schlegel, Hölderlin, and Hegel, to name but a few—found inspiration in Kant's account of the power of judgment. Kant's earlier investigation into the extent and limits of knowledge in his *Critique of Pure Reason* had, by contrast, left many readers cold. As Goethe famously put his response to it: "I found pleasure in the portal, but I dared not set foot in the labyrinth itself; sometimes my gift for poetry got in my way, sometimes common sense."[1] And as for Kant's subsequent effort to think through the transcendental grounds for moral action, this too left many unconvinced. In the *Critique of Practical Reason*, Kant had to convince readers that while we would never be able to sensibly discover freedom amid the mechanical workings of everyday life, we still needed to understand the force of its power for directing human choice. G. W. F. Hegel was particularly cool to Kant's account, asking how an experience drained of positive content in

1. Johann Wolfgang von Goethe, "The Influence of Modern Philosophy," in *Goethe: Scientific Studies*, ed. and trans. Douglas Miller (New York: Suhrkamp, 1988), 28–30, 29.

this way might still encourage moral behavior. For, in Hegel's view, "this contradiction, which remains insuperable in the system and destroys it, becomes a real inconsistency when this absolute emptiness is supposed to give itself content as practical reason and to expand itself in the form of duties. Theoretical reason lets the intellect give it the manifold which it has only to regulate; it makes no claim to an autonomous dignity, no claim to beget the Son out of itself."[2]

The third of Kant's *Critiques* felt different, however, for this generation of readers. Yes, Kant's arguments contained the familiar caveats regarding epistemic caution, the need to position claims as speculative, heuristic, orientational tools employed by reflective judgment. But again and again Kant took his readers to the edge of something else, either by relying on hybrid terms like "aesthetic ideas" in order to explain cognitions that were otherwise inscrutable, or by pointing past experience and to indeed the supersensible when it came to understanding the work of genius, the order and unity of nature, or indeed the principles that seemed to be guiding organic life itself. Goethe, for one, described this book as "opening up a wonderful period"[3] in his life, even as he complained about Kant's various caveats, declaring that Kant "had a roguishly ironic way of working: at times he seemed determined to put the narrowest limits on our ability to know things, and at times, with a casual gesture, he pointed beyond the limits he himself had set . . . leaving it to us to decide how to enjoy the freedom he allows us."[4] And Hölderlin, largely in response to his reading of the *Critique of Judgment*, went so far as to call Kant "the Moses of our nation."[5]

But if the *Critique of Judgment* enjoyed the sort of immediate embrace denied to the earlier works, readers have nonetheless struggled since its first appearance to understand Kant's method for organizing the book itself. Even a casual glance reveals Kant to have been at pains to model the structure of the text on the two earlier *Critiques*. Difficulties show up immediately, however, upon closer examination. One of the central puzzles here concerns the connection between the two halves of Kant's book, between Kant's "Cri-

2. Georg Wilhelm Friedrich Hegel, *Faith and Knowledge*, trans. and ed. Walter Cerf and H. S. Harris (Albany: State University of New York Press, 1977), 81.

3. Goethe, "Influence of Modern Philosophy," 29.

4. Goethe, "Influence of Modern Philosophy," 31.

5. Friedrich Hölderlin, "An den Bruder, Homburg, 31 Dezember 1798," in *Sämtliche Werke und Briefe in drei Bänden* (Munich: Hauser Verlag, 1992), 2:723–730, 726.

tique of Aesthetic Judgment" in part 1, and his "Critique of Teleological Judgment" in part 2. For a number of Kant's readers, the best approach to the problem has been to look for a throughline. Ernst Cassirer, for example, believed that the theme best connecting the two halves of Kant's *Critique of Judgment* was that of "life," since, as Cassirer understood the basis of Kant's analysis, aesthetic intuition allows us to discover those "formative forces on which the possibility of the beautiful and the possibility of life equally rest,"[6] with the concept of "life" joining, therefore, Kant's major analyses of aesthetic and teleological judgment. Rudolf Makkreel developed Cassirer's insight at length, arguing that "the idea of life pervades the entire structure of the *Critique of Judgment*," given that, for Kant, "life is not a mere biological phenomenon to be set apart from spirit. In conceiving life, Kant does not think in terms of a dualism; organic life and the life of the mind constitute a continuum allowing a scale of positive and negative values."[7] Angelica Nuzzo is similarly disposed to seeing life as a bridge concept. In her words, "the idea of life and the relation that our embodied *Lebensgefühl* entertains with the reflective faculty of judgment is the leading idea of Kant's inquiry in both the critique of aesthetic and the critique of teleological judgment."[8]

Despite this sense of the basic importance of the concept of "life" for Kant, the many ways in which Kant makes use of it remain significantly understudied as an area of sustained investigation. The purpose of this collection is thus to highlight the ways in which "life" functions, not only as a concept running throughout Kant's works, but insofar as it serves as a connecting thread across Kant's discussions of beauty and nature in the *Critique of Judgment.* One of the clearest examples of life as a concept uniting Kant's discussions of nature and art can be found in his account of "genius." Kant develops his position on this in stages, circling back a number of times to pick up an earlier point once other parts of his analysis have fallen into place. What emerges is not just a portrait of the genius at work, but attention to the products of such talent, and the impact these have on us in our encounter with fine art. By the end of Kant's book, the parallel between the account here and Kant's later description of organic nature feels

6. Ernst Cassirer, *Kant's Life and Thought*, trans. James Hayden (New Haven, CT: Yale University Press, 1981), 279.

7. Rudolf A. Makkreel, *Imagination and Interpretation in Kant: The Hermeneutical Import of the "Critique of Judgment"* (Chicago: University of Chicago Press, 1990), 103.

8. Angelica Nuzzo, *Ideal Embodiment: Kant's Theory of Sensibility* (Bloomington: Indiana University Press, 2008), 285.

inevitable. Our compulsion to see a divine intelligence at work in nature's apparent unity and purpose, our amazement at the way in which organisms are somehow both animated and organized in a way that is purposive yet free, these experiences have already been introduced to Kant's readers in his initial discussion of our encounter with the types of fine art that can only be produced by genius.

The genius displays the type of native talent, according to Kant, that can be neither learned nor taught to others. It is indeed this kind of sui generis aspect of the genius that distinguishes the originality of a Goethe from even the learned brilliance of a scientific mind like Newton's. This sort of exemplary, rare capacity identifies a genius as nature's favorite (§49),[9] even as the genius remains themself capable of explaining neither the specific means by which they achieve perfection in their own work nor how they might train others to yield a similar perfection in their own artistic productions. Kant maintains that a beautiful work of fine art is judged to be so for its perfect synthesis of freedom and material form—that is, of the supersensible and the sensible realms—on the one hand, and its effect on the viewer, on the other, insofar as the work yields an experience that cannot be wholly grasped by way of determinate perception. As in the case presented by a natural organism, therefore, the work of fine art hides the specific means, the "rules" by which the artwork has been created by the genius in the first place (§45). When we look at an organism, the manner by which it is "ruled" by the form of its species is hidden from our view; when we encounter a work of fine art, like a poem, for example, it is its constraint according to the rules of prosody and meter that remains unseen. Kant is clear when it comes to the importance of these rules for the material construction of the work of art, for it is by these means that the artist is able to transform what would otherwise be the lawless freedom of their genius, into a work that has at last been perfected by means of law and judged thereby according to the rules of taste (§48). It is in this sense, Kant explains, that taste clips the wings of genius (§50). But just as the genius remains at a loss as to how they have managed, from out of

9. Unless otherwise noted, all citations are to paragraph number of Kant's *Critique of Judgment*, followed by volume and page number of the Akademie Ausgabe of Kant's works, namely, Immanuel Kant, *Gesammelte Schriften* (Berlin: de Gruyter, 1901–). (Subsequently cited page references to Kant's works are also to volume and page number of this edition.) Unless otherwise indicated, quoted translations are from Kant's *Critique of Judgment*, trans. Werner Pluhar (Indianapolis: Hackett, 1987).

their own nature, to produce a work of fine art that is wholly perfect in its joining together spirit and law, so too is the subject in their encounter with the works produced by genius.

As Kant describes it, the pleasure we feel in our experience of fine art is a response to the way in which our cognition is thrown into a state of play in the encounter. Unable to reduce a piece of fine art to some kind of conceptual determination of it, our imagination breaks free of its usual role in relationship to understanding. In this moment, as Cassirer puts it, "the imagination is in possession of its own autonomous realm into which no conceptual demand and no moral imperative may intrude."[10] An artwork that has spirit is able to animate the mind of the person who encounters it, Kant tells us, quickening their own spirit into a kind of cognitive free play. In this aesthetic encounter with freedom in the work of art, the imagination is led to produce its own counterpart to the rational ideas of God or immortality that have been produced by reason; in this case, however, the idea is aesthetic. As Kant understands it, our encounter with a work of fine art causes the imagination to produce a multitude of kindred presentations, presentations overflowing the imagination's attempt to pin down its experience conceptually. The result of this is the imagination's exhibition of an "aesthetic idea," Kant explains, "a presentation that makes us add to a concept much that is ineffable, but the feeling of which quickens our cognitive powers" (§49, 5:316).[11] And the fine art with the greatest capacity to affect us in this way, Kant argues, is poetry.

In poetry, language becomes more than letters, it is infused by the spirit of its creator, since "it owes its origin almost entirely to genius and is least open to guidance by precept or examples." Because, moreover, poetry "fortifies the mind," giving the mind a sense of its own nature as "free, spontaneous, and independent of natural determination," poetry, as Kant sees it, "lets the mind feel its ability to use nature on behalf of and, as it were, as a schema of the supersensible" (§53, 5:326). What is this like? Hans Georg Gadamer describes it as the moment when the artwork comes forth. "One reads a poem," he explains, "one reads it again. One goes through it, and it goes

10. Cassirer, *Kant's Life and Thought*, 324.

11. While not focused on the role played by genius in particular, John Zammito does tease out the link he sees between Kant's appeal to *Geist* in section 49, and his later discussion of the feeling of moral respect captured by one's *Geistesgefühl* in section 54. See John Zammito, *The Genesis of Kant's Critique of Judgment* (Chicago: University of Chicago Press, 1992), 292–305.

along with one. It is as if it began to sing, and one sings along with it."[12] Only a genius could produce a poem like this. It is, moreover, in this way that our encounter with the work of art is at the same time an enlivening event, a feeling of spirit and thus of the furtherance of life itself for Kant.

As the investigations in this collection will aim to make clear, Kant's appeal to the "feeling of life" and its various relata so far as the mind experiences them—animation, enlivening, and quickening—provide us with an exemplary guideline for understanding not just one of the organizing principles within the *Critique of Judgment* itself, but indeed of the overall significance of freedom for Kant when it comes to our experience of the world we encounter every day.

The opening chapter provides a broad overview of Kant's project in the third *Critique* with attention paid along the way to its influence on Kant's immediate successors in the German idealist and Romantic traditions and on mid-century continental philosophers. Focusing initially on the tight connection between life, playfulness, and freedom, Dennis Schmidt teases out the manner in which "the feeling of life is what thinking feels when thinking is aware of itself" insofar as "the mind for itself," as Kant puts it, "is solely, wholly life (the principle of life itself)" (§29, 5:278). After this, the discussion takes up Kant's appeal to the vocabularies of birth and gestation (*beleben, Belebung*), the importance of the symbol and its "hypotyposis" for understanding Kant's approach to life, and, finally, the best way to approach Kant's effort to connect beauty and the good. As Schmidt explains, "What binds us to the good is this intensification of life and it is this bond and its reflexive fold back into the consciousness of one's own existence, rather than any knowledge—either practical or theoretical—that exposes a sense of what Kant called a 'moral feeling [which] is something merely subjective and which yields no knowledge' " (*Metaphysics of Morals*, 6:400).

In chapter 2, James Risser offers a separate overview, this time from the point of view of Kant's own account of it in the two "Introductions" written for the third *Critique*. In the "Introductions," Kant foregrounds the architectonic connection between this last *Critique of Judgment* and the two earlier investigations devoted first to the extent and limits of human knowl-

12. Hans Georg Gadamer, "Artworks in Word and Image," *Theory, Culture and Society* 23, no. 1 (1992): 57–83, 75. For some further discussion of Gadamer's account of this see Jennifer Mensch, "The Poem as Plant: Archetype and Metamorphosis in Goethe and Schlegel," *International Yearbook for Hermeneutics* 13 (2014): 85–106.

edge, the *Critique of Pure Reason* (1781), and second to the transcendental basis for moral decision making and action, in the *Critique of Practical Reason* (1788). Accordingly, much of the discussion there is focused on accounting for the systematic unity of reason's collective activities, and, in particular, on understanding the most difficult task faced by reason in all three of the *Critiques*, namely, the bridge between a transcendentally free subject and its experience of a world constrained in every case by the laws of mechanical determinism. The key to understanding the possibility of a bridge between the two realms as "something more than wishful thinking," according to Risser, is seeing how the concept of life is mobilized by Kant in two ways. In Kant's account of aesthetic judgment, it is the "free play" and "quickening" of the mind in its experience of beauty (or via catharsis in our experience of the sublime) that explains the bridge between empirical experience and a sense of our transcendence from it. In the discussion of teleological judgment, we approach nature by way of analogy, projecting this sense of our own freedom from mechanical determination onto nature. This analogy orients us, allowing us to reflectively entertain the possibility of not just nature's underlying unity and purpose—that is, of our experience of organic life as itself transcendentally free, or as somehow "both cause and effect of itself" (§65, 5:372), as Kant puts it—but indeed to discern the existence of a moral teleology or guideline for understanding the history of humankind's freedom itself.

Courtney Fugate opens his discussion with something of a puzzle for his readers: given that the third *Critique* is best-known in part for its wide-ranging discussion of our approach to nature—to its organisms, its apparent unity, order, purpose—alongside Kant's response to appeals made in the life sciences to "hylozoism," "vitalism," and even a "*Bildungstrieb*," surely here is where we will find a robust account of the concept of "life" as Kant understands it. And yet, as Fugate notes, for Kant's most striking and original uses of the concept we might need to look beyond the *Critique of Judgment* to Kant's other works, including his own handwritten notes and lecture transcripts, precisely in order to see where the stakes for the concept's appearance in the third *Critique* actually lie. In order to orient the discussion more properly toward a sense of Kant's "creative adaptation and resuscitation of a traditional concept," the chapter opens with a brief but clear overview of the way philosophers before Kant have made room for it in their own metaphysical systems. In this part of the discussion, Fugate focuses on the traditional way that life has been connected by philosophers to the soul as an animating principle at work as much in plants as in animals, with a key shift in this approach appearing only after Thomas Aquinas. In Kant's case, it seems clear that Christian August Crusius was an important influence, and Fugate's detailed analysis is especially interesting, suggesting room for further investigation. As he summarizes Crusius's position, "when we communicate, we do not simply influence the mind of another; we rather cause them to literally come alive in a certain specific way, a way that should correspond to what it means to think a certain idea or to have a certain feeling of the kind we intend to communicate." In the remainder of his discussion, Fugate patiently takes the reader through Kant's notes and reflections, including comments he is recorded to have said in his lectures on the concept, before turning to Kant's discussion of the "form of life" that emerges in the process of aesthetic judgment. Much as the autonomous moral agent is said by Kant to be both author of and subject to the moral law (*Groundwork of the Metaphysics of Morals*, 4:431) or the organism suggests an analogy whereby it might be somehow "both cause and effect of itself," when the mind is engaged in a judgment of taste, Fugate argues, we recognize another kind of reciprocity wherein taste is serving both as object and as law to itself (e.g., §36, 5:288). In what sense? As Fugate explains, "taste makes its claims only on other judgments of taste made by other subjects, subjects who *claim* to have the very same basis for making the reciprocal demand on our own judgments of taste. In other words, we share this form of life by mutual participation in a normative practice that is intrinsically self-regulating and autonomous."

In chapter 4, J. Colin McQuillan provides more connections for readers interested in understanding Kant's sources and influences when it comes to the concept of life. In McQuillan's reconstruction, Kant's appeal to a "feeling of life" and employment of a "quickening" (*eine Belebung*) to describe the state of the cognitive faculties engaged in aesthetic judgment emerge, in fact, out of Kant's critique of Alexander Baumgarten and Georg Friedrich Meier's aesthetics. In Baumgarten's formulation, the science of aesthetics was engaged just as much in the perfection of sensible cognition as the scientific pursuit of the truth led to the perfection of intellectual cognition. Key to understanding Baumgarten's aesthetics, however, was the role played by "liveliness," and this was especially prominent in his analysis of poetic art. Much of Baumgarten's work on aesthetics can be said to have received its fullest portrait in the work of his student Meier, whose *Foundations of All Beautiful Sciences* offered a systematic account of aesthetics, including a comprehensive discussion of the aesthetic perfection of life. Meier describes the "sensible life of thoughts"[13] in terms of their connection to the faculty of desire: when living cognition is distinct, it moves the will as the higher faculty of desire; when cognitions are indistinct, by contrast, then feelings of pleasure and pain are aroused insofar as these are linked to the lower faculty of desire. McQuillan describes Kant's response to such accounts as a mixture of hostility and debt. While Kant's rejection of the clarity-distinctness criterion for judging sensibility is well known from his inaugural dissertation (1770), the previous analyses make it also clear how much use Kant will make of his predecessors' work when it comes to conceiving the state of the mind in aesthetic judgments. Even if Kant rejected Baumgarten's tie between judgment and perfection and identified the free play imagination and the understanding as the site of mental quickening (versus the lower faculties of desire, as Meier had it), it is certainly fair to say that the framework, and especially the key notion of life, was already a key part of the discussion by the time Kant came to join the conversation.

In her contribution, Kristi Sweet is interested in convincing readers to reconsider a part of Kant's account that has been mostly ignored by his many commentators, namely, his discussion of the ideal of beauty. In section 16 of Kant's analysis of aesthetic judgment, he had distinguished between the unconstrained natural beauty of a flower (an object whose contemplation remains free from any sense of its purpose) and an object like a horse or a use-specific building, where any consideration of beauty is merely accessory or "adherent" to the object's purpose. This means, to use Kant's own example, that while we might like the embellishments provided by the tattoos on a New Zealander, such appreciation falls away once we consider the purpose of this kind of object. What sort of purpose is Kant thinking of here? Kant spends the following section trying to clarify, and this is the focus of Sweet's analysis. Humans are unique among objects in their having intrinsic purpose, meaning that when we view them as objects, we are engaged in a judgment that is both aesthetic and intellectual insofar as our rational idea of humanity's inner purpose is indeed the means by which we aesthetically judge the outer appearance of a person. When we judge someone to be beautiful, in other words, this can only be the result of a harmony having been achieved between inner purposes and outer countenance (against which decorative tattoos, for example, become

13. Georg Friedrich Meier, *Anfangsgründe aller schönen Künste und Wissenschaften* (Halle: Carl Hermann Hemmerde, 1748–1750), Abs. 7.

irrelevant for judgment). What this analysis points to above all is Kant's ongoing effort to discern freedom's appearances in the world, in this case via the embodied human being whose inner virtue and goodness animates their speech, gestures, and overall way of being.

There is a similar conceptual framework in play when discussing our sensible experience of the sublime. For just as the rational idea of moral perfection can be exhibited in its idealized form via the morally beautiful human being, our sensible experience of the sublime also rests on a rational idea, one demanding our attention and respect. As Rachel Zuckert analyses Kant's account of the dynamic sublime—the terrifying but also thrilling experience of powerful natural events like earthquakes and volcanoes—what we discover is that this experience is another vehicle by which we might make contact with our intelligible self. In our encounter with the dynamic sublime, we inhabit two standpoints, recognizing at once our dual nature as a finite embodied being and as a moral subject invulnerable to nature's power. As she puts it, "the human subject recognizes, indeed feelingly inhabits, her nature as a sensible, vulnerable, living being, and yet also the absolute break with—the 'inhibition' and redirection of—such life that comprises her nature as a practically rational being." It is an exhilarating experience, as Kant describes it, and as captured so nicely also in Rudolf Makkreel's formulation: the sublime is "felt instantaneously as a *Lebensgefühl* and judged reflectively as a *Geistesgefühl*."[14] Amid all this, Zuckert is careful to point out that culture plays a structural role in the experience of the sublime, according to Kant, since the rational idea of our moral self is not innate in some kind of Cartesian sense but rather something to be cultivated in us over time (§23, 5:245; §29, 5:264–65). "One must have articulated moral ideas to experience the full, Kantian, meaningful dynamic sublime," Zuckert explains, "because those ideas are not implicitly within or (therefore) 'revealed by' the imaginatively thrilling experience. Rather, it is only by *supplying* moral ideas to one's imaginative experience that one can find that experience morally significant."

In Chapter 7, Robert R. Clewis takes readers into the heart of the experience of the sublime as he teases apart the best way for understanding the mental processes undergirding it; a natural companion to Rachel Zuckert's investigation now that we have the broad outlines in place. Like Zuckert,

14. Rudolf A. Makkreel, "Sublimity, Genius and the Explication of Aesthetic Ideas," in *Kants Ästhetik/Kant's Aesthetics/L'esthétique de Kant*, ed. Herman Parret (Berlin: de Gruyter, 1998), 615–29, 622.

Clewis opens his discussion with reference to Edmund Burke's theory of the sublime as a precursor to Kant's own interest in it. While Kant ultimately dismisses Burke's theory for its having taken a "physiological" and "psychological" route, Clewis notes Kant's evolution on this point, given his initial willingness to tie the experience to our physiological enhancement. As Kant reportedly put it to students taking his new course on "Anthropology" in 1772, the experience of the sublime both elicits respect and borders on fear ("Anthropologie Parow," 25:388) and can thus be physiologically linked to one's sense of either the promotion or hindering of one's vitality: "Regarding the sublime, it unhinges the nerves, and causes pain when it is engaged with forcefully. Indeed, one can bring the sublime to the point of terror and breathlessness" (25:389). By the time Kant is ready to publish his thoughts on the topic, his will be a transcendental account of the conditions underlying the possibility of our experiencing the sublime at all. Here Clewis is careful to note that while Zuckert and other commentators are certainly correct in identifying the role played by our rational idea of the moral self in the process, it cannot be the case that we must be directly self-reflective for the experience to unfold. "In the experience of the sublime," he explains, "the mind achieves a kind of self-affection, as reason interacts with imagination in aesthetic play. The sensation created by this play may (or could) be observed self-consciously," but it need not be.

In her account of the dynamic sublime, Rachel Zuckert comments on the role played by one's culture when it comes to cultivating an awareness of humanity's moral vocation, on the one hand, and one's own role as a moral agent bound by the moral law in pursuit of that vocation, on the other. It is because of this background requirement, Zuckert explains, that while we might assert that all humans *should* experience the sublime (tied, as it is, to our native respect for the moral law for Kant), we cannot in practice require that everyone would in fact do so (§29, 5:265). This is the point in Kant's account where Dilek Huseyinzadegan wants to begin her own investigation. For as her analysis shows, Kant's exposition of the sublime, while meant to demonstrate what should at least in theory be a universal human capacity, relies in fact on what Huseyinzadegan identifies as an "anthropological deduction" and thus ties Kant's account much more closely to the older discussion in his *Observations on the Feeling of the Beautiful and Sublime* (1764). Kant, in her words, "is not explaining the way in which this feeling can relate to its objects a priori, which would amount to a transcendental deduction. Rather, he is showing us that the sublime is acquired through being prepared by previous experience and through reflection on one's moral purpose—which is how he defines an empirical deduction (A85/B117)." For Huseyinzadegan, this means that Kant's account of the sublime is not universal but indeed parochial, an account of how only certain people can experience it. This "corrupts the transcendental nature of the judgments of the sublime and shows that the modality of these judgments is contingency: they depend on a kind of culture that understands morality to be a function of freedom, where supersensible ideas constitute the basis of the feeling of the sublime." What does this all mean? As Dilek Huseyinzadegan sees it, it "means that cultural, ethnic, or racial judgments continue to play a central role in the formation of Kant's, and by extension, modern aesthetic theory."

In Chapter 9, Rodolphe Gasché pays close attention to the way in which "community" takes on a key role in the third *Critique*. Positioning aesthetic judgment as something that is intrinsically interwoven with others, Gasché explains that "the prefix *Bei-* in *Beistimmung*, *Beitritt*, or *Beifall* clearly emphasizes that what is demanded, or solicited, of others is to join the one who judges through assent" since "all these terms with the prefix *Bei-* imply that others are expected and asked to come together not only in approval of the judgment, but to enter into a relation with the judging subject intent on forming on this occasion a sort of community." What underlies the possibility of this demand or solicitation? For Kant, "common sense" emerges as the transcendental condition for the possibility of communicability and thus serves as the a priori basis upon which the universality of aesthetic judgments can be made, judgments that in turn provide the basis for our call to others. In Gasché's words, "Life in community with others is the horizon with respect to which a judgment of taste is uttered, and that by appealing to communal consent of others also furthers life together." Here, however, Gasché is careful to distinguish Kant's precise notion of a "sensus communis" from the "common understanding" invoked by thinkers associated with the Scottish Enlightenment. Indeed, it is telling, Gasché insists, that Kant shifts his terminology from the German *Gemeinsinn* to, first, the Latin *sensus communis* in section 40, and then to *gemeinschaftlich* (communal) in his analysis, since it reveals Kant's intentions on this point. Kant's *sensus communis* is not concerned with the senses any more than it is with the common: "It is only through a (negative) relation to others in which one occupies the place of others by stripping one's own judgment from everything private, hence from everything non-communicable and non-universalizable, that one puts oneself in the place of others. As a result of such abstraction, one's judgment demonstrates communal sense." And this communal sense, Gasché argues, is part of what makes us human.

"The sensus *communis* as an idea of life," he emphasizes, "is one of being alive mentally, of being together in spiritual fashion, the pleasure of which is the only one that suits human beings as human beings and is as such universally communicable."

Like Courtney Fugate, Rudolf Makkreel is interested in thinking about why there is much more time devoted to describing the life of the mental faculties in play during aesthetic judgment than one would expect Kant to have spent on accounting for our experience of the life all around us in the natural world. In order to answer this question, Makkreel starts with a short review of Kant's shifting notion of life across his works before taking up the difference in Kant's account of cognition between the *Critique of Pure Reason* and the *Critique of Judgment* with respect to the imagination. Focusing on the discussion of "magnitude" in the two works allows him to get to Kant's later account of the mathematically sublime. In the third *Critique*, "the displeasure of being perceptually frustrated by a great magnitude now impels our imagination to feelingly project the '*whole vocation* of the mind' (§27, 5:259)," he explains. "The ordinary sense-based and gathering mode of 'comprehension' (*Zusammenfassung*) of the imagination is replaced with a felt flash-like 'comprehension' (*Comprehension*) that opens up the supersensible potential of the life of the mind." This account of comprehension reveals its centrality for understanding Kant's ultimate approach to organic life, for according to Makkreel, reflective comprehension is the means by which we can anticipate an internal, adaptive "reciprocity" at work in nature: it "provides a source of orientation to supplement our *determinate* understanding of the mechanisms of nature with what will be shown to be an *indeterminate* reflective comprehension of organic reciprocity." What does such reciprocity entail? Here Makkreel appeals first to Kant's description of *Gegenbildung* as one of the formative functions of the imagination, since it is *Gegenbildung* that allows the imagination to generate analogies, that is, "to discern symbolic rather than literal counter-parts in different contexts." With this method we identify internal purposiveness as an adaptive and reciprocal activity at work in an organism, and we do so in a way that avoids reliance on mechanical *causality*. Pointing instead to the relational category of *community*—and responding thereby to Hannah Ginsborg's critique of Kant's seeming reliance on an argument from design—Makkreel argues that "what especially characterizes organic purposiveness for Kant is the internal purposiveness among its various organs. This involves an organizational adaptation that need not be governed by the normative oughts associated with design." Indeed, "there is something pre-fixed or static about completing a design, which goes against the self-modificatory powers of an organism." The intrinsic natural perfection of an organism (§65, 5:375), according to Kant, is thus best understood via reflective comprehension to be "a self-modifying and adaptive perfection in which different coexisting contextual forces converge and intersect."

Susan Shell's account of the state moves the discussion away from the mental grounds of our sense for communal life toward an analysis of Kant's work to reimagine the political community as a whole. Tracking Kant's emerging view, Shell is convinced that the language used by Kant when describing the organism—that is, as a system best understood to be an organized and self-organizing being—is similarly working as a model in Kant's approach to the state. There is indeed a long history of political theorists from Thomas Hobbes to Burke to Johann Gottfried Herder using organic imagery when dissecting the body politic, and Shell opens with a brief rehearsal before settling on the importance of Jean-Jacques Rousseau for Kant's own formulation, paying close attention in particular to the insights gleaned from his reading of *Émile*. In the wake of this, Shell remarks on the significance of Kant's appeal to "autonomy" in 1785's *Groundwork of the Metaphysics of Morals*, arguing that with this new concept Kant "adds a refining element to this account of the formation, misformation, and transformation (*Bildung*, *Missbildung*, and *Umbildung*) of the body politic." From here we see Kant increasingly torn between two kinds of models. On the one hand, and in a nod toward Rousseau's description of the "general will" that unifies the body politic from within, Kant offers his readers a view of the state according to which "a monarchical state is represented by an ensouled body, if it is governed by the inner laws of the people, and a mere machine (like a hand-mill) if governed by an individual absolute will" (§59, 5:352). On the other hand, Kant is excited by the possibilities for thinking about the body politic in light of the American experiment unfolding abroad. Having fought off a despotic will imposed on them "mechanically" by King George, the colonists created a whole new kind of constitution. In this version of the state, as Kant described it, "each member should freely serve in such a whole not merely as a means but also and at the same time as an end, co-effecting the possibility of the whole, the idea of which, in turn, determines each with respect to both place and function" (§65, 5:375n). This was something different: it was the state as a self-organizing being versus something animated but also led by the monarch as entelechy. Shell goes on to look at Kant's use of terms like "paternal soil" when describing land or "maternal womb" for the commonwealth, before closing with the fresh difficulties facing Kant in the wake of Burke's successful critique of the French Revolution and the Terror that followed. Despite these, Kant was unwilling to entirely abandon the American model, working instead to understand the means by which a people might work to improve their systems of self-governance.

While many of the contributions to this volume have made reference to Kant's account of our feeling of the furtherance of life as a result of the free play of the imagination and the understanding during aesthetic judgement, Michael Olson reminds readers that Kant spent time as well on the invigorating effect of this free play on our bodily feeling of health. As Olson puts it, for Kant, "games of chance, music, and witty conversation each engender a free play of sensations reminiscent of the free play of the imagination and the understanding in judgments of beauty." But even if these are embodied sensations and are thus in some sense downgraded in comparison to the "disinterested" pleasure to be had in one's encounter with the beautiful, Kant seems to have recognized that their existence marks a pivot point between aesthetic and teleological reflection. In this way health takes on a liminal character for Kant, from an initial mediation between our mental quickening and the body's enhanced physiological well-being to serving as the structural hinge between the two parts of Kant's analysis. Citing Rudolf Makkreel on this point, Olson explains that "having brought life to the level of bodily health we are now ready to observe the transition in the *Critique of Judgment* from the aesthetical to the teleological." With this in mind, Olson returns readers to Kant's early career, demonstrating Kant's long-standing interest in questions regarding health, disease, and the ways in which not just pleasure but pain too increases our feelings of the promotion of life, in investigations spanning 1767's *Essays on the Maladies of the Head* to Kant's late endorsement of John Brown's theory of health and illness in 1798's *Anthropology from a Pragmatic Point of View*. Returning at last to the third *Critique*, Olson examines Kant's comments in section 54 against the backdrop of his contemporaneous lectures on anthropology. "The feeling of health Kant associates with agreeable experiences like lively conversation and hearing a good joke is not a feeling of a stable state of health," he tells us. "It is rather the gratification that results from promoting life by agitating the organs, which brings us closer to the ideal equilibrium of health. In other words, what Kant glosses with the phrase 'feeling of health' in the *Critique of Judgment* is actually a kind of shorthand for 'feeling of the promotion of life and a return to health.' "

In "Kant and Organic Life," Joan Steigerwald investigates Kant's significance for life science theorists in the lead up to what would become the field of biology. Contending that Kant's importance lay not in his particular solutions to the questions surrounding generation, reproduction, and inheritance, Steigerwald argues instead that it was the compelling way in which Kant formulated the problems facing such inquiries that opened up possible routes for investigations by scientists and writers coming after him. Thus it was Kant's "conception of the self-organizing capacities of organized beings and his reflections on the judgments productive of that conception in the *Critique of Judgment*," she explains, "it was this conception of the reciprocity of means and ends, of cause and effect, as characteristic of organisms that was cited repeatedly by naturalists, physiologists, and philosophers attempting to develop a science of life at the turn of the nineteenth century." Now, why is it the case, Steigerwald asks, that we have an account of organic life in a book about judgment as opposed to one about nature? It's a good question and much of the chapter is spent on its answer. In short, Kant's account of organisms is one modeled on the activities of *judgment* and is therefore more about us than it can ever be about anything else. The kinds of judgments we make about organisms "out there," moreover, are singularly reflective of our own way of thinking about them "in here." Kant "argued that we arrive at the concept of natural purpose only through the activity of judgment, as it reflects on our empirical investigations of organisms and their possible conceptualization. Moving between theoretical cognition and practical reason, yet unable to settle in either, critically reflecting on the concepts of natural mechanism and concepts of rational purpose, neither of which provides a determinate grasp of organisms, we arrive at the indeterminate concept of natural purposes." And this concept, according to Steigerwald, sets up a parallel between the activity of judging and the object of this judgement. "In closely considering the self-organizing capacities of organized beings and reflecting on the modes of judgment through which we attempt to make sense of these capacities, Kant concluded that both are guided by thinking in terms of reciprocal means and ends or causes and effects." With this much established, Steigerwald spends the rest of the chapter briefly tracing Kant's influence in this vein on Friedrich Wilhelm Joseph Schelling and Carl Friedrich Kielmeyer.

In her contribution to the volume, Felicitas Munzel takes up Kant's turn toward moral teleology in the final sections of the *Critique of Judgment*, asking how we might best understand Kant's approach toward moral life. Kant's well known distinction between heteronomy and autonomy has created the impression of a sharp division between the realm of feeling and the moral law, but Munzel opens her discussion with a reminder that

Kant deliberately scheduled his ethics lectures to run during the semesters when he taught anthropology, since, as he had explained already in 1785's *Groundwork of the Metaphysics of Morals*, anthropology was simply the empirical counterpart to ethics; in his words, "morality requires anthropology for its application to human beings" (4:412). What does this mean? As Munzel reconstructs his discussion from the *Critique of Practical Reason* to the *Metaphysics of Morals*, she argues that Kant's account of the feeling of life finds, in fact, its most realized presentation in the discussion of our aptitude for "personality," that is, in the human capacity to behave as a morally accountable person whose motives are led by a rational embrace of the moral law. As she summarizes Kant's path at one point, "Understanding moral feeling as an aesthetic concept that is of a piece with the feeling of the sublime that, in turn, yields an intense feeling of the promotion of life, allows one to better comprehend the full import of Kant's identification of moral feeling as 'morality itself, subjectively regarded' (*Critique of Practical Reason*, 5:76." This moral feeling—or "moral vital force," as he describes it in the *Metaphysics of Morals*—must be cultivated, according to Kant, for as he puts it: "it is of great importance to draw attention to this attribute of our personality and to cultivate as best as one can, the effect of reason on this feeling" (5:117). Munzel's is a rich discussion and a perfect ending to the volume, opening as it does onto the next stage of Kant's thoughts on the cultivated feelings of an embodied but morally positioned human life.

Chapter 1

From the Beginning

Kant on the Feeling of Life Itself

DENNIS J. SCHMIDT

> Die Schöne Dinge zeigen an, daß der Mensch in der Welt passe.
>
> —Immanuel Kant, *Handschriftlicher Nachlaß Logik* (R1820a, 16:127)[1]

There is something truly revolutionary, utterly radical and new, about Kant's *Critique of Judgment.* It begins by unfolding what would seem to be the most interior and intimate of experiences—the purely subjective feeling of a quite peculiar and specific pleasure that is recognizably different from other pleasures and so becomes the occasion for reflection. This reflection eventually comes to understand that this pleasure is a consequence of what Kant calls "the feeling of life," and this realization is where the third *Critique* begins.[2] Unpacking that moment—its conditions, delimitations, and

1. Immanuel Kant, *Handschriftlicher Nachlaß Logik*, Bd. 16 of *Kant's gesammelte Schriften*, ed. Königlich Preußische Akademie der Wissenschaften (Berlin: Georg Reimer, 1914), 127.

2. In what follows I will limit myself almost exclusively to the Judgment of Taste, and not discuss the Judgment of the Sublime. This limitation is strictly self-imposed, but should not be taken as an indication that the sublime is less significant for the largest concerns of the *Critique of Judgment* than the beautiful. Kant will—wrongly, I

consequences—ultimately leads to the insight that this pleasure, this first signal of beauty, needs to be understood as showing how we belong in the world as moral beings. That claim only encompasses what is said in part 1 of the *Critique of Judgment* and so it refers only to the first stage of what that text as a whole exposes. Part 2 reframes the question of our moral being in the world by rethinking the character of the appearance of nature and by showing how we, "favored by nature," not only find a home in the world of appearances but also find ourselves encouraged to "further our culture" by means of nature itself (§67, 5:380n). Taken together, the two parts of the *Critique of Judgment* could be said to expose the deep kinship of the starry sky and the moral law.[3]

But Kant puts his finger on the real pulse and heartbeat of the third *Critique* simply and perfectly when he writes, "beautiful things indicate that human beings belong in the world."[4] The point is that beauty helps us understand how we are at home in the world and with one another. It opens a new way of seeing how beings defined by freedom, beings who live in a kingdom of other such beings, are to be understood also as belonging to a natural world that we, free beings, neither define nor control.[5] In the

believe—suggest that is the case when he writes that "the concept of the sublime in nature is not nearly as important and rich in consequence as that of the beautiful in nature" (§23, 5:246). Were one to address the sublime in the context of this concern with the feeling of life, then one would do well to look to the "First Introduction" to the third *Critique* where Kant calls the Judgment of the Sublime a "Critique of the Feeling of Spirit" (*Geistesgefühl*) (20:250). The *Geistesgefühl* here is a clear counterpart to the *Lebensgefühl* that begins the Critique of the Judgment of Taste. [Editor's note: This aspect of Kantian theory is touched upon by Rachel Zuckert in this volume.]

3. This of course refers to the remark Kant makes in the *Kritik der praktischen Vernunft* at 5:161, in *Kant's gesammelte Schriften*, Bd. 5, ed. Königlich Preußische Akademie der Wissenschaften (Berlin: Georg Reimer, 1913), 1–163. On this remark, and the connection that is hidden there, see my "Thank Goodness for the Atmosphere," *Research in Phenomenology* 50, no. 3 (2020): 370–85. [Editor's note: For discussion of this remark in connection to Burke see Robert Clewis's chapter in this volume, note 29.]

4. Kant, *Handschriftlicher Nachlaß Logik*, R1820a (16:127).

5. Understood in this way, the third *Critique* offers a new perspective and casts new light on the riddle that defines the third antinomy of the first *Critique*—the question of the place of a being defined by freedom, living in a realm of nature defined by causality. On this point, see María del Rosario Acosta López, "Beauty as an Encounter between Freedom and Nature: A Romantic Interpretation of Kant's *Critique of Judgment*," *Epoché* 12, no. 1 (2007): 63–92.

end, one needs to recognize that the *Critique of Judgment* is a work saturated by a concern with understanding just how we are to live in a world as moral beings.

It is clear that the third *Critique* is a work of immense reach and vision, and it is no surprise that its publication was felt as a seismic event for those who recognized its radicality. Among those who did see the real promise of the *Critique of Judgment* were Georg Wilhelm Friedrich Hegel, Friedrich Hölderlin, and Friedrich Wilhelm Joseph Schelling who, six years after the publication of the third *Critique*, would together compose a manifesto in which they declared that "the highest act of reason, the one through which it encompasses all ideas, is an aesthetic act," and that "truth and goodness only become sisters in beauty"[6] and that for the future "the whole of metaphysics falls within *moral theory*."[7] Inspired by the most radical and far-reaching promises of the third *Critique*, the efforts of early German idealism were aimed at pressing forward with those promises. However, it is clear that this revolutionary impulse that gave rise to German idealism was quickly tamed, in part at least, thanks to the way in which those same young inheritors of Kant's work developed its legacy. Over time the full revolutionary force of the vision articulated in the third *Critique* has been dimmed even as its contributions and influence have echoed throughout the subsequent history of philosophy. Interpretations of the *Critique of Judgment* have been inspirations for many—Hegel, Schelling, Friedrich Schiller, Friedrich Nietzsche, Martin Heidegger, Theodor W. Adorno, Hans-Georg Gadamer, and Jacques Derrida, to name just a few—but these same efforts to appropriate Kant's insights have tended to lose sight of some of Kant's most profound concerns so that much of the promise found in that work remains undeveloped.

In the remarks that follow, my intention is to call attention to what I take to be the most philosophically surprising and even disruptive insights

6. Georg Wilhelm Friedrich Hegel, "Das älteste Systemprogramm des deutschen Idealismus," in *Werke: Auf der Grundlage der Werke von 1832–1845*, ed. Eva Moldenhauer and Karl Markus Michel (Frankfurt a. M.: Suhrkamp, 1971), 1:234–36, 235. Just three years after this, Hölderlin will call Kant "the Moses of our nation." Friedrich Hölderlin to Karl Christoph Friedrich Gok, January 1, 1799, in *Sämtliche Werke und Briefe*, ed. Michael Knaupp (Munich: Hanser Verlag, 1992), 2:726. See also Jacques Taminiaux, *La nostalgie de la Grèce à l'aube de l'idéalisme allemand: Kant et les Grecs dans l'itinéraire de Schiller, de Hölderlin et de Hegel* (La Haye: Martinus Nijhoff, 1967), 23–45.

7. Hegel, "Das älteste Systemprogramm," 234.

of the *Critique of Judgment*—those insights that proved so energizing to the young Hegel, Schelling, and Hölderlin. Their ambition was great—to move Kant's third *Critique* forward into new horizons—my ambition now is rather modest: to simply try to understand some of those features of the *Critique of Judgment* that might need a closer look. To this end, I want to begin with the apparent starting point for this text, namely, the feeling of life, and then draw a bit more clearly the line from that fragile and contingent pleasure, which we can neither summon nor demand, to the realization that in the end "beautiful things indicate that human beings belong in the world."

While the experience that Kant announces as distinctive and so takes as the guiding thread of his analyses is found in the "feeling of life," the choice of that beginning needs to be understood as made in response to an unusual question: the question of reflective judgment.[8] The question is whether we can identify a form of judgment that does not begin with a universal law or principle, but rather with something given in its singularity, its "thisness," and that is nonetheless a priori? In other words, is there a judgment, a decision, that does not work by means of "subsuming the particular under the universal," but "ascends from the particular to the universal" ("Introduction," 5:179). Any such judgment, in order to qualify as a priori, would not be able to refer to anything empirical, it would not "be able to borrow from experience" ("Introduction," 5:180), and so any such judgment would need to give itself the law of its own judging. It would be purely, merely, subjective.[9] It could only refer to, and legislate over, itself, which is what it means to say that it would be "heautonomous" ("Intro-

8. Forgetting that the turn to the judgment of taste is made *in order to address the question of reflective judgment* is one of the ways in which the larger, ultimately moral, concerns of the third *Critique* are obscured. Aesthetic experience and the judgment of taste are exemplary of reflective judgment, but it is not the sole form of such judgment. Giorgi Tonelli argues that the discovery of the problematic of reflective judgment is the key to the eventual shape of the third *Critique*. On this, see Giorgio Tonnelli, "La formazione del testo della *Kritik der Urteilskraft*," *Revue Internationale de Philosophie* 8, no. 30 (1954): 423–48, as well as John H. Zammito, *The Genesis of Kant's "Critique of Judgment"* (Chicago: University of Chicago Press, 1992), 4–7.

9. For a fine discussion of the importance of the word "merely" (*bloß*) for Kant, see Rodolphe Gasché, *The Idea of Form: Rethinking Kant's Aesthetics* (Stanford, CA: Stanford University Press, 2003), 18–24.

duction," 5:185).[10] The question that opens the third *Critique* is whether such reflective judgments are possible as a priori judgments.

Refining this question, Kant makes clear that "what is merely [*bloß*] subjective in the presentation of an object, i.e., what constitutes its relation to the subject, not the object, is its aesthetic constitution" ("Introduction," 5:189). This aesthetic character of an experience is a feeling that, in the end, is simply a matter of pleasure or displeasure. But the real shift, the real beginning comes when Kant announces the distinctive character of the judgment of taste, that is, the decision that something is beautiful. This is first announced when Kant says that "what is strange and different [*Abweichende*] about a judgment of taste is only this: that it is not an empirical concept, but rather a feeling of pleasure (consequently, not at all a concept), which through the judgment of taste . . . is assumed [*zugemutet*] of everyone" ("Introduction," 5:191). In short, the distinctive character of the judgment of taste for answering the question of reflective judgment is simply asserted. The justification of this assertion will only be found in its analysis and deduction. What needs to be borne in mind is that taste only emerges as an exemplary case of how to understand the larger question of how reflective judgments can be said to be a priori. This larger question, which is guided by the moral orientation of the *Critique of Judgment*, should not be forgotten.[11]

---

10. Kant's use of this word, which highlights the reflexive pronoun (ἑαυτο), is a way of emphasizing the purely subjective character of such judgments: the rule is given by and followed by the subject itself. There is an interesting parallel with this notion of heautonomy in part 2 of the *Critique of Judgment* when Kant describes a natural product as "both cause and effect of itself" (§65, 5:372). The difference between "heautonomy" and "autonomy" is not insignificant but goes beyond the scope of my concerns now. On this see Gilles Deleuze, *La philosophie critique de Kant* (Paris: Presses Universitaires de France, 2004), 70; Henry E. Allison, *Kant's Theory of Taste: A Reading of the "Critique of Aesthetic Judgment"* (Cambridge: Cambridge University Press, 2001), 41–42, 62–64, 169–70. See also Frederick Beiser, *Schiller as Philosopher: A Re-examination* (Oxford: Oxford University Press, 2005), 64–68, for a discussion of the use of this term in Schiller and how it is not to be confused with Kant's use of the term.

11. It should also not be forgotten that aesthetic judgment is composed of a judgment of taste *and* the judgment of the sublime. To be sure, their relationship is not easily defined and Kant himself will seem to diminish the full significance of the sublime for the question of judgment when he says that the "concept of the sublimity of nature is not nearly important or rich in consequences as that of the beautiful" (§23, 5:246); however, to ignore the question of sublimity—as Kant himself will largely do—is one of

The beginning of the analytic of taste is clear, but it is remarkably condensed and full of consequence. After stressing that judgments of taste are not cognitive, not logical judgments, but simply aesthetic and so based upon a feeling proper to the subject itself, Kant says that there is a "feeling of life" (*Lebensgefühl*) that "grounds a thoroughly unique capacity for discriminating and judging" and that it is a feeling in which the "mind [*Gemüth*] becomes conscious of feeling its own state" (§2, 5:204).[12] In other words, the feeling of life is *what thinking feels when thinking is aware of itself.*[13] Kant will reinforce this point when he says later that "the mind [*Gemüth*] for itself is solely, wholly life (the principle of life itself)" (§29, 5:278). As Kant reminds the reader, there are many varieties of pleasure, and when he does this, he mostly shifts to the language of "liking" (*Wohlgefallen*), but this quite strange pleasure that is defined as the "feeling of life" is different, and it calls attention to its difference from everyday experience insofar as it interrupts the normal workings of cognition. In this feeling of life, the mind (*Gemüth*) folds back upon itself in a unique way, intensifying its own sense of itself. It is a feeling in which I become aware of myself in a new way. The feeling of life is, first and foremost, a quite distinctive form of self-disclosure of the subject, one in which the heautonomy of the subject will be established.[14]

The word *Lebensgefühl* is introduced as the starting point of the *Critique of Judgment*, and as such one would expect that the word would appear often and be at the center of much of what follows. That is, however, not the case. In fact, the word only appears once again in the text and then

---

the ways in which the most radical dimensions of the third *Critique* are shut down. Saying this, I also note the limitations of my own remarks in this essay and will only excuse them by saying that they need to be read as simply a first stage in a larger problematic.

12. The word *Gemüth* is poorly translated as "mind"; however, I do not have a better translation to propose. Part of the problem is that the word "mind" in English has a set of associations that pull away from wider senses of *Gemüth*. Another remark by Kant that hinges so much on understanding just how to think this word is the celebrated remark, "Zwei Dinge erfüllen das Gemüth mit immer neuer und zunehmender Bewunderung und Ehrfurcht, je öfter und anhaltender sich das Nachdenken damit beschäftigt: der bestirnte Himmel über mir und das moralische Gesetz in mir" (*Kritik der praktischen Vernunft*, 5:161). I will return to this word and to this other remark later.

13. See Gasché, *Idea of Form*, 26; Jean-François Lyotard, *Leçons sur l'analytique du sublime* (Paris: Galilée, 1991), 13–17.

14. On the character of this self-disclosure of the subject in such an experience, see my *Lyrical and Ethical Subjects* (Albany: State University of New York Press, 2005), 7–18.

it is used in a somewhat confusing manner.[15] However, section 9 poses a question that he says "is the key to the critique of taste and so deserves full attention" (5:216), and here the question is whether this feeling, this special pleasure, precedes the judgment of beauty or is its result. The answer is unambiguous and easily explained: This pleasure is the consequence of the "universal communicability of a mental state [*Gemütszustand*]," otherwise, its validity would only be private, not a priori—it would depend upon the contingency of the subject and the immediacy of the givenness of the object. In short, Kant's initial remark that "the decision about whether something is beautiful or not . . . refers to the subject and his feeling of pleasure or displeasure" (§1, 5:203)[16] can no longer be taken as unproblematic. Likewise, the notion of the feeling of life will need further qualification if it is to be understood as the starting point of aesthetic experience. This is the task of section 9, and in order to accomplish this task Kant introduces two notions that are decisive in explaining just what the feeling of life means: play (*Spiel*) and quickening (*Belebung*).

Reflective judgment finds its universal validity by rigorously, exclusively, giving attention to a purely subjective feeling—a feeling that is not essentially attached to anything "objective" or outside of the subject. The summit of this feeling, its most developed possibility, announces itself as the feeling of life itself and this possibility unfolds as the judgment of taste, as the experience of the beautiful. In the analytic of this experience, Kant offers four "clarifications" (*Erklärungen*) of the beautiful: it is without any interest in the existence of the object (§6, 5:211);[17] it is universal, but not

15. The second reference appears in the "General Comment" at 5:277. Here Kant is interested in attempting to compare his "transcendental exposition of aesthetic judgments with the physiological one by someone like *Burke*," and the remark about the "feeling of life" in this context is not very helpful in his remarks on physiological issues, nor in unpacking the notion of the feeling of life. For a fine discussion of this confusing passage, see Rudolf Makkreel, *Imagination and Interpretation in Kant: The Hermeneutical Import of the "Critique of Judgment"* (Chicago: University of Chicago Press, 1990), 103–6. [Editor's note: See also Robert Clewis's attention to precisely this aspect of Burke's discussion in this volume.]

16. Here the contrast with Plato, who argues that the pleasure we take in beauty is linked with the erotic and desire, opens up some interesting points. In particular, reading *Philebus* in conjunction with Kant on this point highlights something in both Kant and Plato.

17. This often-misunderstood point simply emphasizes that the object is not the source of the feeling that defines taste and that even the "reality" of the object does not matter—it can, for instance, be "imaginary," but it cannot be a matter of "desire."

able to be grasped by a concept; it has the form of being in accord with purposivity, but does not present any purpose; and the beautiful is a form of liking (*Wohlgefallen*) that is felt as necessary. These four clarifications are "inferences" (*Folgerungen*) of the experience, the feeling of life, that is at the heart of this judgment; strictly speaking, they do not characterize that experience itself. Rather, the phenomenology of aesthetic experience continues when Kant writes that if this purely subjective experience is to be universally communicable—that is, if reflective judgments are possible a priori—then it must find its basis in the "state of mind [*Gemüthszustand*] which is encountered [*angetroffen*] insofar as the relation of the representational powers [*Verhältnis der Vorstellungskräfte*] to each other refers to [*beziehen auf*] cognition in general" (§9, 5:217). The full import of this remark and its legitimation will wait until the Deduction, especially sections 39 and 40, where the communicability of this feeling is justified. But here, in section 9, more is said about the feeling of life itself. This begins when Kant says, "When this happens, the cognitive powers which are set into play, are in a free play because no determinate concept restricts them to any particular rule of cognition" (5:217). [18] The feeling of life is a form of play.

While Schiller has had a significant influence in the way in which the notion of play is to be understood here, I believe that there is much to be learned from Gadamer's discussion of the concept of play in *Truth and Method*;[19] in particular, Gadamer calls attention to two features of play

18. For excellent discussions of the importance and priority of play, as well as the problematic of pleasure, see Makkreel, *Imagination and Interpretation*, 90–92; John Sallis, *Kant and the Spirit of Critique* (Bloomington: Indiana University Press, 2020), 206–14.

19. See Hans-Georg Gadamer, *Gesammelte Werke*, vol. 1, *Wahrheit und Methode: Grundzüge einer philosophischen Hermeneutik* (Tübingen: Mohr Siebeck, 1986), 107–39. There are problems with Gadamer's treatment of the third *Critique* in *Truth and Method*, above all, Gadamer continues the long tradition of transferring the question of the aesthetic experience to the realm of the work of art and so excluding the centrality of the question of the beauty of nature. On Gadamer's interpretation of Kant in *Truth and Method*, see my "Aesthetics and Subjectivity: Subjektivierung der Ästhetik durch die Kantische Kritik," in *Hans-Georg Gadamer: Wahrheit und Methode*, ed. Günter Figal, Klassiker Auslegen 30 (Berlin: Akademie Verlag, 2007), 29–43. When he shifts the focus of aesthetic experience from the beautiful to the work of art, Gadamer aligns himself with a tradition that begins with Hegel, who opens his *Vorlesungen über die Aesthetik* by saying: "Diese Vorlesungen sind der *Ästhetik* gewidmet; ihr Gegenstand ist das weite *Reich des Schönen*, und näher ist die Kunst, und zwar die *schöne Kunst*, ihr Gebiet. . . . Durch diesen Ausdruck nun schließen wir sogleich das *Naturschöne* aus." Georg Wilhelm Friedrich Hegel, *Vorlesungen über die Ästhetik 1*, in *Werke: Auf der Grundlage der Werke*

that are especially helpful in understanding how Kant enlists the idea of play for an understanding of the feeling of life. First, Gadamer emphasizes that play is a movement, an activity or event, that has no purpose other than its own self-presentation or self-affirmation. One might say simply that play has no purpose independent of itself and is intent only on its own repetition.[20] Second, Gadamer notes that, while play needs to be essentially free, it is not on that account unruly. Quite the contrary, real play is a free relation to its own structure, its own rules.[21] What Gadamer's insights into the character of play contribute to understanding how we are to hear that notion in Kant is centered in both a distinctive kind of movement and a freedom at ease with law.

But Kant's remark about the feeling of life as a matter unfolding in the pleasure of play is taken even further when he says that we become conscious of this in the sensation of the "quickening [*belebten*] of powers of the mind [*Gemütskräfte*]" (§10, 5:219). This quickening of the mind gives rise to no concept, no cognition; indeed, its possibility seems to depend upon the unburdening of the mind[22] so that it is no longer engaged in cognizing the world. In other words, for there to be a judgment of beauty, one cannot be occupied by the effort to "know" what one is judging—a different "state of mind" (*Gemützszustand*) is needed.

---

von 1832–1845, Bd. 13, ed. Eva Moldenhauer and Karl Markus Michel (Frankfurt a. M.: Suhrkamp, 1986), 19–20; *Vorlesungen über die Ästhetik 1*, in *Sämtliche Werke*, Bd. 12, ed. Hermann Glockner (Stuttgart: Frommann-Holzboog, 1988). Theodor W. Adorno is one of the few to note and take into account the implications of this exclusion of nature and this substitution of the question of art for the question of beauty. On this, see his *Ästhetische Theorie*, in *Gesammelte Schriften*, ed. Rolf Tiedemann, Bd. 7 (Frankfurt a. M.: Suhrkamp, 1972), 97–98.

20. This is a point that Kant will echo when he says that "we *linger* [*weilen*] in our contemplation of the beautiful, because this contemplation reinforces and reproduces itself" (§12, 5:222). It is worth noting that this movement is not in the first instance defined as a change of place.

21. This point finds an echo in Kant's remark that in this experience we find a "lawfulness without a law" ("General Remark," 5:241).

22. This is what I take Kant to be suggesting when he speaks of this as *erleichterten Spiele* (§10, 5:219). The translation of *erleichterten* as "facilitated" by both Werner Pluhar and Paul Guyer is correct but misses the sense that the faculties of the mind are unburdened by the demands of cognition. One might say simply that we are typically too busy, too burdened by cognizing the world, to let this interruption happen. For the judgment of taste to happen, the mind cannot be burdened by its own attempt to know—it must be open to a different way of judging.

The word *Belebung* is so on point and so well chosen. It is also the case that the English translation of this word as "quickening" is especially appropriate; in fact, it is almost more to Kant's point than the German word.[23] The word "quick" refers to the incipience of life, to the first moment in which the movement of the fetus is felt by a pregnant woman;[24] it is a word that refers not only to the incipience of life, but also to its heart (as in the remark that something "cuts to the quick"); it is a word that stands as the counterpart to death (as in "the quick and the dead"). Its connection with suddenness and speed is also significant: when Kant refers to *eine Belebung* there is something of a suddenness, a transformation that is not easily broken down into stages of a transition, about what is named. Here, in this quickening of the mind, we find the intensification and the movement of life that is the real signal of the beautiful.[25]

More could be said about possibilities opened by this notion of quickening that Kant does not pursue, but there is one possibility in particular that is worth at least noting; namely, the connection between quickening and birth. What is important about this connection is that it highlights the way in which this experience, this quickening of the life of the mind, opens up something new. That is why Schelling described the experience of the beautiful as opening a "second empire" and why Gadamer spoke of it as

23. For an interesting discussion of this word in Kant's anthropology lectures and notes on ethics in the 1770s, see Paul Guyer, *Kant's System of Nature and Freedom* (Oxford: Oxford University Press, 2005), 129–31. One finds, for instance, Kant writing in 1776–8, "was belebt (oder das Gefühl von der Beförderung des Lebens) ist angenehm." "Reflexionen zur Moralphilosophie," in *Handschriftlicher Nachlaß: Moralphilosophie, Rechtsphilosophie und Religionsphilosophie*, Bd. 19 of *Kant's gesammelte Schriften*, ed. Preußische Akademie der Wissenschaften (Berlin: de Gruyter, 1934), 92–317, R6862 (19:183).

24. And in this context, it has a complicated and contentious history that takes up both Aristotle (*On the Generation of Animals*) and Aquinas. It is interesting to note that in her teaching copy of the *Critique of Judgment* (she used the Bernhard translation), Arendt crosses out Bernhard's translation of *Belebung* as "excitement" and inserts "quickening." See "Kant—Critique of Judgement," *Hannah Arendt Personal Library*, posted March 8, 2019, https://blogs.bard.edu/arendtcollection/kant-critique-of-judgement.

25. Although there are significant differences between Kant and Plato on the beautiful, the sense that beauty is an intensification of appearance, of life, is shared. On this, see Plato's discussion of τὸ ἐκφανέστατον (the highest shining of appearance) in *Phaedrus* (250d). On this, see especially John Sallis, *Spacings—of Reason and Imagination in Texts of Kant, Fichte, Hegel* (Chicago: University of Chicago Press, 1987), 90ff.

a *Zuwachs am Sein*—an "increase in Being."[26] The experience that belongs to our sense of the beautiful introduces something new, some change that cannot be explained with reference to the order of what is already available to us. Put in other words, we are not left unmoved or unchanged by this judgment, this experience, of beauty that first announces itself as the feeling of life.[27]

The full extent of this change in the subject, the character of what this quickening amounts to, points to the largest achievement of the *Critique of Judgment*[28] and even beyond to other of Kant's works.[29] While my remarks here do not extend to these larger consequences, one point is important to note now since it stands as a reminder of the deepest source of unity in the third *Critique*.

That which is quickened, brought into being and reinforced by the pleasure it inaugurates, is the awareness of our largest concern, our moral vocation. In the third *Critique*, Kant will refer to this repeatedly and in various ways. So, he will speak of our "moral predisposition" (*die moralische Anlage in uns*) (§86, 5:446) or "the whole vocation of the mind" (*die ganze*

26. Gadamer's choice of the phrase *Zuwachs am Sein* also carries a reference to birth, since the expression *Zuwachs bekommen* refers to the welcoming of a newborn into a family. One should read Socrates's comment in *Phaedrus* that faced with beauty one "sprouts wings" and sees what one did not see previously (252c). On this, see my *Idiome der Wahrheit* (Frankfurt a. M.: Klostermann, 2014), 185–200.

27. An interesting comment on this point is found in Zammito, *Genesis*, 114–15, where he suggests that "we redesign the given in aesthetic experience."

28. One should especially note the importance of this notion of quickening in Kant's discussion of genius, which is introduced with this remark: "Spirit, in its aesthetic meaning, refers to the quickening principle in the mind [*belebende Prinzip im Gemüte*]. But that by which this principle quickens the soul [*die Seele belebt*], the material it enlists to this end, is what sets the powers of the mind into a movement that accords with purposivity [*die Gemütskräfte zweckmäßig in Schwung versetzt*], i.e., in a play which sustains itself on its own and even strengthens the powers for such play" (§49, 5:313). Just prior to this remark Kant speaks of "a free movement" (*eines freien Schwunges der Gemütskräfte*) and his use of the phrase "free movement" is clearly a way of speaking of the same movement as defined play. *Schwung* also carries a sense of beginning, of putting life into something, such as in the expressing *in Schwung kommen*.

29. On this, see Jennifer Mensch, *Kant's Organicism: Epigenesis and the Development of Critical Philosophy* (Chicago: University of Chicago Press, 2013), especially the very interesting discussions of "birthplace" (129–35) and the remarks on a "vital moral force" (203, 215–16).

Bestimmung des Gemüts) (§27, 5:259) or "the ultimate purpose of our existence: our moral vocation" (*was den letzten Zweck unseres Daseins ausmacht, nämlich der moralischen Bestimmung*) (§42, 5:301)—there are many other such references. But the point is invariably that we become newly aware, and in a unique way, of the essentially moral task of our existence. It is important not to collapse the difference between moral judgment and aesthetic judgment; however, it is just as important that we recognize that the kinship between these forms of judgment is not overlooked, since something emerges at that point that is found nowhere else.[30] We do not become aware of any imperatives or of any moral law; we are not made "morally better" (*nicht sittlich besser*), "but we are humanized" (*doch gesittet machen*) (§83, 5:433), we are opened up to who we are as human beings. If then we claim that we are changed by this experience of beauty it is that we become more of who we are destined to be as moral beings.

Two further features of the feeling of life that are closely related to one another need to be discussed: first, the impulse to communicate this feeling; and, second, the vivid presence of others that belongs to this feeling. The feeling of life *includes* the conviction that it not only *can be shared* but *needs to be shared*—this need belongs to the feeling itself. This purely subjective feeling includes a sense of one's connection with others and of the impulse to put that feeling in language.[31] Kant's discussion of the universal communicability of the pleasure we take in the beautiful and of the companion sense that such a pleasure is necessarily able to be shared is curiously brief given the profound import and consequence of these points. Most of the discussion is found in sections 39 and 40.[32]

The urge to communicate does not imply that communication will be successful, only that one needs to understand it as something that one

30. Most importantly, what emerges is something that theory itself cannot awaken: "The astonishment [we feel] in beauty . . . seems to affect the mind by arousing the moral feeling . . . and moral ideas" (Die Bewunderung der Schönheit . . . scheinen . . . auf das moralische Gefühl . . . und also durch Erregung moralischer Ideen auf das Gemüth zu wirken) (5:482n).

31. Here it should be noted that "language" does not necessarily refer to words, but can equally be a matter of gesture, of sound, and of any form in which an effort to communicate is possible.

32. An insightful appreciation of this point is found in Hannah Arendt, *Lectures on Kant's Political Philosophy* (Chicago: University of Chicago Press, 1982), 68–72. Arendt's recognition of the real significance of *sensus communis* as Kant develops it is a key to much of her own political thought and deserves more attention.

is "ideally" able to accomplish. What founds this urge is the sense that the source of the pleasure one takes in the beautiful is not particular, not related to any contingency of one's being an individual, but is based solely in one's being a human being: "This pleasure must necessarily rest upon the same conditions for everyone, because they are the subjective conditions of the possibility of cognition at all" (§39, 5:292). Or put more bluntly: "Beauty holds only for human beings, i.e., beings who are animal and also rational, but not merely as rational (e.g., spirits), but at the same time as animal" (§5, 5:210). [33] The experience of the beautiful is essentially human and it is felt as such, as something that one understands as shared. This *sensus communis* announces itself in this feeling of life as a sort of belonging: one feels oneself as able to share this feeling with others.[34]

The importance of this *sensus communis* should not be underestimated, and yet it is difficult to justify precisely since it is so fundamental. In the end, the possibility of reflective judgment rests upon this common sense, and no further, no objective, evidence can be given beyond the self-evidence of the feeling of life: "Thus I can say that only under the presupposition that there is a common sense (by which we do not understand any external sense, but rather the effect that emerges out of the free play of our cognitive powers), only under such a presupposition of such a common sense, do I say that judgments of taste can be made" (§20, 5:238). However, there is some evidence of the effect of this presupposition upon us that is to be found in the drive to communicate. This impulse to share the experience of the feeling of life, this urge to connect with others, is the real expression and evidence of such a *sensus communis*: "Taste can be called *sensus communis* with more legitimacy than can sound understanding. . . . One could even define taste as the ability to judge something that renders our feeling in a given presentation *universally communicable* without the mediation of a concept" (§40, 5:295).

33. This means that neither animals nor gods can have the experience of beauty.

34. Kant does not give an extended account of this *sensus communis* in any explicit sense. It is known and understood more by its absence: stupidity, "something for which there is no remedy." *Kritik der reinen Vernunft*, in *Kant's gesammelte Schriften*, Bd. 4, ed. Königlich Preußische Akademie der Wissenschaften (Berlin: Georg Reimer, 1911), 1–252, A133/B172, 3:132n. A similar remark is found in the *Anthropology* where Kant writes, "the sole universal hallmark of insanity is the loss of a sense of the common (*sensus communis*) and the sense of idiosyncrasy (*sensus privatus*) that takes its place." *Anthropologie in Pragmatischer Hinsicht*, in *Kant's gesammelte Schriften*, Bd. 7, ed. Königlich Preußische Akademie der Wissenschaften (Berlin: Georg Reimer, 1917), 117–333, 7:219.

That there is a connection between communicability and a *sensus communis* is clear; however, Kant does not make the real character of this connection as clear as one might wish.[35] What is clear, though, is that any such communicability will need to be uncommon, it will need to be somehow different than our ordinary ways of communicating that rely upon concepts of the intellect. The exclusion of the concept from the judgment of taste, its inadequacy and inappropriateness for articulating the feeling of life, has been made clear repeatedly,[36] but what has not yet been made quite clear is how such communicability will take place. The profoundly human impulse to communicate this sense of the feeling of life and the sense of belonging and being in common that emerges brings with it the challenge to communicate differently. What sort of "language" is spoken?

The question of the role and character of language in aesthetic judgment is both important and complex. It is also a quite concealed topic in the text itself. My intention is not to even attempt to discuss this topic, but I do want to note what is the key point for my concern with tracing the notion of the feeling of life and its real consequences; namely, that this feeling, this play of the mind in which one feels an increase, an enlargement of the mind—if followed carefully—asks me to think and speak differently, it interrupts ordinary experience. Something new is exposed and the schematism of experience that founds conceptual cognition is stymied by this task.

The language and logic of cognition—the concept and the schematism of experience—are interrupted in aesthetic experience, and they prove themselves insufficient to account for such experience since cognition closes off the conditions of that experience. Put simply: the experience of beauty

35. There is one curious phrase that could, perhaps, be developed. In section 42, Kant refers to the "cipher-writing through which nature speaks to us figuratively in its beautiful forms" (5:301) and he refers to "a language which language brings to us and which seems to have a higher meaning" (5:302). The sense that we are being addressed by the beautiful—above all beautiful nature—is clear. This hint of a language, a cipher language of higher meaning but not mediated or captured by the language of the concept, is not something that Kant pursues at all. This sense that beauty *addresses us* is, however, something that is developed in interesting ways by Maurice Merleau-Ponty in *L'Oeil et l'esprit* (Paris: Gallimard, 1964) and Adorno in *Aesthetische Theorie*. On this, see my *Between Word and Image* (Bloomington: Indiana University Press, 2013), 136–47. One might even begin to think the work of art as the most far-reaching form of such a drive to communicability.

36. This, for instance, is the primary concern of sections 6–9.

requires a different state of mind (*Gemütszustand*), and although cognition is interrupted, thinking continues—just differently. Ultimately, one is able to find "an ecstasy [*Wollust*] for one's spirit [*Geist*] in a path of thinking [*Gedankengang*] that one can never fully unfold" (§42, 5:300). In order to explain the language and logic of this different way of thinking, Kant introduces two key and yet rather puzzling notions: the aesthetic idea and the symbol.

The aesthetic idea is introduced in conjunction with the notion of genius.[37] While the phrase itself is strange and seems to be an oxymoron—an idea is what cannot be found in experience and that which is aesthetic is a matter of a feeling that is merely subjective—Kant does not seem to be concerned about the peculiarity of this notion. Indeed, at one point, he even suggests that "one easily sees that it is the counterpart of a rational idea" (§49, 5:314) as if the clarity of this point needs no further explanation.[38] And what explanation he does give is not immediately helpful. After noting that "spirit is the animating principle in the mind" (*das belebende Prinzip im Gemüte*), Kant continues by explaining that "this principle is nothing other than the capacity [*Vermögen*] of presenting [*Darstellung*] aesthetic ideas which I understand as that representation [*Vorstellung*] of the imagination that gives rise to [*veranlaßt*] much thought, but without any determinate thought, i.e., concept, able to be adequate to it," and then, most significantly, he continues by saying that, "consequently, no language can fully express this and make it comprehensible" (§49, 5:313–14).[39] In short, this notion

---

37. While the first reference to the aesthetic idea appears in section 17 (5:233)—a fascinating outlier in the analytic of taste and deserving of careful attention—the remarks about the aesthetic idea there are never explained and the use of the phrase seems almost incompatible with all else that is said about the aesthetic idea. Because the remarks in section 17 are not only quite opaque, but also seemingly remote from later uses of the phrase, I will not refer to its appearance there.

38. In fact, the very idea that the aesthetic idea and the rational idea are "counterparts" is not only not "easily seen," but it is quite debatable. This point goes beyond my concerns in this essay, but the fuller discussion of the question of the aesthetic idea would do well to take the asymmetry between these "ideas" very much to heart.

39. This remark finds a fascinating echo in Hegel's 1800 text "Systemfragment," where he writes: "Der Geist ist belebendes Gesetz in Vereinigung mit dem Mannigfaltigen, das alsdann ein belebtes ist." Georg Wilhelm Friedrich Hegel, "Systemfragment von 1800," in *Werke: Auf der Grundlage der Werke von 1832–1845*, ed. Eva Moldenhauer and Karl Markus Michel, Bd. 1 (Frankfurt a. M.: Suhrkamp, 1971), 419–27, 421.

of the aesthetic idea, which is introduced in order to explain how spirit is to be understood as the capacity (*Vermögen*) that constitutes genius, seems to cloud more than it clarifies.[40]

The full set of questions posed by the notion of the aesthetic idea goes beyond my concerns in this essay.[41] Likewise, there is an important complication for my own argument that I will ignore; namely, that the aesthetic idea is a notion proper to the production of art, not to the reception of beauty. While it belongs to the "Critique of Aesthetic Judgment," it answers a question that emerges in the inquiry into genius, not taste, so that strictly speaking its relation to the feeling of life is a complex one at best.[42] In the end, what matters most is the problem, the question, that the aesthetic idea addresses: the problem of how to understand the character of a way of thinking that is not defined by either the language or logic of concepts.

Kant is clear, consistent, and insistent: "No expression which is defined by a determinate concept can be found for" an aesthetic idea; furthermore,

---

40. So far as I can tell, the only uses of this phrase "aesthetic idea" are found in these passages on eight scattered pages in the *Critique of Judgment*. Adding to the problem of understanding this notion, one of Kant's clear declarations of its meaning—"the aesthetic idea can be called an *inexponible* representation of the imagination" (§57, 5:342; emphasis is Kant's)—enlists and even emphasizes a word that Kant seems to have invented, "inexponible." That word does not appear in German before Kant, nor does it appear in Latin (the word "exponible," which Alexander Baumgarten uses in his logic, is found in Latin independently of its use by Baumgarten). That word is only used by Kant twice in his corpus, both times in the effort to explain the "aesthetic idea," and it is never used in German except in discussions of Kant. So, the explanation of "aesthetic ideas" is explained with reference to a word that has no meaning, is not found in any dictionary, and is never explained by Kant. The best clue as to what this word might mean is that it is followed by the parallel remark about the rational idea as "indemonstrable."

41. While not a great deal has been written about this notion that really investigates what it might mean, there are some quite interesting pieces that provide good starting points for that investigation. See, for instance, Rudolf Lüthe, "Kants Lehre von den ästhetische Ideen," *Kant-Studien* 75, no. 1 (1984): 58–77; Michel Chaouli, "A Surfeit in Thinking: Kant's Aesthetic Ideas," *Yearbook of Comparative Literature* 57 (2011): 55–77; Makkreel, *Imagination and Interpretation*, 112–23.

42. The claim that "beauty . . . requires the presentation of aesthetic ideas" is well argued by Chaouli, "Surfeit in Thinking," 63–64. The details of that claim and its support, which begins with the importance of the notion of spirit, do not need to be laid out here, since, in the end, my argument is that there is a clear line to be drawn from the beginning of the "Critique of Aesthetic Judgment" in the feeling of life, to the disclosure that beauty is the symbol of morality. That this line might move through both taste and genius does not alter the basic shape of that argument.

the aesthetic idea "lets us add to [*hinzu denken*] a concept much that is beyond words [*unnennbar*], the feeling of which quickens [*belebt*] the cognitive capacities and binds language—as otherwise merely letters—with spirit" (§49, 5:316).[43] In the aesthetic idea, the mind expands itself beyond the language of concepts—the language that is the mother tongue and special excellence of philosophy—and, confronted with this limit of language, the mind begins to recognize the need for a language that is as expansive as what the aesthetic idea presents. Kant will not say much about this language; however, his comments on poetic speech come very close to pointing to poetic language as what is needed: "It is really poetry in which the capacity of aesthetic ideas can show themselves in their full measure" (§49, 5:314).[44] What is important to bear in mind is that the presentation of the aesthetic idea, like the experience of the feeling of life, is not simply indifferent to the concept, and not simply waiting for its eventual conceptualization, rather such aesthetic ideas, like the feeling of life, actively *resist* the concept. If they are to find their way to language, if the drive of communicability is to satisfy itself, then a different sense of language will be needed.

---

43. The language of this passage is notable. *Hinzu denken*, *unnennbar*, *belebt*, *Sprache*, *als bloßem Buchstaben*, and *Geist verbindet* are all words and phrases that highlight the exceptional nature of aesthetic ideas while pointing to the important way in which such ideas challenge ordinary ways of speaking. A few years after the publication of the third *Critique*, Johann Gottlieb Fichte will publish a text entitled "Ueber Geist und Buchstab in der Philosophie" (1794) that addresses much that is found in Kant's remark here. Johann Gottlieb Fichte, *Fichtes Werke*, ed. Immanuel Hermann Fichte, Bd. 8, *Vermischte Schriften und Aufsätze* (Berlin: de Gruyter, 1971), 270–300.

44. This will be a key claim driving Romanticism, especially as it was developed by the Schlegel brothers and those involved in the *Athenaeum* journal project, as well as by Samuel Taylor Coleridge. It is important to differentiate between conceptual inventiveness and poetic language. Kant is conceptually quite inventive in the third *Critique*—the notion of the "aesthetic idea" is a fine example of this—but that does not mean that Kant's language is poetic. Some of the most fascinating radicalizations of Kant's insights in the third *Critique* are found in Hölderlin. One thinks especially of his strange and difficult text (1799) that begins: "Wenn der Dichter einmal des Geistes mächtig ist, wenn er die gemeinschaftliche Seele, die allem gemein und jedem eigen ist, gefühlt und sich zugeignet . . ." (When the poet is at last in charge of the spirit, when the poet feels and appropriates for himself the communal soul which is common to each and every person . . . ; this sentence continues for 97 lines). Friedrich Hölderlin, "Wenn der Dichter einmal des Geistes mächtig ist," in *Sämtliche Werke und Briefe*, Bd. 2, ed. Michael Knaupp (Munich: Hanser Verlag, 1992), 77–78. Much of Hölderlin's theoretical writings press forward the possibility of the sort of poetic thinking that moves beyond what Kant himself will discuss.

Aesthetic experience, which unfolds in the feeling of life and the aesthetic idea, sets the mind in motion. Kant describes this movement as a "quickening," as the incipience of life, as a sort of birth of something new that enlarges the mind. It draws upon that which Kant calls *unnennbar*—beyond words, unnameable—and yet it is not on that account to be considered as unformed. Aesthetic experience is not unformed, not inchoate, not without its own compelling force; rather, it is simply formed differently and in such a way that "one is able to think so much more than one can put into words" (§49, 5:315). Kant acknowledges that aesthetic experience cannot be formed according to the schematism that lies at the heart of the experience he has described in the first *Critique*. The experience analyzed there culminates in the possibility of knowledge, and it can be articulated according to the language of the concept. Aesthetic experience, on the other hand, is not able to be schematized—its resistance to the concept is only one reason for this limit—but it can be symbolized.

Kant's discussion of symbolic hypotyposis in section 59 is the summit of the "Critique of Aesthetic Judgment," and it is here that the real destiny of the feeling of life that opens this project is announced, and there is no ambiguity about this: "Now I maintain that the beautiful is the symbol of the ethically good" (5:353). However, what is also unambiguous is that Kant's earlier effort in section 4 to sharply distinguish the disinterested pleasure of taste from the interest bound up with the pleasure we take in the good has not been abandoned: "The beautiful prepares us to love something—even nature—without interest; the sublime to esteem it even against our (sensible) interest" ("General Comment," 5:267). In section 4, Kant refers to the relation to the good that we can have through the rational will. In section 59, a different relation that we have to the good is established. This achievement, as Kant explains it, rests upon the bond uniting the symbol and ethicality (*Sittlichkeit*). There is much that is confusing about this section, and, if one were to read Kant ungenerously, one could say that this is the point at which Kant fails to justify his most profound claims. For instance, the reason for the *necessity* of this is never made clear, and the subsequent discussion of the symbol is woefully inadequate and often quite simply wrong even according to Kant's own sense of that notion.[45] However, the real insight

45. For more details about this, see my "Einige Betrachtungen zu Sprache und Freiheit aus einem hermeneutischen Blickwinkel," in *"Dimensionen des Hermeneutischen": Heidegger und Gadamer*, ed. Günter Figal and Hans-Helmuth Gander (Frankfurt a. M.: Klostermann, 2005), 59–73; "On the Incalculable: Language and Freedom from a Hermeneutic Point

of this section and the way in which it exposes the deepest sense of the experience of beauty for us has already been prepared for in the analysis of the feeling of life and the discussion of the aesthetic idea. Both of these notions share a number of features that point to the need to understand experience as configured differently than in the schematism. There are four such features to be noted. First, aesthetic experience *interrupts and arrests* ordinary experience; it brings us to "linger" (*weilen*) (§12, 5:222). Second, this interruption, this shift to a different order of experience, entails a sense of increase, of an expansion, of the mind, a *quickening* that is akin to a sort of birth. Third, a defining element of this experience is that it is shared, that it is rooted in what I *share with other human beings*. Fourth, the *urge to communicate* this extraordinary experience, to bring it to language pushes ordinary language to its limits. Taken together these features of aesthetic experience point to the need to understand the logic of a different sort of "translation of reflection" (§59, 5:353), one that does not operate according to the schema, but the symbol.[46] It is on the basis of this operation that Kant can say that "taste is basically an ability to judge the sensibilization of moral ideas [*Versinnlichung sittlicher Ideen*]" (§60, 5:356). The question that is most important to ask at this point is simple: Why does this "ethicality" (*Sittlichkeit*) need to present itself symbolically here, and what emerges in this presentation of the ethical that is not able to emerge according to the schematism of experience? One might put this question somewhat differently and ask why the symbol opens one up to the ethical.

---

of View," *Research in Phenomenology* 34 (2004): 31–44. See also Tzvetan Todorov, *Theories of the Symbol*, trans. Catherine Porter (Ithaca, NY: Cornell University Press, 1982). What is most missing from Kant's discussion is the relation of the symbol to nature, for example, his rather puzzling comment about the "cipher-writing . . . through which nature speaks to us figuratively in its beautiful forms" (Chiffreschrift . . . wodurch die Natur in ihren schönen Formen figürlich zu uns spricht) (§42, 5:301). It is this relation that distinguished the symbol from allegory, which is conventional, and that is so important for the way Johann Wolfgang von Goethe will take up the notion of the symbol in discussions of beauty and of nature.

46. The emphasis on this point is, of course, at the heart of Cassirer and the neo-Kantian school that emerged out of Marburg. But there is a way in which this point has received a different emphasis insofar as the logic of metaphor has taken on a similar role. One sees this already in Hölderlin's theoretical work when he speaks of the "metaphor of an intellectual intuition" or lyric as the "continuous metaphor of a feeling." The question of the metaphoricity of thinking is a key one and is even hinted at by Kant in his remarks on the vocabulary of philosophy—ground, substance, flowing (consequence)—however, this question goes beyond the concerns of this paper.

What needs to be remembered is that the aesthetic experience that Kant finds in the trail of the feeling of life and set forth in the aesthetic idea is an experience that enlarges, expands, and increases the mind while simultaneously exposing insurmountable limits and confronting the mind with what will forever exceed it. This is the great paradox at the heart of aesthetic experience. Just as reason has a "peculiar fate," so too does the aesthetic experience that begins with the remarkable and arresting "feeling of life." To understand the special destiny of this unique feeling, one needs to acknowledge that it is deeply and solely a *human possibility*: "Beauty is valid [*gilt*] only for the human being, i.e., beings who are animal, but also rational" (§5, 5:210). Strangely, it is at this most human of experiences that we are put in contact both with others with whom we share in common this sense, but also with that which exceeds and surpasses us. We are instructed about the sort of beings we are and about that which is larger than what such beings can know and control. Nature opens itself to us in a different way, not as what we cognize, but as the place in which we find ourselves.[47] The second part of the *Critique of Judgment* is dedicated to exploring this place, and it too will end on a note both of finitude and affirmation: "Faith (as *habitus* not as *actus*) is reason's moral way of thinking in affirming [*Fürwahrhalten*] that which is inaccessible to theoretical cognition" (§91, 5:471). The first part has reminded us that "beautiful things indicate that human beings belong in the world."

There is, of course, much more to be said. Above all, the systematic unity of the *Critique of Judgment*—the relation that binds its two parts together—needs to be clarified. Doing that, bringing together the sense of freedom that defines part 1 and the vision of nature developed in part 2, shows the real reach of this book and the extent to which it rewrites and reframes established pillars of Kant's critical project. Doing this also shows just how much Kant is engaged in thinking nature not as the realm of objects causally related, but as the movement of life itself.[48] While there

---

47. Thus, "we can call it the favour [*Gunst*] in which nature holds us when it distributed not only what is useful, but even more what is beautiful" (§67, 5:380). See also "General Comment": "How can one explain why nature has so extravagantly spread beauty everywhere, even at the bottom of oceans?" (5:279).

48. Since Aristotle began *Physics* B.2 by laying out an analogy between physis and techne, that analogy and its consequent technomorphism of nature, has become a standard way to think the being of nature. Kant challenges this when he writes: "One says far too little when one speaks of nature and its capacity in organized products by calling nature an *analogue of art*. . . . Perhaps one comes closer to this inscrutable character of nature

is a great deal in the third *Critique* that is in need of closer attention, I want to conclude by raising a question that moves beyond the text itself, but emerges out of it.

The question is simple: What, for Kant, binds us to the good that has been presented in the beautiful? In some ways the answer is equally simple: a unique pleasure. The pleasure that follows from the free play and quickening of the mind that define the feeling of life is utterly singular. It is not linked with any interest or desire, any concept or expectation. It is a gift one cannot demand, bid into being, or even request. Ultimately, even in the case of the products of genius, even in the work of art, it is the gift of nature, and, as Kant says, it "indicates that human beings belong in the world." Importantly, it is not the same pleasure that one experiences in "doing good," in the good will or in duty, and this difference is important.[49] This pleasure *changes us*, it does not leave us unmoved, untouched, unaffected—in the end, it can educate us. This education is not a matter of winning some knowledge or grasping the nature of duty or an imperative. It is much more a matter of a cultivation, a *Bildung*, an understanding that folds back into existence.[50] The change that happens is perhaps better described as an intensification: of the feeling of life, of the limits of one's capacity to speak of and to that feeling, and ultimately of one's sense of oneself as a human being.

What binds us to the good is this intensification of life, and it is this bond and its reflexive fold back into the consciousness of one's own existence, rather than any knowledge—either practical or theoretical—that exposes a sense of what Kant called a "moral feeling [*das moralische Gefühl*] [which] is something merely subjective and which yields no knowledge" (*Metaphysik*

---

if one calls it an *analogue of life*" (§65, 5:374).

49. One is right to hear echoes of Socrates's remark to Protarchus in *Philebus* (64e) that "now the power of the good has taken refuge [καταφεύγω] in the nature of the beautiful."

50. Here one should draw a connection with Kant's remark at the end of the second *Critique*: "Two things fill the mind [*das Gemüth*] with always renewed and increasing admiration and reverence the more often and sustainedly I am to think about them: the starry sky over me and the moral law in me. . . . I see them before me and *connect them immediately with the consciousness of my existence* [*verknüpfe sie unmittelbar mit dem Bewußtsein meiner Existenz*]" (*Kritik der praktischen Vernunft*, 5:161–62; emphasis added). This immediate bond of this state of mind with the simple consciousness of one's own existence describes the same sort of education I am referring to here. It is an education insofar as it changes one and, above all, one's understanding of one's place in the world. It is, strictly speaking, an education that is not a matter of any special knowledge.

der Sitten, 6:400).[51] Kant, in his generosity, suggests that "no human being is without any moral feeling, for if one were completely unreceptive to it one would be morally dead [*sittlich todt*]" (6:400). In the context of the third *Critique* this amounts to saying that no human being is without a feeling for the beautiful. Even if that is true, it will remain a question as to just how well one is able to cultivate this feeling of life, this astonishing pleasure that goes to the heart of being human in the world.

51. See also the remarks at *Die Religion innerhalb der Grenzen der bloßen Vernunft*, in *Kant's gesammelte Schriften*, Bd. 6, ed. Königlich Preußische Akademie der Wissenschaften (Berlin: Georg Reimer, 1914), 1–202, 6:27, 6:114; *Die Metaphysik der Sitten*, in *Kant's gesammelte Schriften*, Bd. 6, ed. Königlich Preußische Akademie der Wissenschaften (Berlin: Georg Reimer, 1914), 203–493, 6:387, 6:399.

Chapter 2

The Furtherance of Life as the Bridge between Nature and Freedom in Kant's Critical Philosophy

James Risser

An Overview of Kant's Project in the *Critique of Judgment*

Kant's *Critique of Judgment* is without doubt a most peculiar book. In the "First Introduction" to the book, Kant poses his problem in its most comprehensive form. This *Critique* is to complete the critical philosophy, but it soon becomes evident that this is by no means a simple completion. With reference to his earlier work in this regard, Kant begins by noting that he has already achieved a completion with respect to the system of philosophy. This system is in fact divided into two parts, formal and material, where "the material (or real) part considers systematically the objects we think about, insofar as we can have rational cognition of them from concepts" ("First Introduction," 20:195).[1] Given the distinction of objects, the system of phi-

1. All citations in the body of the text are to paragraph number (when applicable), then Akademie edition volume and page number, of Kant's *Kritik derUrteilskraft,* in Immanuel Kant, *Gesammelte Schriften*, Bd. 1–22 edited by Preussische Akademie der Wissenschaften; Bd. 23, Deutsche Akademie der Wissenschaften zu Berlin; ab Bd. 24,

losophy is divided into a theoretical and practical philosophy—a philosophy of nature and a philosophy of morals. But this completion of the system of philosophy as the system of rational knowledge does not complete the system of higher cognitive faculties that ground philosophy. To complete the *critical* philosophy will require completing an examination of the *faculty* for a priori cognition. From his two earlier *Critiques*, Kant has examined two of the three faculties of a priori cognition and has discovered that they both successfully legislate a priori and thus contribute to rational knowledge. The faculty of understanding contains constitutive principles for the manifold of intuitions in the realm of nature and the faculty of reason contains a constitutive law for the manifold of desires in the realm of freedom. The issue now is to examine whether judgment as the third cognitive faculty along with understanding and reason also has the possibility of a priori cognition.

In Kant's examination of the faculty of judgment relative to the demands of a critical philosophy, we see immediately the peculiarity of this book through the complication that it presents from the outset. There is an initial complication that stems from the unique character of judgment, which stands as the middle term between understanding and reason in the system of higher cognitive faculties.[2] Kant states that the faculty of judgment, unlike the faculties of understanding and reason, is not an independent faculty of cognition, since "it is merely a power of subsuming under concepts given from elsewhere" ("First Introduction," 20:202). As such, the faculty of judgment does not have a designated domain for a priori legislation, as do understanding and reason in relation to nature and freedom, respectively. Still, Kant claims that, although the faculty of judgment does not have a domain for special legislation, it may contain nonetheless, by analogy to the other higher cognitive faculties, an a priori principle. In fact, the discovery of this principle is sufficient for judgment to be included in the system of the pure faculty of conceptual cognition, although not in the system of philosophy in its theoretical and practical parts. Since it has no field of objects as its realm, however, the a priori principle that issues

Akademie der Wissenschaften zu Göttingen (Berlin, 1900–). Translations are from Immanuel Kant, *Critique of Judgement*, trans. Werner S. Pluhar (Indianapolis: Hackett, 1987). Other volumes noted accordingly.

2. Formally, Kant distinguishes the three terms relative to a capacity for thinking: understanding is the capacity for knowledge of the universal, the judgment is the capacity for the subsumption of the particular under the universal, and reason is the capacity for the determination of the particular through the universal ("First Introduction," 20:201).

from judgment can be so only in a "subjective respect." Thus there is the complication of a necessary conformity to law (an a priori principle) that is in some sense subjective.

This complication concerning the faculty of judgment is immediately compounded by the fact that Kant does not limit himself to identifying this a priori principle in order to exhaust the possibility of a priori principles, as we see clearly from the introduction; he also wants to bring the principle to bear on what he considers the fundamental problem of the critical philosophy as a whole, namely, the problem of its unity. Kant tells us there is an "immense gulf" that separates the sensible realm of the concept of nature and the supersensible realm of the concept of freedom, since the first has no influence on the latter and yet the latter should (*soll*) have influence on the former ("Introduction," 5:176). The construction of a bridge between these two realms is precisely what the third *Critique* is to accomplish. This bridge must be more than a simple joining together such that, through the joining, what stands on each side no longer stands in opposition. Such a simple joining with respect to freedom and nature has already been established by reason in the first *Critique* in the resolution of the third antinomy. Rather, the constructing of a bridge would entail establishing a unity in the precise sense that "the concept of freedom [should] actualize in the world of sense the purpose enjoined by its laws, and consequently it must be possible to think of nature as being such that the lawfulness of its form will harmonize with at least the possibility of [achieving] purposes that we are to achieve in nature according to laws of freedom" ("Introduction," 5:176). Unlike a simple joining that merely holds up for view the relation of the two realms, this unity would effect a transition (*Übergang*) from one realm to the other, at least with respect to thought.

Such a transition, which is without the help of theoretical or practical reason, is made, according to Kant, by a certain force, as if thinking were complying with an order: the domain of the concept of freedom should have an influence on the domain of the concept of nature. This order, which is effectively an order with respect to conformity, Kant identifies as coming from the life of the mind (*Gemüt*). But, as we shall see, this means at once that the order is to be effected for the sake of the furtherance of that life. While exactly what this entails remains to be seen, it is important to note here at the outset that the transition to be effected is deemed to be necessary for that life—a necessity that cannot be ascribed to it on a strictly logical basis, but only with respect to a kind of practical necessity, as if it were issuing from a demand of freedom. To say it again, the concept of freedom is meant to actualize in the world of sense the purpose proposed by its laws; and even if it cannot be shown that causality through freedom is actually resident in nature, its effect "should exist" ("Introduction," 5:196). This "should" is the demand of freedom, and, accordingly, the constructing of the bridge is undertaken in the name of freedom. To put it more strongly: the bridge is a constructing by freedom, where freedom is understood as the consciousness of a being that comes to itself only by making the world its own. Such constructing will not be an easy matter, for what is at stake now is not the fact that there is legislation under the concept of freedom, but the exercising—or better, the accomplishing of—its legislation. The constructing, in other words, must show how freedom can come to bear on the order of nature, without violating the particular legislation of nature's order.

Now, in describing the bridge in this way, Kant seems to have further compounded the complication introduced by the faculty of judgment. It is not an easy matter to see how this bridge can be built, since it is in fact a bridge built by judgment that, in Kant's initial description of it, has little connection to a demand of freedom. Kant's construction here begins with an analogy: just as judgment in its logical use makes possible a transition from understanding to reason, so Kant argues we can suppose that judgment will bring about a transition from the realm of natural concepts to the concept of freedom. The key distinction that Kant now makes is that between judgment in its reflective rather than determining capacity, since the unity sought extends beyond the analytic unity that a determinant judgment provides. That is to say, for the sake of the bridge-building, the functioning of judgment must be inverted: in its function of subsumption, the reflective judgment engages in a movement from the particular in nature to the universal, rather than the other way around, in order to establish the possibility of a more fundamental ordering in the order of nature. The faculty of judgment, in other words, is being asked to bring about a unity of the laws of nature relative to a higher unity that stands in relation to the law of freedom, and as such the unity cannot itself be determined by a law of nature. Since the unity cannot be obtained by borrowing an a priori law from experience, judgment, we are told in a remarkable phrase, can only provide the law "from and to itself" ("Introduction," 5:180). The reflective judgment thus mediates between nature and freedom by considering the empirical laws of nature in accordance with a unity "as [they would have] if they too had been given by an understanding (even though not ours) so as to assist our cognitive powers by making possible a system of experience in terms of particular natural laws."

In giving the law, that is to say, the rule, to itself, we can better understand Kant's claim that the a priori rule of judgment is subjective in some sense, but what is not yet understood is how this rule adheres to the demand of freedom. At this point, all we can say is that the furtherance of life that would issue from the demand of freedom is caught up in the formative activity of the reflective judgment. To say more than this requires that we take a look at the actual a priori rule of judgment, but here too, as we will soon see, we will not have freed ourselves from complication. Kant identifies the subjective a priori principle of judgment as the purposiveness of nature. Kant actually formulates this principle in the same language he uses for the description of the general nature of the principle: The purposiveness of nature is a rule whereby "we present nature as if an understanding contained the basis of the unity of what is diverse in nature's empirical laws" ("Introduction," 5:181).[3] If this description of the rule does not yet tell us precisely how the gulf between freedom and nature is bridged, it does seem to tell us something about the character of the demand for unity that is demanded by freedom. The principle of the purposiveness of nature is in effect a principle posited in the subjunctive mood and has accordingly the character of a fiction.[4] No human understanding actually contains this ground of understanding, and we can only use the concept to reflect upon the unity of nature. The representation of purposiveness is that of a formal purposiveness of nature, and not an actual purposiveness of nature. It is a purposiveness that will allow nature to harmonize with the purpose to be effected in it according to the law of freedom.

Certainly, we have reason to pause here and ask whether the systematic ordering has become too much of a construction and whether Kant, caught within the parameters of this construction, is now engaged in a little wishful thinking, that is to say, he is being left with what amounts to a desire for unity and freedom's effectiveness, since the unity is pursued and in fact

3. In the subsequent section of the introduction to the *Critique of Judgment*, Kant explains the transcendental status of the principle and defines the transcendental concept of purposiveness of nature as "neither a concept of nature nor a concept of freedom, since it attributes nothing whatsoever to the object (nature), but [through] this transcendental concept [we] only think of the one and only way in which we must proceed when reflecting upon the objects of nature with the aim of having thoroughly coherent experience. Hence it is a subjective principle (maxim) of judgment" ("Introduction," 5:184).

4. The notion of "fiction" here follows the sense of the "as if" presented by the neo-Kantian Hans Vaihinger. See *The Philosophy of the 'As If,'* trans. C. K. Ogden (London: Routledge & Kegan Paul, 1935).

promulgated in the face of the recognition that it can never be actually known to be so. And if wishful, what then are we ultimately to say about the bridge that is to be built? It is this theme of the ultimate effectiveness of the unity that is the concern of the remainder of my remarks, and, of course, to pursue this theme properly we have to enter still further into the compounding complications of the *Critique of Judgment.*

The Importance of Aesthetic Judgment

At this point in the introduction, Kant puts forward a division within the reflective judgment such that the unity it is to provide must now take into consideration not just two things, freedom and nature, but three: freedom, art, and nature. Why three rather than two at this point certainly has something to do with the way in which Kant came to compose the *Critique of Judgment.* From early on, Kant had an interest in aesthetics—more properly, what one should call an empirical aesthetics, since he did not think that a *critique* of aesthetic taste was possible. Although he wrote to Marcus Herz in 1771, indicating that he intended to write a work on aesthetics, as late as 1781, he considered this critique of taste an unlikely possibility. But by 1787, Kant had found what he was looking for. He wasable to write a critique of taste because he had found a distinct a priori principle that would give a rule to the feeling of pleasure and displeasure involved in taste. When Kant then names the three parts of philosophy that have a priori principles he does not include aesthetics, but names them as theoretical philosophy, teleology, and practical philosophy. The obvious question is how Kant moves from his intended purpose to write a critique of taste to teleology and how the two areas, which come to constitute the main division in the *Critique of Judgment,* namely, aesthetics and teleology, actually relate to each other.

Certainly, from what we have already seen, the very idea of a system plays a crucial, if not determining, role in this regard.[5] Quite simply, Kant was able to find an opening for completing the systematic unity of reason once he realized that a critique of taste would complete the system of human powers (*Gemütsvermögen*), namely, the feeling of pleasure and displeasure, cognition, and desire. In the investigation of taste, Kant's concern began to telescope outward to judgment and the possible judgment of beauty in

5. For an insightful discussion of this issue, see John H. Zammito, *The Genesis of Kant's "Critique of Judgment"* (Chicago: University of Chicago Press, 1992), 169–77.

nature, which in turn opened up to the idea of a teleological judgment and how the two kinds of judgment might stand together in a process of reflection. The beauty of nature suggests that nature is artistically designed, and this idea of teleology opens the way for an "ethical turn." This ethical turn announced itself under the heading of the supersensible. If judgment is to make possible the transition between nature and freedom, it can do so only in relation to the concept of a unifying supersensible ground of nature—a ground that would in some fashion then truly unite human life. For Kant what is indispensable to human life is not the fact of its actuality but its accomplishing of an actuality that requires an orientation, if not a practice, that is always more than the mere thought of the supersensible. Judgment provides this orientation in the concept of purposiveness. Thus the *Critique of Judgment* is written and justified as part of the critical system on the grounds of an a priori principle, namely, the purposiveness of nature that in fact can only be ascribed to aesthetic judgment, since the teleological judgment, which presupposes a concept of the object, is not a pure reflective judgment. And yet, if the "Critique of Aesthetic Judgment" holds privilege in this regard, it must be tempered by the fact that a critique of aesthetic judgment is ultimately secondary to Kant's ongoing concern for ethical life.

The Link between Purposiveness and Pleasure

This brief look at the motivation and context for writing the third *Critique* does not resolve the complex issues surrounding its philosophical presentation. To work our way through them so as to resolve the issue of the bridge, we can proceed in stepwise fashion. First of all, we need to see how the concept of purposiveness is linked to a judgment of taste as a judgment of the beautiful, and how this link serves the issue of the bridge. The key to this link is the more basic link that Kant establishes between the concept of purposiveness and a feeling of pleasure. With this word "purpose" (*Zweck*) we assume that Kant means the conscious adaptation to an end, as if purpose is simply deliberate creation. But in its eighteenth-century use the word had a broader meaning; it pertains as well to the harmonious unification of the parts of a manifold.[6] Understood in this way, the adaption to an end also implies that, in relation to conscious adaption, the part is

6. See Ernst Cassirer, *Kant's Life and Thought*, trans. James Haden (New Haven, CT: Yale University Press, 1981), 287.

not just adjacent to another part, but has its existence connected to that other part. This broader notion of purpose is not immediately evident when Kant defines purpose in the *Critique of Judgment*. The definition states that "a purpose is the object of a concept insofar as we regard this concept as the object's cause (the real basis of its possibility); and the causality that a *concept* has with regard to its *object* is purposiveness (*forma finalis*)" (§10, 5:219–20). From this definition we get the clear sense that purpose pertains to intelligent agency: "Purpose is the *relation* between a concept and an object whereby the concept acts as the cause of the actuality of the object."[7] What is attained in the actuality of the object by the reflective judgment, which means attained for itself, since the understanding cannot prescribe this causality to nature, is an ordering—an order of design where nature is not a mere aggregate. Now, as we note from section six of the introduction, Kant simply asserts that the attainment of this logical purposiveness of nature is bound up with a feeling of pleasure. The assertion appears to rest on Kant's claim that pleasure always results from the fulfillment of a design or aim (*Absicht*), not unlike the way we feel pleasure in accomplishment. And it would also appear to be the case that pleasure is naturally connected to the sense of harmony in the broader notion of purpose. Thus it can be said that in discovering the contingent *orderliness* of nature—contingent because ultimately it is an order we read into nature—we feel pleasure.

Accordingly, Kant defines pleasure in the *Critique of Judgment* as "a state or affection of the mind [*Zustand des Gemüts*] in which a presentation is in harmony with itself [and] which is the basis either for merely preserving this state itself (for the state in which mental powers further one another in a presentation preserves itself) or for producing the object of this presentation" ("First Introduction," 20:230–31). It would follow, of course, that the feeling of displeasure would pertain to the lack of harmony. This definition of pleasure from the "First Introduction," though, does not say very much, but elsewhere we find Kant to be more illuminating. In the *Anthropology*, Kant distinguishes between inner sense as the mere power of perception and an interior sense as the feeling of pleasure and displeasure that Kant then defines as "our susceptibility to be determined by certain representations, either to hold onto them or to drive them away" (7:153).[8]

7. Zammito, *Genesis*, 90.

8. Immanuel Kant, *Anthropology from a Pragmatic Point of View*, in *Anthropology, History, and Education*, ed. Robert B. Louden and Günter Zöller (Cambridge: Cambridge University Press, 2007), 227–429, 7:117–333.

Pleasure is thus a state that involves a maintenance of attraction. Perhaps even more illuminating is Kant's remark on pleasure in the *Lectures on the Philosophical Doctrine of Religion* where he distinguishes pleasure from desire, as a more originary relation to things. Pleasure, he writes, "consists rather in the relation of my representations to the subject, insofar as these representations determine the subject to actualize the object. Insofar as it first determines the subject to the desire, it is called *faculty of desire*; but insofar as it first determines the subject to desire it is called *pleasure*" (28:1060).[9] Here pleasure is not just a maintenance but is involved in making in general.

With this basic link in view, let us pursue the link between purposiveness and pleasure in Kant's turn to the aesthetical in section 8 of the introduction. Kant writes:

> When an object is given in experience, there are two ways in which we can present purposiveness in it. We can present it on a merely subjective basis: as the harmony of the form of the object (the form that is [manifested] in the *apprehension* (*apprehensio*) of the object prior to any concept), with the cognitive powers. . . . But we can also present it on an objective basis: as the harmony of the form of the object with the possibility of the thing itself according to a prior concept of the thing that contains the basis of that form. ("Introduction," 5:192)

In the first case, judgment relative to purposiveness is aesthetic, that is to say, the representation of the object is made entirely in reference to the subject, and in this case the purposiveness rests on the "immediate pleasure in the form of the object." In different words, the representation of purposiveness in an object is directly connected to a feeling of pleasure, and in this case the pleasure expresses nothing other than the subject's harmony with the cognitive powers that come into play in the reflective judgment. Accordingly, pleasure expresses a subjective formal purposiveness of the object, one that can only "prompt" the concept of purposiveness in nature. A judgment of aesthetic taste as a judgment about the beautiful is then defined as one in which the form of the object in the mere reflection upon it is judged as the ground of a pleasure.

---

9. Immanuel Kant, *Lectures on the Philosophical Doctrine of Religion*, in *Religion and Rational Theology*, trans. Alan W. Wood and George di Giovanni (Cambridge: Cambridge University Press, 1996), 335–451, 396, 28:993–1126.

So, at this point, we have the following distinctions before us: there is in the effort of a bridge-building a demand on the side of the law of freedom that is taken up by judgment in its reflective capacity, which in turn posits a concept of purposiveness as a concept of intelligent order, which in turn is felt in an aesthetic reflective judgment when, in relation to the mere form of purposiveness, there is the harmonious free play of the cognitive faculty (the interplay of the imagination and understanding). It remains to be seen, though, how the link between purposiveness and the feeling of pleasure directly serves the issue of the bridge and the demand of freedom. For this we have to take into consideration the real import of the feeling of pleasure as it is presented in the aesthetic reflective judgment. That import concerns the intention of Kant to remove the feeling of pleasure from the realm of empirical psychology. The sense of this is given to us when Kant defines the aesthetic judgment all over again in the first section of the "Critique of Aesthetic Judgment." The aesthetic judgment is one in which "the presentation is referred only to the subject, namely to his feeling of life, under the name feeling of pleasure or displeasure" (§1, 5:204). What is different here is Kant's insertion of the phrase "the feeling of life."

If we ask ourselves what this life is that is referred to here, we have to assume that it is something more than biological life. But how much more is not at all clear, since life in relation to pleasure and displeasure is certainly a component of biological life. In the *Anthropology* Kant in fact defines life as the alternation of states of pleasure and pain, and his explanation of this alternation is itself interesting. He appears to describe both, but most certainly with respect to pain, as a vital force. Thus, immediately we can say that the life at issue in aesthetic judgment—the life that ultimately involves by definition the life of the mind (*Gemüt*)—is life in its vivification, that is to say, life in its making alive of life. Pleasure is thus not a blind feeling, but the feeling of life being promoted. And pain, he tells us, must precede pleasure since in its opposition to pleasure it is "spur of activity in which we feel our life" (7:231). This same idea—the idea that what is at issue in pleasure is not simply the feeling of life but the furtherance of life—is also expressed by Kant in the *Nachlaß*. There Kant writes: "Everything comes down to life—whatever vivifies [*belebt*] is pleasurable. Life is unity; hence all taste has as its principle the unity of vivifying sensations." To this Kant then adds, most dramatically so for us: "Freedom is original life and its coherence [*Zusammenhang*] is the condition for the harmony [*Übereinstimmung*] of all living; hence that which promotes the feeling of universal life is the cause of pleasure. Do we feel ourselves at home in universal life?"

("Notes on Moral Philosophy," N6862, 19:183).[10] The vital force of life is not merely biological, but a force relative to the highest order of life, namely, freedom.[11] Accordingly, we can say that the demand of freedom taken up by the aesthetic reflective judgment is translated into a feeling of pleasure as the feeling of intelligent life relative to its promotion.

Beauty and the Furtherance of Life

A further step, which can only be outlined here, is to see how the beautiful carries out this furtherance of life and constitutes the "prompt" for the purposiveness of nature. That the beautiful concerns the furtherance of life is explicitly indicated by Kant in section 23 where he contrasts the beautiful with the sublime. In contrast to the sublime in which there is a feeling of a momentary check to the vital forces, the feeling with respect to the beautiful, Kant tells us, "carries with it directly a feeling of the furtherance of life [*Beförderung des Lebens*]" (§23, 5:244). This furtherance of life appears to be possible only under the condition where life is in accord with itself, which is precisely what is displayed by the beautiful. Here, then, we can ask: How does the beautiful display itself, and precisely what is displayed by the beautiful?

Regarding the first half of this question, we know that Kant makes the following distinctions. First, "there are two kinds of beauty: free beauty (*pulchritudo vaga*) and merely accessory beauty (*pulchritude adhaerens*)" (§16, 5:229). In the case of the former, there is no definite concept of what the object judged beautiful ought to be, whereas, in the latter, the beautiful is conditioned by such a concept. From this distinction one should not assume that Kant wants to privilege free beauty over accessory or adherent beauty; rather, it is simply the case that in a free beauty we judge the purposiveness

10. Immanuel Kant, "Notes on Moral Philosophy," in *Notes and Fragments*, ed. and trans. Paul Guyer, trans. Curtis Bowman and Frederick Rauscher (New York: Cambridge University Press, 2005), 405–478, 443 (translation altered).

11. In his *Lectures on Ethics*, Kant writes: "Freedom, on the other hand, is the capacity which confers unlimited usefulness to all the others. It is the highest degree of life. . . . The inner worth of the world, *the summum bonum*, is freedom according to a choice that is not necessitated to act. Freedom is thus the inner worth of the world" (27:344). Immanuel Kant, "Moral Philosophy [Collins]," in *Lectures on Ethics*, ed. Peter Heath and Jerome Borges Schneewind, trans. Peter Heath (Cambridge: Cambridge University Press, 1997), 37–222, 125.

of the form apart from any conceptualization. In fact, Kant gives accessory beauty a certain preference in that it can exhibit an ideal of beauty. The ideal of beauty is an archetype of taste that rests on an indeterminate idea that can be presented "only in an individual exhibition" (§17, 5:232). Such an ideal would then be fixed by a concept of purposiveness internal to the possibility of the object. Such an ideal, Kant tells us, is only found in the human relative to the humanity of the person, and this entails that in the ideal of beauty there is an expression of morality

Secondly, Kant tells us elsewhere that unless we connect the beautiful arts with moral ideas, which alone carry with them a self-sufficient satisfaction, the beautiful arts serve only as a diversion (§52, 5:326). Kant's comment here points to his subtle distinction between an intellectual interest in the beautiful and an interested pleasure that cannot be a determining ground for a judgment of taste. There can be an immediate interest in beauty, albeit only indirectly. Kant says that taking an immediate interest in natural beauty is always the mark of a good moral character, since it indicates a disposition to moral feeling relative to the beautiful forms of nature (§42, 5:298–99). And, quite interestingly, in relation to this notion Kant then claims that art is called beautiful only if it looks like nature (§45, 5:306).

Thirdly, the beautiful displays itself as sensible illustration. This is, of course, the idea that the beautiful is a symbol of the moral good. Its importance for Kant cannot be underestimated, for it is only in this capacity for symbolic sensible illustration that our pleasure in the beautiful includes

> a claim to everyone else's assent, while the mind is also conscious of being ennobled. . . . The morally good is the *intelligible* that taste has in view . . . for it is with this intelligible that even our higher cognitive powers harmonize. . . . In this ability [taste], judgment does not find itself subjected to a heteronomy from empirical laws, as it does elsewhere in an empirical judging, just as reason does regarding the power of desire. . . . And because the subject has this possibility within him, while outside [him] there is also the possibility that nature will harmonize with it, judgment finds itself referred to something that is both in the subject himself and outside him, something that is neither nature nor freedom and yet is linked with the basis of freedom, the supersensible, in which the theoretical and practical power are in an unknown manner combined and joined into a unity. (§59, 5:353)

In the particular vividness of the beautiful—a vividness in relation to a felt accord—the mind is strengthened, *as if* it has received confirmation that it is universal life. For it is now referred to something within and without. In the experience of the beautiful, the mind stands in relation to the unity of being—the supersensible ground that unites freedom and nature.

It cannot go unnoticed that in each of these distinctions Kant links the beautiful to the good, as if the good is sheltered in the beautiful. What is ultimately displayed in the beautiful, then, is the intelligent order that we can now call transcendental freedom.

The Furtherance of Life as Moral Destination

To take yet another step towards resolving the issue of the bridge, we need to make note of that aspect of the demand of freedom that, in effect, connects the idea of beauty to moral destination. That is to say, if we ask, with respect to this demand, why freedom should take place in the world, why nature should be compatible with intelligent order, the answer, one must suppose, is that it should take place, not just for the sake of itself, but for the sake of its perfection. This idea is precisely what is developed in the second part of the *Critique of Judgment* and thus serves as a focal point for connecting the aesthetic judgment on the beautiful to the teleology of nature, a connection that must ultimately be expressed in terms of the furtherance of life.

With respect to the beautiful, this life is "determined" in relation to feeling that, as the feeling of pleasure, seeks its own furtherance, a furtherance that is connected to our awareness of freedom in the world of sense. In relation to this determination, we now want to say that the teleology of nature approximates, at a certain level, Kant's philosophy *of* life, and it is this determination that connects the two parts of the *Critique of Judgment*. If the first part of the *Critique of Judgment* pertains to the feeling of the furtherance of life, the second part draws our attention to what that furtherance of life actually entails, namely, the formativity of human life. In the formal objective purposiveness of the second part of the *Critique*, the mind's encounter with the world is something other than amazement (*Verwunderung*), as the shock of incompatibility. It is, as Kant tells us in section 62, an experience of admiration (*Bewunderung*)—an amazement that continually recurs after the doubt is gone. This amazement that is a look of purposive agreement (*Einstimmung*) enlarges the mind; "it makes it suspect, as it were, that there is something else above and beyond those presentations of sense, something which, although we do not know it, might hold the ultimate basis for that agreement" (§62, 5:365). Kant then suggests that what is being admired in this agreement is what we commonly call beauty. Here it is not a matter of aesthetic judging, but an intellectual judging, which has its own manner of enlivening.

So, what precisely is this philosophy of life, this furtherance of life relative to nature? In the opening section of the "Critique of Teleological Judgment," Kant claims that the order of nature can be comprehended only if purpose is added to its known order, namely, the order of mechanical causation. Then in section 63 Kant makes an important distinction between intrinsic and extrinsic purposiveness. An intrinsic purposiveness is simply the purposive organization found in all organic forms, while extrinsic purposiveness is the purposiveness of something in nature relative to something else; that is to say, a suitability for the purposes of other living beings. This kind of purposiveness raises the question of whether nature as a whole can be viewed as working toward a universal end. This possibility in turn depends on another possibility, namely, whether there is a being that could be regarded as the ultimate purpose (*letzter Zweck*) of nature, one for whom all nature would then be a means (§83, 5:429). Kant argues that such a being could only be a human being, since this being alone "can form a concept of purpose" relative to a system of purposes. And this is to say that human intelligent life is essentially that of a formative activity adapting nature to its ends.

But what then are we to say about the ultimate purpose of nature as it pertains directly to this being that is in fact ethically an end-in-itself, a final purpose (*Endzweck*) that so considered is independent of nature? Kant tells us in section 83 that the ultimate purpose is to *prepare* the human for what she or he must do in order to be a final purpose. Kant then tells us that the ultimate purpose is in fact culture—ethical life—as if to say that secret agreement that expands the mind is in some way connected with formation, with bringing about our formation as the very idea of the furtherance of life. Without ethical life nature would then be in vain. Or, to say this differently by inverting the formulation, nature is that which is to be amenable to the history of freedom. Accordingly, we can say that the preparation for the ultimate end is not a matter of contemplation, but of practical activity. And, as a final note, Kant wants to then consider the highest good with respect to this activity. This good, the *summum bonum*, is happiness, and our striving after this good—a striving that requires in this account the notion of God—would place us before the thorough-going harmony of human and natural purposiveness (§87, 5:450). It would constitute life's ultimate being at home in the world, or, what one might call, as the appropriate term for harmonious order, justice. In looking back, we see that this idea was anticipated in beauty. The furtherance of life, it now appears, is something beyond feeling; it is the activity of intelligent life's own coming to itself through the direction of reflective judgment.

For Kant, the bridge-building that takes the form of a demand for intelligent life is a very peculiar kind of demand. As if looking into a mirror, intelligent life continues to be encouraged by what it sees. It refuses the struggle that others see in the relation between freedom and nature. In the demand to be at home in the world, it looks to nurturing itself, finding encouragement as it looks at nature. Nature is beautiful, Kant tells us, because it looks like art, and art can only be called beautiful if it looks like nature, that is, if it looks like nature's purposiveness, which is really already intelligent life. There is here no "pain of beauty" that might foreshadow an enmity between freedom and nature, no secret justice of destruction. Still, the furtherance of life has its own reward.

Chapter 3

Pure Aesthetic Judging as a Form of Life

Courtney D. Fugate

Kant's metaphysical understanding of life presents us with something of a puzzle.[1] On the one hand, the concept itself appears only rarely in the writings published during his lifetime. One might expect to find some application of it in the "Critique of Teleological Judgment"; but there Kant denies not only that we can legitimately attribute life to organisms, but even that we can legitimately attribute an analogue of life to them (§65, 5:374–75).[2] The reason Kant gives for this denial here and elsewhere—namely, that the very concept of matter is incompatible with the concept of life—indeed might make one suspect that the concept has no role to play in the critical

1. My inspiration for taking up this topic long ago was first Martin Moors and then again later Rudi Makkreel. I would like to dedicate this chapter to both of them with gratitude. I have also gained much from the pioneering work, John H. Zammito, *The Genesis of Kant's "Critique of Judgment"* (Chicago: University of Chicago Press, 1992), ch. 15. An earlier treatment of this topic can be found in Courtney D. Fugate, *The Teleology of Reason* (Berlin: de Gruyter, 2014). Makkreel was perhaps the first to suggest in print that Kant's analysis of judgments of taste may be fundamental to understanding his wider conception of life. See Rudolph A. Makkreel, *Imagination and Interpretation in Kant: The Hermeneutical Import of the "Critique of Judgment"* (Chicago: University of Chicago Press, 1990), ch. 5.

2. Here and in the following, I cite all Kant's writings using the form "volume:page number" of *Kant's gesammelte Schriften*, ed. Königlich Preußische Akademie der Wissenschaften (Berlin: Georg Reimer/Walter de Gruyter, 1902–).

philosophy at all. On the other hand, when the concept of life does appear in Kant's writings, it does so in the most striking and original of ways, ways that are in part the basis of Georg Wilhelm Friedrich Hegel's penetrating remark that "with his concept of *internal* purposiveness, *Kant* has resuscitated the Idea in general and especially the Idea of life."[3] If we look to Kant's personal notes and the transcripts of his lectures, we also find a very complex and precise set of views on this topic, a set of views that Kant clearly continued to develop over his long career.

But as it turns out, this initially puzzling duality between Kant's published and unpublished views on the concept of life is a fairly common feature of his entire corpus. As recent research has demonstrated plentifully, what first appear as fresh and spontaneous remarks in the published writings are in fact often the conclusions of decades of analysis and reflection. Usually, the latter reflect both a deep engagement with the views of his predecessors, contemporaries, and critics, and an effort to adapt these views to the radically new context of his own critical philosophy.

In this respect, the concept of life is no different; or so I will argue. Indeed, as I will show in this chapter, Hegel was correct in taking this as a truly exemplary case of Kant's creative adaptation and "resuscitation" of a traditional concept. Much could be said on this topic, but here I will focus in particular on how Kant's attempts to integrate the concept of life into his critical philosophy silently structure his analysis and deduction of pure aesthetic judgments regarding the beautiful. In the first section, I will lay the ground by recalling the basic outlines of the history of the concept of life in the Western metaphysical tradition. In the second, I will turn to Kant's general theory of this concept. In the final section, I will show that when seen from within this wider context, the deduction of pure aesthetic judgments is in essence the deduction of a unique form of human life.

The Problem of Life in the Metaphysical Tradition Prior to Kant

Historically, the philosophical concept of life has always signified the internal activity that is characteristic of some substances. In Plato and neo-Platonism, this inner activity was identified with a process of mediation between an

3. Gottfried Wilhelm Friedrich Hegel, *The Encyclopaedia Logic*, trans. Theodore F. Geraets, W. A. S. Suchting, and H. S. Harris (Indianapolis: Hackett, 1991), 280.

idea and what partakes of or participates in that idea, and thus also between the universal and the particular, the one and the many, the first principle and its effects. But, above all, the Platonic conception of life identified it with self-motion, which it was believed always began from an invisible and indeed intellectual principle, namely, the "soul."[4] In the Aristotelian tradition, the concept of life continued to serve much the same function. Indeed, in accordance with his desire to bring form and matter into a closer connection, Aristotle expanded the explanatory role of life despite his rejection of the central Platonic conception of self-motion. In his writings, the distinction between different kinds of substances is understood not in terms of the distinct ideas in which they participate, but instead in terms of the distinct forms of internal or natural activity that they exhibit. This gave rise in turn to a hierarchical understanding of the forms of life according to which distinct, more independent, and better kinds of beings were understood to be characterized by distinct, more independent, and better kinds of living activities. In accordance with his usual "pros hen"[5] understanding of metaphysical concepts, this also meant that for Aristotle one such form—namely, that belonging to the unmoved mover—was most perfect and independent and therefore most properly to be called "living."[6]

In the medieval period, this two-fold root of the concept of life was codified and provided a Christian inflection through the writings of St. Thomas Aquinas. In *De veritate*, he introduces his own view, stating, "we say that something lives in the proper sense if it has a principle of motion or of any activity whatsoever within it, for the primary reason why things are said to be alive is that they seem to have something within them moving them in some kind of motion."[7] As we learn further in *Summa theologiae*, the distinguishing feature of living beings is first discovered in examining the "characteristic life of animals." From these it is evident that life begins when they begin to move themselves from within and ceases when they

4. For more on this see Joachim Ritter and Karlfried Gründer, eds., *Historisches Wörterbuch der Philosophie*, Bd. 5 (Basel: Schwabe, 1980), 53–56.

5. The feature of Aristotle's doctrine of being and its relation to his concept of life is presented excellently in Joseph Owens, *The Doctrine of Being in the Aristotelian "Metaphysics"* (Toronto: Pontifical Institute of Mediaeval Studies, 1963), 107–37, 461–66.

6. Aristotle, *Metaphysics*, 12.7.1072b.

7. St. Thomas Aquinas, *The Disputed Questions on Truth*, vol. 1, *Questions I–IX*, trans. Robert W. Mulligan (Chicago: Henry Regnery, 1952), 198.

cease to do so.[8] This motion is not accidental to and externally produced in such beings, but instead is natural and arises from within them. Hence, although all motion of natural bodies bears some similarity to life, they are not said to be living in a proper sense; for their nature is to be at rest and hence their motion, which is always produced from without, is a departure from what is natural to them.[9]

From this it would appear that life is a kind of activity, namely, one that begins from within. But this is incorrect according to Aquinas. Words are applied to things mainly because of their external appearances, but that does not mean that words should be taken to indicate these appearances alone. For example, "body" appears to us as a three-dimensional thing, but to define body as a three-dimensional thing only would be to classify it as a species of quantity.[10] Similarly, although we encounter life through various kinds of activities, by "life" we actually refer to a "substance which of its nature has the power of moving itself or giving itself any kind of impulse to activity." Thus, life is not an activity, but instead something that belongs preeminently to certain kinds of substances, by virtue of which they are *able* to bring about motion or activity from within. In stating this, Aquinas also underscores the deep connection between the very nature of the substance, and thus the *kind* of substance it is, and the specific activities through which its life becomes apparent. For although all motion has similarity to life, as was stated above, only that which truly originates in the living nature of the substance can be called "living" in a proper sense.

As in many matters, Aquinas also follows Aristotle in outlining a hierarchy within the various possible forms of life. As he explains, the more perfectly it can be seen that a thing acts from itself, "the more perfectly does it possess life."[11] Now action from within can have various determinations, namely, (1) the form by which it is moved, (2) the end for the sake of which it moves, and (3) the carrying out of the activity itself. Plants are of the lowest kind, as both (1) and (2) are fixed by nature for these and it is only (3) that arises from within them. Next are animals, which in addition to (3) are also moved by a form that they themselves acquire through the senses. Still higher are the beings with intellect, for in addition to (1) and

8. St. Thomas Aquinas, *Summa theologiae*, vol. 4, *Knowledge in God (1a. 14–18)*, ed. Thomas Gornall (Cambridge, UK: Blackfriars, 1964), 115.

9. Aquinas, *Summa theologiae*, 117.

10. Aquinas, *Summa theologiae*, 119.

11. Aquinas, *Summa theologiae*, 123.

(3), these also act in view of ends, "which they provide for themselves," and hence they "have a more complete kind of life in that their self-movement is more complete."

But that is not all; the activities of beings with intellect can also be more or less complete in inverse proportion to the extent to which their principles and ends are provided for them by nature. The human intellect, for instance, is self-moved in that it initiates motions, acts from forms it acquires sensibly, and devises the ends to be pursued in particular actions. However, "by nature" it has certain "first principles, about which it has no choice, and the ultimate end, which it is not free not to will."[12] Moreover, as human knowledge is impossible without input from the senses, the human mind is in this way also dependent upon something provided from without.[13] None of these defects, however, are found in God, whose being is identical with his intellect. Hence, according to Aquinas, God moves from his own form toward himself as end and is indeed identical with this end and with what he knows. This activity alone is truly complete in the sense of being entirely from itself and toward itself. And although God's life cannot be other than it is (i.e., his being is necessary), it is necessary not because any of its determinations are provided from without (as is the case with the human intellect, for instance), but rather because they arise from his own nature entirely. For this reason, although all beings from plants to those with intellect can be said to "live" in a proper sense, only "God has life in the most proper [*maxime proprie*] sense."[14]

Before moving forward, it will be helpful to say something about how the concept of a soul fits into this discussion. Following Aristotle, Aquinas also regards the soul as the substantial principle of life in a natural body. The need for such a principle, he argues, is evident from the fact that natural bodies are only moved by something external to them. Hence, if there is life in a natural body, this must be by virtue of a substance that lives within it. Such a substance is simply called the "soul," and it, rather than the body, is the *proper subject* of life in beings that possess a body. Beings without bodies, on the other hand, such as angels and God, do not require such a principle to act, but instead act of themselves. Hence, they are not said to have "souls" in a proper sense, although they certainly have

12. Aquinas, *Summa theologiae*, 125.

13. St. Thomas Aquinas, *Summa contra gentiles*, book 4, *Salvation*, trans. Charles J. O'Neil (Notre Dame, IN: University of Notre Dame Press, 1975), 81.

14. Aquinas, *Summa theologiae*, 123. See also Aquinas, *Summa Contra Gentiles,* 81.

life. "Soul" is therefore to be understood as a concept that depends on the further concept of a relation; "soul" is what we call the inner principle of activity *insofar as* it acts upon the body.

Turning now to the modern period, it is striking to see just how little philosophical attention was devoted to the concept of life, at least up to Kant's time. For the most part, we find it relegated to the dustbin of history along with all the other so-called "occult qualities" to which the moderns were often vehemently opposed. On the continent, the sole major figure to deal with it is Gottfried Wilhelm Leibniz, who, however, left behind only the doctrine that all substances are intrinsically living along with some notoriously obscure comments about the need to retain the conception of an entelechy. Closer to Kant's immediate milieu, Christian Wolff and his followers seem to have had even less to say on the topic than did Leibniz. The only exception that I have been able to locate and who would have been relevant to Kant's intellectual development is Christian August Crusius, whose treatment of this concept is the most detailed and extensive of any German philosopher of his time.[15]

Crusius's concept of life, which I can treat here only briefly, is remarkable for the way in which it combines the kind of theory found in Aquinas with concerns distinctive to the modern period. "Under life," he explains, "we understand that capacity of a substance, by virtue of which it can be active in many ways based upon an internal ground."[16] The main motivation behind this definition is the recognition that, according to early modern physics, material substances do in fact exhibit activity from a relatively internal principle. Their distinguishing characteristic lies instead in that this activity is always determined in a fixed spatial direction, and thus lacks the "capacity" to be active in "many ways." Ultimately, Crusius sees life then as consisting in the capacity of a substance to be active by means of several fundamentally distinct powers.

This definition, Crusius claims, agrees perfectly with common usage if only we recognize that in the latter it is sometimes employed "properly," at other times "tropically." It is applied properly to spirits, since these necessar-

15. I am not here considering the possible influences on Kant's views on life that come from outside of metaphysics proper, many of which are discussed in Jennifer Mensch, *Kant's Organicism: Epigenesis and the Development of Critical Philosophy* (Chicago: University of Chicago Press, 2013).

16. Christian August Crusius, *Entwurf der nothwendigen Vernunft-Wahrheiten* (Leipzig: Gleditschens Buchhandlung, 1766), §§458, 942–43.

ily have at least two fundamental powers, namely, will and understanding, and thus also to embodied spirits, that is, animals. It is applied tropically, however, to bodies, plants, and powers. "When we call an animal living: We say 'life' of the entire *Supposito* §24. But we hold only the soul to be the *Subjectum quo* of life, and say that the body becomes enlivened by the soul. . . . As long as the body is enlivened by the soul: Then also life itself is ascribed to the body through a trope *κατά συμπάθειαν*, i.e., *participative*, and through a participation."[17]

Thus, the phrase "life of the body" is not to be taken literally when it refers to biological activities such as the beating of the heart. These would be better described as "indications of the enlivened body." The use of the term in respect to plants, however, Crusius regards as entirely figurative or tropical, since these have no souls and the only basis for using the word "life" in respect to them lies in their external similarity to animal bodies. Finally, for Crusius it is clear that a physical power in a state of activity, which in this period was often referred to as a "living power" (*lebendigen Kraft*), can only be called such tropically, and should instead be said not to have "life" (*Leben*), but "liveliness" (*Lebendigkeit*) to avoid confusion.

According to this important precursor of Kant, then, the true *subjectum quo* of life is always the soul or spirit. But what about the activities of souls? Are they not living as well? To explain this final use of the term "life," Crusius draws on the classical distinction between existing in a first actuality and existing in a second actuality, explaining: "Life can be present either *actu primo*, or *actu secundo.* It is present *actu primo*, if the powers required for life exist in the subject, but presently do not act. But when they also actually act: then life is there *actu secundo.* Thus, life in *actu secundo* consists in the liveliness of the spiritual powers." As he further remarks, "since the will in a spiritual being is the ruling power," life is in fact present in *actu secundo* "when any single living activity of the will is present."[18]

Already from this, we can see that Crusius, like Aquinas, is concerned to distinguish different senses of life, arguing that some are proper, while others are figurative. But also like Aquinas, and despite his more modern approach, Crusius embraces his own version of the traditional hierarchy of forms of life, taken in a proper sense, based upon the degree or perfection of this activity. Crusius's hierarchy, however, is much more complex and in fact runs along three distinct axes. The life of a being can be of a higher

17. Crusius, *Vernunft-Wahrheiten*, §§458, 945.

18. Crusius, *Vernunft-Wahrheiten*, §§460, 949–50.

or lower kind, and this kind in turn can be developed such that its life is increased or diminished with respect to both the number of its powers and the perfection of these powers. In terms of kind, living beings range all the way from those that are "merely passive" in the sense that no living activity (*actu secundo*) is present in them unless they are stimulated by sensations, to those that are self-active, in which case they can enliven themselves without this.[19] Human beings, Crusius maintains, are of the latter kind. In terms of magnitude, or the number of powers, a living being is capable of activating and developing its powers such that it can exercise more powers at a time. Finally, in terms of perfection, the powers can increase in strength, become better internally connected, and can be developed so that the less noble powers and drives are subject to those that are more noble, such as conscience. The key to developing the last two, that is, the number and perfection of powers, lies in freedom; for on Crusius's view, it alone is absolutely spontaneous and thus capable of directing, recruiting, and, as it were, forming the other human powers and drives so that they develop in both magnitude and perfection. In this sense, freedom is the proper and highest ruling principle of life within spirits, although by itself it is not necessarily of the greatest strength or magnitude.

This theory of Crusius is quite original, and certainly goes beyond anything found in Aquinas. Equally original is Crusius's attempt to provide an extensive taxonomy of the different ways in which the powers of living beings may be internally connected, each of which he associates with a special law that is either entirely spiritual or rather mixed, "leges pneumaticae vel mixtae."[20] Such laws can either be empirical, or metaphysical, which latter outline only the possible laws of such beings. The further details of this theory do not presently concern us here, except insofar as they constitute an original and quite advanced theory of how the activities of a living being can operate in connection with one another; for instance, how the enlivening of certain mental faculties can depend upon the life in others, how the development or perfection of one may depend upon another, and how the life of freedom can be exercised to form the entire life of an individual.

Finally, to be noted here is the remarkable fact that Crusius chooses to treat the possibility of the communication of ideas and sentiments, which he takes to be the true essence of language and the basis of society, within this metaphysics of the laws of life. Ideas and sensations, Crusius argues, are

19. Crusius, *Vernunft-Wahrheiten*, §§467, 963–64.

20. Crusius, *Vernunft-Wahrheiten*, §§459, 948.

immaterial activities within the soul and, as such, they cannot be produced passively in us through the laws governing the interactions of material substances. Thus, when we communicate, we do not simply influence the mind of another; we rather cause them to literally come alive in a certain specific way, a way that should correspond to what it means to think a certain idea or to have a certain feeling of the kind that we intend to communicate. Now, like all other activities of living beings, this manner of enlivening must be governed by laws, in this case, those describing how the "power to sense can become combined also with a liveliness of the understanding that in other parts is independent from all movement."[21] The laws in question are contingent, and hence empirical, and also "mixed," meaning they span the gap between the mechanism of the body and the powers of the soul. "If a spirit is to be social," Crusius explains, "then he must be able to share his thoughts and his state of mind [*Gemüthszustand*] with others, and others with him, through sensations." But human beings can only communicate through the motions we produce with our bodies. Hence, "the sharing of thoughts must happen through certain motions, which serve as signs of thoughts, namely, in that the matter signified occurs to the other spirit in the sensing of the sign. This is what is essential in language."[22] The laws governing this sharing of life through language constitute a special class, and hence are unique and irreducible to those of any other kind of activity. Thus, for Crusius, the sharing of thoughts and sentiments is a relatively autonomous form of activity, that is to say, a relatively autonomous form of life.

As we will soon see, Kant took a special interest in the complexities of a theory of life, and in this he no doubt drew considerable inspiration from these innovations found in Crusius.

Kant's Underlying Theory of Life

Since, as a general rule, nothing in Kant's unauthorized writings should be given more weight than those thoughts he actually selected for publication, it is best to begin with the few such remarks he makes about life. In the *Metaphysical Foundations of Natural Science*, published in 1786, Kant states that "*life* is the faculty of a *substance* to determine itself to act from an *internal principle*, of a *finite substance* to change, and of a *material substance*

21. Crusius, *Vernunft-Wahrheiten*, §§465, 957.

22. Crusius, *Vernunft-Wahrheiten*, §§465, 957–58.

[to determine itself] to motion or rest, as change of its state. Now we know no other internal principle in a substance for changing its state except *desiring*, and no other internal activity at all except *thinking*, together with that which depends upon it, the *feeling* of pleasure and displeasure, and *desire* or willing" (4:544).[23]

In the first lines of this passage, Kant endorses—as he does on many occasions—the traditional metaphysical concept of life. But at the same time, he partially follows Crusius in indicating what this definition means for a specifically material substance when we take into account the principle of inertia: Life for such a being must be understood as a faculty to be active in more ways than just according to one spatial direction, and thus to violate that principle and to change its own state spontaneously, whether this be one of motion or rest. However, as Kant further explains, since the principle of inertia is a fundamental presupposition of all natural science, it follows that attributing life to material substance would mean the "death of all natural philosophy" (4:544).[24] Thus, "the inertia of matter is, and means, nothing else than its lifelessness, as matter in itself" (4:544). Kant's endorsement, it turns out, therefore comes with a seemingly devastating caveat; life as such cannot be located in nature regarded as appearance, and to the extent that the concept of soul depends on the ability of an internal principle to affect the body, it too seems to lose all objective reality. That a principle of life cannot be attributed to bodies or matter as such, is indeed one of the permanent and fundamental limitations of his theory.

The purpose of the second part of this passage is less clear unless seen within the context of Kant's more general theory of meaning. Crusius had already made the claim, based on metaphysical grounds, that a living being must at least possess both intellect and will. Kant reaches the same result here, but by the following argument: the definition of life is that of a capacity for acting from an internal principle. But the only internal principle we can properly *conceive of* is thinking. Now, acting from an internal principle of thought is precisely *desiring*. Therefore, life, if it is to mean anything at all, must be the concept of a substance with a faculty of desire. Kant thus arrives at the same conclusion as Crusius, but by means of a critical rather than a metaphysical argument and so without any commitment to the existence of such beings.

23. Immanuel Kant, *Metaphysical Foundations of Natural Science*, ed. and trans. Michael Friedmann (Cambridge: Cambridge University Press, 2004).

24. Cf. *Critique of Judgment*, §73, 5:395.

This is the origin of Kant's real definition of life, which is found in several of his published writings. The *Critique of Practical Reason*, for example, has it that " 'life' is the faculty of a being to act according to the laws of the faculty of desire" (5:9n).[25] This is sometimes referred to as Kant's "narrow" definition of life.[26] However, Kant himself does not generally speak in terms of either a narrow or a broad definition and, if I am correct, then this is really the only definition of life he thinks possible. Moreover, as Kant explains later in the same passage, this must be the *broadest* formulation of such a real definition, since "it is composed only of marks belonging to pure understanding, i.e., categories, which contain nothing empirical." Essentially the same definition is stated in a variety of ways throughout Kant's writings and always as if it were the true and only definition.[27]

Now, similar to what we saw in Aquinas and Crusius, life is here described as a kind of second-order faculty belonging to a substance or a being considered as a whole, a faculty by virtue of which it may have other faculties for specific kinds of activity, and most especially a faculty of desire. So, while the faculty of desire and life are distinct, there is by definition no living being for Kant to which a faculty of desire is not also attributed. For this reason, Kant states in some contexts we can just define a living being as one having a faculty of desire.[28]

The same generality applied to his definition of life also applies to the definitions of desire and pleasure, which immediately follow the definition of life stated in the second *Critique*: "The *faculty of desire* is a being's *faculty*

25. Immanuel Kant, *Critique of Practical Reason*, in *Practical Philosophy*, trans. and ed. Mary J. Gregor, 133–272 (Cambridge: Cambridge University Press, 1996). Here I have changed the translation of *nach* as "in accordance with" to "according to."

26. See Pluhar's editorial note in *Critique of Judgment*, §73, 5:394, p. 276n7.

27. I cite (and translate) Kant's so-called "Reflexionen," and other texts, according to *Kant's gesammelte Schriften*, ed. Königlich Preußische Akademie der Wissenschaften (Berlin: Georg Reimer/Walter de Gruyter, 1902–); here "Metaphysik Mrongovius," in *Kant's Vorlesungen, Kant's gesammelte Schriften*, Bd. 29, ed. Akademie der Wissenschaften zu Göttingen (Berlin: de Gruyter, 1983), 743–940, 29:894; "Reflexionen zur Anthropologie," in *Handschriftlicher Nachlaß: Anthropologie*, Bd. 15 of *Kant's gesammelte Schriften*, ed. Berlin-Brandenburgische Akademie der Wissenschaften (Berlin: Georg Reimer, 1913), 55–654, R574, 15:248; R1034, 15:465; R1050, 15:469; "Reflexionen zur Metaphysik," in *Handschriftlicher Nachlaß: Metaphysik*, Bd. 17 of *Kant's gesammelte Schriften*, ed. Preußische Akademie der Wissenschaften (Berlin: de Gruyter, 1926), 227–745, R3855, 17:313–14; "Metaphysik Volckmann," in *Lectures on Metaphysics*, trans. and ed. Karl Ameriks and Steve Naragon (Cambridge: Cambridge University Press, 1997), 287–96, 28:448–49.

28. See, for example, "Metaphysik L_2," in *Lectures on Metaphysics*, 297–354, 28:587.

to be by means of its representations the cause of the reality of the objects of these representations. Pleasure [*Lust*] is the *representation of the agreement of an object or of an action with the subjective conditions of life*, i.e., with the faculty of the *causality of a representation with respect to the reality of its object* (or with respect to the determination of the powers of the subject to action in order to produce the object)" (5:9n).

These definitions are also repeated, in various forms and nearly always with a reference to life, throughout Kant's published and unpublished writings. In other contexts, however, Kant goes much more deeply into his analysis of the latter in particular. In a series of reflections and notes from the late 1770s, for instance, he explains that we cannot actually feel life itself, and so pleasure cannot simply be said to be a feeling of it.[29] What we do feel, however, is the *exercise* of life in our actions, and most particularly in the feelings of pleasure or displeasure, which indicate the furtherance or hindrance of this exercise. In the "Metaphysik Mrongovius" transcripts, he is reported to have explained this special connection between life and feeling as follows: "Since pleasure is agreement with the faculty of desire, it is also agreement with life, and displeasure [is] conflict with life" (29:894).[30]

Now, because of the indirectness of this relation, there is, according to Kant, no simple way to read off, as it were, the meaning of pleasure and displeasure in regard to life itself; for although pleasure and displeasure generally indicate the furtherance or hindrance of life or liveliness in the part being exercised, this exercise may in fact lead to a decrease in the overall faculty for further action, and thus to a decrease of life in the whole, which is something Crusius had already noted.[31] For the same reason, we must often distinguish our feeling of the furtherance of life or of liveliness

29. "Reflexionen zur Anthropologie," R561, 15:244; R582, 15:251; R586, 15:252–53; R587, 15:253–54; R1487, 15:717–26; "Moralphilosophie Collins," in *Vorlesungen über Moralphilosophie*, Bd. 27 of *Kant's gesammelte Schriften*, ed. Akademie der Wissenschaften der DDR (Berlin: de Gruyter, 1974), 237–473, 27:381; "Moral Mrongovius," in *Vorlesungen über Moralphilosophie*, Bd. 27 of *Kant's gesammelte Schriften*, ed. Akademie der Wissenschaften der DDR (Berlin: de Gruyter, 1979), 1395–581, 27:1512; "Anthropologie Friedländer," in *Vorlesungen über Anthropologie*, Bd. 25 of *Kant's gesammelte Schriften*, ed. Berlin-Brandenburgische Akademie der Wissenschaften (Berlin: de Gruyter, 1997), 469–728, 25:499; "Anthropologie Mrongovius," in *Vorlesungen über Anthropologie*, 1209–1429, 25:1319.

30. Cf. "Reflexionen zur Anthropologie," R823, 15:367–68.

31. See "Reflexionen zur Anthropologie," R570, 15:247; R580, 15:249–50; "Anthropologie Friedländer," 25:506.

(*actu secundo*) from what furthers life itself as a whole (*actu primo*). This is obvious in the cases of opium or drunkenness, for instance, which provide an initial stimulation and rush of pleasure, just before rendering us insensible.[32] And quite generally, Kant points out that we can feel very good while being ignorant of the fact we are in fact near to death (*The Conflict of the Faculties*, 7:100).[33] On the other hand, pain may signal the hindrance of life in some part of our body, but at the same time improve overall health. What this shows is that, although pleasure and pain do indicate the state of life and its promotion or hindrance in some respect, their true significance depends upon how the activities they indicate add to or subtract from the life of the whole.

As we will see in a moment, Kant generalizes this idea far beyond such empirical examples. But to understand how, we must first examine the distinctive hierarchy of the forms of life that he develops in his reflections and notes to replace the ones articulated by his predecessors. Much like them, Kant thinks of life in terms of a hierarchy arranged according to the degree of activity present in each. The first and lowest degree of life is found in animal nature, which at most contains an *analogon rationis*, or an analogy of reason ("Metaphysik Volckmann," 28:450) and an *arbitrium brutum*, or brute faculty of choice. Such life, even in the human body, is essentially "incomplete," without spontaneity, and subject to "external necessitation as in a machine," while its desire is "heteronomous," governed by instinct, and dependent on pleasure for its activation ("Metaphysik Volckmann," 28:251). Furthermore, and very significantly, it is entirely private or restricted to the individual. This form of life departs so far from the traditional meaning that Kant sometimes suggests it should not be referred to as life at all. The highest kind of life, by contrast, is that of spirit, which belongs to free beings with understanding and will, who, by virtue of these, have the ground of their actions more fully within themselves ("Metaphysik L_1," 28:205; "Reflexionen zur Anthropologie," R824, 15:368).[34] God, understood as *primus motor*, is the only "original and unconditioned life" and the source of all life, as

32. Immanuel Kant, *Die philosophischen Hauptvorlesungen Immanuel Kants: Nach den neu aufgefundenen Kollegheften des Grafen Heinrich zu Dohna-Wundlacken*, ed. Arnold Kowalewski (Munich: Rösl, 1924), 177.

33. Immanuel Kant, *The Conflict of the Faculties*, in *Religion and Rational Theology* (Cambridge: Cambridge University Press, 1996), 233–328.

34. Immanuel Kant, "Metaphysik L_1," in *Vorlesungen über Metaphysik und Rationaltheologie*, Bd. 28 of *Kant's gesammelte Schriften*, ed. (Berlin: de Gruyter, 1968), 167–350.

Aristotle had claimed; "all other life depends upon the determining causes in time" ("Reflexionen zur Metaphysik," R4786, 17:727–28). Nevertheless, the human being, as a *free* being, partakes of a "spiritual" life as well; for through this property "the chain of determining causes is in every case cut" ("Reflexionen zur Metaphysik," R3855, 17:313–14). Such life is "complete" ("Reflexionen zur Anthropologie," R567, 15:246) and highest because it is free ("Anthropologie Friedländer," 25:560) and possesses "spontaneity in accordance with practical laws, and its nature is not determinable merely organically and physically, but also morally" ("Reflexionen zur Metaphysik," R5995, 18:418–19).[35] Instead of being governed by instinct and by "a foreign and implanted idea," human beings possess *arbitrium liberum*, or free choice, and direct themselves "autonomously," that is, "according to their own idea, which can originate from themselves *a priori*, and their causality is freedom."

Finally, in contrast to animal life, which is private, spiritual life is intrinsically and objectively universal:

> The sufficiency of free choice is the complete life. The more it is in agreement with itself, the more is its choice, according to its nature, in agreement with the wills of others, and the more it is a ground of the unification of others' choice with our own: the more it agrees with the universal principle of life, the less its obstacles also, and the greater the influence on the relations of free choice of others. The free will that at the same time unifies itself with others possesses the greatest life. ("Reflexionen zur Anthropologie," R567, 15:246)

Freedom is the original life and in its coherence the condition of the agreement of all life; hence, what furthers the feeling of universal life, or the feeling of the furtherance of universal life, produces a pleasure ("Erläuterungen zu A. G. Baumgartens *Initia philosophiae practicae primae*," 19:6862).[36]

---

35. Immanuel Kant, "Reflexionen zur Metaphysik," in *Handschriftlicher Nachlaß: Metaphysik*, Bd. 18 of *Kant's gesammelte Schriften*, ed. Preußische Akademie der Wissenschaften (Berlin: de Gruyter, 1928), 3–725.

36. Immanuel Kant, "Erläuterungen Kants zu A. G. Baumgartens *Initia philosophiae practicae primae*," in *Kant's gesammelte Schriften*, Bd. 19, ed. Preußische Akademie der Wissenschaften (Berlin: de Gruyter, 1934), 5–91, 19:6862.

In short, "whatever harmonizes with freedom agrees with the whole of life" ("Metaphysik L_1," 28:251).[37] Of course, in saying this, Kant is not indicating that freedom agrees with all life and so even with the liveliness that damages and decreases life in the whole, but instead that what harmonizes with freedom agrees with the highest life, that is, the life that is greatest in terms of magnitude and perfection. This, again, is a view anticipated by Crusius.

In a small essay published in 1796, Kant explicates these two kinds of life, that is, the animal and the spiritual, and their relation insofar as this concerns the human being's need for philosophy. Here Kant explains that animal life, though it be merely mechanical and not yet practical, still serves to stimulate and drive us towards the development of our capacities. Nevertheless, this life is a constant fluctuation "poised upon a knife-edge," and as such it requires philosophy as therapy and medicine in order "to preserve the equilibrium which we call health" ("Proclamation of the Imminent Conclusion of a Treaty of Perpetual Peace in Philosophy," 8:414).[38] But, beyond this, philosophy investigates reason and ultimately "proves its [i.e., freedom's] reality and truth in effects that are presentable in experience" (8:416), thereby revealing the "hyperphysical basis of man's life" (8:417). "This life-principle," Kant explains, "is not founded on concepts of the *sensible* . . . ; it proceeds initially and at once from an Idea of the *super-sensible*, namely *freedom*, and from the morally categorical imperative." The philosophy that establishes and teaches this highest principle of life is alone capable of establishing "perpetual peace" and a state of health among rational beings. In a word, life is unity,[39] and so the principle of the highest and greatest life, which is established by philosophy, is also the principle of the highest and greatest unity of all rational beings.

Between the animal life, of which the human being partakes as a bodily being, and this spiritual life, of which it partakes as a free and moral being,

---

37. See also "Anthropologie Friedländer," 25:560; "Reflexionen zur Anthropologie," R824, 15:368; R946, 15:419; "Erläuterungen zu Baumgartens *Initia*," 19:6871, 6870.

38. Immanuel Kant, "Proclamation of the Imminent Conclusion of a Treaty of Perpetual Peace in Philosophy," in *Theoretical Philosophy after 1781*, ed. Henry E. Allison and Peter Heath, trans. Peter Heath (Cambridge: Cambridge University Press, 2002), 451–60.

39. Immanuel Kant, *Opus postumum*, ed. Eckart Förster, trans. Eckhart Förster and Michael Rosen (Cambridge: Cambridge University Press, 1993), 21:211; "Anthropologie Friedländer," 25:561; "Erläuterungen zu Baumgartens *Initia*," 19:6862.

there is finally the unique "human" life that she partakes of as a member of her species. In his notes, Kant always situates and clarifies this form of life by contrast with the other two, higher and lower, forms of life.[40] Unlike animal life, human life is not private, but essentially social. This it shares with spiritual life. But unlike spiritual life, human life is associated not with desire, but always with taste and so with sensibility. In terms of its basis, however, human life again distinguishes itself from the animal in that it is not the life of our bodily senses, but rather is "the life of our cognition" itself ("Reflexionen zur Anthropologie," R806, 15:351–58), and as such is a kind of life shared by all cognitive subjects insofar as they have intuition and understanding. Taste, or the feeling of this life, therefore depends not on the intrinsically private stimulation by sensations, but instead on their formal or intuitive aspect insofar as this harmonizes with the higher cognitive faculties, and with understanding in particular. Furthermore, since spiritual life concerns "the understanding and freedom," and more generally whatever genuinely stems from an internal principle of spontaneity, "humanity [or human life], consists in that animality is subordinated to the spiritual" ("Reflexionen zur Anthropologie," R824, 15:368).

Now, as indicated above, all three forms of life are subject to the distinction between what enlivens, and hence pleases, in the part, and what in fact contributes to the life of the whole. For Kant this distinction runs along two axes, one running horizontally within each form, and the other vertically among the forms. Just as physical pleasure may damage physical life as a whole if it is not controlled and kept in balance, a faculty of genius, which Kant identifies with the enlivening principle in fine art, can damage social life if it is not controlled and kept in balance by the faculty of taste. Even in the moral realm, the "state of *health* in the moral life" can be damaged by "an affect, *even one aroused by the thought of what is good*, [which] is a momentary, sparkling phenomenon that leaves one exhausted" (*Metaphysics of Morals*, 6:406; emphasis mine).[41] This is, so to say, the horizontal axis of Kant's hierarchy.

The vertical axis is built from a comparison of the three forms with one another. In all cases, life is a principle of unity, and what contributes to

40. "Reflexionen zur Anthropologie," R567, 15:246; R779, 15:341; R806, 15:351–58; R823, 15:367–68; "Reflexionen zur Metaphysik," R4237, 17:471–72; "Metaphysik L_1," 28:248.

41. Immanuel Kant, *The Metaphysics of Morals*, ed. Mary J. Gregor (Cambridge: Cambridge University Press, 1996.)

the fundamental unity of our powers contributes to life itself. But as we have also seen, the unity in the three forms of life is not of the same scope; animal life is limited entirely to the unity of the individual body, while human life extends to the unity of our kind, and moral life extends universally to the unity of all rational life as such. Therefore, in the human being, who partakes of all three forms, the two lower forms of life only truly contribute to life in the highest sense when they are controlled and kept in balance through freedom, and hence in agreement with the unity of our rational nature and so ultimately with the moral law as the principle of that unity.

Now, since he regards feeling as signifying the furtherance or hindrance of life, it is not surprising that we also discover Kant articulating a hierarchy of feeling that strictly parallels the vertical axis above. In one sketch, he writes, for instance: "The lowest feeling is in that which is considered merely in relation to the private sense. More elevated is that which pleases the communal sense (taste). . . . The highest is that which is derived from the unity of the universal satisfaction *a priori.* 1. Sensible feeling. 2. Taste (*sensus communis*). 3. Moral feeling. All three please immediately" ("Reflexionen zur Anthropologie," R1487, 15:654).

A bit later in the same sketch, we read that "everything that furthers the feeling of life, be it of animal (wellbeing) or human or of spiritual life, pleases." Another related reflection states, "the feeling of the furtherance or hindrance of life is liking and disliking. . . . But we have an animal, a spiritual and a human life. Through the first, we are capable of gratification and pain (feeling), through the third, of liking through sensible judgment (taste), through the second, of liking through reason" (R823, 15:367–68). In R824 (15:368), Kant explains similarly, "the feeling of life in perception is great, but I feel an even greater life in an enlivening that is voluntary, and I feel the greatest *principium* of life in morality." Thus, in parallel with the forms of life, the sensible feeling of animal life is private, the moral feeling of spiritual life is objectively universal, and the pure aesthetic feeling or the taste of human life is universal, but both sensible and subjective ("Metaphysik L_1," 28:248–49). Kant sometimes expresses this idea by describing taste as social feeling or the feeling of human life.[42] Just after distinguishing the three kinds of life in "Metaphysik L_1," Kant is reported to have said that "*human pleasure* is feeling according to a universal sense, by means of the sensible power of judgment; it is a middle thing and is cognized from sensibility through the idea" (28:248).

42. *Die Philosophischen Hauptvorlesungen*, 223.

From the above, we can see that Kant developed a highly articulated theory of life over his career, one that should shed light on his analysis of taste. But now we must face a typical Kantian question: With what right do we ascribe objective reality to any of these concepts? Kant's position on animal life is somewhat murky. In some texts he seems to accept it based on an analogy with the life we experience within ourselves. But in the third *Critique*, he seems to deny that animals can be said to be living even by such an analogy (§65, 5:375). As for spiritual life, and the feeling of it, their objective reality is evidently established along with the reality of freedom and the moral incentive in the second *Critique*. As Kant states in one text, "the moral law reveals to me a life independent of animality and even of the whole sensible world" (5:162). But what about human life? It is my central thesis that the application of this concept receives its sole critical foundation in the "Critique of Aesthetic Judgment," to which I now turn.

Kant's Deduction of Human Life

The theory of life just presented is in fact just a basic sketch of the main contours of Kant's thoughts on this topic, as they occurred to him in various contexts over the course of the critical period. The vast majority of the texts, some of them quite important, have not been analyzed or even mentioned here for want of space; although I am confident that they would not overturn the general points made above.

Nevertheless, it has been shown that when Kant began to write the *Critique of Judgment*, he had long been thinking about the connection between life and feeling. He had even developed a fairly detailed view on how the judgment of taste fits into this larger picture. Already in the early 1770s, he was prepared to state, for instance, that the beautiful "promotes the inner life, since it sets the powers of cognition into activity" ("Anthropologie Collins," 25:181).[43] Seen from this point of view, it was clear to Kant that in making a judgment of taste, we not only "postulate" the universality of our aesthetic pleasure, but on a deeper level, we also postulate the existence of a form of life belonging to us not as animals alone, nor as spirits alone, but instead as human beings in which the nexus of the animal and the spiritual (i.e., the moral) is essential and definitive. In taste itself, he states in

43. "Anthropologie Collins," in *Vorlesungen über Anthropologie*, Bd. 25 of *Kant's gesammelte Schriften*, ed. Berlin-Brandenburgische Akademie der Wissenschaften (Berlin: de Gruyter, 1997), 7–238.

1790 without further comment or justification, the "presentation is referred only to the subject, namely, to his feeling of life, under the name feeling of pleasure or displeasure, and this forms the basis of a very special power of discriminating and judging" (§1, 5:204). Taste is so "very special," on his view, because it consists in the power to judge whether the pleasure arising from one's own feeling of life is at the same time universally valid for all other human beings, and so also whether this feeling is really one of the furtherance of a specifically shared human form of life.

Seeing taste from the vantage point of the concept of life thus provides us with another way to understand the critical project concerning the former. "The critique of taste," as Kant explains, "is a *science* if it derives the possibility of such judging from the nature of these powers as cognitive powers as such. It is with the latter alone, with a transcendental critique, that we are here concerned throughout. Its aim is to set forth and justify the subjective principle of taste as an a priori principle of the power of judgment" (§34, 5:286). The "Critique of Aesthetic Judgment," in other words, seeks to justify the normative claims "postulated" in judgments of taste by justifying the subjective principle that they presuppose. But this subjective principle is nothing but the special form of human life, the furtherance of which is supposedly felt in aesthetic pleasure. Hence, the critique aims to justify this form of human life "as an *a priori* principle of the power of judgment." But what can this mean? It cannot mean, of course, that Kant wishes to demonstrate the existence of this form of life. If such were even possible, it still would not support the *normative claims* of taste, nor would the proof be "scientific" in the sense of the quotation above. As we will see more fully below, the normative claims contained in judgments of taste, when taken together, amount to the claim that we are able to make judgments that rest entirely on such a form of life. And to justify this *claim*—which in fact concerns the supersensible principle within us, about which knowledge is impossible—Kant believes that he need only to show that we do in fact make it and that making it is consistent with the constitution of our mental faculties and the limitations these impose upon judgment itself.

The "Analytic of the Beautiful": The Four Moments and the Form of Life

As we have just seen, Kant articulates the formal features of human life by comparing it with, and positioning it between, animal and spiritual, or moral, life. Strikingly, the employment of this same method is one of the most prominent features of the "Analytic of the Beautiful" as explicated in the four moments, which latter articulate the distinct claims made in a judgment of taste insofar as they are reflected in its form. What I propose to do in this subsection is to explain how each of the first three moments corresponds to one of three essential features of the form of human life, so that together they amount to the *claim* that taste rests on an entirely distinctive form of life that is shared among all human beings as such.

In the first moment of the beautiful, Kant distinguishes the pleasure found in a judgment of taste from the pleasure of the agreeable, that is, physical pleasure, and liking of the good, that is, the approval we give to something either as a means or morally. The pleasure of taste is distinct from the former, but like the latter, in that it claims to rest on reflection. On the other hand, it is distinct from the latter, but like the former, in being aesthetic and singular. Yet it differs from both in claiming to be essentially unrelated to any possible interest. With the agreeable, the physical pleasure based upon our bodily constitution comes first and subsequently generates an interest when we reflect upon it. With the good, reflection itself generates an interest, and from this arises a liking, which in the moral case is presented to us as a feeling determined by consciousness of the moral law itself. The pleasure of taste, by contrast, is neither determined by the constitution of something outside of our minds and over which we have no control, nor is it determined by our will, which, although within our control, is not free with respect to what it approves. Thus, although moral life contains a higher degree of spontaneity, indeed the highest, the approval involved in moral life, in respect to us as human beings, is not free at all. The freedom of moral life is only the freedom of the will, *and for this reason*, not the freedom of pleasure or liking. Therefore, as Kant explains, "of all three kinds of liking, only the liking involved in taste for the beautiful is disinterested and *free*" (§5, 5:210). The freedom of this liking *as such* thus already indicates, according to Kant, that it is distinct in kind from both the agreeable and the good, and therefore holds "only for human beings, i.e., beings who are animal and yet rational, although it is not enough that they be rational (e.g., spirits) but they must be animal as well." Now, freedom, or spontaneity, is one of the essential features of life, as we saw above, and here in the first moment, Kant effectively articulates the claim that the principle of aesthetic judgment is a free and spontaneous, and hence independent, activity. It goes beyond animal life in the degree of its spontaneity, but it differs from spiritual life in the specific form of its freedom.

Kant introduces the second moment of the beautiful by noting that it is implied already in the first as follows. If judgments of taste claim to be free in the sense above, then they claim independence from all external determining factors, and hence from all particular or private ones deriving from the agreeable feeling of animal life. If such a judgment is possible, then it is, at the very least, intrinsically universal for all judging subjects, and the life of which it is a feeling must be a form of life that each human being partakes of equally. But being also intuitive and singular, the judgment of taste cannot be based upon concepts, and so must be distinct from the approval of what is good, which is universal, but ranging over all rational beings as such. This "remarkable" and "strange" feature consists, then, in the claim that each judgment—precisely due to its freedom—exemplifies a *universal rule*, not for judging the features of objects, which would be easy to explain, but rather for the aesthetic judgings of all other human beings. Kant describes the claim to such "subjective universality" as equivalent to the belief that one has a kind of "universal voice," which is "only an idea," albeit one that enables us to speak for others in a way that "*requires* . . . agreement from everyone, as an instance of the rule" (§8, 5:216). From this, we can see that the second moment of the beautiful goes beyond the first by introducing *the concept or idea of a higher rule* of which each genuine judgment of taste is thought to be but an instance or example. Moreover, this higher rule governs only the judging of subjects in the absence of anything else that would determine such judgment, whether this be something bodily or something purely conceptual.

Now, life as *actu primo* is in all cases a principle of unity that provides an internal rule and measure of all its own activities *actu secundo*. This is already implied in Kant's definition of life in terms of a being having causality based upon representations. The unity and structure of the representation in such a being provides the normative form or exemplary model for the products brought about through its life's activities. Taste, as we have just seen, also attests to just such a rule or principle for evaluating the expressions of human life: the rule underlying it is thought as the exemplary model providing the standard for such evaluation.

But what precisely is the matter of this form of life? If such is not the body and not the will itself, then what exactly is the form of life the life of? Kant answers this question at the end of the second moment through a comparison with the other two forms of life. Taste cannot have its principle in the physical constitution of our senses, and hence in animal life, or else it would be private. Only cognition is truly universal. But taste cannot consist in cognition either, and so cannot be a feeling attesting to our spiritual life. The only remaining possibility—Kant concludes—is that taste contains a feeling of the life of the indeterminate subjective basis making possible cognition *in general*. Now, in all *human* beings, but not necessarily in all *rational* beings, this subjective basis consists in the unity or harmony between the imagination's faculty for apprehending sensible intuition and the understanding's faculty for unifying this in turn under a concept. Furthermore, since this harmony also must not be restricted to any determinate cognition, it must be a free or indeterminate harmony of these two faculties in general insofar as they are conditions of cognition. If my interpretation is correct, then Kant refers taste to human life precisely because the matter of its activity can only be the two faculties of cognition found in all human beings as such, but not necessarily all rational beings, namely, imagination and understanding.[44] And it is the furtherance of this same life that he then makes reference to when he speaks of the mutual enlivening of these mental faculties in their free play (§21, 5:238–39).[45] Not surprisingly, Kant here traces the *form* of judgments of taste, namely, their free lawfulness, which itself is analogous to the form of life, back to the concept of an actual principle of life standing at the basis of such judgments.

Kant introduces the third moment by defining purposiveness in its most general form as "the object of a concept insofar as we regard this concept as the object's cause (the real basis of its possibility); and the causality that a *concept* has with regard to its *object* is purposiveness (*forma finalis*)" (§10, 5:220). The connection of this to Kant's definition of life is patent; a living being *actu primo* is one capable of having purposes, and the form of its causality, that is, of its life *actu secundo*, is purposiveness. As we should expect by now, Kant identifies the special purposiveness underlying taste by distinguishing it from the forms deriving from purposes based on animal life and on spiritual or moral life. These last two forms of purposiveness involve determinate purposes. Taste, however, as it cannot be based on nor give rise to a purpose, can only consist in a purposiveness that is indeterminate or

44. Whether on Kant's view this claim applies to both imagination and understanding, or rather only to the former of this pair, is a difficult matter to decide.

45. An important discussion of the development of Kant's views on this matter is found in Paul Guyer, "Kant's Aesthetics in his *Lectures on Metaphysics*," in *Kant's "Lectures on Metaphysics": A Critical Guide*, ed. Courtney D. Fugate (Cambridge: Cambridge University Press, 2018), 156–78.

without purpose. Notably, Kant never in fact explains why we must attribute purposiveness to taste. Presumably, the reason is that taste claims to be a spontaneity according to a rule or idea, and hence to be based upon a causality of the mental powers exhibiting some kind of lawfulness in their free activity, and this alone implies an indeterminate form of purposiveness. In any case, life in general is a causal principle of unity, and taste, Kant here declares, "does have causality in it, namely, to keep [us in] the state of [having] the presentation itself, and [to keep] the cognitive powers engaged [in their occupation] without any further aim" (§12, 5:222). The purposiveness of taste, which is the form of the enlivened activity of the mental powers, is thus peculiar in that it aims at nothing but the continuation and reproduction of its own intrinsic form of causality.

As we saw from the second moment, taste claims to rest on a spontaneous or free rule or idea. Now, from the third, we can also see that this rule or idea is not merely the norm for some product created through the act of judgment, like the concept of a shelf in the mind of a carpenter would be for the shelf actually built; rather, it is the idea and norm of judgment's *own* activities. The life that we feel in a judgment of taste aims at nothing beyond itself. Its inner rule or criteria is only the promotion of its own free activity. Therefore, whatever form of life taste may exemplify, the rule or norm in question is nothing other than the internal measure for judging all other activities of judgment as instances of that very same life. Like all forms of life, taste is self-regulating and self-formative.

Kant's Deduction of the Form of Human Life as the Principle of Taste

Judgments of taste not only make claims, they make claims a priori. And for this reason, Kant believes, they require a deduction. But not all the claims of taste require justification. There is no need, for instance, to justify their status as singular and aesthetic, any more than it is necessary to justify the pleasure we take in the agreeable, that is, in our feeling mere animal life, since the last makes no claims on the judgment of *anyone else*. What requires a deduction, according to Kant, is specifically "*the universal validity of this pleasure*," that it is "valid for everyone" (§37, 5:289).

Kant's very brief solution to this problem rests on two fundamental ideas, both of which were adumbrated already in the second moment of the beautiful. The first is that the deduction really only needs to show that *if* there are such judgments, then these must be valid for everyone. He doesn't presume to show there actually are such judgements. This is where the second fundamental idea comes in: among the essential claims of taste is the claim that it takes into account nothing but the sensible form of the object, and as such can be based only upon the same mental faculties we presuppose in all other *human* beings (not all animals, not all rational beings). If there are judgments of taste, and if there is a feeling of life that accompanies them—that is, if the claims made in such judging truly obtain—*then* that feeling can only be a feeling of a life that is present equally in all human beings *as such*. This pleasure is neither restricted to private conditions, nor is it determined by our higher rational nature, as in the case of moral feeling. It is instead a feeling that belongs specifically to humanity insofar as it is active, responsive and thus alive in the individual, finite cognizer. Taste can therefore be defined as "our ability to judge a priori the communicability of the feelings that (without the mediation of a concept) are connected with a given presentation" (§40, 5:296).

Why does Kant include this seeming repetition of the second moment? And what does it add to his theory of human life? The point is one about deduction or justification. The second moment shows that judgments of taste make a claim to universality and what motivates this claim. The present deduction, however, explains that—due to the special character of taste itself—the basis upon which we claim universality is at the same time sufficient to *justify* this claim. Why? Because taste makes its claims only on other judgments of taste made by other subjects, subjects who *claim* to have the very same basis for making the reciprocal demand on our own judgments of taste. In other words, we share this form of life by mutual participation in a normative practice that is intrinsically self-regulating and autonomous. "Taste," Kant states in another context, "lays claim merely to autonomy" (§32, 5:283), "where it is, subjectively, object to itself as well as law to itself" (§36, 5:288). The feature or norm of human life exhibited in taste, in other words, is nothing but the inner characteristic form of the faculty of judgment's own free activity and, as such, it requires no further or external justification for making its claims upon itself.

Human Life as the Solution to the "Dialectic of Aesthetic Judgment"

As Kant makes clear, the dialectic of taste is not like the dialectics in either of the other two *Critiques*. Since taste does not concern concepts and does not make conceptual claims, it cannot give rise to a dialectic directly. However, indirectly, in the act of transcendental reflection upon the possibility of judgments of taste, there nevertheless arises "a dialectic of the critique of taste (rather than of taste itself) concerning the *principles* of this critique" (§55, 5:337). That is to say, in this act of transcendental reflection, "conflicting concepts arise naturally and inevitably."

This is a remarkable claim for several reasons. First, it shows that transcendental reflection in this case is actually *an original source of concepts* regarding the principles of taste. In other words, these concepts arise only from within this reflection, and would not have been discoverable from any other source. As Kant states elsewhere, the analysis of taste reveals "to him [i.e., the transcendental philosopher] a property of our cognitive power which without this analysis would have remained unknown" (§7, 5:213). Second, it claims that these concepts arise "naturally and necessarily" in the course of our reflections on taste itself and upon its principles. We are forced, so it seems, to adopt different "points of view in judging" (§57, 5:339), which, only when conceptualized by the transcendental philosopher, produce an unavoidable antinomy.

The fact that this critique is itself an original source of concepts for us has a parallel, if at all, only in the dialectic of the first *Critique*, where the speculative antinomies force us to introduce the concept of things considered as noumena. However, in that case, the antinomy that arises is between presumably objective principles for cognizing objects, and it is a difficulty for common human reason, not for the transcendental philosopher. By contrast, in the dialectic of taste, as Kant informs us, the situation is reversed; the antinomy arises only for the transcendental philosopher, and not at all for the common practitioner of taste who judges without concepts. Hence, in this case alone does transcendental philosophy first disclose cognition of a dimension of human nature.

The antinomy faced by the transcendental philosopher is this: (thesis) taste is not based on concepts, for otherwise it would not be singular and aesthetic, and one could demonstrate the truth or falsity of an aesthetic judgment (which cannot be done); (antithesis) taste is based on concepts, for otherwise it could not be universal and necessary, and we could not demand others judge as we do (§57, 5:339). From this we can see three things. First, the thesis and antithesis here result from nothing more than a particular way of combining the claims made by taste into two opposing statements, which Kant sometimes refers to as taste's claims and counterclaims. Second, none of the moments of taste, which explicate the claims made by one who presumes to make a judgment of taste, actually consist in the claim that taste is or is not based on concepts. Rather, it is the transcendental philosopher who first introduces the idea that taste is or is not based upon a concept; and she does this precisely in order to make sense of the claims of taste by investigating the possibility of their principle. Third, in view of the question of life, we can see that the two opposing statements have a very special significance. The thesis amounts to the claim that the principle of taste is animal life (§57, 5:339), while the antithesis amounts to the claim that it is spiritual or moral life. Together, these claims thus seem to conflict and to cancel one another out, thereby undermining the coherence, and thus the validity, of *any* principle of taste, and so also of all the claims made by taste in the four moments.

According to Kant, in order to "save its claim" in each case (§57, 5:340), we must here introduce an entirely new notion, namely, one of an indeterminate concept of a supersensible basis for judgment that lies within every human subject. Only such an indeterminate concept of the "supersensible substrate of humanity," he asserts, allows us to *positively* resolve all of judgment's claims by reference to a single principle. The antinomy discovered in the course of this critique thus compels "us against our will to look beyond the sensible to the supersensible as the point [where] all our a priori powers are reconciled, since that is the only alternative left for bringing reason into harmony with itself" (§57, 5:341).

In summary, the form that taste claims for itself, as explicated in the four moments, results in a demand being placed on the transcendental philosopher to admit the idea of an ultimate subjective basis of all cognitive activities in human beings, that is, a shared principle and form of cognitive life that is uniquely human. As we have seen, the legitimacy of this concept is established by Kant neither empirically, nor metaphysically, but instead *critically* through the science of the beautiful, which is nothing other than the transcendental critique of the aesthetic power of judgment itself. As for the idea of this special form of life "as the sole key for solving the mystery of this ability [i.e., taste] concealed from us even as to its sources, we can do no more than to point to it; but there is nothing we can do that would allow us to grasp it any further" (§57, 5:341).

Chapter 4

The Aesthetic Perfection of Life in Baumgarten, Meier, and Kant

J. Colin McQuillan

Some readers might associate the phrase "the aesthetic perfection of life" in the title of this chapter with Nietzsche's appeal to the "great and rare art" of "giving style to one's character" in *The Gay Science*, with Michel Foucault's injunction to "create ourselves as a work of art," or with related discussions of philosophy as a "way of life" and "art of living" in works by Pierre Hadot and Alexander Nehamas.[1] These associations are only natural, given the ambiguities of the term "aesthetics," its proximity to "the philosophy of art," and the way that "lifestyle" has become such a pressing contemporary concern—not least among philosophers.

In fact, the phrase, as it is used in the title of this chapter, refers to an older way of thinking about the role that the concept of "life" plays in aesthetics, one that emerged in German philosophy in the middle of the eighteenth century. It was during this time that aesthetics was introduced as a new part of philosophy by Alexander Baumgarten. Baumgarten did not

1. Friedrich Nietzsche, *The Gay Science*, trans. Walter Kaufmann (New York: Vintage, 1974), §290; Michel Foucault, *Essential Works, 1954–1984*, vol. 1, *Ethics, Subjectivity and Truth*, ed. Paul Rabinow (New York: New Press, 1997), 262; Pierre Hadot, *Philosophy as a Way of Life: Spiritual Exercises from Socrates to Foucault*, ed. Arnold Davidson (Malden, MA: Wiley-Blackwell, 1995); Alexander Nehamas, *The Art of Living: Socratic Reflections from Plato to Foucault* (Berkeley: University of California Press, 2000).

conceive of aesthetics as a philosophy of art or a critique of taste; on the contrary, he understood aesthetics as a science that would guide sensible cognition to perfection.[2] And he took the perfection of sensible cognition to be analogous to, but distinct from, philosophical knowledge of the truth—the perfection of intellectual cognition. All of this might sound terribly academic and theoretical, which it surely is, and was, at the time when Baumgarten was writing; yet that does not mean it has nothing to do with "life."

In what follows, I will reconstruct the conception of "life" that one finds in the works of Alexander Baumgarten, Georg Friedrich Meier, and Immanuel Kant in order to highlight the role this concept played in the origins of modern aesthetics.[3] I will show that, in his *Reflections on Poetry* (1735) and *Metaphysics* (1739), Baumgarten regarded "liveliness" as an essential feature of poetry in particular and sensible cognition in general; that he elevated life, in his *Aesthetics* (1750/1758), to the status of a perfection that contributes to the beauty of sensible cognition; that Meier further developed Baumgarten's conception of "life" as an aesthetic perfection in his *Foundations of All Beautiful Sciences* (1748–1750); and that Kant challenged Baumgarten's and Meier's way of thinking about the relationship between sensibility, perfection, and life in aesthetics in his lectures on metaphysics, anthropology, and logic in the 1770s, and, later, in his critical philosophy—especially the *Critique of Judgment* (1790).[4] Kant's hostility to Baumgarten's and Meier's

2. On the differences between aesthetics, the philosophy of art, and the critique of taste, see J. Colin McQuillan, *Early Modern Aesthetics* (New York: Rowman and Littlefield, 2015), chap. 2–4.

3. I would like to thank Marcus Willaschek, Gabriele Gava, Claudia Blöser, and the other members of the Frankfurter Kant-Arbeitskreis for helpful comments on an earlier draft of this chapter.

4. Quotations from Baumgarten are based on the following translations: Alexander Baumgarten, *Reflections on Poetry*, trans. Karl Aschenbrenner and William B. Holther (Berkeley: University of California Press, 1954); Alexander Baumgarten, *Metaphysics: A Critical Translation with Kant's Elucidations, Selected Notes, and Related Material*, ed. and trans. Courtney D. Fugate and John Hymers (London: Bloomsbury, 2013). Translations of passages in Baumgarten's *Aesthetica* [*Aesthetics*], 2 vols. (Frankfurt a. d. Oder: Johannis Christian Kleyb, 1750/1758) and Meier's *Anfangsgründe aller schönen Künste und Wissenschaften* [*Foundations*], 3 vols. (Halle: Carl Hermann Hemmerde, 1748–1750), are my own, although Alexander Baumgarten, *Ästhetik*, trans. Dagmar Mirbach (Hamburg: Felix Meiner Verlag, 2007), has been an invaluable resource. All quotations from Kant include references to the volume and page number in *Kant's gesammelte Schriften*, ed. Königlich Preußische Akademie der Wissenschaften (Berlin: Georg Reimer/Walter de Gruyter, 1902–). Translations from Kant's lectures and published works are based on

conception of aesthetics did not, however, prevent him from employing the concept of "life" in new and interesting ways in his own work. In the end, I hope to show that Kant's appeals to the "feeling of life" (*Lebensgefühl*) and the "enlivening" (*Belebung*) of the cognitive faculties in aesthetic judgment in the third *Critique* derive from his earlier critique of Baumgarten's and Meier's aesthetics.[5]

Baumgarten's *Aesthetics*

"Life" is thematized in three works that are central to Alexander Baumgarten's new science of aesthetics. By following the passage of this concept from Baumgarten's poetics, in the *Reflections on Poetry*, to his empirical psychology, in his *Metaphysics*, and, finally, to the (quasi-) systematic presentation of his new science in the *Aesthetics*, we can see how life came to be understood as an aesthetic perfection.

In Baumgarten's dissertation, *Reflections on Poetry*, the "liveliness" (*vivacitas*) of poetry is addressed in a series of propositions near the end of the text, immediately preceding the introduction of aesthetics as a new science. According to Baumgarten, a lively representation is one that allows us "to perceive many parts either simultaneously or in succession" (§112). This might seem like a strange way to define liveliness, but Baumgarten uses painting and rhetoric to confirm the appropriateness of his definition. He notes that "a picture painted in the most variegated color" is called "a

---

Immanuel Kant, *Critique of Judgment*, trans. Werner S. Pluhar (Indianapolis: Hacket, 1987); Immanuel Kant, *Theoretical Philosophy, 1755–1770*, trans. and ed. David Walford, with Ralf Meerbote (Cambridge: Cambridge University Press, 1992); Immanuel Kant, *Lectures on Logic*, trans. and ed. J. Michael Young (Cambridge: Cambridge University Press, 1992); Immanuel Kant, *Lectures on Metaphysics*, trans. and ed. Karl Ameriks and Steve Naragon (Cambridge: Cambridge University Press, 1997); Immanuel Kant, *Critique of Pure Reason*, trans. and ed. Paul Guyer and Allen W. Wood (Cambridge: Cambridge University Press, 1998); Immanuel Kant, *Lectures on Anthropology*, ed. Allen W. Wood and Robert B. Louden, trans. Robert R. Clewis, Robert B. Louden, G. Felicitas Munzel, and Allen W. Wood (Cambridge: Cambridge University Press, 2012).

5. A very different approach is employed by Courtney D. Fugate, who traces Kant's reference to "the feeling of life" back to Gottfried Wilhelm Leibniz and Crusius. Courtney D. Fugate, "Life and Kant's 'Critique of Aesthetic Judgment,'" in *Recht und Frieden in der Philosophie Kants: Akten des X. Internationalen Kant-Kongresses*, ed. Valerio Rohden et al. (Berlin: de Gruyter, 2008), 609–21.

lively painting," while a speech "offering all sorts of perceptions to occupy us, as much in the sound as in the meaning" is called "a lively speech." These examples, along with Baumgarten's definition, suggest that the liveliness of a poem derives from the multiplicity of its parts and the complexity of their relations. Yet there is more to this concept than the identification and definition of one of the many qualities of a poem. In the very next proposition, Baumgarten considers a definition of the poem, formulated by Daniel Heinrich Arnoldt in his *Attempt at a Systematic Guide to German Poetry in General* (1732), that makes liveliness an essential feature of poetry. Arnoldt defines poetry as "speech which, by attention to tonal qualities (meter), represents a thing as vividly as possible and which with its whole power of comprehension insinuates itself into the soul of the reader, so that it can move him in a definite way."[6] One might expect Baumgarten to compare this definition with the definition of the poem that he presents at the beginning of his *Reflections on Poetry*, where he says poetry is "perfect sensible speech" (§9). Instead, he notes that Arnoldt's definition includes three aspects of poetry—meter, maximum liveliness, and action that moves the reader's soul—that are demonstrated elsewhere in the *Reflections on Poetry.* Meter is the measure of speech that produces pleasure in the ear, so Baumgarten holds that it is essential to the perfection of poetry as sensible speech (§§102–4). The liveliness of poetry is, moreover, guaranteed by the extensive clarity of poetic representations, which affirms that "when, in representation A, more is represented than in B, C, D, and so on, but all are confused, A will be said to be *extensively clearer* than the rest" (§16). Baumgarten argues that speech is more poetic when it is clear than when it is obscure and that sensible speech is necessarily confused, because it is sensible, rather than intellectual, so he concludes that extensively clear representations, which represent more than other confused, sensible representations, are also more poetic than other representations (§§12–17).[7] The most

6. Daniel Heinrich Arnoldt, *Versuch einer systematischen Anleitung zur Deutschen Poesie überhaupt* (Königsberg: Johann Stelter, 1732), §4, quoted in Baumgarten, *Reflections*, §113.

7. The claim that poetry contains "extensively" clear representations is based on a contrast Baumgarten draws with logic, which contains "intensively" clear representations. The intensive clarity of logical representation is obtained through analysis, which explicates the predicates contained in a concept, making the concept more distinct. The extensive clarity of poetic representations is obtained through synthesis, by compounding representations, leaving both the original and the additional representations confused. See J. Colin McQuillan, "Clarity and Distinctness in Eighteenth Century Germany: Metaphysics, Logic, Aesthetics," in *Leibniz en Dialogo*, ed. Manuel Sánchez and Miguel Escribano

extensively clear representations will, therefore, be found in perfect sensible speech—poetry—satisfying the maximum liveliness condition of Arnoldt's definition. Finally, Baumgarten takes himself to have demonstrated that poetry moves the reader when he argues, in the *Reflections on Poetry*, that poetic representations are "representations of present changes in that which is to be represented" (§25). Because poetic representations are sensible, they are confused, and, because they are confused, they affect us as "marked degrees of pleasure or pain," which we represent to ourselves, again, confusedly, as good or bad. Emotions are aroused by representing something as pleasurable or painful, good or bad, so the final condition of Arnoldt's definition is satisfied by Baumgarten's arguments in the *Reflections on Poetry.* Rather than rejecting Arnoldt's definition and insisting on the superiority of his own, Baumgarten shows that the two definitions of poetry are equivalent to one another—they both agree that liveliness is essential to poetry.

At the end of the *Reflections on Poetry*, after considering the relationship between Arnoldt's definition of poetry and his own, and dismissing another definition proposed in Johann Georg Walch's *Philosophical Lexicon* (1726), Baumgarten introduces his new science of aesthetics. He argues that, because philosophical poetics is "the science guiding sensible speech to perfection," it necessarily presupposes another science, since we must already possess the sensible representations "that we communicate in speech" (§115). He recommends calling the science of sensible representation "aesthetics," because it concerns "things perceived" through the faculty of sensibility, as opposed to logic, "the science of knowing things philosophically," which serves "for the direction of the higher cognitive faculty in apprehending the truth" (§§115–16). Baumgarten denies that logic can explain the sensible representations that are found in poetry, because logic, "by its very definition, should be restricted to the rather narrow limits to which it is as a matter of fact confined" (§115). In other words, logic is concerned with the cognition of the higher cognitive faculty, the understanding, which is directed toward philosophical knowledge of the truth, so the sensible cognition of the lower cognitive faculty, sensibility, necessarily falls outside the scope of logic, and must be the object of a different science. Baumgarten does not have much to say about this science in the *Reflections on Poetry*, apart

(Seville: Themata, 2017), 149–59. See also Rudolf Makkreel, "Baumgarten and Kant on Clarity, Distinctness, and the Differentiation of our Mental Powers," in *Baumgarten and Kant on Metaphysics*, ed. Courtney D. Fugate and John Hymers (Oxford: Oxford University Press, 2018), 94–109.

from naming it (aesthetics), identifying its object (sensible representation), and articulating its two main parts as general rhetoric, which concerns the "unperfected presentation of sensible representations," and general poetics, which is "the science which treats generally of the perfected presentation of sensible representations" (§117).

He has more to say about aesthetics in the *Metaphysics*, however, which was published only three years later. There we see that aesthetics is included within metaphysics—"the science of the first principles of human knowledge" (§1)—as a part of psychology—"the science of the general predicates of the soul" (§501)—and, more specifically, empirical psychology—the part of psychology that "deduces its assertions based upon experience that is nearest to hand" (§503). The empirical psychology chapter of the *Metaphysics* includes a catalog of all the cognitive faculties, from the lower faculties—sensibility in general, as well as the particular faculties of sense, imagination, perspicaciousness, memory, invention, foresight, judgment, anticipation, and characterization—to the higher faculties—understanding in general and reason in particular (§§519–650). Baumgarten also discusses the kinds of cognition with which these faculties are concerned. In the discussion of the lower cognitive faculty in general, also known as the faculty of sensibility, he says, for example, that sensible cognition can be obscure or confused, but not distinct (§520). Cognition becomes distinct when the marks of a concept—the predicates that constitute its definition—are represented clearly (§522). Cognition that represents the marks of a concept more clearly than another cognition possesses "intensively greater clarity" than the other cognition (§631). Sensible cognition is obscure or confused, so it cannot represent the marks of a concept distinctly and does not possess intensive clarity. Still, it is perfectly consistent to say that confused sensible cognition possesses "extensively greater clarity" than obscure sensible cognition, because it represents more than an obscure cognition, however confusedly its marks may be perceived (§531). Baumgarten maintains that extensively clear cognition is more "lively" (*vividus*) than intensively clear cognition because it is "stronger" (*fortior*) than an intensively clear cognition—the liveliness of a cognition being dependent on its strength, and the strength of a cognition being defined by its quantity, so that "the more marks a perception embraces, the stronger it is" (§517, §532). He also argues that extensively clearer cognition is more perfect than cognition that is less extensively clear, because it is less obscure, clearer, and, thus, stronger and livelier (§532). Aesthetics—"the science of knowing and presenting with regard to the senses" (§533)—is the science concerned with this perfection, though that is stated more explicitly in Meier's German translation of the *Metaphysics* (1766), where aesthetics is said to be "the science of the rules of the perfection of sensible cognition and of its meaning" or "the science of the beautiful, which deals with the improvement of all the lower cognitive powers."[8]

Baumgarten's *Aesthetics* builds on, but also subtly modifies, the arguments of the *Reflections on Poetry* and *Metaphysics.* As in his earlier works, Baumgarten presents aesthetics as the science of the confused sensible cognition of the lower cognitive faculty. He continues to distinguish aesthetics from logic, the science of the distinct intellectual cognition of the higher cognitive faculty. However, he no longer appeals to the concept of extensive clarity to draw this distinction or to account for the liveliness of sensible cognition. Extensive clarity is replaced by a list of several cognitive perfections that contribute to the overall beauty of sensible cognition—a name for aesthetic perfection that is absent from both the *Reflections on Poetry* and *Metaphysics.* "Life" (*vita*) is among the perfections of sensible cognition that Baumgarten enumerates in the *Aesthetics,* alongside richness, greatness, truth, clarity, and certainty (§22). However, he provides no definition or explanation of the aesthetic perfection of life anywhere in the text. The "Synopsis" that Baumgarten includes in the first volume (1750) indicates that the final section of the "Heuristic" chapter of the first, theoretical part of the *Aesthetics* would be devoted to "the life of aesthetic cognition" (*vita cognitionis aesthetica*), but, in the preface to the second volume (1758), he explains that illness prevented him from completing his treatment of aesthetic certainty and the sections on aesthetic life, which he calls "the loveliest beauty of agreeable cognition," as well as the chapters on methodology and semiotics that were to conclude the first part of the text (§§596–601). Given the incompleteness of Baumgarten's *Aesthetics,* all we can know about his conception of life as an aesthetic perfection is what can be derived from a few passing references elsewhere in the text. For example, in the section in which he introduces the six perfections of sensible cognition, Baumgarten says that beautiful cognition is comprised by these perfections, to the extent that they are "in agreement with each other in a representation, e.g., richness and greatness with clarity, truth and clarity with certainty, and all the rest with life, insofar as the different parts of cognition agree" (§22). This implies that aesthetically perfect or beautiful cognition is complex rather than

8. Alexander Baumgarten, *Metaphysik,* trans. Georg Friedrich Meier, ed. Dagmar Mirbach (Jena: Dietrich Scheglmann Reprints, 2004), §395. See also Baumgarten, *Metaphysics,* §533.

simple, a point that is confirmed in a later passage, where Baumgarten refers to "life, the foremost gift of beautiful cognition," as "that which manifests itself beautifully in its manifold kinds and degrees" (§188).

The complexity of aesthetic life is important, because it corresponds to the definition of liveliness that Baumgarten proposes in the *Reflections on Poetry* and the *Metaphysics.* However, it is unlikely that complexity is the specific difference of cognition that possesses the aesthetic perfection of life, since the complexity of beautiful cognition seems to be explained by its richness, a perfection that Baumgarten defines as the "copiousness, abundance, multitude, treasure, wealth" (§115) of beautiful cognition. This definition suggests that cognition that represents more is richer and, therefore, more perfect than cognition that represents less, so it is unlikely that Baumgarten continues to hold, in the *Aesthetics*, that the liveliness of a representation or cognition is a function of its quantity, as he had in the *Reflections on Poetry* and *Metaphysics.* Perhaps, then, it is not the quantity of sensible cognition that defines its life, but the agreement of the different cognitive perfections to which Baumgarten refers in the passage introducing the perfections of beautiful cognition. Recall that he had said cognition is beautiful insofar as its perfections are "in agreement with each other in a representation," which suggests that it is as important for its perfections to be consistent with one another as it is for there to be many of them. This supposition is plausible, because Baumgarten will say, in his discussion of the characteristics of the "happy aesthetician," that the lower cognitive faculty attains a "higher life" through the agreement that is present in beautiful thoughts (§78). However, it is also possible that the aesthetic perfection of life concerns neither the quantity nor the consistency of sensible cognition, but its relation to motivation and action. This is suggested by a section introducing a chapter on aesthetic persuasion, which is included in the second volume (1758), but not in the synopsis of the *Aesthetics* that Baumgarten included in the first volume (1750). After indicating that he wishes to proceed from aesthetic certainty to aesthetic persuasion, Baumgarten says persuasion is related to action, but also has a place within theoretical philosophy, which distinguishes it from aesthetic life (§829). This passage suggests that Stefanie Buchenau may be right when she says aesthetic life ultimately concerns the "practical efficacy" of sensible cognition.[9] Still, given the unfinished state of the text, it remains unclear whether Baumgarten's conception of the aesthetic perfection

9. Stefanie Buchenau, *The Founding of Aesthetics in the German Enlightenment* (Cambridge: Cambridge University Press, 2013), 144.

of life concerns the quantity, the consistency, the efficacy, or some other characteristic of beautiful cognition, which we have not, as yet, surmised.[10]

Meier's *Foundations*

In the preface to the first edition of his *Foundations of All Beautiful Sciences*, Georg Friedrich Meier says, "if this text has the luck to win the world's approval, I am bound by the love of honor to say that the greater part of this honor does not belong to me; on the contrary, the reader owes the foremost and greatest honor to the famous Professor Baumgarten in Frankfurt an der Oder, my eternally worthy teacher" (*Foundations*, Vorrede). Meier explains that Baumgarten began to formulate his plan for a new science of aesthetics while he was still in Halle but continued developing it after his move to Frankfurt an der Oder. Baumgarten had laid out this plan in a "Collegium on Aesthetics" that Meier had studied.[11] However, because Baumgarten never published his "Collegium," and because the *Foundations* was published two years before the first volume of Baumgarten's *Aesthetics* appeared in print, Meier's debts to Baumgarten are not always clear. Some scholars have accused Meier of "watering down" Baumgarten's ideas;[12]

10. Paul Guyer claims in his *History of Modern Aesthetics*, that Baumgarten's conception of the aesthetic perfection of life is primarily concerned with "our emotional response to art" and that it establishes "a connection between the cognitivist paradigm for aesthetic experience upheld by Christian Wolff and the emotional impact of art emphasized by Jean-Baptiste DuBos in France and by Lord Kames in Britain at the end of Baumgarten's life." This claim is, I assume, built on the plausible assumption that Baumgarten's account of aesthetic life would correspond to what we find in volume 1, chapter 7 of Meier's *Foundations*. Paul Guyer, *A History of Modern Aesthetics*, vol. 1, *The Eighteenth Century* (Cambridge: Cambridge University Press, 2014), 319, 331–32, 337–39.

11. Bernhard Poppe published a German translation of Baumgarten's *Kollegium* from a handwritten manuscript in *Alexander Baumgarten: Seine Bedeutung und Stellung in der Leibniz-Wolffschen Philosophie und seine Beziehungen zu Kant* (Borna-Leipzig: Robert Noske, 1907), 65–258. Although Poppe points out that this manuscript can date from no earlier than 1749, and more likely comes from 1750 or 1751, it is likely that Meier had access to an earlier version of this or a similar text. While the manuscript translated by Poppe mentions life as a perfection of sensible cognition, it includes no more discussion of this perfection than the published text of the *Aesthetica*.

12. Hans Rudolf Schweizer claims that Meier "watered down" Baumgarten's aesthetics in *Ästhetik als Philosophie der Sinnlichen Erkenntnis* (Basel: Schwabe, 1973), 13. Frederick Beiser rejects this claim in *Diotima's Children: German Aesthetic Rationalism from Leibniz to Lessing* (Oxford: Oxford University Press, 2009), 122–23, 295n18.

though, for our purposes, Meier's *Foundations* possess something crucial that is missing from Baumgarten's *Aesthetics*—a complete and systematic account of the aesthetic perfection of "life."

Following Baumgarten, Meier begins his *Foundations* with a discussion of the new science that he will be presenting. In the introduction, Meier defines aesthetics as "the science . . . that concerns sensible cognition and its general characteristics" (§2). According to Meier, aesthetics includes "the rules of perfections and beauties in general" as well as "the doctrine of the soul, especially concerning the nature of the lower sensible cognitive faculty" (§3). This account actually provides the first two volumes of Meier's *Foundations* with their structure.[13] The first part of the text, "On the Beauties of Sensible Cognition," is entirely devoted to the perfections of sensible cognition, while the second part, "On the Sensible Faculties," discusses the faculties that are included among the lower cognitive faculty. The first part, which corresponds to the first (1748) volume of the *Foundations*, includes chapters on the beauties of aesthetic cognition in general, as well as aesthetic richness, magnitude, probability, and certainty. It also includes chapters on the "liveliness" (*Lebhaftigkeit*) and the "sensible life" (*sinlichen Leben*) of thoughts (*Gedanken*), before concluding with a chapter on the beautiful spirit. The second (1749) volume contains the second part and includes chapters on the sensible cognitive faculties in general, as well as the faculties of attention, abstraction, the senses, the imagination, wit, perspicaciousness, memory, invention, taste, foresight, anticipation, characterization, and the lower faculty of desire. Here we can already see how Meier's account of the cognitive faculties differs from Baumgarten's *Metaphysics*. In addition to reordering the presentation of the faculties, Meier includes chapters on the faculties of attention and abstraction that are not present in Baumgarten; divides the faculties of wit and perspicacity as well as the faculties of foresight and anticipation; and includes a faculty of taste that is not present in Baumgarten. Meier's account of the "beauties" of sensible cognition also deviates from Baumgarten's *Aesthetics* in important ways. Although he

13. Like Baumgarten's *Aesthetics*, Meier's *Foundations* is devoted to theoretical aesthetics, though, unlike Baumgarten's *Aesthetics*, it is not organized around the differences between heuristics, methodology, and semiotics. All three of these subjects are discussed in the third (1750) volume of the *Foundations*, though Meier treats them very differently than Baumgarten does. Instead of discussing the perfections of sensible cognition in the section on heuristics, for example, Meier explains the differences between aesthetic concepts, judgments, and conclusions. This constitutes a significant structural difference between Meier's *Foundations* and Baumgarten's *Aesthetics*.

insists, at the beginning of the *Foundations*, that beauties are perfections, Meier replaces Baumgarten's account of the aesthetic perfection of "truth" with the beauty of aesthetic "probability," or, perhaps, "verisimilitude" (§2). He also distinguishes between "the liveliness of thoughts" (Abs. 5) and "the sensible life of thoughts" (Abs. 7) in ways that seem to correspond to Baumgarten's accounts of the perfections of "light" and "life," but which depart from this terminology.

When he introduces the beauty of "liveliness of thoughts" (*Lebhaftigkeit der Gedanken*) in the first chapter of the *Foundations*, Meier initially identifies liveliness with extensive clarity. He argues that representations become more lively when we clarify representations by increasing their number, instead of increasing the clarity of the marks contained in a concept (§33).[14] Lively cognition remains confused, so it is sensible rather than intellectual; however, it is still more perfect and, thus, more beautiful than less lively cognition, because it represents more than other sensible cognitions (§23, §28, §30, §33). Later, in the chapter on the beauty of liveliness, Meier clarifies that liveliness is also called "aesthetic intelligibility" and "aesthetic light" (§119); that higher degrees of aesthetic light are called "aesthetic brilliance"; that particular determinations of liveliness are called "aesthetic colors"; that cognitions lacking aesthetic color are "dry, thin, and sober" (§120); and that cognitions lacking aesthetic light are obscure and covered in "shadow" (§123). In order to promote liveliness in cognition, Meier recommends, as a general rule, considering "all abstract and universal conceptions and truths, whether they are higher or lower genera or species, not in the abstract, but, rather, concretely" (§128). Thinking concretely allows clearer, more determinate representations to stand in for more obscure, drier ones (§129). Meier encourages his readers to use these substitutions, or tropes, whether in the form of synopsis or synecdoche (§130), examples (§131), or metonymy, metaphor, and irony (§§133–35), to make cognition not just clearer, but livelier, since lively cognition reveals the similarities and differences, agreements and disagreements, connections and relations, that are present in our thoughts, as a whole and in their parts (§137). He then proceeds to discuss a series of figures, which function differently than tropes, because they render cognition clearer and livelier without substituting one representation for another (§138). Meier considers figures of speech

14. Because it is ultimately grounded in the quantity of representations in our cognition, Meier traces the origin of the beauty of liveliness of thoughts to their richness, apparently grounding one beauty in another. See §124.

(§139), description (§140), oxymoron (§141), paralepsis (§142), and climax (§143), before making some recommendations for avoiding errors of lively representation (§144). He concludes with a series of rules for representing novelty, which Meier calls "the most beautiful of all the aesthetic colors" and also "the most secure medium for promoting liveliness" (§146), since the liveliness of all the other tropes and figures is increased by being "new and wonderful" (§147). Meier does not provide a summary or a unified account of liveliness at the end of the chapter; yet he seems to think the liveliness of cognition depends on its extensive clarity, concreteness, and novelty, which are increased and improved by the use of tropes and figures.

When Meier introduces the "sensible life of thoughts" (*sinlichen Leben der Gedanken*) in the first chapter of the *Foundations*, he says, "a cognition is alive when it causes pleasure or pain, desire or aversion, through the intuition of a perfection or imperfection" (§35). Meier adds that "living" (*lebendig*) cognition includes more variety and agreement than dead cognition, because it "contains an intuitive representation of the good and bad" and "its parts include the sufficient ground for the movement of the faculty of desire." This leads him to conclude that living cognition is not only the concern of the cognitive faculty, but also the faculty of desire, and, therefore, "fills the entire soul." Elaborating on these points in the chapter on the sensible life of cognition, Meier claims that, when living cognition is distinct, it moves the higher faculty of desire—the will (§178). When living cognition is indistinct, it arouses the lower faculty of desire, which is moved by feelings of pleasure and pain. Following Christian Wolff and Baumgarten, Meier takes these feelings to be the effect of certain kinds of representations.[15] Representing something as good, that is, as containing, increasing, or promoting perfection, will give rise, in the lower faculty of desire, to feelings of pleasure (§180). Representing something as lacking, diminishing, or hindering perfection, or bad, will make us feel pain. Meier's chapter contains a series of rules for arousing these feelings, which he calls "aesthetic affections" (§§181–87). He argues, for example, that in order to move the aesthetic affects, one must seek to awaken either a sensible pleasure or pain, or both together (§181); that one must represent objects as good

15. In this respect, Baumgarten and Meier follow Wolff closely. For a general account of Wolffian moral psychology, see Jerome B. Schneewind, *The Invention of Autonomy: A History of Modern Moral Philosophy* (Cambridge: Cambridge University Press, 1998), 431–42. For a more detailed consideration of Baumgarten and Meier's moral psychology, see Clemens Schwaiger, *Alexander Gottlieb Baumgarten: Ein Intellektuelles Porträt* (Stuttgart: Frommann-Holzboog, 2011), §25, §35.

or bad in order to awaken feelings of pleasure or pain (§182, §184); that the goodness or badness of objects is indicated by the beauty or ugliness of their representation (§183, §185); that cognition that is indifferent to these things is dead (§186); and that one must represent objects in a way that appeals to the senses in order to move the aesthetic affects (§187). Then he considers the determining grounds of sensible desire in order to confirm the correctness of the rules he has proposed. According to Meier, sensible desire is moved by attention (§190) and perspicaciousness (§191), as well as natural drives (§192) and the passions (§193). Meier denies that it can be swayed by reason or the will, the higher cognitive and volitional faculties, since they have nothing to do with the senses. However, he does acknowledge that sensible desire can be moved by other sensible perfections, such as the beauties of richness (§194), verisimilitude (§§199–200), and certainty (§§203–4). He also emphasizes the role that foresight and anticipation (§201); liveliness (§202); and surprise (§203) play in moving sensible desire. After enumerating his rules for arousing aesthetic affects and the determining grounds of sensible desire, Meier discusses the four kinds of "affecting and moving arguments" that appeal to the emotions (§§205–7) as well as the "pathetic and moving figures" that affect our souls (§§209–11). Finally, in the final section of the chapter, before moving on to his discussion of the beautiful spirit, Meier reminds readers that he has, at this point in the text, completed his survey of "the six major beauties of all sensible thoughts" (§212). He promises that rhetoricians and poets will be able to leave behind the pedantic formulas of the *ars topica* and apply the knowledge of the different kinds and modifications of these beauties to great advantage.[16]

Kant's Lectures

Kant does not cite Baumgarten's *Reflections on Poetry* or *Aesthetics*, nor does he discuss Meier's *Foundations*, in any of his published writings. However, he used Baumgarten's *Metaphysics* and Meier's *Vernunftlehre* as textbooks in

16. Buchenau provides a very helpful overview of Baumgarten's related criticism of the classical *topica* in the *Aesthetics* (§§130–41), where Baumgarten argues that the *topica* fails to provide a true "art of invention" and remains a mere "art of recollection" (§130). Buchenau, *The Founding of Aesthetics*, 144–51.

his lecture courses in Königsberg for almost forty years.[17] And the transcripts of Kant's lectures on metaphysics, anthropology, and logic contain several criticisms of Baumgarten and Meier's aesthetics, which have important implications for their conception of "life" (*Leben*) as an aesthetic perfection.

Kant's debts to and hostility toward Baumgarten are evident in his lectures on metaphysics. In transcripts of these lectures, Kant criticizes Baumgarten for including a chapter on empirical psychology in his *Metaphysics*, arguing that it reflects a fundamental misunderstanding of the nature of metaphysics.[18] While Baumgarten defines metaphysics as "the science of the first principles of human knowledge,"[19] Kant insists that it is more properly defined as "the science of pure reason" ("Metaphysik L_1," 28:223).[20] As a science of "pure" reason, metaphysics is solely concerned with a priori cognition—cognition that arises in the mind independently of experience. A posteriori cognition derived from experience and, in particular, sensation is not "pure" and, therefore, has no place in metaphysics, according to Kant's definition. Empirical psychology is, for Baumgarten, the part of psychology that "deduces its assertions based upon experience that is nearest to hand,"[21] so it follows from Kant's definition that it should not be included in metaphysics. This leads Kant to take a skeptical view toward a

17. Georg Friedrich Meier, *Georg Friedrich Meiers . . . Vernunftlehre* (Halle: Johann Justinus Gebauer, 1752).

18. Immanuel Kant, "Metaphysik L_1," in *Lectures on Metaphysics*, 17–106, 28:223. The following discussion is based on the transcript known as the "Metaphysik L_1," which dates from the mid-1770s. I focus on only one transcript for reasons of economy, but I believe that this transcript, along with the transcripts of the lectures on anthropology and logic that I discuss below, are sufficiently representative of Kant's views during the period under consideration to serve the purposes for which I am using them.

19. Baumgarten, *Metaphysics*, §1.

20. The conception of metaphysics that Kant proposes in this lecture corresponds to the definition he employs in both the 1770 inaugural dissertation *On the Form and Principles of the Sensible and the Intelligible World* (in *Theoretical Philosophy, 1755–1770*, 373–416, §8, 2:395) and the first *Critique* (Axx/Bxxii–xxiv), indicating it was important for Kant to emphasize the "purity" of metaphysics—its independence from experience and its nonempirical character. This view was not common among other rationalist philosophers, including Wolff, who emphasized the importance of both experience and experiments in metaphysics in general and in cosmology in particular. See Alberto Vanzo, "Christian Wolff and Experimental Philosophy," *Oxford Studies in Early Modern Philosophy* 7 (2015): 225–55.

21. Baumgarten, *Metaphysics*, §503.

number of Baumgarten's claims, particularly his account of sensible cognition. Instead of using the confusion of sensible cognition to distinguish it from the distinctness of intellectual cognition, Kant maintains that sensible cognition "arises either entirely from the impression of the object, and then this sensible cognition is a representation of the senses themselves, or sensible cognition arises from the mind, but under the condition under which the mind is affected by objects, and then sensible cognition is an imitated representation of the senses" (28:230). Sensible cognition is defined by its origin in sensible affection, so it need not be confused. Indeed, Kant will argue, against German rationalists from Gottfried Wilhelm Leibniz and Wolff to Baumgarten and Meier, that sensible cognition can be distinct without ceasing to be sensible, while intellectual cognition can be confused without ceasing to be intellectual (28:229).[22] Again, it is the origin of cognition in sensibility or the understanding that makes it sensible or intellectual, rather than its confusion or distinctness. Kant recognizes that this undermines Baumgarten's aesthetics, which attributes a specific set of perfections to confused sensible cognition; yet he continues to employ a version of Baumgarten's distinction between the aesthetic and logical perfections of cognition in his lectures. Instead of saying that aesthetically perfect cognition is confused sensible cognition that is beautiful or that logically perfect cognition involves philosophical knowledge of the truth, however, Kant maintains that logically perfect cognition agrees with the object, while aesthetically perfect cognition agrees with the subject (28:247). By "agreement" Kant seems to mean that logically perfect cognition accurately represents and, thus, corresponds to its object, while aesthetically perfect cognition arouses feelings of pleasure in the subject, leaving the subject in a more "agreeable" state.[23] Kant makes an interesting reference to the concept of life to explain aesthetic pleasure in a subsequent passage, noting that "objects are accordingly beautiful, ugly, etc., not in and for themselves, but rather in reference to living beings," so that "there must be a faculty in the living being for perceiving such properties in objects." He continues, saying that

22. I have traced the course of this objection through Kant's precritical and critical works in J. Colin McQuillan, "A Merely Logical Distinction: Kant's Objection to Leibniz and Wolff," *Epoché* 20, no. 2 (2016): 387–405.

23. I discuss Kant's references to aesthetically perfect cognition in greater detail in J. Colin McQuillan, "Baumgarten, Meier, and Kant on Aesthetic Perfection," in *Kant and His German Contemporaries*, vol. 2, *Aesthetics, History, Politics, and Religion*, ed. Daniel O. Dahlstrom (Cambridge: Cambridge University Press, 2018), 13–27.

"pleasure and pain is thus a faculty of the agreement or of the conflict of the principle of life with respect to certain representations or impressions of objects." Kant thinks we derive pleasure from beautiful things because they agree with the "principle of life" (*Princip des Lebens*) within ourselves and not because those objects are perfect or because sensible cognition is "livelier" than other cognitions.

Kant's objections to Baumgarten's empirical psychology and his conception of aesthetics should not, however, be mistaken for general opposition to these subjects. Kant clarifies, in his metaphysics lectures, that empirical psychology should not be abandoned; on the contrary, he thinks it should be developed as an independent discipline devoted to the empirical study of humanity.[24] That is why Kant made the chapter on empirical psychology in Baumgarten's *Metaphysics* the basis of the lectures on anthropology that he began delivering in 1772.[25] In the transcripts of these lectures, Kant provides an account of the distinction between sensible and intellectual cognition that is more sympathetic to Baumgarten, remarking that "distinctness is a work of the understanding and clarity is a work of the senses, for distinctness is based on reflection" ("Anthropology Friedländer," 25:482).[26] Attributing distinctness to the understanding brings Kant closer to his rationalist predecessors than some of the passages in his metaphysics lectures, but he still does not say that sensible cognition is necessarily confused—only that it possesses clarity and, later, intensity (25:485). Kant's account of the perfections of cognition in his anthropology lectures also deviate from what we saw in Baumgarten and Meier and then in his metaphysics lectures. Instead of distinguishing between logical and aesthetic perfections, Kant says the

24. For Kant's views on empirical psychology, see Thomas Sturm, "Kant on Empirical Psychology: How Not to Investigate the Human Mind," in *Kant and the Sciences*, ed. Eric Watkins (Oxford: Oxford University Press, 2001), 163–84; Rudolf A. Makkreel, "Kant on the Scientific Status of Psychology, Anthropology, and History," in *Kant and the Sciences*, ed. Eric Watkins (Oxford: Oxford University Press, 2001), 185–201; Thomas Sturm, *Kant und die Wissenschaft vom Menschen* (Paderborn: Mentis, 2009), esp. 183–260; Patrick Frierson, *Kant's Empirical Psychology* (Cambridge: Cambridge University Press, 2014).

25. On the origin of Kant's anthropology lectures, their relation to Baumgarten's empirical psychology, and the debates they occasioned, see Holly Wilson, *Kant's Pragmatic Anthropology* (Albany: State University of New York Press, 2006), 17–26.

26. The following discussion is based on the transcript known as the "Anthropologie Friedländer," which dates from the 1775–1776. Immanuel Kant, "Anthropology Friedländer," in *Lectures on Anthropology*, 37–256.

perfection of cognition is determined by "1. the relation of cognitions to the object, 2. the relation of cognitions to the subject, 3. the relation of cognitions among one another" (25:483). He associates truth, certainty, and distinctness with the perfection of cognition in relation to the object, while "facility, liveliness, and novelty" pertain to the perfection of cognition in relation to the subject. Kant notes that we do not have "better" cognition of an object when we find it "easy, novel, and lively" since the difference between objectively perfect and subjectively perfect cognition "concerns the human being himself, and not the object." Kant explains this difference in more detail when he turns from the cognitive faculties to the faculty of feeling pleasure and pain later in the transcript. Kant insists that the faculty of feeling pleasure and pain is distinct from the cognitive faculty, because "to cognize something and to be pleased with something are two different things" (25:558–59). Thus, Kant says, "I can have a representation of something, but the effect which things have on the whole of the mind, is the faculty of pleasure and pain" (25:559). Enjoyment or pleasure is "the feeling of the promotion of life" (*Beförderung des Lebens*), while pain is "the feeling of the hindrance of life" (*Gefühl von der Hinderung desselben*). In a passage reminiscent of the *Critique of Judgment* that he would publish almost twenty years later, Kant explains that "life is the consciousness of a free and regular play of all the powers and faculties of the human being." He maintains that anything that promotes the free play of the human being's powers and faculties will be a source of pleasure, because it will promote "life" (*Leben*). And he says beauty is particularly conducive to this kind of pleasure, insofar as it "furnishes a certain pure gratification" ("Anthropology Collins," 25:177).[27] Interestingly, in a way that distances him from Baumgarten and Meier, but also recalls the third *Critique*, Kant says beauty has no effect on sensibility (25:178).[28] Instead, the gratifications associated with beauty arise "in accordance with appearance compared with

27. Immanuel Kant, "Anthropology Collins," in *Lectures on Anthropology*, 11–26.

28. Kant is not always consistent about this point, as is evident from his logic lectures (cf. "The Blomberg Logic," in *Lectures on Logic*, 1–246, 24:45). However, I take the view in this passage to correspond to Kant's distinction between aesthetic pleasure and sensible agreeableness in the third *Critique* (§3), which I take to be a rejection of "sensibilism"—the view that aesthetic pleasure is grounded in sensibility. I defend this view in J. Colin McQuillan, "Outer Sense, Inner Sense, and Feeling: Hutcheson and Kant on Aesthetic Pleasure," in *Kant and the Scottish Enlightenment*, ed. Elizabeth Robinson and Chris W. Suprenant (New York: Routledge, 2017), 98–107.

feeling." This seems to be another way of saying that beauty is a source of pleasure because of the way it affects the subject's faculty of feeling; yet it helps to highlight some of the differences between Baumgarten, Meier, and Kant. While Baumgarten and Meier associate beauty with perfect sensible cognition, Kant separates beauty from sensibility. Beauty is important for Kant because of its effect on our faculty of feeling pleasure and pain, which is pleased by things that promote life, understood as the consciousness of the free play of our faculties, and not as one of the perfections or beauties of sensible cognition.

Kant's logic lectures are based on Meier's *Vernunftlehre*, rather than his *Foundations*, but they contain a number of remarks that are relevant to understanding his critique of Baumgarten's and Meier's aesthetics.[29] In the transcript of one of these lectures, Kant denies that aesthetics can be a science, because it does not contain any rules that can be demonstrated "by themselves, apart from all use, *a priori*" ("Logik Blomberg," 24:25).[30] He does not say so explicitly, but a series of passages emphasizing that "the science of taste" is among those cognitions "whose form is not rational" (24:24) also indicates that Kant thinks cognition associated with beauty and taste must be empirical, since it is not governed by a priori rules. When he discusses the aesthetic perfection of cognition, Kant builds on the claim, also found in his lectures on anthropology, that aesthetic perfection consists in "agreement with subjective laws and conditions" (24:43). He explains that "a cognition agrees with the subject when it gives us much to think about and brings our capacity into play" and also when it "has an effect on our feeling and taste" (24:44). This leads him to conclude that cognition is aesthetic when it "affects our feeling (by means of pleasure or pain)" (24:48). However, he also says that "an aesthetic perfection is a perfection according to laws of sensibility" (24:45), so that "the greater art of taste consists in now making sensible what I first expounded dryly, in clothing it in objects of sensibility, but in such a way that the understanding loses nothing thereby." This is obviously inconsistent with what Kant says in his anthropology lectures; yet we should not be too hasty to accuse Kant of contradicting himself. His account of the relations between aesthetic perfection and sensibility is simply a gloss on Baumgarten and Meier's

29. The following discussion is based on the transcript known as the "Logik Blomberg," which dates from the early 1770s (see note 27 of this chapter).

30. I examine Kant's reasons for denying that aesthetics can be a science, in his logic lectures and other texts, in J. Colin McQuillan, "Kant, the Science of Aesthetics, and the Critique of Taste," *Kant Yearbook* 9 (2017): 113–32.

identification of the aesthetic and the sensible, as is his claim that "the beauty of all good poetic representations . . . is sensed only in confused concepts, and it loses its value just as soon as the concept is made distinct" (24:51). In several places, he tries to make this view consistent with his emphasis on the effect of the beautiful on our faculty of feeling pleasure and pain, as when he says, "feeling is stirred by confused cognition, and on that account it is very hard to observe it, so that in general a science of it, i.e., *aesthetica*, has very many difficulties" (24:49), or when he identifies aesthetic perfection with "sensible pleasure and feeling" and says, "what excites our sensible feeling is aesthetically perfect" (24:60). These passages conflate the faculty of sensibility and feeling that Kant takes pains to distinguish in his anthropology lectures and also at several points in his logic lectures. For instance, he will say that "the activities of the soul consist of cognition, feeling, and desire" (24:31) and that "the principal capacities of our cognition are properly the following: (1.) understanding, (2.) feeling, and (3.) desire" (24:58). The second of these formulations could be said to conflate sensibility and feeling, since sensibility is usually considered a cognitive faculty, but Kant here seems to identify the cognitive faculty with the understanding. In any case, it is clear that Kant was not always consistent in his criticism of Baumgarten and Meier in his lectures and did not always defend a consistent position of his own. It is likely that Kant's own views were not clearly or fully formed during this period and that he treated his lectures as an opportunity to experiment with different philosophical positions, even when he was lecturing on Baumgarten's *Metaphysics* and Meier's *Vernunftlehre*.

Kant's *Critique of Judgment*

The passages from the transcripts of Kant's lectures on metaphysics, anthropology, and logic that I discuss in the previous section all date from the 1770's—a period when Kant was deeply engaged with Baumgarten and Meier, but before he published the *Critique of Pure Reason* and began incorporating his own critical philosophy into his lectures. In the lecture transcripts from this period, we can see that, even before he arrived at the positions he would defend in the first *Critique*, Kant had already raised important objections to the most basic premise of Baumgarten's and Meier's aesthetics—the confusion of sensible cognition. He also began formulating novel views, insisting that aesthetic cognition is empirical, that it is not governed by a priori rules, and, thus, cannot be the subject of a science.

Kant's lectures also establish a close connection between beauty, taste, and feeling that he continued to defend, even in contexts where he equivocated about other aspects of aesthetics—whether, for example, aesthetic cognition belongs to the faculty of sensibility or the faculty of feeling pleasure and pain. Finally, Kant developed a novel way of connecting aesthetic pleasure to life—the claim that aesthetic perfection is a function of the relation between the subject and its cognition, which gives rise to pleasure because it promotes life, which is understood, in a very unusual way, as the free play of the subject's faculties and powers.[31]

We can see traces of these innovations in works from the 1780s and 1790s that are central to Kant's critical philosophy. In a footnote to the "Transcendental Aesthetic" in the first edition of the first *Critique* (A, 1781), Kant repeats an argument from his logic lectures, when he says that Baumgarten's attempt to bring "the critical estimation of the beautiful under principles of reason" had failed, because "the putative rules or criteria are merely empirical as far as their sources are concerned, and can therefore never serve as *a priori* rules according to which our judgment of taste must be directed" (A21). Kant softens his judgment in the revised version of the footnote that he includes in the second edition (B, 1787), claiming only that "only the most prominent sources" of aesthetic judgment are empirical and denying that they are governed by any "determinate *a priori*" rules (B35). These qualifications open a space for another innovation that Kant introduces in the third *Critique*, where he breaks with the position he had defended in his lectures and in the first *Critique*, proposing that there is,

31. This conception of life is unusual, because it is notably different from the one Kant regularly employs in his moral philosophy, where life is defined as "the faculty of a being to act in accordance with laws of the faculty of desire." See Immanuel Kant, *Critique of Practical Reason*, in *Practical Philosophy*, trans. and ed. Mary Gregor (Cambridge: Cambridge University Press, 1996), 133–271, 5:9. It is also different from the conception of life that Kant employs in the second part of the *Critique of Judgment*, on teleological judgment, where life is understood in relation to the purposive arrangement and interaction of the parts of an organism. On the relation of these conceptions of "life" to Kant's aesthetics, see Rudolf A. Makkreel, *Imagination and Interpretation in Kant: The Hermeneutical Import of the "Critique of Judgment"* (Chicago: University of Chicago Press, 1990), 90–99. On Kant's conception of life in relation to biology, see also Rachel Zuckert, *Kant on Beauty and Biology: An Interpretation of the "Critique of Judgment"* (Cambridge: Cambridge University Press, 2007), 100n20. See also Jennifer Mensch, *Kant's Organicism: Epigenisis and the Development of Critical Philosophy* (Chicago: University of Chicago Press, 2013), 51–69.

indeed, an a priori principle of aesthetic judgment—the principle of purposiveness ("Introduction," 5:180–81).[32]

Although Kant's discovery of the principle of purposiveness represents a fundamental change in his views on aesthetics, many aspects of the "Critique of Aesthetic Judgment" in the third *Critique* are still familiar from his lectures. For example, Kant's insistence, that "a judgment of taste is wholly independent of the concept of perfection" (§15, 5:226) is merely an extension of his earlier arguments that the aesthetic perfection of a cognition is not derived from its relation to an object, nor can beauty be identified with the perfection of confused sensible cognition. Instead of trying to reformulate Baumgarten's distinction between the aesthetic and logical perfections of cognition to accommodate these changes, Kant simply abandons the concept of aesthetic perfection. Similarly, Kant's claims that the ground of a judgment of taste "*cannot be other* than *subjective*" (§1, 5:203) is consistent with the subjectivism of his discussions of aesthetically perfect cognition in his lectures. The distinction he draws between aesthetic pleasure and sensible agreeableness is also closely related to the claim, in the lecture transcripts, that beauty is associated with the faculty of feeling pleasure and pain, rather than the cognitive faculty. These aspects of the third *Critique* prove that Kant's critical aesthetics is still bound up with the criticisms that he articulated in his lectures during the precritical period of Baumgarten and Meier's conception of aesthetics as a science devoted to the perfection of sensible cognition.

32. Kant explains his discovery of this principle in a letter to Reinhold, indicating that it was the "systematicity" of the three faculties of the mind (the cognitive faculty, the faculty of feeling pleasure and pain, and the faculty of desire) that led him to the discovery of the a priori principles of aesthetic judgment, after he had already discovered the a priori principles of the faculties of cognition and desire in the first and second *Critique*. See Immanuel Kant to Carl Leonhard Reinhold, December 28 and 31, 1787, in *Correspondence*, trans. and ed. Arnulf Zweig (Cambridge: Cambridge University Press, 1999), 271–273, 10:514–15. Guyer attributes this discovery to Kant's concern with teleology, while Patrick Frierson sees it as an extension of Kant's psychological taxonomies, which are mostly elaborated in his lectures. Paul Guyer, "Beauty, Freedom, and Morality: Kant's *Lectures on Anthropology* and the Development of his Aesthetic Theory," in *Essays on Kant's Anthropology*, ed. Brian Jacobs and Patrick Kain (Cambridge: Cambridge University Press, 2003), 135–63; Patrick Frierson, "A New Sort of *A Priori* Principles: Psychological Taxonomies and the Origin of the Third *Critique*," in *Kant and the Faculty of Feeling*, ed. Kelly Sorensen and Diane Williamson (Cambridge: Cambridge University Press, 2018), 107–29.

Of all the perfections that Baumgarten and Meier attribute to aesthetic cognition, it is perhaps "life" (*Leben*) that is most important for Kant. Baumgarten was never able to complete his discussion of the aesthetic perfection of life in the *Aesthetics*, but Meier provided an extensive discussion of sensible life in his *Foundations*, connecting the sensible life of thoughts to the lower faculty of desire, the representation of good and bad things, and the feelings of pleasure and pain that are aroused by these representations. Kant never cites this discussion, but he maintains the connection between life and feeling that is found in Meier's *Foundations*. At the beginning of the "Analytic of the Beautiful," for example, Kant says that judgments of taste are "referred only to the subject and to its feeling of life, under the name of the feeling of pleasure or pain" (§1, 5:204).[33] Kant's reference to the "feeling of life" (*Lebensgefühl*) in this passage has perplexed many commentators, but it is not surprising when one recalls the metaphysics lectures, where Kant said, "pleasure and pain is thus a faculty of the agreement or of the conflict of the principle of life with respect to certain representations or impressions of objects" (28:247). Since the impressions of objects that affect our faculty of feeling pleasure and pain, and agree or conflict with our principle of life, are not beautiful or ugly in themselves, but only with respect to our status as "living beings," the subjectivism of Kant's conception of beauty in the third *Critique* can be seen as an extension of his critique of Baumgarten and Meier.

The distinctions Kant draws between aesthetic and moral judgments in subsequent passages indicate that he intended to keep the faculty of feeling pleasure and pain separate from the faculty of desire, instead of following Meier and uniting them.[34] The key difference between aesthetic and moral judgment, which justifies Kant's distinction between the faculties of feeling and desire, is that moral judgments involve interest. We have a moral interest in goodness, which makes some objects desirable, but which

33. Kant's conception of a "feeling of life" and its "life-enhancing" character is discussed in detail in Makkreel, *Imagination and Interpretation*, 91–93.

34. Kant rejects the distinction between the higher and lower faculties of desire in the second *Critique*, arguing that the two faculties cannot be distinguished by the origin of pleasurable representations in the faculties of sensibility or the understanding. Instead, he insists that only the lower faculty can be moved by feelings of pleasure and pain, while the higher faculty, which is to be identified with reason, determines itself through "the mere form of a practical rule," without reference to feelings of pleasure and pain. Kant, *Critique of Practical Reason*, 5:22–25.

also presupposes their existence (§4, 5:211). Such an interest is not found in aesthetic pleasure, which is only related to the subject and is, as such, "devoid of all interest" in objects and their existence (§2, 5:204–5). Later in the text, Kant will also associate the feeling of aesthetic pleasure with the "enlivening" (*Belebung*) of the cognitive faculties that takes place in free play through the "reciprocal harmony" of their mutual interaction (§9, 5:219). This echoes Kant's remarks in the anthropology lectures, where he says, "life is the consciousness of a free and regular play of all the powers and faculties of the human being" (25:559). Nothing like this is to be found in Baumgarten or Meier, though Kant's conception of enlivening could, perhaps, be compared to Meier's account of the sensible life of cognition, since they both bring different faculties together and give rise to feelings of pleasure. Still, it would be a mistake to reduce Kant's account of free play to Meier's conception of sensible life. Kant's account of the enlivening of the faculties involves the imagination and understanding, rather than sensibility and the lower faculty of desire. Nor does Meier have anything like Kant's conception of "free play," in which a presentation that "has a merely subjective determining ground" and "does not involve the concept of an object," is related to "cognition in general" (§9, 5:217). No less unprecedented is Kant's claim that, because "no determinate concept restricts them to a particular rule of cognition" in their relation to cognition in general, we are able to "feel" the way the imagination and understanding "harmonize" with one another in judgment—even though there is no determinate object to judge (§9, 5:218). These claims are clearly very different from Meier's account of the relationship between "living" (*lebendig*) cognition and feelings of pleasure and pain, which grounds aesthetic pleasure in confused sensible representations of objects that increase the perfection of our cognition. And yet Kant's account of the enlivening of the cognitive faculties in the free play of the imagination and understanding appears to derive from a lecture, based on Baumgarten's empirical psychology, that associates pleasure and life in a way that is similar to Meier, even if the exact relationship between Meier's views and Kant's is neither clear nor direct.

In the end, I would like to suggest that Kant's critique of Baumgarten and Meier led him to reject the idea that aesthetic pleasure is grounded in confused sensible cognition, as well as the idea that life is an aesthetic perfection of sensible cognition. The same critique also helps to explain important aspects of the critical aesthetics that Kant presents in the third *Critique*. The subjectivism of his conception of beauty; the distinctions he draws between the cognitive faculties, the faculty of desire, and the faculty of feeling pleasure and pain; and, last but not least, his appeals to "the feeling of life" and the "enlivening" of the cognitive faculties through free play, can all be traced back to the critique of Baumgarten's and Meier's aesthetics in Kant's lectures on metaphysics, anthropology, and logic from the 1770s. The path from Kant's lectures to his critical aesthetics is complicated and convoluted, but there are still markers along the way, in the transcripts of his lectures, which indicate that this is the route he took.

Chapter 5

The Ideal of Beauty and the Meaning of "Life" in Kant's Philosophy

Kristi Sweet

In the section of *the Critique of Practical Reason* entitled "On the Wise Adaptation of the Human Being's Cognitive Faculties to His Practical Vocation," Kant argues that from the perspective of our moral goodness, it is beneficial to us that we do not have knowledge of God's existence. If we had such knowledge, he suggests, "most actions conforming to the law would be done from fear, only a few from hope, and none at all from duty" (5:147).[1] To describe such heteronomy, namely, the appropriation of an external ground for action that merely conforms to the morally good, Kant writes, "everything would *gesticulate* well, but there would be no *life* in the figures." In one regard, Kant would seem here to violate what he insists upon elsewhere, namely, that we are not granted any access to the intentions of others. The suggestion in this passage is that there is an outward appearance of a person's motivations. With this, and perhaps what is more

1. Immanuel Kant, *Critique of Practical Reason*, in *Practical Philosophy*, ed. Mary J. Gregor, trans. Allan W. Wood (Cambridge: Cambridge University Press, 1996), 133–272. In-text citations will refer to the Akademie edition of Kant's work, including the volume and page number.

compelling as a suggestion, is Kant's naming of a specific kind of causal relation between the will and the body, namely, that of *life*.[2]

Kant's insistence that there is a difference in the movements of human bodies depending on their moral worth goes to the heart of a central question of his practical philosophy: whether or not freedom can be efficacious in the natural order. Reason, in its practical context, demands that its ends be realized in nature; the world must be transformed into a place fit for rational beings such as ourselves. Reason, however, finds nature obdurate in the face of its efforts to make the world into what it ought to be. The question of whether or not nature can be made into something other than what it is recurs throughout Kant's practical philosophy, from the postulates of practical reason to his thinking on culture and history. While the question of freedom's effectiveness shows up continually throughout Kant's practical opus, it is the central and defining topic of the *Critique of Judgment*. In the third *Critique*, Kant argues that there is a third, independent but mediating sphere of reflective judgment between freedom and nature. This sphere is meant not only to allow us to think that freedom may have influence in the natural order—to provide a "bridge" between freedom and nature—but also to complete Kant's philosophical system. Freedom's effectiveness, according to the third *Critique*, is taken to be possible through the mediating sphere of judgment. However, throughout the text, Kant repeatedly points beyond the limits of the critical project and the judgments described in the text as reflective. It is to *life*—understood as the *direct* or *unmediated* forcefulness of freedom in the natural order[3]—that the text continually gestures. It does this because, while the system is complete, reason nevertheless demands a more thoroughgoing kind of unity of freedom and nature exemplified in *life*.

One of the key moments where Kant gestures toward life in the third *Critique* is in his discussion "On the Ideal of Beauty." Scholars have long wrestled with (or alternatively dismissed) this section of the third *Critique*, which seems, to some, to be forced into the text on account of Kant's desire

---

2. Distinctive of my approach in this essay is that I take my point of departure from the question of what "life" is. While there has been other really excellent work on Kant on life, much of it begins with the feeling of life we have in judgments of taste. Perhaps the best example of this is Rudolf Makkreel's treatment of life and its role in Kant's philosophy in *Imagination and Interpretation in Kant: The Hermeneutical Import of the "Critique of Judgment"* (Chicago: University of Chicago Press, 1990).

3. I use "forcefulness" here quite literally—it is freedom as an effective force that is in question.

to speak to a debate of his age. In this chapter, I will offer an account of the ideal of beauty as a moment of Kant's text that points toward life—a kind of unity demanded by reason that even the completion of the system does not yield. In this, I will suggest we understand the ideal of beauty as a site of unity between freedom and nature that reason demands, but that nevertheless exceeds the bounds of the critical system. Insofar as it presents a real unity of freedom of nature, too, it does serve as an exemplar of what beauty itself suggests. Moreover, from the perspective of practical reason, the ideal of beauty suggests that the will potentially has the force completely to determine and even ground the ultimate natural obstacle to our moral goodness, namely, the body.

This chapter will unfold in three parts. First, I will lay out how Kant takes the judgments of the third *Critique* to offer a way for freedom and nature to be mediated in their relation, and at the same time to complete his philosophical system. With this, Kant establishes three independent spheres of truth, beauty, and goodness. Second, I will suggest that despite the completion of the system, Kant nevertheless repeatedly gestures out beyond this system to *life*. Life will be seen to be a unity of freedom and nature that exceeds what is permitted within the critical system. Lastly, I will turn to the ideal of beauty as one moment of such a gesture. In the section "On the Ideal of Beauty," Kant describes a person whose material being is thoroughgoingly determined by the force of freedom in his or her will. As the ideal of beauty offers an "original pattern" of all things we find beautiful, it presents to the reader not only the unity of force and matter in a human life, but also reminds us that it is this unity to which all judgments of taste point.

The Completion of the Critical System

In the "Transcendental Dialectic" of the *Critique of Pure Reason*, Kant is clear about the demands of reason. Reason, Kant argues, demands the unconditioned. It is a "need" of reason to "assume that when the conditioned is given, then so is the whole series of conditions subordinated to one another, which is itself unconditioned, also given (i.e., contained in the object and its connection)" (A307–8/B364). With this, reason demands completeness and unity in all things. That is, reason seeks always the whole of what is, wherein the whole is unified in the connection between its constituent parts. It is this driving and implacable need of reason that gives birth to two millennia of metaphysical speculation, and ultimately to what Kant calls "transcendental illusion" (A293/B350). Even with critique—the cognizance of one's own cognitive limits and the disciplining of one's reason—this press of reason remains. It gives rise to what Kant names our peculiar fate: we are destined to ask questions we cannot answer.

Reason's demand for completeness and unity extends into all spheres of human life; it is not merely confined to our cognition of the natural order. Reason in its practical use likewise demands such completeness. We see this most concretely in Kant's articulation of the highest good as a thoroughgoingly moral world, brought about through the free causality of a good will. The moral world takes shape ultimately in the ubiquity of political right (cosmopolitanism) and the enactment of an ethical community (a rational religion). The absoluteness of the charge for freedom to transform nature into a rational whole is clear in Kant's logic. Paul Guyer puts it simply, "it would be irrational for us to act as duty commands if we did not believe that the realization of the object it turns out to command is at least possible."[4] Kant's commitment to this is clear. He goes so far as to argue that if freedom cannot transform the natural order to conform with the dictates of reason, that is, if the highest good in the world is not possible, "then the moral law, which commands us to promote it, must be fantastic and directed to empty imaginary ends and must therefore in itself be false" (5:114).

The demand for completeness and unity further takes shape with respect to the system of human faculties of mind. Kant introduces the need for such an arrangement in the first *Critique*. "The Architectonic of Pure Reason" is concerned with just such systematicity in the delineation and use of our faculties. He opens the section with a nod to wholeness conceived *organically*. That is, the system of human faculties is conceived as an organism—a totality of parts organized with respect to the use of the other parts, ultimately with respect to the one end. In this, he writes, "the whole is therefore articulated (*articulatio*) and not heaped together (*coacervatio*)" (A833/B861). Articulation, borrowed here from its principal use in medicine, means to join together, as in articulating bones together at the joint.[5] This issue of joining faculties into a system is one of, if not

4. Paul Guyer, "From Nature to Morality: Kant's New Argument in the 'Critique of Teleological Judgment,'" in *Kant's System of Nature and Freedom* (Oxford: Oxford University Press, 2005), 314–42, 315.

5. This understanding is still in use today, when we describe a skeleton as articulated.

the, central driving forces of the third *Critique*, too. He is concerned that without such a joining, the "mental powers form no system, but only an aggregate" ("First Introduction," 20:206).[6] He goes on to note that such a system is "of the utmost importance for the use of reason in all contexts" (preface to first edition, 5:168).

The question of whether or not freedom can be efficacious in the natural order is, for Kant, answered in the possibility of systematizing the faculties of the human mind and the two parts of philosophy—practical and theoretical. Moreover, this is the question the third *Critique* seeks to answer in establishing a third, "joining" sphere of judgment.

Kant conceives of the sphere of judgment as *mediating* between freedom and nature, between practical and theoretical philosophy. His conception of the mediating relation comes out most clearly in his discussion of territory and domain in the introduction to the text. It is through his geographical and geopolitical metaphorics in this section of the text that he most directly addresses how he conceives of the possibility of freedom and nature, practical and theoretical philosophy, being joined. Kant begins by defining the broadest relation of human faculties to what there is in the world. "Insofar as we refer concepts to objects without considering whether or not cognition of these objects is possible, they have their field" ("Introduction," 5:174).[7] Within this broadest relation of concepts to objects, Kant goes on to name two more. First, "the part of this field in which cognition is possible for us is a territory (*territorium*)." Second, within the territory of what is possible are two legislative spheres—spheres in which our faculties have jurisdiction, where their laws are applied to objects. "That part of the territory over which these concepts legislate is the domain (*ditio*) of these concepts and the cognitive powers pertaining to them."

There are two domains that are established on the territory; part of the territory, however, remains extrajurisdictional. The two domains that Kant names are those governed by the concepts of freedom and the concepts of nature. Kant suggests that these two domains are "set up" or erected (*errichtet*) on the territory. The territory, as it were, is the *ground* upon which the two domains of practical and theoretical philosophy are built. The grounding or

6. Immanuel Kant, *Critique of Judgment*, trans. Werner Pluhar (Indianapolis: Hackett, 1987).

7. I have modified Werner Pluhar's translation, substituting "field" for his "realm." Field not only more adeptly captures the German *Feldes* but upholds more continuously the geographical metaphors Kant here employs.

foundational character of the territory is given, too, in Kant's association of *territorium* with *Boden*: soil, or, historically, bottom. Rudolf Makkreel aptly names the territory as the "base of what can be experienced by humans."[8] What is crucial is that the two domains share a common terrain upon which they are built. And, this terrain constitutes its own sphere for Kant—there are sets of objects that reside "out in the territory," as it were, and are not annexed to either of the other two spheres. Most prominently, these are things that are beautiful, and organisms. The territory, then, the extrajurisdictional sphere that appears between the domains of freedom and nature, yet also provides the annexed ground on which those domains are built, thus provides a way across—a transition or *Übergang*—between the other two spheres.

It is thus with the addition of a third or mediating sphere of reflective judgments that Kant completes his philosophical system and allows for us to think the possibility of freedom having an influence on the natural order. Each sphere for Kant retains its legislative independence. Yet, the three spheres relate to each other through the shared grounding and possible mediation of judgments of reflection. Truth—the theoretical sphere of cognition—beauty—the aesthetic sphere of reflective judgment—and goodness—the practical sphere of freedom, remain separate from each other in their sets of concepts and objects.

With this, the kind of satisfaction that reason gets remains incomplete. Freedom's influence on nature is still indirect, insofar as it is mediated. In Kant's system, freedom does not come into direct contact with the natural order. What we get is precisely what is promised in the introduction to the third *Critique*:

> Hence an immense gulf is fixed between the domain of the concept of nature, the sensible, and the domain of the concept of freedom, the supersensible, so that no transition from the sensible to the supersensible (and hence by means of the theoretical use of reason) is possible, just as if they were two different worlds, the first of which cannot have any influence on the second; and yet the second *is* to have an influence on the first, i.e., the concept of freedom is to actualize in the world of sense the purpose enjoined by its laws. Hence it must be

8. Rudolf A. Makkreel, *Orientation and Judgment in Hermeneutics* (Chicago: University of Chicago Press, 2015), 65.

> possible to think of nature as being such that the lawfulness in its form will harmonize with at least the possibility of achieving the purposes that we are to achieve in nature according to the laws of freedom. ("Introduction," 5:176)

What is promised is the *possibility* of *harmonization*. And indeed, in the third *Critique*, nature appears to us as generally purposeful. Nature's purposivity—judged merely reflectively—allows us to think that it is possible that nature itself may have a supersensible substratum that accords with the ends of freedom. This does not suggest, though, that freedom may reach out into nature and transform it into something rational. Indeed, Kant clearly, decisively, and self-consciously opts for *harmonization* instead of *unity* with respect to freedom and nature. Those who followed in his wake in the German idealist tradition were critical of him for just this. "Nature and freedom are not identical" in Kant, writes Günter Figal on the matter.[9] Rather, "the supersensible is given in the sensible and natural aspect of aesthetic experience in such a way that it does not oppose the sensible; supersensible freedom arrives in intuition with the sensible of aesthetic experience without being able to unify with the latter."

Life: Unity beyond the Critical System

In completing the philosophical system and, with it, the system of human faculties, Kant remains committed to reason's peculiar fate. While the system is complete, reason fails to attain that for which it principally strives—to become, through its own efforts, the animating force of the world. Despite Kant's consistency with respect to this commitment, there are a few, notable instances where the kind of unity reason desires breaks through in his writing. The name for the kind of causal unity reason seeks to have with respect to the natural order is life. In this section, I will lay out Kant's view of life, and how it lies beyond the confines of the critical philosophy. In the next section, we will see how the ideal of beauty is an instance of *life*, and of the possibility of reason attaining the absolute dominion over what is exterior to it.

---

9. Günter Figal, *Aesthetics as Phenomenology: The Appearance of Things* (Bloomington: Indiana University Press, 2015), 29.

Kant has a long-standing interest in the question of life. He begins his philosophical career as a twenty-one-year-old student with an essay, "Thoughts on the True Estimation of Living Forces."[10] In this essay, he makes an intervention into the *vis viva* debate, which had been waged already for more than fifty years by the time of his writing.[11] The *vis viva* debate took shape around attempts to understand how force related to matter, specifically by way of the task of measuring such forces in moving bodies. The debate began in 1686, when Gottfried Wilhelm Leibniz published a short piece entitled "A Brief Demonstration of a Notable Error of Descartes and Others Concerning a Natural Law."[12] In it, Leibniz argues against René Descartes with respect to his characterization of force; this essay is typically taken to initiate a distinction between kinematics and dynamics. Kinematics studies the motion of bodies with respect to what is externally measurable. Dynamics, by contrast, studies the inner forces that are taken to be the underlying cause or source of the movement. The latter is what comes to be associated with living forces—the forces that animate or enliven a thing to motion. These are what Leibniz identifies as "essential forces," which, as Kant notes, "inhere" in a body ("True Estimation of Living Forces," 1:17). In this, a material body possesses, or is possessed by, the force that is the source of its motion. Kant's own discussion comes to take shape in part around the question of whether or not a body is moved by forces external to it or internal to it (1:139ff.). What is compelling is not so much Kant's view; rather, the fact of his inaugural interest in the question of the relation of force to matter is what is really at issue.

Even in his early essay, Kant sees the question of the relation of force and matter as one with broader relevance. Living force is the force that is essential to a body when it becomes activated, that is, vivification. Kant

---

10. Immanuel Kant, "Thoughts on the True Estimation of Living Forces and Assessment of the Demonstrations That Leibniz and Other Scholars of Mechanics Have Made Use of in This Controversial Subject, Together with Some Prefatory Considerations Pertaining to the Force of Bodies in General," in *Natural Science*, ed. Eric Watkins, trans. Jeffrey B. Edwards and Martin Schönfeld (Cambridge: Cambridge University Press, 2012), 1–155.

11. For detailed examinations of this debate, please see Carolyn Iltis, "Leibniz and the *Vis Viva* Controversy," *Isis* 62, no. 1 (1971): 21–35; David Papineau, "The *Vis Viva* Controversy: Do Meanings Matter?," *Studies in History and Philosophy of Science* 8, no. 2 (1977): 111–42; Mary Terrall, "*Vis Viva* Revisited," *History of Science* 42 (2004): 189–209.

12. Gottfried Wilhelm Leibniz, "A Brief Demonstration of a Notable Error of Descartes and Others Concerning a Natural Law," in *Philosophical Papers and Letters*, ed. Leroy E. Loemker (Dodrecht: Kluwer, 1989), 296–302.

himself notes that the difficulty in conceiving how this force comes to life and affects material being also has import for practical life. He writes: "A similar difficulty becomes apparent when the question is raised as to whether the soul, too, is capable of setting matter in motion. . . . For the question whether the soul can cause motions, that is, whether it has moving force, is transformed into the question whether its essential force can be determined toward an externally directed action, that is, whether it is capable of acting outside itself on other entities and producing changes" (1:20).

The question of a living being and its animation, then, is the question of how a force—something immaterial—can come into causal contact with and ultimately affect something material.

While Kant's question with respect to living beings holds with the philosophical tradition beginning with Aristotle in *De anima*, what is important is not only that he is concerned with it from the beginning. Rather, it is how he comes to define life by way of living forces. Life, for Kant, comes to be defined by a specific kind of union between force and matter. In this, he follows Leibniz closely.

Kant comes, however, to deviate from Leibniz and others in the early modern tradition with respect to whether or not we can investigate, let alone even think, the possibility of life as it is conceived. Kant, with the transcendental turn, comes to reject a science of living beings; the movement of matter can only be investigated according to mechanistic causalities. He holds a strict distinction between force and matter, and it is beyond the scope of human thinking to cognize a unity in their relation. In his *Metaphysical Foundations of Natural Science*, in 1786, Kant reiterates his now established view about the issue. Kant defines matter thus, "matter is the movable in space" (4:480).[13] "Motion," he goes on, "is the change of [a thing's] outer relations in a given space" (4:482). Matter also "fills a space" (4:496), as movable, it "has moving force," and "can be an object of experience" (4:554). But matter, "as such," Kant writes, is "lifeless" (4:544). By this he means that it is inert; it has "no internal determinations or grounds of determination" (4:453). Matter, then, qua matter, is always subject to that which is external to it, whether that externality is other matter or some living force. Matter is inert: it does not act but is acted upon. From the perspective of scientific inquiry, moreover, matter, qua matter, is only amenable to mechanical accounts of its being, that is, the kind of accounts

13. Immanuel Kant, *Metaphysical Foundations of Natural Science*, trans. Michael Friedman (Cambridge: Cambridge University Press, 2004).

that are made possible as knowledge under the regime of the analytic in the *Critique of Pure Reason*.

Kant thus rejects the *life* sciences, the sciences that purport to account for movement of an object whose determination to motion originates in itself. "Life," he writes, "is the faculty of a substance to determine itself to act from an internal principle" (4:544). Such motion includes not only the force to move from one place to another, but the nutritive movements of sustenance, growth, healing, and reproduction. In fact, as Jennifer Mensch highlights in her study of Kant's intellectual development with respect to thinking organic life and the possibility of the life sciences, Kant continually found the challenge of thinking living being to be beyond the scope of our capabilities.[14] Of the problem, Kant writes, "the various appearances of life in nature and the laws governing them, constitute the whole of that which it is granted us to know. But the principle of this life, in other words, the spirit-nature which we do not know but only suppose, can never be positively thought, for, in the entire range of our sensations, there are no data for such positive thought" ("Dreams of a Spirit-Seer," 2:351).[15]

Perhaps the most telling mature discussion of what life is, what it is not, and what we can know about it can be found in Kant's description of organisms in the third *Critique*. In writing the third *Critique*, Kant already—and still—rejects the life sciences as earlier conceived. He revisits the question of the biological sciences, however, and the possibilities for investigating living beings under the auspices of reflective judgment. As such, the orientation for such an investigation remains out in the territory for Kant. What we do get, however, is the concept of an organism; organisms, for Kant, are constituted by what he names internal purposiveness. In virtue of its internal purposiveness, an organism is a natural end—it is "both cause and effect" (§64, 5:371) of itself; each part "reciprocally produces the other" (§65, 5:374); each part exists "*for the sake* of the others and of the whole" (§65, 5:373). Living being, organic life, is "self-organizing." To be a living being is to cause one's own existence, both as a member of a species and as an individual. In this, an organism has a kind of self-determination of its existence—in continuing its existence in living, and in determining the form of its existence materially.

14. Jennifer Mensch, *Kant's Organicism: Epigenesis and the Development of Critical Philosophy* (Chicago: University of Chicago Press, 2013), esp. ch. 3.

15. Immanuel Kant, "Dreams of a Spirit-Seer Elucidated by Dreams of Metaphysics," in *Theoretical Philosophy, 1755–1770*, trans. and ed. David Walford, with Ralf Meerbote (Cambridge: Cambridge University Press, 2003), 301–59.

This organic arrangement of materiality is given by what Kant names a "formative force." He rejects, though, that this is the same thing as *life*. He writes, "hence an organized being is not a mere machine. For a machine has only *motive* force. But an organized being has within it *formative* force, and a formative force that this being communicates [*mittheilt*] to the kinds of matter that lack it (thereby organizing them)" (§65, 5:374).[16] Here, the formative force that organizes a being into a living being is one that arranges the parts of the thing with respect to its whole being and its capacity to persist in being. The causality belonging to the formative force, though, is not therefore life. Kant will first reject that this power is akin to art—art has its causality from outside of itself. He will only suggest, however, that perhaps this "inscrutable property" is "an analogue of life" (§65, 5:374). The problem he articulates here is the very same one he is "astonished" by in his precritical writings on the topic: Either, he suggests, we endow matter with a "property (hylozoism) that conflicts with its nature. Or else we must supplement matter with an alien principle (a soul) *conjoined* [*Gemeinschaft*] to it" (§65, 5:374–75). In either case, what *life* is for Kant emerges out of a dichotomy that may remain hidden without close inspection. Life here is a *union* between the property of animation or self-determination and material nature. Hylozoism simply ascribes a soul to matter itself, thereby rendering it not matter proper, or we take the soul to be able to come into a union with the matter. These two models of relation differ from the formative force, which merely "communicates" (*mittheilt*) with the matter. Kant's formulation of the formative power is crucial, as it suggests that there remains a distance between the force and the matter. The force that organizes a living being is transmitted to or gotten across to the matter, but it does not come into a union with it. This is a strange kind of causality, and Kant concludes that "the organization of nature has nothing analogous to any causality known to us" (§65, 5:375).

Life, then, names a certain kind of unity of force and matter, wherein force activates the matter. This unity, this causal relation, is not one that the human faculties are fit to think, however. Living beings, organisms, cannot even be thought properly under the auspices of life—we must still remain in the dark about the way that the formative power communicates itself to the matter it forms. Despite this, Kant will return to the possibility of life, to the possibility of such a unity, intermittently throughout his opus. In his

16. I have modified the translation slightly. Rather than render *mittheilt* as "imparts" I use "communicates." It better presents the distance maintained in the relation of force to matter that Kant is describing.

"Reflections on Moral Philosophy" we find, for example: "Everything finally comes down to life; that which animates, or the feeling of the promotion of life, is agreeable. *Life is unity* [*Das Leben ist Einheit*]; hence all taste has as its principio the unity of animating sensation" (R6862, 19:183; my emphasis).[17]

Ideal of Beauty and "Life in the Figures"

Judgments of taste and judgments of organicity both remain squarely within and ultimately complete the critical system. They are reflective judgments that suggest to us the purposivity of nature, and with this, the possibility that nature itself has a supersensible substratum rendering it amenable to the ends of freedom. The notion of a supersensible substratum here, however, is merely a reflective and regulative one; it does not constitute the appearance of beautiful things or organisms. We have already seen that the press of reason tends toward the positing of life—a unity of force and materiality for which our cognitive capacities are ill-suited. Thus, judgments made out in the territory may speak to this need of reason, but they do not satisfy it.

The ideal of beauty, by contrast, is one such example of *life* breaking through the confines of the critical system in an effort to satisfy reason's demands. Even more than this, it affords us the opportunity to see what is ultimately at stake practically for Kant when *human life* is at issue, namely, the possibility of freedom's efficaciousness in the natural order, specifically with respect to the human body. In the end, this possibility can only be represented, as we shall see, aesthetically. In this section, I will reconstruct Kant's argument for the ideal of beauty, drawing out the absolute determination of the natural by the rationale that he suggests here.

Scholarship has long neglected or even derided Kant's section "On the Ideal of Beauty." Henry E. Allison's reading of the third *Critique* does not treat it at all.[18] Paul Guyer suggests that rather than tell us anything about beauty, Kant "was searching for nothing less than vehicles for the representation of the primacy of practical reason itself."[19] As Rachel Zuckert

17. Immanuel Kant, "Notes on Moral Philosophy," in *Notes and Fragments*, ed. and trans. Paul Guyer, trans. Curtis Bowman and Frederick Rauscher (Cambridge: Cambridge University Press, 2005), 405–78.

18. Henry E. Allison, *Kant's Theory of Taste: A Reading of the "Critique of Aesthetic Judgment"* (Cambridge: Cambridge University Press, 2001).

19. Paul Guyer, "Feeling and Freedom: Kant on Aesthetics and Morality," *Journal of Aesthetics and Art Criticism* 48, no. 2 (1990): 137–46, 143.

points out, too, "paragraph 17 is the paragraph of the *CJ* most infrequently discussed in the scholarly literature, often passed over in silence." Even more than this, Kant's treatment of "human beauty" in this section is, when taken up, "much maligned."[20] By contrast, my examination of the section will highlight how, in fact, the ideal of beauty is a genuine ideal. More than this, too, it exemplifies that even in the completion of his system, Kant continually refers beyond the system to *life*.

Kant introduces his discussion "On the Ideal of Beauty" in the third moment of the "Analytic of the Beautiful" within the context of his much-celebrated treatment of purposiveness without a purpose. The systematic significance of the ideal of beauty has remained elusive for Kant scholars. In one respect its dismissal as integral to the text makes sense—Kant suggests that the need for a model of an ideal of beauty is produced through reason and its attendant "indeterminate idea of a maximum" (§17, 5:232). Yet, the ideal as Kant articulates it is—despite what at first glance appear to be contradictions with earlier claims about the beautiful—the highest instantiation of the beautiful for Kant. In addition, it is Kant's notion of purposiveness without a purpose that generates the interpretation of Kant's aesthetics as a kind of formalism—that is, what is beautiful is so due solely to its form—yet the ideal of beauty poses a counter argument for the supremacy of content as determinative for a standard of beauty. What is compelling about the ideal of beauty is twofold. First, it is the culmination of what beauty, constrained by reflection, merely suggests, namely, the union of force and matter. Second, it is the very substance of what Kant puts forward as the ideal—the morally good person. Kant submits not only that the judging of beauty requires an ideal that operates as a kind of measure for the beautiful but also that this ideal be developed out of the concept of human freedom.

As elsewhere, Kant takes pains in the opening paragraph of section 17 to remind his readers that there is "no objective rule of taste" (5:231). That is, there is nothing in our concepts, or in the object, to which we could appeal in order to demonstrate that an object has met some criterion that would designate it as beautiful. As judgments of taste are predicated on pleasure and not on concepts, Kant asserts that, "if we search for a principle of taste that states the universal criterion of the beautiful by means of determinate concepts, then we engage in a fruitless endeavor, because we

20. Rachel Zuckert, "Boring Beauty and Universal Morality: Kant on the Ideal of Beauty," *Inquiry* 48, no. 2 (2005): 107–30, 125n6, 108.

search for something impossible and intrinsically contradictory." Despite the impossibility of a rule or proof that could be offered for the beautiful, Kant nevertheless asserts that we must each, for ourselves, produce a "highest model" or an "archetype" of taste (5:532). While there is no criterion we can apply in each instance of beauty, there still must be an ultimate measure or height that it can reach. It is reason that generates a need in us to produce an idea of what is maximally beautiful—the most beautiful thing we can imagine. The archetype of the maximally beautiful "which everyone must generate within himself" is that "by which he must judge any object of taste, any example of someone's judging by taste, and even the taste of everyone else" (5:232). This archetype, though, if it is going to serve as a measure, cannot remain a mere idea. Rather, it must take shape in an *ideal*—a concrete and individual instantiation of the idea. Kant explains the difference between these in the first *Critique*. While human wisdom "in its entire purity" is an idea, the sage, he writes, is an ideal of this wisdom. Namely, the ideal is an "original image" that serves for the "thoroughgoing determination of the copy" (A569/B597). The ideal of beauty, as the maximum beauty we can imagine, thus provides us with an example or prototype of the original pattern of what we find beautiful; this example guides us in judging all objects of beauty. In this, the beautiful points to and reminds us of the possibility of its original pattern. It is, as it were, a kind, copy, or imprint of the original.

But what is it that is maximally beautiful, and that serves as a standard or original image of the beautiful? Kant begins his analysis by first rejecting the possibility that what he has previously delineated as a "free" beauty, which corresponds with a "pure" judgment of taste could fill such a role. For many readers of Kant, this is a stunning turn. The "pure" judgment of taste, which has been intimated to be the highest kind of beauty, is hereby dismissed as a candidate for that which is maximally beautiful. With this, Kant rejects formal beauty—as a "pure" judgment of taste is made with regard only to the form of the object as appearing to have a purpose, and not being grounded on a concept—as the original pattern of beauty. Rather, he writes that, "we must be careful to note, first of all, that if we are to seek an ideal of beauty then the beauty must be *fixed*, rather than *vague*, fixed by a concept of objective purposiveness. Hence this beauty must belong not to the object of an entirely pure judgment of taste, but to the object of a partly intellectual one" (§17, 5:232).

Kant advocates for the maximally beautiful to involve a concept because for there to be an ideal of something, there must be some idea (i.e., a concept of reason) on which it is based. It is the idea of the thing that provides the end "on which the object's internal possibility rests" (§17, 5:233), and therefore the measure of what the object is supposed to be. This is nothing other than the idea of perfection. As there must be *some* thing the object ought to be, for it to be an ideal, he denies the possibility that things like flowers, furnishings, or gardens could attain an ideal.

The one thing whose end is determinate enough to admit of perfection and thus ideality is the human being. The human being, Kant observes, "has the purpose of its existence in itself," and as such is "alone among all objects in the world, who admits of an ideal of *beauty*, just as the humanity in his person, as an intelligence, is the only thing in the world capable of the idea of *perfection*" (§17, 5:233). The human being, whose end exists in and of itself, is thus capable of providing for itself its own measure of what it ought to be. We set our ends out of our own freedom; as human beings, we have an absolute relation to ourselves and to everything else insofar as we are the source of what we are and what our ends are. Only humans, then, can admit of perfectibility and perfection.

Those familiar with Kant's theory of beauty will be surprised at the apparent equivocation of perfection with beauty, as Kant clearly denies any kind of conditioning relation between these two things. In explicitly denying that the beautiful pleases in virtue of a concept, Kant forecloses the possibility that a thing could be beautiful on account of its perfection. How is it, then, that Kant believes the perfection of the human being can be beautiful and not merely a kind of knowledge—an occasion for the determination of a concept—or even merely a recognition of moral goodness that would effect respect in us?

The very thing that allows for human beings to be capable of perfection is the very same thing that allows the idea of humanity to admit of being beautiful. It is our capacity for freedom that grants human life the possibility of perfection; it is on account of freedom that our existence has its end in itself. At the same time, freedom is less like a determinable concept such as those of the faculty of the understanding and more like what Kant will later outline as an aesthetic idea in his discussion of art and genius. Mere concepts, on the first *Critique* account, are determinable empirically; this means that in grasping what is represented, the concept is fully determined in reality. There is nothing left over, left out, or remaindered. Freedom, on the other hand, is the absolutely unconditioned quality of the human will; it is an unconditioned causality, a cause in and of itself. As such, freedom does not belong to the domain of appearances and cannot be grasped in a representation in the way a mere concept can. Indeed, freedom, Kant reminds us, is "not capable of being presented empirically" (5:15). Freedom shows up to us as a demand, an imperative of the will, but, according to Kant, we cannot even conceptualize this demand. It presents itself in moral feeling, and the formulations of the moral law, he writes, are simply ways we bring the unconditioned closer to intuition. Freedom, then, cannot be grasped conceptually, nor be presented empirically; insofar as it can be presented, however, it admits of being presented aesthetically.

What does it mean to understand human freedom, in the context of the ideal of beauty, as an aesthetic idea? In his description of fine art, Kant does not argue that the formal qualities of an artwork make it beautiful, as one might expect. Rather, he submits to the reader that it is the content or aesthetic idea of an artwork—the idea that is presented aesthetically—that makes it beautiful. Kant elucidates aesthetic ideas with reference to a "rational idea," which he names as their counterpart. Aesthetic ideas, Kant writes, "strive toward something that lies beyond the bounds of experience, and hence try to approach a presentation of rational concepts" (§49, 5:314).[21] What distinguishes an idea of reason from an aesthetic idea is simply this: aesthetic ideas are attempts to make ideas of reason representable to our senses. Beautiful art is nothing other than the presentation of something that, strictly speaking, cannot be presented in its full determinacy. An idea of reason exceeds our capacity for conceptual determination, and thus its presentation to our senses in the aesthetic domain—if done well—can occasion a feeling of the beautiful in us. Because, as Kant describes it, an idea of reason "cannot be adequately presented," it "prompts the imagination to spread itself over a multitude of kindred presentations that arouse more thought than can be expressed in a concept determined by words" (§49, 5:315). Aesthetic ideas occasion the free play of the faculties that constitute the judgment of taste. Freedom as an aesthetic idea, then, is freedom insofar as it admits of being presented at all.

The presentation of freedom takes shape in the morally good human being. In "On the Ideal of Beauty," Kant describes the attainment of moral perfection—the thoroughgoing determination of the body by freedom. Kant describes the morally good human being as beautiful insofar as freedom animates his or her figure—one's movements, one's gestures, one's comport-

21. Here I have chosen to translate *Darstellung* as "presentation" and not follow Pluhar's "exhibition."

ment. He writes that it is "the *rational idea,* which makes the purposes of humanity, insofar as they cannot be presented in sensibility, the principle for judging its figure [*Gestalt*], which reveals these purposes, as their effect in appearance" (§17, 5:233). Kant is clear: the freedom that cannot be presented to our senses determinatively nevertheless can have an effect in the figure of a human being who is morally good. There is something, Kant intimates, in the morally good person's embodiment that renders perceptible the moral ideas that guide it. Further on he repeats the description of the ideal of beauty in the human figure as "the visible expression of moral ideas" (§17, 5:235). In the ideal of beauty, the moral idea of freedom is rendered sensible in the human form.

Kant's discussion of the ideal of beauty suggests that the body of a person determined wholly through freedom is organized not only by its physical or organic ends but principally by moral ends. In this, the freedom that constitutes the activity of moral goodness arranges the physical parts of the body. Freedom, though, exceeds the mere physical relation of the parts to the whole, and imbues the movements, gestures, indeed the entire physical bearing of the morally good person with a moral aesthetic quality. Through the enactment of freedom in moral goodness, the morally good person may form their body through freedom's union with the body. If freedom can be a force that organizes our bodily movements, then we can, as Kant indicates, discern "goodness of soul, or purity, or fortitude, or serenity," in the actions of someone else. However, Kant does not seem to think that all morally good persons can achieve such a standard, indicating that there is something expressed aesthetically in the ideal beyond simply performing morally good acts. That is, one may enact one's freedom in what one does, yet not necessarily attain the height of beauty in so doing. He writes that, "in order for this connection to be made visible, as it were, in bodily expression (as an effect of what is inward), pure ideas of reason must be united with a very strong imagination in someone who seeks so much to judge, let alone exhibit it." Like the genius—a rare individual among human beings—the morally good person who is capable of such beautiful embodiment must be able to "[create], as it were, another nature, out of the material that actual nature gives it" (§49, 5:314). The morally good person whose freedom forms his or her embodiment makes a unique aesthetic impression on us. The way they carry themselves in their actions exceeds the judgment that they simply act well—their morally good actions are attractive and pleasing in the humility and grace that they express.

The human body, on this account, is organized in all of its activity—all of its liveliness—by the form of freedom. There is nothing that this body does that is not governed by and willed through freedom. What we see when we are brought into contact with the ideal is not a human body, but freedom personified. This is to say that something like the supersensible—an idea—thoroughly dominates the material or sensible aspect of the thing.

We may also say that in the ideal of beauty, freedom is what *animates* the body. In this regard, Kant associates the liveliness of the human being with *spirit*.[22] Indeed, Kant joins the notion of spirit with life in multiple contexts, but foremost when speaking of human life. When Kant writes of beautiful art, he describes spirit as something substantively presented, a kind of presence in the material of the work. He writes about works that are artistic, but lack spirit: "A story may be precise and orderly yet have no spirit. An oration may be both thorough and graceful but have no spirit. Many conversations are entertaining, but they have no spirit" (§48, 5:312). Within human beings, it is spirit that brings the mind to life, "*spirit* in an aesthetic sense is the animating principle in the mind" (§49, 5:313–14). And perhaps most directly, in his "Treaty of Perpetual Peace in Philosophy," he writes: "By means of reason, the soul of man is endowed with a *spirit* (*mens, nous*) so that he may lead a life adapted, not merely to the mechanism of *nature* and its technico-practical laws, but also to the spontaneity of *freedom* and its morally-practical laws. This life-principle . . . proceeds initially and at once from an Idea of the *super-sensible*, namely *freedom*" (8:417).[23]

Spirit emerges in certain moments of Kant's philosophy as the animating principle of human life. Spirit is the name Kant gives to the force of freedom that comes into union with and imbues materiality with itself. Spirit, as life force, does not merely communicate with matter; it acts on and through material being. Spirit thus appears to be the supersensible that

---

22. My analysis here appears to go against John H. Zammito's very fine work to distinguish *Lebensgefühl* from *Geistesgefühl*. Zammito takes the *Lebensgefühl* to be about the mere fact of living, and not the human (i.e., moral) life of freedom. I think that for Kant, human *life* is always given in freedom. John H. Zammito, *The Genesis of Kant's "Critique of Judgment"* (Chicago: University of Chicago Press, 1992), 292–305.

23. Immanuel Kant, "Proclamation of the Imminent Conclusion of a Treaty of Perpetual Peace in Philosophy," in *Theoretical Philosophy after 1781*, ed. Henry E. Allison and Peter Heath, trans. Peter Heath (Cambridge: Cambridge University Press, 2004), 451–60.

has taken hold of and is directing materiality. Angelica Nuzzo describes the principle of life as that which "discloses the traces of the supersensible within the sensible."[24]

Kant further describes the possibility of human freedom having the force ultimately to transform material nature in his writing on medicine. While Kant does not go so far as to argue that reason can reach down into the cells of our materiality and alter them, he does argue that one's reason has "the sheer power . . . to master his sensuous feelings by a self-imposed principle determin[ing] his manner of living" (*The Conflict of the Faculties*, 7:100–101).[25] The force of our will can change the way we feel about things, that is, it can alter our natural inclinations. With this, it transforms our natural constitution. Kant notes that he himself tended toward hypochondria, something for which he writes he had a "natural disposition." Hypochondria is "the exact opposite of the mind's power to master its pathological feelings" (7:103). He suggests that while the mechanical oppression in his chest about which he had become melancholic remained, he overcame his feelings, thus employing the mind's power to do just this. The effect, he writes, is this: "The result was that, while I felt the oppression in my chest, a calm and cheerful state prevailed in my mind, which did not fail to communicate itself to society, not by intermittent whims (as is usual with hypochondriacs), but purposely and naturally. And since one's life becomes cheerful more through what we freely do with life than through what we enjoy as a gift from it, mental work can set another kind of heightened vital feeling against the limitations that affect the body alone" (7:104).

This is a remarkable passage. It brings together many of the themes treated thus far. Kant notes that the disposition he has rationally chosen is public, and that it appears to others both as purposeful and natural. This would indicate that it appears both chosen and thoroughgoing, as if it was a second nature (we can recall here the idea of making a new nature out of the nature that is given to us). The choice has worked its way onto and into the physical bearing. With this, too, Kant identifies the work of reason in this context to influence one's feelings with a "heightened vital feeling."

---

24. Angelica Nuzzo, "Leben and Leib in Kant and Hegel," *Hegel-Jahrbuch* 2 (2007): 97–101, 98.

25. Immanuel Kant, *The Conflict of the Faculties*, in *Religion and Rational Theology*, ed. Allen W. Wood and George di Giovanni (Cambridge: Cambridge University Press, 1996), 233–328.

That is, the activity of the will in altering one's feelings and inclinations yields nothing other than a feeling of life.[26]

Returning to the ideal of beauty, we can see how it is at once a possibility that lies outside of the critical philosophy, yet does, in fact, function as the absolute measure of the judgments that do complete the system. As an original pattern, the ideal of beauty stands as the epitome or culmination of what all judgments of taste are; beautiful things are beautiful insofar as they represent or copy this ideal. The substance of the ideal is unity of force and matter, of freedom and nature. In it, freedom determines and dominates the human body. The appearance of such "spirit" in matter is precisely what we find beautiful in fine art—the extent to which an artist can achieve such a feat of imagination is the extent to which a work will be beautiful.

Conclusion

We can now make sense of Kant's distinction between those who "gesticulate well" and those for whom there is "life in the figures." Those characterized by *life* are those able to determine their material being—their bodies—through the force of their own free will. It is not simply that one's body moves as effect of the will, that is, that the will communicates with the body to move here or there. Rather, one's freedom, or, more specifically, one's desire for the good or good intentions, is the spirit that infuses the body in its movements. In this, the force of freedom is not simply external, as one billiard ball causing the movement of another. The force of one's freedom vivifies the body.

Judgments of reflection—including judgments of taste—are taken by Kant to complete the system of philosophy. They do this in virtue of the mediating role they play between freedom and nature. In this, freedom and nature do not, as it were, come into contact with one another; freedom cannot reach out beyond itself and determine the natural order to be other than how it is. In leaving behind the possibility of thinking life, as a determining relation between force and matter, Kant commits himself to

26. On Kant's remarkable debate with the medical faculty, and their engagement with him, please see John H. Zammito, "Kant and the Medical Faculty: One 'Conflict of the Faculties,'" *Epoché* 22, no. 2 (2018): 429–51. In this piece, Zammito further draws our attention to Kant's claim that human beings walk upright as a result of our rational and social vocations (432).

this problem. Yet, reason cannot extirpate its own tendency toward thinking the possibility of such a union.

All beautiful things are, in some sense, copies of the original pattern of the ideal of beauty. As such, beautiful things suggest the possibility of their ideal, the possibility of life. In this, those very judgments that complete the system of philosophy in their reflective mode, still point beyond themselves to an ideal that can ultimately satisfy reason's demand for the unity of force and matter.

With this, the ideal of beauty and also judgments of taste suggest to us not only that nature may be amenable to the ends of reason. Rather, they suggest that freedom has the force and the possible relation to nature to determine material being through its own efforts. Under the auspices of life, reason has not only the authority but also the ability to achieve its own ends rather than rely on nature, or providence, to realize them.

Chapter 6

The Momentary Inhibition and Outpouring of the Vital Powers

Kant on the Dynamic Sublime

Rachel Zuckert

> The feeling of the sublime is a pleasure that arises only indirectly: it is produced by the feeling of a momentary inhibition of the vital powers followed immediately by an outpouring of them that is all the stronger.
>
> —Immanuel Kant, *Critique of Judgment* (§23, 5:245)[1]

In the *Critique of Judgment*, Kant influentially portrays the sublime as a pleasurable-painful experience of human limitations but also of human power, of human smallness and vulnerability within nature, but also rational transcendence of it—and so of the division in the human psyche between sensibility

1. Unless otherwise noted, all citations are to paragraph number of Kant's *Critique of Judgment*, followed by volume and page number of the Akademie Ausgabe of Kant's works, namely, Immanuel Kant, *Gesammelte Schriften* (Berlin: de Gruyter, 1901–). (Subsequently cited page references to Kant's works are also to volume and page number of this edition.) Unless otherwise indicated, quoted translations are from Kant's *Critique of Judgment*, trans. Werner Pluhar (Indianapolis: Hackett, 1987). I have modified the punctuation of the quoted passage. Here and throughout, I change "vital forces" to "vital powers" (translating *Lebenskräfte*).

and reason.[2] As is well known, Kant identifies two genres of such experience: the mathematical sublime is the experience of large objects difficult to take in perceptually, while the dynamic sublime is the terrifying but also thrilling experience of extremely powerful objects. The most frequent, compelling, and apparently central examples of the sublime in Kant's treatment—thunderstorms, dangerous oceans, volcanoes—are cases of the dynamic sublime. But in scholarly discussion, Kant's treatment of the mathematical sublime looms much larger. Some of this interest is prompted by the paradoxical suggestion in that account that human beings might be sensibly aware of that which transcends sensibility, or (in Jean-François Lyotard's influential terms) could "present the unpresentable."[3] But here scholars also follow Kant, who works out his account of the mathematical sublime in detail, and then just gestures to ways in which the dynamic sublime might be understood similarly.

In this chapter, I propose to focus instead on the dynamic sublime, to suggest that it merits closer and more puzzled attention. I shall argue, first, that the dynamic sublime is less analogous to the mathematical sublime than Kant suggests, and that his account of the dynamic sublime therefore suffers from a problem, which I shall call an "explanatory gap." This problem may also, I shall argue, be framed historically: Kant argues that his account of the sublime is superior to that provided by Edmund Burke, according to which the sublime is an experience of imagined threat, which rouses one's self-preservative powers. But if Kant's account suffers from an explanatory gap, then his claim to replace the Burkean account would seem to fail. Indeed, I shall argue, Kant's text suggests that, despite his explicit rejection of Burke's view, he continues to understand the experience of the dynamic sublime in Burkean terms.

---

2. Kant also discusses the sublime in his early *Observations on the Beautiful and the Sublime* and anthropology lectures; these ancillary treatments will not be discussed here. Immanuel Kant, *Observations on the Beautiful and the Sublime*, in *Observations on the Feeling of the Beautiful and Sublime and Other Writings*, ed. Patrick Frierson and Paul Guyer (Cambridge: Cambridge University Press, 2011), 9–62; Immanuel Kant, *Lectures on Anthropology*, ed. Allen W. Wood and Robert B. Louden, trans. Robert R. Clewis, Robert B. Louden, G. Felicitas Munzel, and Allen W. Wood (Cambridge: Cambridge University Press, 2012).

3. See Jean-François Lyotard, "Answering the Question: What Is Postmodernism?," in *The Postmodern Condition*, trans. Regis Durand (Minneapolis: University of Minnesota Press, 1984), 71–82. Lyotard uses this tantalizing idea to account for difficult aesthetic experiences of disharmony, blankness, failure, and so on, offered by modernist or postmodernist art.

The chief aim of this chapter is, accordingly, to identify and historically to situate a problem in Kant's account of the dynamic sublime. But I shall also propose a kind of response to it: I shall not propose a solution to the problem, but rather shall suggest that it is unavoidable, given Kant's understanding of practical reason. And I shall sketch an alternative view of Kant's account that accommodates both the (unavoidable) explanatory gap and Kant's own Burkean descriptions of the sublime: that the experience of the Kantian dynamic sublime is a reflectively reinterpreted, symbolically enriched Burkean experience of the sublime. In this reinterpreted experience, the human subject recognizes, indeed feelingly inhabits, her nature as a sensible, vulnerable, living being, and yet also the absolute break with—the "inhibition" and redirection of—such life that comprises her nature as a practically rational being. Hence, I think, the centrality of the dynamic sublime for Kant: as an experiential, felt self-recognition of the moral subject as such.

I begin with an overview of the Kantian account of the sublime, including what the dynamic and mathematical sublime have in common and the distinctions between them. I then raise the problem (the explanatory gap) in the second section, and, in the last section, propose my response.

The Kantian Sublime, an Overview

As in his treatment of beauty, Kant's object of analysis in his account of the sublime is in the first instance the judgment of the sublime, that is, "This [object] is sublime." Like the judgment of beauty, this judgment is aesthetic—based on feeling—and yet purports to have universal subjective validity, that is, to make a claim on all other subjects to find the object so, to share one's feelings in response to it (§23, 5:244).[4] And, though Kant wavers somewhat on this point (for reasons I will mention), he largely appears here, as in the case of the beautiful, to aim to justify this claim to universal subjective validity. As my introductory remarks indicate, however, Kant also treats the sublime as a kind of *experience*, which grounds and is expressed in the judgment of the sublime. Kant thus also aims to describe such experience phenomenologically, and to explain how human beings can have it, in transcendental-psychological terms.

4. Kant also claims here that the feeling is disinterested, taken in the mere "exhibition" of the object as it promotes the functioning of cognitive powers. I return to this claim briefly below.

The central claims in these three Kantian projects concerning the sublime—phenomenology, explanation, and justification—are as follows. Phenomenologically, the experience of the sublime is affectively charged, combining pleasure and displeasure.[5] These feelings arise, Kant claims, in response to the perception of a sensibly overwhelming natural object, which perception evokes rational ideas. So the phenomenological, representational "contents" of the experience of the sublime might include, for example, Wordsworth's natural chasm that seems to reveal the infinity of being, or an experience of the massive power of a waterfall as instantiating God's majesty.[6]

According to Kant's transcendental-psychological explanation, such experience is generated by the sensible faculty of imagination—the faculty that composes the perception of the chasm as large, the waterfall as powerful—together with the faculty of reason, which furnishes the rational ideas (for example, of infinity or moral majesty) with which such perceptions are connected. The functioning of imagination and reason also is meant to explain the affective character of the experience. In such experiences, the imagination is challenged in perceiving the object; thereby the subject becomes painfully aware of her sensible limitations. But she also becomes aware of the superiority of reason to those limitations; hence the elevating pleasure of the experience.

Indeed, Kant concludes that, properly speaking, it is not the natural object that is sublime, but rather the faculty of reason. The chasm and waterfall (or the sensible perceptions of them) do not in fact present ideas of infinity or moral majesty. Such ideas of reason, and their objects, lie beyond mere sensible experience, beyond nature. The faculty of reason is the source of those ideas, and therefore also the true focal object of one's painful-pleasurable admiration. Correspondingly, the judgment of the sublime ("this waterfall is sublime") does not mean, properly speaking, that the natural object is admirable (sublime); that attribution is "subreption" in Kant's technical terms. Rather, it claims that others ought also to feel displeasure and elevation in perceiving this object, which feelings ultimately

---

5. As Paul Crowther notes, Kant is not entirely clear about the relationship between pain and pleasure in this experience. See *The Kantian Sublime: From Morality to Art* (Oxford: Clarendon Press, 1989), 123–25.

6. I adapt this Wordsworth example (from *The Prelude*) from Guy Sircello, "How Is a Theory of the Sublime Possible?," *Journal of Aesthetics and Art Criticism* 51, no. 4 (1993): 541–50, 547; the waterfall example expands upon Kant's discussions of natural power experienced as instantiating God's powers at §28, 5:260–61, 263.

comprise each subject's response to her own rational capacity (§23, 5:245; §25, 5:250; §26, 5:256; §28, 5:264).[7]

As noted, Kant is tentative concerning the justification of such claims. At points, he suggests that it is not legitimate to demand of *all* others that they have similar experiences or feelings because experiencing the sublime requires culture, in the form of developed rational ideas with which the mind must be "filled" (§23, 5:245–46), so that they may be evoked by sensible perceptions. Thus, perhaps, those for whom such "culture" is unavailable cannot be legitimately required to have the feelings of the sublime (§29, 5:265).[8] But insofar as he does offer it, such justification draws upon Kant's psychological explanatory account in at least two ways.

First, as noted, Kant traces the experience of the sublime to the activities of imagination and reason: it is generated not by special cognitive skills, but by capacities that all may be presumed to share (§23, 5:244). In principle, then, such experiences *can* be had by all subjects, and so may be legitimately required of them.

Second, Kant suggests that the feelings in the experience of the sublime are akin to the moral feeling of respect, or, as he glosses it in the *Critique*

---

7. On subreption, see Michelle Grier, "Kant and the Feeling of Sublimity," in *Kant on Emotion and Value*, ed. Alix Cohen (London: Palgrave Macmillan, 2014), 245–64. This conclusion has led to some ambiguity in scholarly discussion concerning Kant's term, the "sublime state of mind"—which may mean the state of mind of the person who is appreciating something as sublime, but also could refer to a state of mind that is the ("true") object of such appreciation. The difference between the state of admiring and a capacity that is admired, however, should be clear. Here, specifically, the state of admiring in part (perhaps even in entirety) includes sensibility (imagination, feeling), but the object of admiration is reason. To avoid such ambiguity, therefore, I eschew the language of "state of mind," and refer to the experience of the sublime or judgment of the sublime (as instances or expressions of admiration), by contrast to object of feeling/admiration.

8. This passage could, however, be read to say simply that there is less agreement in the case of the sublime than that of the beautiful, because culture is required, though it remains legitimate to demand such agreement. At least since Gayatri Spivak's seminal *Critique of Postcolonial Reason* (Cambridge, MA: Harvard University Press, 1999), many scholars have taken this passage, together with Kant's nearby references to a "savage" or "peasant" who cannot appreciate the sublime (because he lacks sufficient culture), to betray the Eurocentric and classist character of Kant's conception of the sublime, perhaps indeed of the eighteenth-century European discussion of the sublime in general. It may be connected as well to Kant's much-criticized association of the sublime with masculinity (in his earlier *Observations*, but, one might argue, implicitly in the *Critique of Judgment* as well). For renewed attention to such concerns about Kant's account, see Dilek Huseyinzadegan's chapter in this volume.

of Judgment, "the feeling of the inadequacy of our ability to attain to an idea *that is a law for us*" (§27, 5:257).[9] This claim could be understood as extending the just-described argument: not just the psychological activities, but also the consequent *feelings*, in the experience of the sublime are justifiably taken to be universal to all human beings, here because they are of the sort required for moral agency. But Kant particularly emphasizes the connection of the sublime to respect in section 29, where he (somewhat cryptically) attempts to ground "the necessity . . . of the assent of other people's judgments to our own" (5:265).[10] That is, respect seems particularly important for Kant's answer to the question why all subjects not only can but *should* have the experience of the sublime.[11]

This reference to morality brings us to Kant's distinction between the two genres of the sublime, mathematical and dynamic. Tracking Kant's distinction between theoretical and practical reason, this distinction applies to the characteristic objects of the experience of the sublime, as well as to the subject's engagement with them. The mathematical sublime concerns natural objects that are sensibly challenging for *cognition* because they are too large to comprehend sensibly. The dynamic sublime concerns natural objects that are challenging to *action*: they are so powerful that they could frustrate actions to attain natural ends such as happiness, indeed they could kill us. In each case, these challenges to human sensible nature are paired with a transcendent idea of reason, theoretical or practical, respectively. In the mathematical sublime, the subject is aware of the idea of infinity formulated by theoretical reason—in comparison to which idea, Kant writes, "everything else . . . is small" (§26, 5:254), including the object she fails imaginatively to comprehend. In the dynamic sublime, though the subject imaginatively recognizes his sensible vulnerability to the powerful natural object, he is also aware of the idea of morality, which identifies an aspect of himself invulnerable to natural power.

Again, though, Kant claims that the same phenomenology—combination of pleasure and displeasure, humility and elevation—and the same psy-

9. Translation modified to use the direct translation of "inadequacy" for *Unangemessenheit*; I return to this striking term below. See also §26, 5:256.

10. My emphasis; see also §29, 5:266.

11. Here I deploy my understanding of the task of the deduction of judgments of the beautiful: Kant must show that all can *and* should take the requisite sort of pleasure in perceiving an object. See Rachel Zuckert, *Kant on Beauty and Biology: An Interpretation of the "Critique of Judgment"* (Cambridge: Cambridge University Press, 2007), ch. 7.

chological structure—failure of imagination reveals superiority of reason—are true of both cases. It is this claim of parallelism, particularly concerning a purported similarity of psychological structure, that I shall now question.[12]

The Problem

Disanalogy

Kant's psychological account of the mathematical sublime cogently explains (at least) two elements of such experience: (1) how it gains its representational contents, that is, how the subject has a sensible perception of a large object as ungraspably large, and so somehow connected to the idea of infinity, and (2) its affective charge, that is, why perceiving a large object could be both pleasing and displeasing, overwhelming and elevating. I linger a moment on the mathematical sublime to explain.

With respect to the first point: Kant notes that human beings *are* capable of judging the size of large objects like mountains through mathematical reasoning or comparison to other, more graspably sized objects such as trees (§26, 5:253–54, 255). (Though Kant does not explicitly so state, it seems likely that we are also affectively indifferent when engaged in such ordinary cognition of the size of objects.) Thus Kant must explain how or why one would experience an (in fact, in some ways, graspable) object as *ungraspably* large (and so affectively moving). Kant does so by proposing that such experience arises if one aims, specifically, to "comprehend" an object as a whole, in one sensible intuition; some objects, perceived at certain distances, are too large to be so perceived.[13] That aim is in turn prompted by reason's aspirations to totality: theoretical reason demands a comprehensive grasp of objects (or sizes, or quantities) as wholes—as exemplified in the idea of infinity, the totality of quantity (§26, 5:255; §27, 5:257). In attempting to comprehend a large object sensibly, the imagination attempts

12. One might argue that there is also a phenomenological difference between them, between (say) dizziness or confusion and an elevated diffusion into the universal all, on one hand, versus excited, imaginatively generated fear and a tense, courageous-feeling surge of power, on the other.

13. I sum up a complex discussion found at §26, 5:251–52. See Rudolf A. Makkreel, *Imagination and Interpretation: The Hermeneutical Import of the "Critique of Judgment"* (Chicago: University of Chicago Press, 1990), 68–83, for a detailed treatment.

to fulfill that rational demand in its own domain, as it were. Thus, when the imagination fails to do so, the subject can become aware that reason sets more ambitious cognitive demands than her sensible faculties can accomplish—precisely because the imagination was aiming to fulfill those demands. As Kant sums up: the "*inadequacy* of our faculty for estimating the magnitude of the things of the sensible world awakens the feeling of a supersensible faculty in us" (§25, 5:250; my emphasis).[14] Hence the representational "contents" of such experience: the representation of an object as sensibly overwhelming, generated (or striven for) by the imagination, and as related to the infinite, an idea generated by reason and functioning as the guiding aim of the imaginative activity. Hence too the affective charge of this experience, as noted: it displeases because the imagination strives and fails, yet also pleases because thereby, Kant writes, the experience "as it were makes intuitable . . . the superiority of [reason] . . . over the greatest faculty of sensibility" (§27, 5:257).

Kant would seem to have a similar explanatory task in the case of the dynamic sublime. Like Burke before him, Kant emphasizes that in order to have an aesthetic experience of the powerful object, one must know that one is not in fact threatened by it. (Otherwise, one might be too afraid, run for one's life, and so forth, instead of contemplatively appreciating it, in a perceptual-imaginative experience.) Thus, here Kant needs first to explain why one would feel displeasure, specifically fear, given that one knows one is safe, and then why that experience would be pleasurable, and so again why one represents the object as powerful *and* as linked to one's moral capabilities.

Kant indicates that his response to these questions is parallel to that offered concerning the mathematical sublime. Following a description of the psychology of the mathematical sublime, he writes:

> *In the same way* [i.e., just as in the case of the mathematical sublime] though the irresistibility of nature's might [i.e., of the powerful natural object] makes us, considered as natural beings, recognize our physical impotence, it reveals [*entdeckt*] in us at the same time an ability to judge ourselves independent of nature and . . . a superiority over nature that is the basis of a self-preservation . . . different in kind from the one that can

14. My translation.

> be assailed and endangered by nature outside us, whereby the humanity in our person remains undemeaned, even though a human being would have to succumb to that dominance [of the powerful natural object]. (§28, 5:261–62; my emphasis)[15]

Kant adds that "nature is here called sublime merely because it elevates our imagination" to present "cases where the mind can come to feel its own sublimity, which lies in its vocation and elevates it even above nature" (§28, 5:262). This activity of the imagination, Kant claims, "calls forth our power (which does not belong to nature) to regard those things about which we are concerned (goods, health and life)," and over which the natural object would have "dominance," as "trivial" in light of "our highest principles" (§28, 5:262).[16]

The question I wish to raise is whether this suggested parallel holds, that is, whether Kant offers here as cogent an explanation of the phenomenology (representational contents and affective charge) of the experience of the dynamic sublime as he does for the mathematical sublime. We may grant Kant, I think, that the imagination is responsible for the perception of the natural powerful object as threatening (fearful), even while one knows that one is safe. Specifically, Kant suggests that such a perception comes about through imagining oneself confronted by the object, and how its power could adversely affect one's possessions, health or life.[17] Likewise plausible is Kant's suggestion that an "inspirational pleasure" could arise from considering that one's moral humanity cannot be demeaned by the natural power (§28, 5:262).[18]

But—unlike in the case of the mathematical sublime—there is no explanation of why these two contents or feelings should be conjoined, why an imaginatively generated fear for one's natural goods should "reveal" one's moral superiority to nature. For here Kant does not explain *why* one might imaginatively consider one's possible encounter with the powerful object. Specifically, he does not argue that practical reason leads one to do

15. Translation modified. Kant also uses descriptions of the psychology of the mathematical sublime to describe the sublime in general; see, for example, "General Remark," 5:268.

16. Translations in this paragraph are my own.

17. See also "General Remark," 5:269.

18. My translation.

so.[19] Indeed, *must* one be thinking of oneself as a moral agent, attempting to realize moral ends, to imagine oneself as potentially threatened by a powerful natural object? Could one not engage in such imaginative activity quite naturally from a general pragmatic point of view, considering "what if" I were out there in the storm? Nor does Kant offer any reason why the imagined experience of such a threat would prompt *further* imaginative activity, namely (as quoted from §28, 5:262 above), to present to oneself cases in which one would try to resist the natural power for moral reasons. Perhaps one's imagination of oneself as weathering the storm has a moral flavor ("Wouldn't I be brave if I were out there, facing up to it?"). But this moral flavor might have little to do with the idea of acting on higher principles—one may imagine oneself just stuck out there and doing one's best, say—nor that of a moral capacity that would be undamaged by the encounter.

To be clear, I am not suggesting that the two representational contents—one is vulnerable as a natural being, but invulnerable as Kantian moral being—*could* not be conjoined; they are consistent. Nor do I mean to suggest that an experience with such contents would not have the affective charge Kant describes. Rather: the conjunction seems somewhat arbitrary. It is a "leap" to add to one's imagined experience of vulnerability a thought about one's moral capacities or the imagination of oneself as heroically facing up to such natural power for moral reasons. Some subjects may do so, but Kant provides little reason to expect that all subjects would, that it is an integral part of the experience of a powerful natural object as potentially

19. There might be a form of the sublime midway between the mathematical and dynamic, that is, a cognitive attempt to comprehend an object's power imaginatively, which, when frustrated, could make one aware of one's capacity to have the rational idea of infinite power. It is not clear to me that, given his view in the "Anticipations of Perception" chapter of the *Critique of Pure Reason*, trans. and ed. Paul Guyer and Allen W. Wood (Cambridge: Cambridge University Press, 1998), Kant would think that the imaginative comprehension of force would be additive in the way that spatial comprehension of magnitude is, according to the account of the mathematical sublime. But in any case, this would not be the activity of imagination, nor resultant displeasure, involved in the dynamic sublime on Kant's presentation. For Kant describes the subject as considering the object's power in relation to herself, with something like a practical attitude: she considers the object as part of her sphere of action, in comparison to her own power to act, even if she is not per se deliberating about what to do. And, of course, the idea of morality is not the same as that of infinite power. I am grateful to Nora Schleich for prompting me to think further about this possible case.

threatening. In sum: Is a sense of one's moral superiority to nature "revealed" within that imaginative experience, or just added into it (by Kant)? Kant's gestures at parallels between the mathematical and dynamic sublime cover over this explanatory gap. In the former account, but not in the latter, Kant makes a case for the connections among cognitive activities, experiential contents, and feelings.[20]

This explanatory gap in turn generates problems for justifying judgments of the dynamic sublime.[21] As noted above, Kant refers to respect, as connected to the feelings of the sublime, to legitimate judgments based on those feelings. It probably is legitimate on Kant's view to expect all others to consider themselves moral agents and to feel respect for morality.[22] But, we must ask: Why is it legitimate to require others to *conjoin* that moral self-conception or feeling *to* an imaginatively fearful experience of natural power? Why *should* others judge that the storm is sublime (specifically, that it is dynamically sublime in Kant's sense)?[23]

---

20. This lack of parallelism goes unremarked by commentators to my knowledge. Rudolf A. Makkreel, "Sublimity, Genius and the Explication of Aesthetic Ideas," in *Kants Ästhetik/Kant's Aesthetics/L'esthétique de Kant*, ed. Herman Parret (Berlin: de Gruyter, 1998), 615–29, is the single, provocative instance of which I am aware of interpreting the mathematical sublime in light of the dynamic sublime, rather than vice versa. Perhaps as a result, Makkreel also unusually emphasizes the violence of the "regress" of the imagination—which could perhaps be considered a discontinuity or disruption—in Kant's account of the mathematical sublime.

21. And, in fact, also for judgments of the mathematical sublime, since their justification also seems to turn in some way on the kinship between the feeling on which they are grounded and respect—a difficult point meriting further discussion.

22. Kant tends to deny, however, that one could *require* anyone to have moral feeling. Rather, subjects must already be susceptible to moral feeling as part of their original constitution as moral agents (as agents susceptible to moral obligation). See Immanuel Kant, *The Metaphysics of Morals*, ed. Mary J. Gregor (Cambridge: Cambridge University Press, 1996), 6:399. [Editor's note: See Dilek Huseyinzadegan's chapter in this volume for some critical engagement on this point.]

23. See indeed §39, 5:292. Perhaps Kant means something like this, in raising the potential objection to his account that it portrays the experience of the dynamic sublime as being "overly far-fetched and the result of somesubtle reasoning [*vernünftelt*]" (§28, 5:262). If so, his response—pointing to the admiration for warriors, as an exemplary, widely shared form of the dynamic sublime that supports his contention—only reraises the problem. For in such admiration, the subject does not have to come up with the idea of morality and then conjoin it to (or project it into) the imagined experience of encountering a fearful natural object. Rather, he recognizes, admires, and perhaps

Reflecting a similar worry, Thomas Weiskel suggests that Kant's account portrays a self's defense-mechanism: If I am brought to recognize my vulnerability, I may scrabble around to find some way to shore up my self-esteem and land upon the idea of my moral invulnerability.[24] On this view, Kant in some sense explains the connection between experiential contents in the experience of the dynamic sublime—natural vulnerability and moral invulnerability—and consequent feelings. But the connection seems at once associative and self-serving. It is unclear how one could require such feelings of others justifiably.

Burke

This problem may be reformulated in historical terms by putting Kant's account of the dynamic sublime in conversation with that of his most influential predecessor on this topic, Edmund Burke. In his *Enquiry concerning the Origins of Our Ideas of the Sublime and the Beautiful*, Burke characterizes the experience of the sublime as (paradigmatically) a feeling of fear at a powerful object, drawing upon the powerful human drive of self-preservation.[25] Though Burke does not say so explicitly, he too takes it, I think, that the imagination is responsible for arousing such fear, through an associative-stimulative mechanism. His view is something like this: As vulnerable animals, we are on alert for signals of dangers, that is, perceptions (of objects) that we associate imaginatively with danger. Awareness of such signals then leads us to be on our guard; we feel fear, we gird ourselves for potential threats. This self-preservative preparedness in turn contributes to Burke's (not entirely worked out) explanations of the pleasure one feels in such prima facie emotionally negative experiences. He suggests sometimes that one first feels fear and tension in response to a powerful object (perceived as a threat), but then, upon recognizing that one is in fact safe, feels "delight." This is not, Burke claims, a pure positive pleasure, but a comparative pleasure arising from the removal of a pain.[26] Such delight at

---

imaginatively identifies with the moral motivation and strength of the warrior who faces up to death heroically.

24. Thomas Weiskel, *The Romantic Sublime: Studies in the Structure and Psychology of Transcendence* (Baltimore: Johns Hopkins University Press, 1976), 84, 105; I omit many Freudian complexities in Weiskel's analysis.

25. Edmund Burke, *A Philosophical Enquiry into the Origins of Our Ideas of the Sublime and Beautiful*, ed. Adam Philip (Oxford: Oxford University Press, 1990), 1.7.

26. Burke, *Enquiry*, 1.4, 4.7, 4.18.

actual safety (after the experience of fear) might be understood, then, as a pleasure in being alive, a good of which one is normally not aware or appreciative, but here is salient by comparison to its threatened absence, and pleasing because of the removal of that threat.[27]

Alternatively, Burke suggests that the very tension, the very preparedness in response to the fearful object, constitutes a gathering of one's forces, which is itself enlivening and makes one aware of one's powers—and so is pleasurable.[28] On this proposal, it is not so much that we gain delight from realizing that we are safe. Rather, safety makes the pleasure of intensified vitality less costly. Instead of having to brave actual dangers to feel such surges of power, one can feel such intensity and consequent pleasure while safe, because of mechanisms of imaginative association and self-preservative preparedness. For these mechanisms are involuntary and automatic, happening as it were "behind the back of" one's knowledge of one's safety.

Burke's answers, in short, are something like what we would call endorphins or adrenaline—either a surge of pleasure at being released from tension, or a pleasure in the very tension, in the "high" of gathering one's powers in response to a challenge.[29] Both are echoed in Kant's description of the dynamic sublime as "momentary inhibition" and then "outpouring" of vital powers.[30]

Kant claims that his account of the sublime better explains such experience than does Burke's. He explicitly objects to the first Burkean explanation—that one feels delight upon the cessation of fear—on psychological grounds. This would not lead one to linger over the experience or seek it out, Kant claims; rather, one will wish never to be so exposed again (§28,

27. Burke, *Enquiry*, 4.7.

28. Burke, *Enquiry*, 4.6.

29. Of course, one might interpret Burke in a less naturalist-materialist way; see, for example, Stephen K. White, "Burke on Politics, Aesthetics, and the Dangers of Modernity," *Political Theory* 21, no. 3 (1993): 507–27. For an interpretation closer to mine, however, see Vanessa Ryan, "The Physiological Sublime: Burke's Critique of Reason," *Journal of the History of Ideas* 62, no. 2 (2001): 265–79. Kant himself appears to understand Burke in such materialist terms, in that he links Burke's account to physiology and, in that context, praises the Epicurean view concerning the corporeal sources for feelings of the "furtherance or inhibition of the vital powers" ("General Remark," 5:2778).

30. Kant's description of the (mathematical) sublime as involving "vibration, i.e., a rapid alternation of repulsion from, and attraction to, one and the same object" is also reminiscent of Burke (§27, 5:258). See Robert Clewis's chapter in this volume for extensive textual support, concerning Kant's deep agreement with Burke concerning the phenomenology and perhaps vitalist origins, of the experience of the sublime.

5:261). And, of course, Kant attempts to infuse such terrifying yet thrilling experience with more conscious meaning, so as to explain better than Burke does the uplifting, pleasurable character of the experience.

From a Burkean perspective, however, one might ask whether such added meaning explains anything better, whether it is justifiably "added in" at all. If the experience of one's vulnerability—common to both accounts—is not obviously connected to the idea of acting on "higher principles," why think that that idea could explain anything here?[31] If Kant himself conceives of this thrilling experience as arising from the felt "inhibition" and "outpouring" of vital powers—that is, from Burkean mechanisms—why need one invoke moral ideas to explain it? We have returned, that is, to the explanatory gap.

Some Reflections in Response

As indicated above, I do not propose to respond to this problem by filling out an account more properly parallel to that of the mathematical sublime, more independent of the Burkean mechanisms of tension and release. (Say: a reconstructed account of an imaginative expansion—perhaps of all ends one might pursue—somehow demanded by practical reason, then cast down by the imagined encounter with the natural power, but in a way that reveals the demandingness, and thus superiority, of practical reason.)[32] I argue, rather, that the problem I have attempted to bring out—the disanalogy with the mathematical sublime, the explanatory gap—*must hold* on a Kantian view. Unlike theoretical reason, which absolutizes judgments of

31. Sandra Shapshay helpfully classes accounts of the sublime as "thick" or "thin": the former take the experience to have significant cognitive content, the latter to be simply emotional response, see "Contemporary Environmental Aesthetics and the Neglect of the Sublime," *British Journal of Aesthetics* 53, no. 2 (April 2013): 181–98. I agree with Shapshay that Kant's and Burke's accounts fall into the two categories, respectively, but take it that there is a tighter connection between Burke's "thin" account and *some* of the content (human vulnerability) Kant ascribes to the dynamic sublime than the contrast may suggest.

32. Kant himself suggests such a parallel: Just as the imagination is expanded and feels its power in attempting (if, ultimately, failing) to attain to infinity in the mathematical sublime, so can it feel its "might" in engaging with the dangerous object, under direction by practical reason, in the dynamic sublime ("General Remark," 5:269). This parallel seems again problematic, however: In what sense does the imagination show its power here? Just in making the imagined threat vivid? Why would that require being directed by ideas of practical reason?

the understanding—seeking the first, unconditioned cause, or the absolutely great magnitude (infinity)—practical reason does not absolutize natural inclinations or pragmatic judgments concerning how to attain happiness. Rather, it formulates its own, independent moral law.[33] This means that there *will be* a radical discontinuity between consideration of one's natural desires and conditions for their attainment (on one hand) and the idea of one's moral vocation (on the other). Moral ideas will not arise integrally from, or direct, the imaginative expansion of one's everyday desires, as their ultimate, totalized aim. Correspondingly, the imagined frustration of one will not "reveal" the capacity for the other. There can be no parallelism between mathematical and dynamic sublime, of the sort at which Kant gestures.[34]

The radical discontinuity between practical reason and natural life, between imagined vulnerability and the idea of moral invulnerability, does support, however, Kant's claim that one has to have "culture" to experience the dynamic sublime (§29, 5:264; §23, 5:245–46).[35] Such "culture" comprises, Kant writes, a "development of moral ideas" necessary for one to find an object sublime, rather than "repellent" (§29, 5:265).[36] This is too strong, I

33. One might here contrast Kant's claim that the moral law is "given" as a "fact of pure reason" (*Critique of Practical Reason*, 5:47; my translation) with his account of theoretical reason's generation of ideas at the opening of the "Transcendental Dialectic" of the *Critique of Pure Reason*. Practical reason does formulate the idea of the highest good, as the totality of ends of human action, but this totalization incorporates (presupposes, rather than generates the idea of) morality, as a distinctive, supreme end. Immanuel Kant, *Critique of Practical Reason*, in *Practical Philosophy*, trans. and ed. Mary J. Gregor (Cambridge: Cambridge University Press, 1996), 133–272, 5:3–163.

34. This discontinuity means also—I note briefly, and also contra the letter of Kant's account—that one's final attitude in the experience of the dynamic sublime toward the natural object should not be described as finding one's moral capacity to be "superior" to its power (as at §28, 5:261, quoted above). They are simply on different scales. Perhaps it is right that moral intentions, since they are of a radically different order than nature, cannot be "bent" or transformed by natural power; but the moral intentions do not crush the natural power either. Hence I think it more appropriate to speak of the potential "invulnerability" of morality to natural power—which suffices, I believe, to characterize the pleasurable elevation experienced in the dynamic sublime.

35. The second cited passage occurs in section 23, which concerns the mathematical sublime. But the more extensive discussion of this point in section 29 and the example used in section 23 (the violent ocean) connects this point more tightly to the dynamic sublime—as, of course, does the more explicit role of moral ideas therein.

36. In line with Kristi Sweet's view in "Kant and the Culture of Discipline: Rethinking the Nature of Nature," *Epoché* 15, no. 1 (2010): 121–38, one could propose that the "culture of discipline"—the taming of inclinations that helps to make virtue possible—plays

would argue: one may have the Burkean visceral experience of vitalization without culture. But, understood more precisely, it seems apt, given the preceding discussion: One must already have articulated moral ideas to experience the full, Kantian, meaningful dynamic sublime, because those ideas are not implicitly within or (therefore) "revealed by" the imaginatively thrilling experience. Rather, it is only by *supplying* moral ideas to one's imaginative experience that one can find that experience morally significant.

I propose, moreover, to understand this activity of supplying moral ideas to the experience of the dynamic sublime as *interpretation* of that experience—in fact, as interpretation of a Burkean experience of the sublime. That is, I suggest that the Kantian account of the dynamic sublime is best conceived not as *replacing* Burke's account, but as reinterpreting it, on two levels. *Kant* reinterprets the Burkean sublime, and, more importantly, one part of that reinterpretation is the claim that *the moral subject* has an experience of the Burkean sublime, which *she* reinterprets.

As I have noted, Kant's language suggests that his dynamic sublime is fundamentally the Burkean experience: the tremors and thrills of the vulnerable, challenged, enlivened animal, the feeling of the inhibition and outpouring of vital powers. But the "cultured" Kantian subject conceives of herself at once as this natural being and also as radically different from and beyond nature, in virtue of her moral capacities. As a result, I suggest, the subject reinterprets her vitally thrilling experience *as* significant for herself as moral being. She recognizes her responses as feelings of her own animal being, and she reflects upon that feeling in light of her self-understanding as also a moral being, as it were "adding in" moral significance.[37] In Rudolf

---

a role here as well. Perhaps the experience of the dynamic sublime presupposes that one has tamed one's fears enough to be able to have an aesthetic experience of fearful objects. Given Kant's descriptions of "culture" in section 29 (quoted in the text), however, I think the more central conception here is of the "culture of skill" (§83, 5:431–32): the development of human capacities, including the development and sophistication of (practical) reason. Given Kant's association of such culture with social relations, Sabina Bremner interestingly suggested (in private communication) that the experience of the sublime may require some form of socialization—perhaps in order to recognize and feel strongly (as a contrast, or perhaps as a revivification) the individualizing and isolating character of this experience.

37. This proposal is sympathetic to Katerina Deligiorgi's view in "How to Feel a Judgment: The Sublime and Its Architectonic Significance," in *Kant and the Faculty of Feeling*, ed. Kelly Sorensen and Diane Williamson (Cambridge: Cambridge University Press, 2018), 166–83, though I would oppose her apparent suggestion that the subject reflectively

Makkreel's nice formulation, on Kant's account, the sublime is at once "felt instantaneously as a *Lebensgefühl* and judged reflectively as a *Geistesgefühl*."[38]

As Kant emphasizes against Burke, this moment of reflection is decisive for justifying the judgment of the sublime (§23, 5:244). On Burke's account, one either will or will not experience the sublime; the mechanisms he describes will or will not be engaged, one will or will not get the thrills of adrenaline or endorphins. There is no sense of what, beyond such thrills, renders the experience valuable, why it is worth seeking. It is not the *Lebensgefühl* by itself, but the reinterpretation thereof, that would ground such value, warrant claims on others to share or seek out such feelings.

We are now faced, therefore, with a transformed version of my question concerning the connection of ideas of vulnerability and invulnerability, natural sensibility and moral capacity, in the experience of the dynamic sublime. I have suggested that one cannot explain the link of the feelings of one's vital powers to the idea of morality from "inside" the experience of the sublime; one cannot take reason's moral ideas to be necessary to generate that imaginative, affectively charged experience. Rather, I have proposed, one must understand the Kantian subject as reinterpreting her (Burkean) experience in light of her moral self-understanding. So now we must ask: Why should one engage in such interpretation? Why, *as* a moral

---

identifies the cognitive *sources* of feeling, that is, the functioning of imagination and reason (see esp. 174–75). *That* reflection is the province of the (Kantian) philosopher, not the appreciating subject thereby described. On my proposal, the subject's reflection rather adds symbolic content concerning the human condition and morality to her responses of vital feeling. In his chapter in this volume, Robert Clewis argues consonantly, and persuasively, against the line of interpretation favored by Deligiorgi (and many others, as he notes). Some of the considerations he raises may tell against my proposal as well, though I am inclined to think that without some such cognitively "thick" content (to use Shapshay's term), the feelings of the sublime aroused at the Burkean animalistic level will not constitute an experience of interest to Kantian critical philosophy.

38. Makkreel, "Sublimity," 622. Makkreel seems to intend this characterization quite generally, but I take it to be far more apt for the dynamic sublime, based on an experience of Burkean vital feeling, than the (pervasively cognitive, perhaps also reflective) mathematical sublime. I note also that Makkreel's suggestion—of a spiritualized reinterpretation of the feeling of life—seems to be a change from his earlier view in *Imagination and Interpretation* (95–97, 104–5), on which the experience of the sublime combines a displeasure from the inhibition of the vital powers (a feeling of the "vital sense") with a distinct spiritual pleasure derived from the mind. More generally, however, Makkreel consistently treats reflection as a form of interpretation (as I do here as well, following Makkreel).

being, should one *care about* the *Lebensgefühl*, take it to be significant and expect others to do so?[39]

Kant's text suggests two ways to answer these questions: two ways to understand the meaning supplied by the moral subject's reflective reinterpretation of the brute Burkean experience of vital feeling, and so two ways to justify judgments of the dynamic sublime. I discuss each in turn.[40]

One may first return to a suggestion touched upon above: perhaps the Kantian subject interprets the Burkean experience as an imagined moral action, picturing herself as attempting to resist the powerful natural object *for moral reasons*. I argued that such moral motivations are not *necessary* for imagining one's encounter with the natural power—and so such imagining need not reveal one's moral capacity. Nonetheless, from an already-taken-up moral point of view, one could reinterpret one's imagined encounter in this way, and thus feel the outpouring of vital powers "called forth" by perceiving the powerful object as (also) moral courage. And perhaps subjects should seek out such experiences to strengthen their moral sensibility, to cultivate their admiration for moral motivation.[41] Or, in the terms of a contemporary commentator, the moral subject might hereby enlist for Kantian morality the aesthetic appeal of "heroic subjectivity,"[42] redirecting his visceral thrills in enhanced vitality, the feeling of his own power in response to challenges, to moral ends.

Though it does reflect aspects of Kant's description of the dynamic sublime (and has, I think, been the default view of commentators), this view seems to me problematic. It seems phenomenologically to misrepresent the (reflectively reinterpreted, meaningful) experience of the sublime, reducing

39. One might judge instead that a feeling of fear when no fear is appropriate (because one is safe) is irrational, for example.

40. Given that Kant relies on the presumed parallel with the mathematical sublime, and does not acknowledge the unavoidable explanatory gap in the dynamic sublime, he does not work out either of these ways of thinking. I develop them on the basis of aspects of his discussion.

41. Kant writes that the sublime "prepares" one to esteem something contrary to one's sensible interests ("General Remark," 5:267). See Henry E. Allison, *Kant's Theory of Taste: A Reading of the "Critique of Aesthetic Judgment"* (Cambridge: Cambridge University Press, 2001), 342.

42. Robert Doran, *The Theory of the Sublime from Longinus to Kant* (Cambridge: Cambridge University Press, 2015), 258. Alternatively, one might see Kant here as aiming to aestheticize, and thereby defuse, the claims of competitor (i.e., non-Kantian) heroic moralities.

an uplifting, rather abstract or indefinite, even cosmic experience—whether of power as such, of disruption and disharmony, or of the human place in nature—to a confined narrative of specific imagined action. It is also reductive in treating the experience of the sublime as valuable only insofar as it is instrumental to moral education, rather than as aesthetically valuable in the mere (reflectively infused) perception of the object, for its own sake. In other words, it treats the pleasure (or judged value) of the sublime as interested: as derivative from and in service to moral interests. Such reinterpreted experience would seem, moreover, to present not just moral benefits, but also moral dangers on a Kantian view. For the subject so experiencing (interpreting) the sublime may be inclined to take "moral credit" for her imagined heroism, for her mere capacity to act, and so to sink into a self-celebratory passivity, rather than heed the moral demand for action.[43]

I suggest, therefore, a second line of thought: that the appreciating subject takes both the natural power and her own natural responses to it—the Burkean experience of enhanced vitality—as *symbolic* of morality.[44] As is well known, in section 59 of the *Critique of Judgment*, Kant analyzes symbolism as a signifying relation between two objects (sign and signified), established in virtue of an "analogy" between the "rule" used to judge the intuition of one object (the sensible object or sign) and the rule used to reflect upon an "entirely different object" thereby symbolized. "Though there is no similarity between" the two objects themselves, Kant claims, "there certainly is one between the rules by which we reflect on the two and their causality [*Kausalität*]" (5:352).[45] In the case of the dynamic sublime on

43. See *Critique of Practical Reason*, 5:84–85, 155–57. Makkreel similarly notes Kant's denial that one can or should take the sublime positively to present freedom or the human capacity for morality (*Imagination and Interpretation*, 85–86).

44. Kant himself gestures at a different significative understanding of the sublime, writing that in this experience "the imagination strains to treat nature as a schema for" the ideas of reason (§29, 5:265; see also "General Remark," 5:269). Here (I think) Kant means to redescribe the (subreptive) experience of the sublime, the way in which the natural object appears to us to exemplify an idea of reason. Kant's subsequent glosses of such schematization—as involving "effort" of the imagination and as opening up the prospect of "infinity"—suggest that he here again is describing the psychological structure of the mathematical sublime (the imagination strives and fails to present a very large whole, as an almost-exemplar of reason's idea of the infinite), and then treating it as if it unproblematically applied also to the dynamic sublime (where infinity is not immediately relevant, and it is hard to understand the imagination as "striving").

45. Translation modified, to use "causality" for *Kausalität*.

Kant's account, one may discern such a "similarity" of "rules" of judgment concerning two objects (the natural power and morality, as symbol and symbolized, respectively), specifically concerning their "causality." As we recall, in the experience of the (Burkean) sublime, the subject imaginatively experiences the natural power as an obstacle to her action or life, a disruption of her ordinary pragmatic rooting around in the world. Morality too (on Kant's view) threatens the pursuit of happiness; it disrupts and renders trivial the ordinary pursuit of natural ends. Moreover, just as perceiving the natural power "calls forth" the subject's vital powers (in the Burkean experience of the sublime), so can morality redirect an outpouring of the subject's natural powers, unleashing them to pursue a different, nonnatural goal.[46] Thus, I suggest, the Kantian moral subject may interpret the natural power as symbolic of morality: it stands in an analogous relation to—has a similar effect on—her sensible nature. So may we also understand why the experience of the sublime is apparently an appreciation of the natural object as morally majestic or awe-inspiring: it is symbolic of that which has true majesty (the moral law).

But there is a further, corresponding symbolic relation in the dynamic sublime, I suggest: The subject's own feeling—her own self-affection, the causality of representations upon herself—in response to perceiving the natural power may be taken to symbolize respect, "the feeling of the inadequacy of our ability to attain to an idea *that is a law for us*" (§27, 5:257; emphasis in the original).[47] In the Burkean experience of the sublime, the subject feels the inhibition and outpouring of vital powers—feelings of natural vulnerability (inadequacy) and natural vitality. So too do we feel, in respect, that our natural being is inadequate to the moral law, that it does not *measure up to* the demands of morality. (Kant's term in section 27 is *Unangemessenheit.*) For it is not that in some instance, one fails to will morally, but rather that human being as such is divided and discontinuous, that practical reason proposes ends that are radically different from natural ends, of an entirely different order than the aims and means of natural desire. However, just as the imagined encounter with the natural power is *also* enlivening, the radical difference of morality from sensibility also offers the exciting, enlivening prospect of self-given goals distinct from, even poten-

46. Interestingly, Kant refers to a "moral vital power" that causes moral feeling at *Metaphysics of Morals*, 6:400; he hedges, however, by characterizing this description as using "medical terms" (and so as metaphorical?).

47. Translation modified, to use "inadequacy" for *Unangemessenheit.*

tially transformative of, nature. The subject experiencing the sublime may, in sum, take her natural feelings of vulnerability and vitality—the Burkean moment of *Lebensgefühl*—as symbolic of the painful disruption and yet also potentially pleasurable and energizing redirection of her natural being by pure practical reason. She may, to return to Makkreel's formulation, feel such feeling also as *Geistesgefühl*.[48]

This symbolic reinterpretation of the Burkean experience in turn suggests a different way to justify the judgment of the sublime. As (merely) symbolically linked to morality, and thus as meaningful in a way predicated on a prior commitment to morality, the experience of the sublime cannot be understood as justifiably required of others because it is preparatory for moral feeling. Rather, I suggest, the symbolically reinterpreted dynamic sublime is valuable as a moment of felt, inhabited recognition of who one is, of what it is to be a human being. It allows the Kantian moral subject to feel her own nature, in a double sense: In the *Lebensgefühl*, she feels herself as a natural, vulnerable and vital being; under its symbolic reinterpretation, she feels herself as that natural being *also* oriented to pure rational (moral) ends. All human beings (with sufficient "culture") *can* have such experience because we share a living nature, consequent responses, and ability reflectively to reinterpret their moral significance. We all *should* have—should value and seek out—such experience because it offers us as moral subjects an opportunity to be personally, affectively conscious of, to live within, our nature as discontinuous, as sensible yet rational, indeed moral beings; to recognize ourselves in feeling.[49]

The experience of the dynamic sublime does so, moreover, in a context divorced from immediate calls upon the subject to act in accord with the moral law. The feeling of the sublime is therefore distinct from the

48. In line with debates concerning Kant's account of the beautiful, one may ask whether there are two feelings (or, more properly, two instances of combined feelings of pleasure and displeasure)—the first a Burkean feeling, the second consequent upon reflection about the first—or one feeling, which gains a second, spiritualized meaning through reflection. In line with Makkreel's formulation, I incline to the second view, though the first might better fit Kant's characterization of aesthetic feelings as based on reflection. Insofar as it identifies multiple feelings of pleasure and displeasure, the first might also explain Kant's waverings (identified by Crowther, see note 5) on how the feelings are related.

49. On my view—which I cannot spell out here—such "inhabited" self-recognition or identification is the primary function of feeling (as a distinctive faculty of the mind) for Kant.

moral feeling of respect not only in content (it is not a response per se to consciousness of the demands of the moral law), but also in its function in mental life. It is disinterested: not enmeshed in deliberation or motivational for action, not even related to imagined action. It is, rather, contemplative, responding (as Kant writes) to the "mere exhibition [*Darstellung*]" (§23, 5:244) of an object insofar as it allows the imagination to harmonize with a higher cognitive faculty.[50] On this proposal, then, the content and obligatoriness of the experience of the dynamic sublime is anchored in the fact that human beings are and ought to be responsive to morality (that which is symbolized in the sublime). But it is nonetheless valued for its own sake, aesthetically; the judgment of the sublime based on universally shareable and valuable feeling.

In this chapter, I have raised a problem concerning Kant's account of the dynamic sublime: the explanatory gap, the psychological discontinuity between imaginative, affectively charged experience of natural vulnerability and moral ideas purportedly thereby evoked. This discontinuity is not eliminable, I have argued, for it reflects the discontinuity of pure practical reason from natural life and sensible desire on Kant's view. Unlike reason's aspirations to totality (infinity) in the case of the mathematical sublime, then, moral ideas are not integral to the imaginative experience of threatening power or the subject's (Burkean) thrilling vital responses thereto. Rather, moral ideas are connected to such experience through reflective, symbolizing reinterpretation. Indeed, I would suggest that the reinterpreted experience of the dynamic sublime not only symbolically means, but also formally mirrors the discontinuity in human nature (and so perhaps again symbolically means that discontinuity, at a further, formal level). For, just as the feelings of the (Kantian) dynamic sublime both are not and yet also are the (Burkean) feelings of aroused vital powers, so too the Kantian moral subject both is not but also is the limited, threatened living being he feels himself to be in the (Burkean) experience of the sublime. He can contemplate it, reinterpret its responses, and redirect its natural powers according to new, self-given ends; yet those powers are also the ones he will enlist to attempt to realize

50. Kant characterizes the sublime as contemplative at §39, 5:292, but he also contrasts its "movement [*Bewegung*] of the mind" with the calm "contemplation" of the beautiful (§24, 5:247, my translation; see also §27, 5:258). It is not clear how to understand this ambiguity in Kant's treatment of the sublime as (not) contemplative. I mean here only to emphasize that the sublime is an aesthetic experience, not part of action or deliberation, even though the object of contemplation (feeling) is the subject's agency, that is, its living and acting nature.

any ends he pursues. As a moment of inhabited feeling, even enactment, of such discontinuous human nature, then, the dynamic sublime is rightly understood as central to Kant's understanding of the sublime, and indeed to Kant's philosophical thought generally. For it comprises an experience of the specifically human, or (using again Makkreel's formulation) the spiritually reinterpreted feeling of life, a feeling of human life as such, as discontinuous and as thereby both limited and powerful.[51]

51. For helpful comments on earlier versions of this chapter, I am grateful to Katalin Makkai, and audiences at the Leuven Kant conference and at the Aarhus Kant week, particularly Mario Caimi, Noam Hoffer, Guido Kreis, Nora Schleich, Janum Sethi, and Kristi Sweet.

Chapter 7

Imagination, Life, and Self-Consciousness in the Kantian Sublime

Robert R. Clewis

In the paradigmatic cases presented in the third *Critique*, the sublime is elicited by a confrontation with a powerful or massive object that, from a safe distance, threatens a person's sensible well-being or frustrates their imaginative capacities. Given the object's menacing or frustrating qualities, why is the experience of the sublime pleasant and uplifting rather than neutral or even painful and annoying? According to the most common reading, Kant's account appeals to the role played by reason, whose elevated status and superiority is made evident in the experience of the sublime. However, I would like to argue that the expansion of imagination and the release of the vital powers are also sources of the pleasure. In addition, I maintain that this release of vital powers counts as promoting a feeling of life. Both the expansion of the imagination (not simply its *frustration*) and the outpouring of the vital forces in the sublime thus deserve more emphasis in our interpretations of the sublime, and, specifically, should be seen as possible sources of the pleasure in the experience. The question of pleasure raises further questions about the kind of awareness a person has when experiencing the sublime (i.e., is it self-awareness, and if so, in what sense?). I address this issue in the final section of the chapter.

In one of his earlier writings, an essay on medicine and philosophy, Kant tells the following story, which I paraphrase as follows: "The philosopher Pyrrho was on a ship in the middle of a terrible storm. Everyone else was anxious and scared. Pyrrho saw a pig eating calmly from his trough on the ship. Pointing to it, Pyrrho declared: 'The calm of the wise sage ought to be like this'" (*Essay on the Maladies of the Head*, 2:262).[1] This anecdote, if one can lift it out of its original context, can be used to provide an example of what Kant meant by an experience of the sublime—that is, the feeling of exhilaration or uplift before a vast or powerful object or event such as a raging storm. We are invited to imagine—observing from the shoreline or some similar safe place—the ship tossed to and fro and to envision a (human) being exhibiting stoic tranquility in the middle of the raging tempest. While the calm sage would be in the possession of tranquility, *we* would feel an exciting rush while watching the breathtaking scene.

According to the most common reading of the paradigmatic case presented in the *Critique of Judgment*, the sublime is elicited by a confrontation with a massive or powerful natural wonder that threatens or frustrates a person's sensible or imaginative capacities, assuming that the person is at a safe distance or feels safe. However, Kant makes a striking claim in the opening section of the "Analytic of the Sublime." It is not the marvels of nature that are sublime, he claims, thereby rejecting many eighteenth-century British contributions to the topic. Rather, the sublime is to be found in (or "concerns") ideas of reason. "Instead, all we are entitled to say is that the object is suitable for exhibiting a sublimity that can be found in the mind. For what is sublime, in the proper meaning of the term, cannot be contained in any sensible form but concerns only ideas of reason" (§23, 5:245).[2] The claim that sublimity concerns ideas of reason (hence, can be

1. Immanuel Kant, "Essay on the Maladies of the Head," in *Anthropology, History, and Education*, ed. Günter Zöller and Robert B. Louden (Cambridge: Cambridge University Press, 2007), 63–77. All citations to Kant are to the Akademie edition (volume and page number). Pyrrho of Elis flourished between circa 365–360 BCE and 275–270 BCE. The source of the anecdote is Diogenes Laertius: "When his fellow-passengers on board a ship were all unnerved by a storm, he kept calm and confident, pointing to a little pig in the ship that went on eating, and telling them that such was the unperturbed state in which the wise man should keep himself." Diogenes Laertius, *Lives of Eminent Philosophers*, ed. Robert D. Hicks (Cambridge, MA: Harvard University Press, 1925), 2:481 (9.68).

2. Immanuel Kant, *Critique of Judgment*, trans. Werner Pluhar (Indianapolis: Hackett, 1987). I have preserved the contents of Pluhar's insertions in square brackets while silently removing the brackets. Another standard translation is Immanuel Kant, *Critique of the Power of Judgment*, ed. and trans. Paul Guyer, trans. Eric Matthews (Cambridge: Cambridge University Press, 2000).

said to be "found in the mind") is but the beginning of many twists and turns in Kant's theory of the sublime.[3] In this opening section, Kant not only distinguishes the experiences of the sublime and the beautiful, but also introduces a perplexing term, "negative pleasure." He claims the pleasure in the sublime comes from a "momentary inhibition of the vital forces" followed immediately "by an outpouring of them that is all the stronger." Here is the crucial passage:

> The two likings are also very different in kind. For the one liking (that for the beautiful) carries with it directly a feeling of life's being furthered, and hence is compatible with charms and with an imagination at play. But the other liking (the feeling of the sublime) is a pleasure that arises only indirectly: it is produced by *the feeling of a momentary inhibition of the vital forces followed immediately by an outpouring of them that is all the stronger.* Hence it is an emotion, and so it seems to be seriousness, rather than play, in the imagination's activity. Hence, too, this liking is incompatible with charms, and, since the mind is not just attracted by the object but is alternately always repelled as well, the liking for the sublime contains not so much a positive pleasure as rather admiration and respect, and so should be called a negative pleasure. (§23, 5:244–45; emphasis added)

There are many issues packed into this quote, but for the moment I wish to explore why, given this frustration and blocking, the experience of the sublime is pleasant and uplifting rather than neutral or even painful and annoying. This passage quite clearly states that the "liking" is (indirectly)

3. Unfortunately, Kant is not very clear about what, exactly, is sublime. At least four candidates can be identified, and there are probably more. Kant appears to attribute sublimity to: *the ideas of reason* (as just quoted); *reason itself* (which he calls supersensible and absolutely great); the *feeling* that is ingredient to the experience of the sublime; and the moral *determination* (*Bestimmung*) of the human being. Kant sometimes writes as if "sublime" can be predicated of the natural object, but that is obviously not his considered position since such an attribution would involve what he calls a subreptive error. It seems futile to determine which of these candidates is Kant's considered or preferred one, though there are several attempts to do this in the literature. It instead seems more important to keep in mind which sense is being employed in a particular passage or context.

caused by a release of blocked vital forces (*Lebenskräfte*).[4] Strikingly, however, in recent Kant scholarship this is rarely identified as the most prominent source of the pleasure.

Rather, the more conventional view is that the (negative) pleasure in the sublime comes from the person's *realization of the powers of reason*, whose elevated status and superiority is recognized in the experience of the sublime.[5] This common reading seems to enjoy firm textual support. Just to give one example, in the first section of the "Analytic of the Sublime," Kant claims that the "liking" in the sublime is somehow connected to the imagination's being in accord with reason, that is, to its "furthering" the aims of reason (§23, 5:244). Describing the similarities between the experiences of beauty and of the sublime at the very beginning of the "Analytic of the Sublime," Kant writes: "Hence the liking is connected with . . . the imagination, with the result that *one regards* [*betrachtet wird*] this power, when an intuition is given us, as harmonizing with the power of concepts, i.e., the understanding or reason, this harmony furthering the aims of these" (§23, 5:244).[6] While this passage clearly shows that Kant holds that the imagination, in the sublime, is thought to promote the aims of reason (while in the experience of the beautiful it promotes the aims of the understanding), it remains unclear who is doing this so-called regarding ("one regards")—is it the philosopher who, upon reflection, gains insight into the structure and significance of the experience of the sublime, or is it the person who is in the midst of the exhilarating experience itself? I return to this question at the end of the chapter.

In the following, my broader aim is to show that two supplementary explanations of liking or satisfaction should be added to the conventional one, and they not only appear to have philosophical plausibility, but are also in agreement with the text: the expansion of imagination and the stoppage-and-outpouring of the vital forces. If that is right, the expansion of imagination and the release of the vital forces need to be emphasized more, and, in particular, should be identified as possible sources of pleasure in the sublime.

4. One could translate *Lebenskräfte* with "vital forces" (Pluhar) or "vital powers" (Guyer/Matthews), or, for a more literal rendering of *Leben*, one could even render it "life forces."

5. According to some commentators, this realization or awareness is merely felt; according to others, it is recognized in a self-aware psychological act of recognition in which one attends to one's own mental faculties. As I aim to show, the former reading is to be preferred.

6. Translation modified.

This issue has a noteworthy implication for how self-conscious or self-aware the experience of the sublime is.[7] In the last section, therefore, I explore how we should interpret the sensible "awareness" of the person experiencing the sublime. It is true that there is a limited sense in which Kant thinks the sublime is an experience of self-awareness: it is a merely sensible, intuitive, or aesthetic intimation of one's own powers of reason. The interpretation I think we should avoid, however, is that the experience *necessarily* involves (nonsensible) self-awareness and reflexive reflection—which calling it a "recognition" of the powers of reason might seem to suggest.[8] The proposed interpretation both makes Kant's position more appealing and counts as a reasonable interpretation of the text.[9]

Sources of the Pleasures in the Sublime

Stepping away from Kant for a moment, we can observe that in theorizing the sublime in general, several sources of the pleasures in the sublime can be identified. The sources of the liking include the following:

1. A sense of belonging to or having a place in a larger whole or totality, including a moral order

---

7. In this chapter, I use "self-conscious" and "self-aware" interchangeably.

8. Rendering *erkennen* and its relatives as "recognize" (Guyer/Matthews), otherwise a fine translation of the term, may be partly to blame here, for "recognize" (like "realizing") may give the impression that the appreciating subject is explicitly self-aware and directs attention to herself (to her reason) in a discrete psychological act. In the cases under discussion, it would be useful to emphasize the sensing, seeing, or perceiving (not just recognizing) that is connoted with *erkennen*. The connotations of "reflect" may also be partly to blame for the misreadings, as the term suggests psychological acts of explicit, directed attention. To make a final terminological clarification, I note that when such attention is directed to *oneself*, it can be called "reflexive."

9. In this chapter, I leave aside (though I grant the importance of) the kind of "self-awareness" that includes implicit or prereflective bodily self-awareness. On that, see Frédérique de Vignemont, *Mind the Body: An Exploration of Bodily Self-Awareness* (Oxford: Oxford University Press, 2018). Rather, the interpretation I will reject is the one that *necessarily* attributes to the aesthetic judge an explicit act of recognition or a reflexive act of reflection, namely, a subject's explicit attention to her own powers of reason.

2. Rising above everyday affairs and concerns (or freedom from the mundane)
3. The activation and expansion of imagination
4. Engagement of the survival and self-preservation instincts (sometimes theorized in terms of "fight-flight-freeze" responses), provided that one feels safe

I think each of these sources can be found in Kant's account—even the physiologically oriented last source.

(1) The sublime involves a (felt) awareness of the powers of reason. The felt intimation of reason counts as a sensible awareness of the rational being's place in the teleological order (which, for Kant, is a teleological order of reason). In the experience of the sublime, reason finds its place in a teleological whole.

(2) The dynamical sublime makes evident or reveals the relative and nonabsolute worth of "property, health, and life" (§28, 5:262).

(3) The imagination is expanded or enlarged in both the mathematical and the dynamical forms of the sublime:[10] "The imagination thereby acquires an expansion and a might that surpasses the one it sacrifices" ("General Comment," 5:269). There is a "liking for the expansion of the imagination itself" (§25, 5:249; cf. §28, 5:262).

(4) The satisfaction in the sublime is a "negative pleasure" resulting from the dam-and-release of the vital forces. As I will discuss below, this explanation of the pleasure's source occurs at a physiological and nontranscendental level.[11]

The first two sources have a Stoic resonance to them. According to this account, we are part of a larger rational order (a *logos*), and the awareness of this (moral) place is accompanied by a liking or satisfaction (1).

10. Space does not permit me to discuss the differences between the mathematical and dynamical forms of sublimity. The dynamical sublime is the more Burkean form as well as the one Friedrich Schiller and Arthur Schopenhauer emphasized in the wake of Kant's aesthetic theory, connecting it with dramatic tragedy. The mathematical sublime, with its connections to the limits of representation and the unrepresentable, has in contrast received more attention from G. W. F. Hegel and the francophone tradition (especially Jean-François Lyotard).

11. In the following, I will focus on (3) and (4): imagination and the vital forces.

This rational order grounds us and puts into perspective the relative value of everyday affairs such as health and property, indeed, even life itself (2). The third source can be traced back to eighteenth-century British aesthetic theories that discussed the "pleasures of the imagination."[12] The fourth source of the pleasure can be read as one of Kant's responses to Edmund Burke, whom he cites favorably, as we will see. It is also a reaction to the discussion of concepts of life, vital forces, and theories of representation found in German philosophy stemming from Gottfried Wilhelm Leibniz, Christian Wolff, Alexander Baumgarten, and Moses Mendelssohn. Since Kant specifically mentions Burke in this context, however, in my discussion of Kant's relation to his contemporaries, I will limit myself to his response to Burke.

Imagination in the Sublime

According to the *Critique of Pure Reason*, imagination is the faculty for representing an object even without its presence in intuition.[13] Applying this general characterization to the mathematical sublime, we can say that in the experience of this form of sublimity, what the imagination attempts (unsuccessfully) to represent in a single intuition is an idea of reason, such as the idea of a world whole or infinity. It attempts to produce images (or intuitions) of the idea of reason, but it fails since the idea cannot be presented in a single intuition.

It is thus common in the literature to emphasize the *failure* of imagination, which after all Kant says is deflated or exhausted. Kant uses the metaphor of "violence" done to the imagination and to "inner sense." "And yet this same violence that the imagination inflicts on the subject's sensible faculties is still judged purposive for the whole vocation of the mind" (§27, 5:259; see also §23, 5:245). This failure serves to show a "subjective" purposiveness, namely, a finality of the mental faculties: imagination is in the service of reason.

---

12. In *Spectator* paper 411 (June 21, 1712), Addison characterized the "pleasures of the imagination," including present and remembered pleasures and delights. Joseph Addison and Richard Steele, *Addison and Steele: Selections from "The Tatler" and "The Spectator,"* ed. Robert J. Allen (New York: Holt, Rinehart, and Winston, 1970), 398.

13. Immanuel Kant, *Critique of Pure Reason*, trans. and ed. Paul Guyer and Allen W. Wood (Cambridge: Cambridge University Press, 1998), B151.

However, it needs to be emphasized that there is also an expansion of the imagination in both mathematical and dynamical sublimity.[14] The stretching is evident in the mathematical sublime, since the imagination is trying to keep up with or realize reason's ideas of a whole. In the dynamical sublime, too, the imagination is not merely engaged and active, but elevated and raised. "Hence nature is here called sublime [*erhaben*] merely because it elevates [*erhebt*] our imagination, making it exhibit those cases where the mind can come to feel its own sublimity, which lies in its vocation and elevates it even above nature" (§28, 5:262). The imagination is expanded when we have the thought that even if an overpowering force of nature could destroy us, we can nonetheless view even life itself as trivial. The "amazement bordering on terror" in the sublime, "is not actual fear," for the experiencing subject is either in a safe position or feels safe. Rather, "it is merely our attempt to incur it *with our imagination, in order that we may feel that very power's might*" ("General Comment," 5:269; emphasis added).[15]

The idea that the exercise of imagination can be a source of pleasure can be viewed as an instance of the Aristotelian teleological principle that the exercise of a given capacity or faculty, all things being equal, brings pleasure. The pleasure accompanies an instantiation of a capacity's end or purpose, within ordinary limits and constraints (i.e., overlooking exceptions that bring about an undesirable outcome, such as when one looks directly at the sun with an unaided eye). Just as seeing is inherently pleasant since

14. For a similar emphasis on imagination in the sublime, see Samantha Matherne, "Imagining Freedom: Kant on Symbols of Sublimity," in *Kantian Freedom: New Essays on the Kantian Theory of Freedom*, ed. Dai Heide and Evan Tiffany (Oxford: Oxford University Press, 2023). Likewise, Brady emphasizes the expansion of imagination in both kinds of sublimity. Emily Brady, "The Environmental Sublime," in *The Sublime: From Antiquity to the Present*, ed. Timothy Costelloe (Cambridge: Cambridge University Press, 2010), 171–82, 177.

15. Some commentators have noted the expansion of imagination in both forms of the sublime. In the French tradition, Jean-François Lyotard is among the first prominent commentators to do so. Jean-François Lyotard, *Enthusiasm: The Kantian Critique of History*, trans. Georges Van den Abbeele (Stanford, CA: Stanford University Press, 2009); Jean-François Lyotard, *Lessons on the Analytic of the Sublime*, trans. Elizabeth Rottenberg (Stanford, CA: Stanford University Press, 1994). One of the first anglophone commentaries to discuss the role of the imagination in the sublime is Rudolf A. Makkreel, *Imagination and Interpretation: The Hermeneutical Import of the "Critique of Judgment"* (Chicago: University of Chicago Press, 1990), 67–87.

it is the activation or fulfillment of the capacity to see, so also is imagining pleasant since it is the exercise of our capacities for image-making and imagining. In fact, in both forms of the sublime, the imagination is more than activated and exercised: it is stretched and expanded.

The Outpouring of Vital Forces as Life-Promoting

I now turn to the second source of pleasure. First, it would be helpful to recall Kant's view of what occurs in the experience of beauty. With beauty, Kant says, there is "directly a feeling of life's being furthered [*ein Gefühl der Beförderung des Lebens*]" (§23, 5:244). I would like to suggest that we find an analogous intensification of the promotion of life in the case of sublimity, namely, in the theory of the outpouring of vital forces.[16] If so, the "promotion of life" can be seen as a genus that includes the release of "vital forces" (*Lebenskräfte*).

According to what I am calling the "the dam-and-release" account, there is a sense of momentary inhibition followed by a stronger pouring out of the vital forces.[17] Although Kant does not say this explicitly, the feeling of the dam-and-release of the vital forces can be viewed as a feeling of life.

---

16. Makkreel makes a similar point regarding this passage, claiming that the sublime can be said to "deepen our sense of life." Makkreel, *Imagination and Interpretation*, 96.

17. Actually, Kant offers *two* accounts of the "movement" in the sublime: the dam-and-release view, and the oscillation view. The block quote at the beginning of this paper presents the dam-and-release view (§23, 5:244–45). So does the following: "Emotion, a sensation where agreeableness is brought about only by means of *a momentary inhibition of the vital force followed by a stronger outpouring of it*, does not belong to beauty at all. But sublimity (with which the feeling of emotion is connected) requires a different standard of judging from the one that taste uses as a basis" (§14, 5:226; emphasis added). Yet near the first passage cited above, at §23, 5:245, Kant suggests that the distancing is simultaneous with the attraction ("the mind is not just attracted by the object but is alternately always repelled as well"). This would count as the oscillation view, which is expressed a few pages later: "This agitation (above all at its inception) can be compared with a vibration, i.e., with a rapid alternation of repulsion from, and attraction to, one and the same object" (§27, 5:258). Many commentators have noticed that Kant offers two accounts; I will not here discuss which one is preferable, though I admit that the oscillation view contains the more plausible phenomenological description. But since Kant appeals to the dam-and-release view in the passages under discussion in this paper, I emphasize it here.

If this is right, then the promotion of life is a way to characterize not only the experience of beauty, but also of sublimity.

Kant sees the experience of the sublime as starting with an imagined threat to life. In the mathematical sublime, the threat comes as violence to our imagination qua cognitive faculty of presentation. In the dynamical sublime, it comes in the form of violence to our sensible or physical well-being, that is, to our bodies. Because of this imagined threat to life (or to self-preservation), the sublime would be experienced as fearsome or terrifying if we were in actual danger or we did not consider ourselves to be safe. Due to this threatening or menacing quality, Kant, like Burke, at one point viewed the sublime as allied with terror or fear. In the *Observations on the Feeling of the Beautiful and Sublime* (1764), Kant identified the "terrifying" sublime as one of the three types of sublimity (alongside the noble/moral sublime and the splendid).[18] Likewise, in a 1772–1773 lecture on anthropology, Kant reportedly said that "the sublime elicits respect and borders on fear" ("Anthropologie Parow," 25:388),[19] even if the sublime does not reach the point of fear (since one feels safe).

It is crucial to notice the contribution of the imagination, as I emphasized in the previous section. We *imagine* being on the ship in the raging tempest. Most of us, unlike Pyrrho's pig, are unable to feel stoic *apatheia* while on an imperiled ship.[20] But why, even if we are only *imagining* being tossed about in the raging storm, would the experience be pleasant? It is prima facie odd that the response to the possibility of our own deaths, even if imagined, would involve exhilarating pleasure rather than anxiety or fear.

One of Kant's explanations of the pleasure in the sublime, as noted, is the dam-and-release of the vital forces. Like Kant, Burke faces the prob-

18. Immanuel Kant, *Observations on the Feeling of the Beautiful and Sublime*, in *Observations on the Feeling of the Beautiful and Sublime and Other Writings*, ed. Patrick Frierson and Paul Guyer (Cambridge: Cambridge University Press, 2011), 9–62 (2:209).

19. Immanuel Kant, "Anthropologie Parow," in *Vorlesungen über Anthropologie*, Bd. 25 of *Kant's gesammelte Schriften*, ed. Berlin-Brandenburgische Akademie der Wissenschaften (Berlin: de Gruyter, 1997), 243–464: "Das Erhabene erregt Achtung und gränzt an die Furcht" (my translation). See 25:390–91 on the sublime's universality, its resistance to being reduced to rules, and its basis in feeling (*Gefühl*) rather than (like beauty) in proportion.

20. On *apatheia* and awareness of one's safety, it may be promising to compare the experience of the sublime with the experience of dramatic tragedy. In tragedy in general, we have the aesthetic illusion that (by a kind of participation or sympathy) we are at risk, yet since we are spectators of the play, we are safe.

lem of explaining how an experience of a menacing object could involve pleasure, a kind of (mixed) delight, so I would like to pause for a moment to see how he handled this issue. Burke offers two sources of the (mixed) liking: pleasure in the fact that one is (or feels) safe, and pleasure resulting from biophysiological changes (or [4], above).[21]

For Burke, beauty is a "social quality" and belongs to what he calls the society of the sexes, that is, propagation or generation.[22] In contrast, the sublime concerns our self-preservation. "The sublime is an idea belonging to self-preservation," provided that one is or feels safe from danger.[23] It is a kind of pleasure in safety. As far as I can tell, Burke does not clarify whether it is the *awareness* that we are not in danger that gives rise to the pleasure, or instead that it is merely a *necessary condition* on our feeling the pleasure (which strikes me as the more plausible position). In any case, the experience of the sublime is not fear plain and simple, but a kind of modified fear. It is not ordinary positive pleasure, either. Burke calls it "delight"[24] and "delightful horror."[25] In other words, it is a mixed feeling.

In calling the sublime a "negative" pleasure, Kant may thus be echoing Burke's concept of a delightful horror. As I read him, Kant makes the feeling of safety (or actual safety) at most a necessary condition on the experience of the sublime and does not maintain that the person experiencing the sublime takes pleasure *in* the safety itself.

---

21. Burke's account also has elements that suggest pleasure derives from an expanded imagination (3): given the obscurity that (Burke thinks) is inherent in words and poetic language, the imagination has to fill in the gaps. He appears to say nothing about belonging to a larger whole (1) and is likewise silent about rising above the mundane (2). Burke emphasizes the vastness and power of the object but does not identify its greatness or perfection as a source of our liking or pleasure; in other words, he says little about the satisfaction that is to be derived from our sharing or participating in that vastness or power, as one finds for instance in the theories offered by Moses Mendelssohn and William Wordsworth. For the writings on the sublime by Mendelssohn and Wordsworth, see "From 'On the Sublime and Naive in the Fine Sciences,'" and "'The Sublime and the Beautiful,'" in *The Sublime Reader*, ed. Robert R. Clewis (London: Bloomsbury, 2019), 91–101 and 177–83, respectively.

22. Edmund Burke, *A Philosophical Enquiry into the Origin of Our Ideas of the Sublime and Beautiful* (London: R. and J. Dodsley, 1757), 18.

23. Burke, *Enquiry*, 72.

24. Burke, *Enquiry*, 126.

25. Burke, *Enquiry*, 129.

Let us now turn to Burke's second source. From a biophysiological perspective, Burke explains pleasure as a release of blockages and the push-and-pulling of the nerves. "Having considered terror as producing an unnatural tension and certain violent emotions of the nerves; it easily follows . . . that whatever is fitted to produce such a tension, must be productive of a passion similar to terror, and consequently must be a source of the sublime, though it should have no idea of danger connected with it."[26] It is in light of such biophysiological explanations that Kant calls Burke's account "physiological" and "psychological" ("General Comment," 5:277).

What is relevant for our purposes, and perhaps surprising, is that Kant subscribed to similar mechanistic explanations, and indeed reserved a certain place for them even as he adopted a transcendental perspective in the third *Critique*. Furthermore, when we examine his theory of pleasure, we find that he there claims that the sublime is a feeling of the promotion of life.

To see this, let us begin with his understanding of pleasure. For Kant, pleasure is in general a feeling of the promotion of life. According to a lecture on metaphysics from the mid-1770s, Kant reportedly refers to life as "the inner principle of self-activity" and continues: "Now there can be a furthering, but also a hindrance to life. The feeling of the furthering of life is pleasure, and the feeling of the hindrance of life is displeasure" ("Metaphysics L_1," 28:247).[27] Likewise, according to an anthropology lecture from 1775–1776, he is recorded to have said: "A person who does not feel the state of his body is healthy. We only feel the greater hindrances and the furthering of life. Therefore, human beings do not feel their exhalation and blood circulation" ("Anthropology Friedländer," 25:499).[28]

According to a lecture on anthropology from 1772–1773, not only was Kant open to mechanistic explanations of the sublime, but he also connected the sublime to the promotion of life: "Now all of these movements such as those of the beautiful and sublime ultimately proceed on something very mechanical [*mechanisches*]. All these activities promote our life as a

26. Burke, *Enquiry*, 126.

27. Immanuel Kant, "Metaphysics L_1," in *Lectures on Metaphysics*, trans. and ed. Karl Ameriks and Steve Naragon (Cambridge: Cambridge University Press, 1997), 17–106 (translation slightly modified).

28. Immanuel Kant, "Anthropology Friedländer," in *Lectures on Anthropology*, ed. Allen W. Wood and Robert B. Louden, trans. G. Felicitas Munzel (Cambridge: Cambridge University Press, 2012), 37–255 (translation slightly modified).

whole." Kant identifies a stretching of the nerves during the experience of the sublime even to the point of pain (*schmerzt*) and terror (*Schrecken*): "Regarding the sublime, it unhinges the nerves, and causes pain when it is engaged with forcefully. Indeed, one can bring the sublime to the point of terror and breathlessness" ("Anthropologie Parow," 25:389).[29]

Finally, according to a physical geography lecture from the same period (1770), Kant seems to have agreed with the claim that whoever ignores the sublimity and beauty in nature misses out on a pleasure that "makes one's heart palpable" (swells the heart), even as it "raises the intellect."[30]

---

29. "Alle diese Bewegungen nun, die wie das Schöne und Erhabene, lauffen zulezt auf etwas sehr mechanisches heraus. Alle diese Thätigkeit befördert unser Leben im Ganzen." "Was das Erhabene betrift, so spannet solches die Nerven aus und schmerzt, wenn es starck angegriffen wird. Ja man kann das Erhabene bis zum Schrecken und zur Athemlosigkeit bringen." The Burke-inspired passage continues: "Everything wonderful is sublime and therefore pleasing, if it is reported in society; only in solitude does it terrify; indeed even the starry sky, if, when gazing at it, one remembers that all the celestial bodies and suns are like our sun in that a similar multitude of celestial bodies again orbit around them, elicits a feeling of horror and terror when alone, for one imagines that, as a small speck of dust in such an immeasurable set of worlds, one does not even deserve the attention of the all-powerful being." ("Alles wunderbahre ist erhaben und daher angenehm, wenn es in Gesellschaft erzählet wird, allein in der Einsamkeit schreckt es; ja selbst der Gestirnte Himmel, wenn man sich bey deßen Anblick erinnert, daß das alles WeltKörper und Sonnen sind, die wieder eine ähnliche Menge WeltKörper um sich drehen laßen, als unsre Sonne, erreget ein Grausen und Schrecken in der Einsamkeit, weil man sich einbildet, daß man als ein kleines Stäubchen in einer solchen unermeßlichen Menge von Welten nicht verdient von dem Allmächtigen Wesen bemerket zu werden.") Compare this to the footnote on "Carazan" in the *Observations* at 2:209n; and contrast it with the "starry heavens" passage at the end of Kant's *Critique of Practical Reason*, in *Practical Philosophy*, trans. and ed. Mary J. Gregor (Cambridge: Cambridge University Press, 1996), 133–272, 5:161–62.

30. Immanuel Kant, Vorlesungen über Physische Geographie, Hesse (1770), manuscript, 184 recto. The passage reads: "Für den Menschen allein hat Gott die Natur mit Pracht und Schönheit, die alle Kunst weit übertrift, so reichlich bestreuet. Wer nicht darauf achtet, der vernichtet den Endzweck Gottes, und *beraubet sich selbst eines Vergnügens, daß zugleich sein Hertz fühlbar machen und seinen Verstand erhöhen würde*" (emphasis added). This passage, which the note scriber inserted into a separate page (184 recto) is actually a direct quote from the preface to a work of 1766: Nicolaus Ehrenreich Anton Schmid, *Von den Weltkörpern: Zur gemeinnützigen Kenntnis der großen Werke Gottes* (Hannover: Schlüter, 1766), 3. Therefore we should not rely on it too heavily as an indication of Kant's own views. Translations are my own and are cited according to the manuscript page. The student transcriptions of Kant's anthropology and physical geography lectures have been available at the Kant-Arbeitsstelle of the Berlin Brandenburgische Akademie der

There is also textual support in the *Critique of Judgment* for the view that the sublime involves a feeling of the furthering of life. In a (pure) aesthetic judgment, Kant writes, "the presentation is referred only to the subject, namely, to *his feeling of life, under the name feeling of pleasure or displeasure,* and this forms the basis of a very special power of discriminating and judging" (§1, 5:204; emphasis added). While "displeasure" could be read as referring to ugliness, it makes more sense, given the contents, aims, and structure of the third *Critique,* to read such occurrences as referring to the sublime (or else simply to the faculty of pleasure/displeasure in general). After all, the third *Critique* devotes an "Analytic" to judgments of the sublime, but does not offer a similar analysis to the ugly.[31] In addition, Kant holds that "all" representations in us "affect the feeling of life, and none of them can be indifferent insofar as it is a modification of the subject" ("General Comment," 5:277).

The reading that the experience of the sublime not merely affects the feeling of life but also is a feeling of its furthering is confirmed in *Anthropology from a Pragmatic Point of View* (1798). In section 16, Kant divides "the senses of physical sensation" into those of vital sensation (*sensus vagus*) and those of organic sensation (*sensus fixus*) (7:154). Sensations of warm/cold and sensations aroused by the mind (such as sudden hope, fear, and the sublime), he says,

---

Wissenschaften (BBAW) since 2007 (http://kant.bbaw.de/base.htm/geo_base.htm). Access requires username and password, granted upon making an inquiry to the Arbeitsstelle. Several of these lectures have been published by Werner Stark: *Kant's Vorlesungen,* in *Kant's gesammelte Schriften,* Bd. 26, ed. Berlin-Brandenburgische Akademie der Wissenschaften (Berlin: de Gruyter, 2020).

Cf. the marginal notes (*Bemerkungen*) Kant wrote in his personal copy of the *Observations* in the mid-1760s ("Remarks," 20:19), where Kant holds that the sublime "swells the heart," fixes the attention, makes one tense, and eventually is exhausting. See also 20:119, which states that in the feeling of the sublime the powers of a human being become stretched, whereas in the beautiful they contract. The terms splendor (*Pracht*) and beauty (*Schönheit*) are used in the *Observations* to describe the magnificent or splendid sublime (*prächtig erhabene*), in which beauty is mixed with the sublime (e.g., when observing a sunset or architectural marvel). Immanuel Kant, "Remarks in the *Observations on the Feeling of the Beautiful and Sublime,*" in *Observations on the Feeling of the Beautiful and Sublime and Other Writings,* ed. Patrick Frierson and Paul Guyer (Cambridge: Cambridge University Press, 2011), 63–202.

31. There is some debate about whether on Kant's account pure aesthetic judgments of the ugly are possible. However this is settled, it remains incontrovertible that, even if he briefly mentions representing ugly objects in a beautiful manner (§48, 5:312), Kant never offers an extended account of aesthetic judgments of the ugly in the *Critique of Judgment.*

belong to vital sensation. "The shudder that seizes the human being himself at the representation of the sublime, and the horror, with which nurses' tales drive children to bed late at night, belong to vital sensation; they penetrate the body as far as there is life in it." Because the experience of the sublime belongs to vital sensation ("penetrates the body as far as there is life in it") and since it is overall a feeling of pleasure (a liking), which is in general a feeling of the promotion life, it can be said to be a feeling of the promotion of life.[32] It is worth noting, too, that a few sentences earlier, Kant had defined "sensation" (*Empfindung*) such that it is *not* necessarily self-conscious in the sense of involving self-directed attention: "A representation through sense of which one is conscious as such is called *sensation*, especially when the sensation at the same time arouses the subject's attention to his own state" (7:153). The addition ("especially when . . .") implies that sensation need *not* be felt self-consciously or with attention directed toward one's own state. I will return to this issue in the next section.

In light of Kant's praise of the "acute" authors such as Burke ("General Comment," 5:277), there is good reason to think that, at least on one level, he thought there was a legitimate place for mechanistic, psychological explanations. He claims (following Epicurus, he states) that "gratification and pain are ultimately always of the body." At an empirical level, such explanations play an important role, and he seems to have considered them compatible with his transcendental method. Kant's theory of the vital forces as a source of the pleasure proceeds at an empirical level just as does Burke's account of the pulling/pushing of nerves and tissues (which could be updated by contemporary cognitive and neuroscience).

If, even in the *Critique of Judgment*, the transcendental philosopher seems to have continued not only to find a place for, but even to esteem, empirical-mechanical explanations, the standard view of why the sublime is on the whole a pleasant experience, namely, the (felt) awareness of the powers and superiority of reason, can also be supplemented by this empirical explanation of the liking, namely, the dam-and-release of the vital forces, which can in turn be seen as a feeling of the furthering of life. It gives another potential reason why Kant, offering his version of Burkean delightful horror, called the sublime a *negative* pleasure. To conclude

32. For a similar interpretation of this passage, see Makkreel, *Imagination and Interpretation*, 95.

this section, we can observe that Kant displayed a rich engagement with Burke,[33] among other authors.[34]

33. According to the Dohna lecture manuscript on geography from 1792, Kant reportedly invoked the Burkean form of the sublime: "Terrifying sublime: all of nature in its death and dying" (Schrekhaft erhaben die ganze Natur in ihrem Sterben). Immanuel Kant, "Vorlesungen über Physische Geographie, Dohna (1792)," manuscript, 33r. The 1792 date of this claim, if that is indeed when Kant made the assertion, is striking: two years *after* the publication of the third *Critique*, and nearly three decades after Kant's *Observations*. In the latter, Kant names this form of the sublime (terrifying sublime, *das Schreckhaft-Erhabene*) as one of the three forms, alongside the noble/moral (*edle*) sublime and splendid (*prächtig*) sublime (2:209). A 1792 date would indicate that, at least in one of his lectures, Kant was still referring to the terrifying sublime even after the publication of the third *Critique*. While I do not wish to make too much out of a single passage in a set of student lecture notes, it is tempting to take this as some support for the view that the older forms of sublimity survived in *some* fashion alongside the official versions, the dynamical and the mathematical sublime. In *The Kantian Sublime and the Revelation of Freedom* (Cambridge: Cambridge University Press, 2009), I argued that, although in the third *Critique* Kant officially and unquestionably identifies only the mathematical and the dynamical sublime, in his other writings, one could find evidence of another older form of the sublime, namely, the "moral" sublime, the partly intellectual (hence "adherent") but still *aesthetic* response to the moral law or to presentations exhibiting moral content of some kind (the most famous instance being the experience of awe before the moral law, a description of which concludes the second *Critique*; 5:161). My deliberate reconstruction (or recalling) of this aesthetic type for Kant was a product of my way of dealing with the "explanatory gap" in the dynamical sublime (as Rachel Zuckert calls it in her chapter in the present volume), namely, the gap between the experience of raw natural power and the imaginative experience of one's natural vulnerability, on the one hand, and consciousness of the *independence of morality* from natural power, that is, respect for one's moral vocation (or the moral law), on the other. The most that the dynamical sublime disclosed (always in a merely sensory way), I argued, was only *negative* practical freedom (by way of revealing the relative value of natural inclinations, health, life, etc. [with regard to (2) above in text]), not positive practical freedom (moral autonomy). I did not therefore consider it necessary to find a way for the dynamical sublime to cross over such an explanatory "gap," and I let it sit without a tight connection to morality (autonomy, moral vocation) or the moral law (which also struck me as phenomenologically more accurate for the dynamical kind of sublimity). Only the "moral" sublime, where there was no such explanatory gap, could aesthetically disclose or reveal (though of course neither prove nor give a positive image of) positive practical freedom or autonomy. In an experience of the moral sublime (as when we admire the moral resoluteness that is displayed by a fearless, virtuous soldier; §28, 5:262), a subreption was not possible, since the content and object of aesthetic reflection was *already* moral, and, unlike objects provoking the dynamical sublime, *never fear-inducing and menacing*—which is one reason I found it hard to characterize experiences of what I called the "moral" sublime as experiences of the *dynamical* sublime, as the literature tends to do. The moral law, for Kant, can never evoke fear. (I classified the elicitors of the moral sublime in an appendix; see *The Kantian Sublime*, 234.)

34. I cannot here examine all of the thinkers (e.g., Joseph Addison, Lord Kames, Baumgarten, and Mendelssohn) whose aesthetic writings Kant appropriated in the course

An Implication: Interpreting the Sublime Transcendentally

In this section, I would like to suggest that the transcendental-empirical distinction ("General Comment," 5:277) can clarify a misunderstanding that is present in much of the literature, which unfortunately attributes to Kant a position that is less plausible and may not even be one he defended: the view that the experience of the source of the pleasure must be explicitly attended to by the appreciating subject who is undergoing the experience. While Kant may be committed to the view that the power of reason is a transcendental source of the pleasure, this does not entail that one must be explicitly *aware* that it is such a source. To attribute self-directed attention to Kant's theory, I submit, is to build in too much.

But first, let me cite a few passages that seem to support the "self-awareness" reading, that is, the one that requires of the appreciating subject explicit attention to and recognition of her powers of reason. Passages such as this seem to support such a reading: "Though the irresistibility of nature's might makes us, considered as natural beings, *recognize* [*erkennen*] our physical impotence, it reveals [*entdeckt*] in us at the same time an ability to judge ourselves independent of nature, and reveals in us a superiority over nature" (§28, 5:261; emphasis added).[35]

Likewise, there is Kant's take on a person's experience of awe in the presence of God's majesty and omnipotence—an exemplary source of the

---

of his intellectual development, but certainly much more should eventually be said about it. [Editor's note: See J. Colin McQuillan's discussion of Baumgarten in this volume for some further account.] Such an investigation would need to examine the development of a theory of the sublime not only in Kant's published works, but (since his publications after 1764 contain relatively little on aesthetic theory) also in his marginal notes, lecture transcriptions, and correspondence. As we can already see, Kant engages with these figures in his lectures, but his account is quite different from the one in the *Critique of Judgment*. The development of his views of the sublime has received relatively little attention in the scholarship. Discussing Kant's anthropology lecture (Collins 1772–1773), however, Paul Guyer maintains that it ("Anthropology Collins," 25:198) reflects a theory that is quite distant from that of the third *Critique*, the innovations in the latter being the following: the distinction between the "mathematical" and the "dynamical" sublime, the claim that each involves a satisfying harmony between imagination and reason, and the view that in the experience of the dynamical sublime the imagination gives us an intimation of the power of our own practical reason. Paul Guyer, "Beauty, Freedom, and Morality: Kant's *Lectures on Anthropology* and the Development of His Aesthetic Theory," in *Essays on Kant's Anthropology*, ed. Brian Jacobs and Patrick Kain (Cambridge: Cambridge University Press, 2003), 135–63, 156.

35. Yet, notice that this "ability to judge" is only a capacity (*Vermögen*): it is not necessarily actualized.

sublime according to early modern theorists such as John Dennis and Giambattista Vico: "Only if he is *conscious* that his attitude is sincere and pleasing to God, will these effects of might serve to arouse in him the idea of God's sublimity, insofar as he *recognizes* in his own attitude a sublimity that conforms to God's will, and is thereby elevated above any fear of such natural effects, which he does not regard as outbursts of God's wrath" (§28, 5:263–64; emphasis added).

In addition, in the following passage Kant mentions being "compelled" to think and "realizing" that nature, qua experienced, is conditioned rather than unconditioned: "This effort . . . is itself an exhibition of the subjective purposiveness of our mind, in the use of our imagination, for the mind's supersensible vocation. And we are *compelled to subjectively think* nature itself in its totality as the exhibition of something supersensible. . . . For we soon come to *realize* that nature in space and time entirely lacks the unconditioned" ("General Comment," 5:268).

Finally, in explaining why he thinks that the claim to universal validity that is made (at least implicitly) by judgments of the sublime does not require a "deduction" (justification) beyond the "exposition" of the sublime he had just offered, Kant writes the following: "When we speak of the sublime in nature we speak improperly; properly speaking, sublimity can be attributed merely to our way of thinking, or, rather, to the foundation this has in human nature. What happens is merely that the apprehension of an otherwise formless and unpurposive object *prompts us to become conscious* of that foundation, so that what is subjectively purposive is the use we make of the object, and it is not the object itself that is judged to be purposive on account of its form" (§30, 5:280).

On the basis of such passages, many recent interpreters have adopted versions of what I am calling the "self-directed attention" or "self-awareness" interpretation. Some philosophers even make this feature part of their Kantian accounts. For instance, Katerina Deligiorgi at one point suggests that the self-aware recognition of one's rational agency is a constitutive ingredient of the experience of the sublime. "The oddity of the judgment is that the subject term of '. . . is sublime' refers to the object and to the self-aware experience of the judging subject. It becomes less odd if we think of the object as triggering this self-awareness through its thwarting of our exercise of our cognitive powers."[36] This quote represents a view shared by other

36. Katerina Deligiorgi, "The Pleasures of Contra-purposiveness: Kant, the Sublime and Being Human," *Journal of Aesthetics and Art Criticism* 72, no. 1 (2014): 25–35, 32.

prominent commentators (diverse as their views may be) including Jane Forsey,[37] Malcom Budd,[38] and Sandra Shapshay.[39] (It is justly repudiated by Paul Crowther, however.)[40] The following passage by Emily Brady, too, is representative of the "self-awareness" interpretation, as it invokes the notions

---

37. For instance, Jane Forsey, "Is a Theory of the Sublime Possible?," *Journal of Aesthetics and Art Criticism* 56, no. 4 (2007): 381–89, 384: "We *become aware* in that moment that while we may physically perish in a raging sea, there is a part of us that cannot be touched, even by the most violent of natural forces." She continues her commentary on Kant as follows: "The real point of these experiences is the *realization* of our own supersensible nature." And she adds: "What unfolds as truly sublime [for Kant] is our moral being, that part of us that is inaccessible to sensory experience but that we nevertheless become *aware* of in (certain) moments of cognitive failure" (385; emphases added).

38. For Budd, the realization in the sublime occurs "only by *conceiving* of the sensible world of experience as being dependent on its intelligible basis" (emphasis added). Malcolm Budd, "Delight in the Natural World: Kant on the Aesthetic Appreciation of Nature, Part 3, The Sublime in Nature," *British Journal of Aesthetics* 38, no. 3 (1998): 233–51, 241.

39. Sandra Shapshay writes, "the thick/thin distinction tracks predominantly the *cognitive reflection* (or lack thereof) that issues from the encounter" with the sublime (emphasis modified). Sandra Shapshay, "A Theory of Sublime Responses, the Thin and the Thick," in Clewis, *The Sublime Reader*, 329–39, 336. Shapshay classifies Kant as offering a thick response, which means that it involves cognitive reflection. For Shapshay, a "thick" sublime response "involves reflection on the complexities of the relationship between human beings and the world in which we find ourselves" (335). While I find Shapshay's thin/thick distinction very useful for understanding the sublime generally, I do not think that Kant holds that the experience of the sublime *must* be a thick response and self-reflective in this way.

40. Paul Crowther, *The Kantian Sublime: From Morality to Art* (Oxford: Oxford University Press, 1989). Crowther rejects Kant's account of the sublime insofar as it is taken to claim that the experience of the sublime involves "conscious reflection" on the superiority of reason over sensibility (124). Charitably, Crowther does not attribute that view to Kant. Crowther writes that Kant "consistently uses terms that strongly emphasize that we are not explicitly aware of this process. In this respect we are told that imagination '*betrays* its limits and inadequacy' and that the '*inner perception*' of this inadequacy 'makes us alive to the feeling of the supersensible'—'whose pre-eminence can only be made *intuitively* evident' " (124; Crowther's emphasis). Crowther astutely observes that "if Kant had even half-heartedly entertained the possibility that our awareness of the superiority of our rational faculty involved the mediation of conscious reflection rather than an indirect manifestation through feeling, he would have no grounds for his insistence that conventionally we mistakenly ascribe sublimity to the object which provokes it, instead of to our rational being" (124). In other words, there would never be any "subreptions" or mistaken identifications of what is truly sublime (rational being, rather than nature). But Kant clearly thinks that subreptive errors occasionally occur and that we sometimes commit them—otherwise he would not have made the effort to account for them.

of self-reflection and reflexivity: "To this [i.e., two features of the sublime just elucidated], add *self-reflection* understood in terms of *reflexivity*, and we have, arguably, a clearer understanding of the sublime as a distinctive aesthetic experience. . . . As we are affected by sublime qualities, we are forced into a position of admiration for nature, feeling both insignificant *and* aware of ourselves in relation to the power and magnitude of elements of the natural environment."[41] Thus, in their reconstructions of a Kantian account or in their interpretations of his claims, some authors set out to defend the "self-awareness" interpretation, while others adopt the interpretation less explicitly.

There are problems with such an interpretation, however, and on several fronts. If we accept the "self-awareness" or reflexive interpretation, we have to attribute to Kant's account a very odd phenomenology of the sublime. I am not sure I have ever had such an experience of *that* kind of sublimity (and, before reading Kant, I *certainly* did not have one). This view has the very odd implication that until Kant had written his account of the sublime, and people had read it, it was difficult if not impossible to have a genuine experience of the sublime.

The reading sometimes forces commentators to make some peculiar interpretive moves. One such response is to say that one "recognizes" the powers of reason "implicitly." Despite its popularity in some philosophical circles, the notion of implicit recognition strikes me as bordering on incoherence. Recognition by a person (unlike logical entailments among sentences, or commitments to some beliefs given the adoption of other ones) seems to require an explicit act of directed consciousness.

But if interpreters insist that the sublime always involves an explicit, self-conscious recognition of the powers of reason, then it suffers as a description of the experience. In short, the reading faces a dilemma. Either it suffers phenomenologically (where the recognition is explicit, self-directed, and self-conscious), or the awareness remains prereflective and sensory. Thankfully, there is a kernel of truth to the latter horn, as we will see; the problem is that it is not always clearly adopted by defenders of the "self-awareness" interpretation.

---

41. Brady, "Environmental Sublime," 182 (emphasis modified). On 181, she likewise refers to our being "aware of ourselves as overwhelmed" and "a kind of self-reflection" in the experience of the sublime. It should be noted, however, that she also sometimes refers to a "felt awareness" (176) and "felt freedom" (177).

I would like to suggest that a promising way out of this dilemma is to claim that the source of the pleasure (whether the power of reason, stretching of imagination, or the release of vital forces) is not meant to be *identified* by the appreciating subject at all, but is rather elucidated by the philosopher or reflective thinker, who, by identifying the mental processes and capacities that make it possible, offers an account of the experience in question. (One might thus call such an account "transcendental.") In other words, the mental play (the imaginative stretching led by reason) is to be identified as the (transcendental) source of the pleasure by the philosopher, not the appreciating subject.[42] This tack has the advantage not only of being more in line with the experience's phenomenology, it also seems to be more in harmony with Kant's transcendental method.

In the experience of the sublime, the mind is not merely in some respect receptive, but also (in other respects) active and spontaneous.[43] The appreciating subject is not (as with inner sense) merely "affected by the play of his own thoughts" (7:161).[44] Rather, in the experience of the sublime, the mind achieves a kind of self-affection, as reason interacts with imagination in aesthetic play. The sensation created by this play may (or could) be observed self-consciously—my point is that it *need* not be.

The proposed line of interpretation can thus be defended for the following reasons. First, as noted, the "self-awareness" interpretation is a poor fit with the phenomenology of the sublime. Kant's account is more plausible if we interpret his claims in some other way. Likewise, the proposed nonempirical, nonpsychological (but instead transcendental) interpretation seems to accord more with Kant's general philosophical method. As much as he admires Burke, toward the end of his discussion of the sublime, Kant says this about Burke and other empirical accounts: "We can now also compare the transcendental exposition of aesthetic judgments we have just completed with the physiological one, regarding which work has been done by someone like Burke and many acute men among us, so that we may see where a merely empirical exposition of the sublime and of the beautiful may

42. In her contribution to the present volume, Rachel Zuckert makes a similar point.

43. For a similar claim, see Deligiorgi, "Pleasures of Contra-purposiveness," 31–32: "The judging and experiencing subject is passive here. . . . At the same time, an active conception is at work." For this statement to avoid self-contradiction, it should be clarified that certain elements are passive while other ones are active.

44. On a related distinction between inner sense and (pure) apperception, see 7:142.

lead" ("General Comment," 5:277). This claim should make us resist the temptation to read Kant's account of the sublime empirically-psychologically. Rather, Kant clearly adopts a transcendental approach in his discussion of the sublime and views the experience as grounded on an a priori principle (cf. "General Comment," 5:278).

Third, the proposed transcendental reading makes the best sense of the potentially confusing doctrine of "subreption" in the sublime. The subreption is the attribution of sublimity to objects rather than to the rational "idea" of our humanity: "Hence the feeling of the sublime in nature is respect for our own vocation. But by a certain subreption (in which respect for the object is substituted for respect for the idea of humanity within ourselves, as subjects) this respect is accorded an object of nature" (§27, 5:257). The "self-awareness" interpretation risks entailing the odd claim that when you say, "The Grand Canyon is sublime," you are saying something that you do not actually believe. For you are at the same time claiming "My reason is sublime" and "The Grand Canyon is sublime," which is an extremely odd epistemic state to adopt. The proposed reading avoids this confusion, since it holds that the person does not have to be explicitly conscious of, or attend to, their rational superiority every time they have an experience of the sublime. The illusion (from a Kantian point of view) underlying the claim that it is the Grand Canyon that is sublime remains: you commit a subreption when you utter the latter sentence. Still, upon philosophical reflection you might be able to identify the transcendental grounds making the experience possible.

Fourth, there is textual support for the proposed interpretation that the source or principle need not be consciously identified while having the experience of the sublime: "I admit that this principle [the invulnerability and moral vocation ultimately grounding the sublime] seems farfetched and the result of some subtle reasoning, and hence high-flown [*überschwenglich*] for an aesthetic judgment. And yet our observation of man proves the opposite, and proves that even the commonest judging can be based on this principle, *even though we are not always conscious of it*" (§28, 5:262).[45] "The imagination thereby acquires an expansion and a might that surpasses the one it sacrifices; *but the basis* [*Grund*] *of this might is concealed from it*" ("General Comment," 5:269; emphasis added). Thus, the principle underlying the validity of judgments of the sublime (in the first passage), or the source

45. Translation modified.

of the pleasure (e.g., enlargement of imagination, according to the second one), need not be recognized in psychological acts of self-directed attention.

Fifth, there is an alternate way of understanding Kant's use of terms such as "recognize" and "realize." He may be using these terms in a way similar to "reveal" in the following passage from the "Analytic of the Sublime," which is also worth quoting since it shows that Kant holds that the analysis of the sublime belongs to transcendental philosophy (presumably, on the grounds that it employs the power of judgment's a priori principle of purposiveness):

> In this modality of aesthetic judgments—their presumed necessity—lies one principal moment for a critique of judgment. For it is this necessity that *reveals* [*macht . . . kenntlich*][46] an a priori principle in them and lifts them out of the reach of empirical psychology, in which they would otherwise remain buried among the feelings of gratification and pain (accompanied only by the empty epithet of being a more refined feeling). Instead this necessity places them, and by means of them our power of judgment, into the class of those judgments that have a priori principles at their basis, and hence brings them into transcendental philosophy. (§29, 5:266; emphasis modified)

In other words, the basis or ground of the experience is made explicit or revealed by transcendental analysis, though not necessarily to the aesthetic judge. What does it mean to say that the analysis belongs to "transcendental" philosophy? Among other things, it means that the judgment of the sublime is conceived of as making a claim to necessity and (subjective) universality, and it means that the judgment rests on an a priori transcendental principle (the a priori principle of purposiveness).[47] Transcendental analysis explains

---

46. Pluhar's rendering of *macht . . . kenntlich* ("reveals") is to be preferred to the more cognitive-sounding Guyer/Matthews translation "makes us cognizant."

47. Technically speaking, Kant never calls the sublime "communicable" in the way he does beauty, and he does not discuss it in terms of a shared *sensus communis*. Yet there is a way in which it is clearly communicable; this should not be surprising and seems after all implied by the judgment of the sublime's claim to necessity and subjective universality. Rather than being founded in a *sensus communis*, however, the judgment of the sublime is grounded in human nature—Kant goes further (arguably too far) and specifies this as a capacity for *morality* that is shared by all human beings. (In my

the possibility of the experience without claiming that such analysis be psychologically present to the appreciating judge. The normativity attributed to the judgment (its universality and necessity) is not itself an ingredient of the experience of the sublime: it is not part of the experience's content, but rather is *attributed to* the judgment, on the second-order, as it were. The normativity attributed to the judgment of the sublime is *about* the experience; it is not contained in the experience itself.[48]

Before concluding, I wish to take up a point mentioned a few paragraphs above, where I suggested that there was a way in which the awareness of the powers of reason might remain prereflective or implicit. In one sense, the sublime does involve a kind of awareness, but it is indirect and sensory, an aesthetic and intuitive intimation of our rational powers as they interact with our sensible sides. As Henry Allison observes, the sublime "puts

view, Kant should not have said it requires "culture" to feel or judge the sublime, for it seems inconsistent with his claim that it is grounded in human nature and in human capacities for feeling and reason. Dilek Huseyinzadegan's chapter in the present volume examines Kant's inconsistency, albeit from a different stance than the present one.) It would be mistaken to think that the judgment of the sublime is (like the agreeable) merely private or individual, though just this seems to be implied by the widespread, even clichéd, replications of *Wanderer in the Sea Fog* (Caspar David Friedrich, c. 1818) as an alleged exemplar of someone experiencing the sublime; alas, it depicts a solitary wanderer. The experience of the sublime can after all be shared with others, as Francesco Petrarca did when he ascended Mount Ventoux with his brother and fellow trekkers; see Francesco Petrarca, "The Ascent of Mount Ventoux," in Clewis, *The Sublime Reader*, 49–54, 53. And even when one is alone, one can imagine or wish that a friend were there. Moreover, witnessing, in a buzzing crowd of fellow spectators, great feats or accomplishments carried out by performers or athletes can give rise to a powerful and shared experience of the sublime. Finally, one could provide, for Kant, a "deduction" of the necessity and subjective universality of judgments of the sublime that goes beyond his mere "exposition." A key move in such a justification would be the claim that, just as (for Kant) understanding and imagination cooperate harmoniously in cognition and make experience possible, reason and imagination (similarly shared by all humans) interact with each other in ordinary experience and practical-moral life.

48. Representative commentary in the literature (more on beauty than the sublime) that adopts this normativity-as-experience line include the following: Hannah Ginsborg, "Primitive Normativity and Skepticism about Rules," *Journal of Philosophy* 108, no. 5 (2011): 227–54; Hannah Ginsborg, *The Normativity of Nature: Essays on Kant's "Critique of Judgement"* (Oxford: Oxford University Press, 2014); Richard Moran, "Kant, Proust, and the Appeal of Beauty," *Critical Inquiry* 38, no. 2 (2012): 298–329; Arata Hamawaki, "Kant on Beauty and the Normative Force of Feeling," *Philosophical Topics* 34, nos. 1/2 (2006): 107–44.

us in touch" with our "higher self," but it does so "merely aesthetically."[49] Even if at one point she appears to adopt the "self-awareness" (recognition) interpretation, elsewhere Deligiorgi claims that the sublime "is a feeling that gives us access to moral self-knowledge."[50] Finally, although Brady sometimes attributes self-awareness and self-reflection to the experience of the sublime, she also refers to a "felt" awareness and freedom.[51] In short, the sublime offers an aesthetic, intuitive, or sensory intimation of our rational powers (sometimes called "reason" or "freedom") in interaction with our sensible and imaginative capacities, even if it does not offer a cognition or intuition of freedom.

Correcting the noted misreadings (if we can characterize them this way) might have implications for the interpretation of self-consciousness or apperception generally, or even for the meaning and significance of transcendental philosophy. For the misreadings of Kant's aesthetics may have a deeper source: a rationalist (perhaps post-Hegelian) line of interpretation of Kant, perhaps traceable back to Wilfrid Sellars, Robert Brandom, and allied authors, that emphasizes the normativity within experience itself. The latter reading may well rest on a confusion of what is realized in an act of explicit self-awareness (or self-salience) and what *transcendentally* makes that possible. It is hard to put it better than Rebecca Kukla does here: "I think that considerable confusion has arisen because commentators have tried to somehow fit the demand for universality, whatever its normative voice, into the *content* of the judgment of taste. I suggest that it is more helpful to think of this demand as a feature of the *performative force* of the judgment. . . . The *pragmatic function* of this judgment is not to *assert* anything, including anything about universal agreement, but rather to *call for* such agreement."[52] The mistake Kukla identifies is particularly regrettable in the case of such a stirring and energizing experience as the sublime, which Kant at one point characterizes as a kind of "amazement" (Pluhar)

49. Henry E. Allison, *Kant's Theory of Taste: A Reading of the "Critique of Aesthetic Judgment"* (Cambridge: Cambridge University Press, 2001), 343.

50. Katerina Deligiorgi, "How to Feel a Judgment: The Sublime and Its Architectonic Significance," in *Kant and the Faculty of Feeling*, ed. Kelly Sorensen and Diane Williamson (Cambridge: Cambridge University Press, 2018), 166–83, 183.

51. Brady, "Environmental Sublime," 176, 177.

52. Rebecca Kukla, "Introduction: Placing the Aesthetic in Kant's Critical Epistemology," in *Aesthetics and Cognition in Kant's Critical Philosophy* (Cambridge: Cambridge University Press, 2010), 1–32, 14n15 (original emphasis).

or "astonishment" (Guyer/Matthews) ("General Comment," 5:269). It is hard to see how this enlivening and invigorating experience could carry the burden of such heavy cognitive and intellectual content—the latter is best left up to philosophical clarification rather than conceived as belonging to or being part of the content of the experience itself.

In short, neither the normativity of the sublime nor its philosophical ground need be recognized in empirical-psychological acts. Likewise, the sources of pleasure in the sublime need not be identified by the subject in the experience itself. If this reading is correct, this insight may put us in a better position to decipher what is Kant's account from what may be innovative philosophy—perhaps inspired by the Kantian tradition—but not exactly Kant.[53]

53. For comments on parts of this chapter, I thank members of the audience at the University of Pavia, Italy, in June 2018, and am especially grateful to Serena Feloj and Luca Fonnesu. Thanks also to Des Hogan for the invitation to present some of this material in his graduate seminar on the *Critique of Judgment* at Princeton University in March 2017. I thank Antje Kühnast for her invaluable assistance with style and formatting.

Chapter 8

A Matter of Life and Death, or The Anthropological Deduction of the Sublime

Dilek Huseyinzadegan

Kant's "Analytic of the Sublime" in the *Critique of Judgment* is a mess. I say this as I also acknowledge how deeply the poetic and provocative language of the Kantian sublime has influenced the imaginations of many authors, philosophers and nonphilosophers alike, and that, on a phenomenological level, Kant seems to describe here *a universal and eventually life-affirming experience* that we all have with, well, you name it, unrepresentability, radical alterity or otherness, formless nature, boundlessness, infinity, the ineffable, an overwhelming power, and so on. These sections on the feeling and the judgment of the sublime in the third *Critique* are particularly messy, however, because Kant here drops his usual architectonic diligence and proceeds as if the four moments of the sublime are quite self-evident to all, so much so that he will claim later on in the text that the judgement of the sublime does not even require a separate deduction of its universal validity, that its exposition was at the same time its deduction.

Indeed, there is not much disagreement in the scholarship on the sublime that the feeling that Kant is describing in the sections on the mathematical and dynamical sublime is universal. In a way, that which provokes the feeling of the sublime may differ, but that feeling of negative pleasure or terror overcome by actual positive pleasure of safety from and superiority over nature is the defining feature of the sublime, and this feeling is universal—*or so we are told*, even though Kant himself does not provide us with an argument for this supposed universality. I will show that the reason why there is no explicit transcendental deduction of the judgments of the sublime is that there cannot be one: for Kant, they are not in fact universal and thus their modality is not necessity but that of contingency. Taking these judgments as universal even without an explicit transcendental deduction is a mistake that we are forced to make while reading this text: we are "mistaking" the white western European male experience of the sublime for a universal transcultural and thus a transcendental one.[1]

Much has been said about the reason why the judgments of the sublime do not require a deduction that shows exactly how these judgments are universal.[2] Kant mysteriously claims that their exposition was at the same time their deduction, but in his own description of the sublime, there is at best a textual ambiguity between the idea that the sublime requires culture and cognitive cultivation and the claim that it is grounded in a natural predisposition [*Anlage*] in humanity and is therefore universal. I will argue that the messiness that we find in these sections on the sublime and its exposition/deduction has to do not so much with a profound insight as to what Kant considers to be the feeling of the sublime, but *a crucial qualification* undergirding who has a rightful claim to this life-affirming feeling.

In this essay, I will explore this textual ambiguity to show that it can be best resolved by pointing out that Kantian judgments about the sublimity in nature are not universal, and that is why we cannot give a transcendental deduction of them. The point, if I can anticipate, is not that the sublime as such does not describe a universal experience; rather, it is that Kantian sublime is quite specific, particular, and provincial. What we find in the text, rather, is what I will term an "anthropological deduction," namely, an empirical deduction that shows that only a specific type of cultured person has a legitimate right or "entitlement" to the feeling of the sublime as

1. This is not only an epistemic mistake; on this, see Gayatri Chakravorty Spivak, *A Critique of Postcolonial Reason: Toward a History of the Vanishing Present* (Cambridge, MA: Harvard University Press, 1999), 34. On the racialized nature of Kantian (and colonial/modern) aesthetics, see also David Lloyd, *Under Representation: The Racial Regime of Aesthetics* (New York: Fordham University Press, 2019), 44–68.

2. See Paul Guyer, *Kant and the Claims of Taste* (Cambridge, MA: Harvard University Press, 1979), 265–66; Paul Crowther, *The Kantian Sublime: From Morality to Art* (Oxford: Clarendon Press, 1989), 127; Robert Clewis, *The Kantian Sublime and the Revelation of Freedom* (Cambridge: Cambridge University Press, 2009), 138; Thomas Moore, "Kant's Deduction of the Sublime," *Kantian Review* 23, no. 3 (2018): 349–72, 351–53.

Kant describes it. Thus, I argue for two interrelated points: one, no transcendental deduction of the judgment of sublime in the Kantian sense can be given, because the modality of such judgments is contingency, and two, Kant does in fact provide an implicit empirical, that is, an anthropological deduction of these judgments in the text by showing that the feeling of the sublime is contingent upon a specific development of culture and human being. In what follows, I propose that we reconstruct the four moments of the judgment of the sublime and pay our architectonic due diligence. My reading will use Occam's razor; I will go with what Kant *actually* said in the text, rather than what he should have said, and offer the simplest possible explanation of his claims regarding the exposition/deduction of the sublime and the requirement of culture. This reading will also clarify the textual continuity between Kant's claims in the *Observations on the Feeling of the Beautiful and the Sublime* and his supposedly universal account of the sublime in the third *Critique*.[3]

Between the Beautiful and the Sublime

Judgments of beauty and sublimity are two types of pure aesthetic judgments that Kant lays out in the first book of the *Critique of Judgment*. There are various similarities between the two. First of all, Kant tells us that they are both singular reflective judgments that are universally valid for all subjects regarding the feeling of pleasure (§23, 5:244). Neither makes a cognitive claim about the object being judged, so the universal validity of these judgments does not concern cognition, only feeling, meaning that they both describe a universal feeling.

Our judgments regarding the beautiful and the sublime nonetheless differ in many respects: the former is concerned with the *form* of the object, the later with its *formlessness*; the former is a liking that relates the imagination with *the understanding*, the latter signifies a relationship between the imagination and *reason* (§23, 5:244). Most importantly, the feeling of

3. Immanuel Kant, *Observations on the Feeling of the Sublime and Beautiful*, in *Observations on the Feeling of the Sublime and Beautiful and Other Writings*, ed. Patrick Frierson and Paul Guyer (Cambridge: Cambridge University Press, 2011), 9–62. Unless otherwise noted, all citations to the third *Critique* are to paragraph number, then Akademie edition volume and page number, of Kant's *Critique of Judgment*; translations are from the Werner Pluhar translation (Indianapolis: Hackett, 1987).

pleasure that we get in judging the beautiful is immediately life-affirming or life-enhancing, as it is a feeling of life being furthered,[4] whereas the feeling of pleasure in the sublime is indirectly so, in that it signifies "a momentary inhibition of the vital forces followed by an outpouring that is all the stronger" (§23, 5:245). It is important that in both cases we arrive at pleasure, either directly or indirectly, even if our immediate reaction in the case of the sublime is one of repulsion due to "negative pleasure" (§23, 5:244).

In section 24, Kant tells us that his analysis of the judgments of the sublime will consist of four moments; he writes that "since judgments about the sublime are made by the aesthetic reflective power of judgment, [the analytic] must allow us to present the liking for the sublime, just as that for the beautiful, as follows: in terms of *quantity*, as universally valid; in terms of *quality*, as devoid of interest; in terms of *relation*, (as a) subjective purposiveness; and in terms of *modality*, as a necessary subjective purposiveness" (§24, 5:247; my emphases).

Given Kant's usual architectonic tendencies, we are led to believe that what will follow are four sections, each dedicated to an explication of one of these four moments, as was the case in the "Analytic of the Beautiful."

However, this does not turn out to be the case, and things start to get messy here, especially messy for someone like Kant, who is often so diligent to make things work, placing everything to its rightful place in the edifice of the critical system. For starters, the "Analytic of the Sublime" seems to be organized around the binary of the mathematical and dynamical sublime rather than the four moments. For instance, instead of an explicit section on quantity, we have the mathematical sublime—a section that does not really talk about the universal validity of the judgments of the sublime, as promised earlier. Then, section 27, "On the Quality of the Liking in Our Judging of the Sublime," talks not directly about disinterestedness, as we may expect from the introductory remarks above,[5] but about the peculiar quality of the displeasure caused by the vibration and agitation of the mind (§27, 5:258). This agitation eventually turns into pleasure, and the feeling of the sublime is all the more life-affirming because of the purposive arousal of the rational ideas (§27, 5:260).

4. Rudolf A. Makkreel, *Imagination and Interpretation in Kant: The Hermeneutical Import of the "Critique of Judgment"* (Chicago: University of Chicago Press, 1990), 5. On the feeling of life as a pervasive theme in the third *Critique*, see especially 88–107.

5. See also Henry E. Allison, *Kant's Theory of Taste: A Reading of the "Critique of Aesthetic Judgment"* (Cambridge: Cambridge University Press, 2001), 324.

Most importantly for my argument here, when we get to section 29, "On the Modality of a Judgment about the Sublime in Nature," instead of explaining, as he had promised, how these judgments carry with themselves "a necessary subjective purposiveness," Kant tells us that

> we cannot with the same readiness [as in the case of the judgment of beauty] count on others to accept our judgment about the sublime in nature. For it seems that, if we are to pass judgment on that superiority of [such] natural objects, *not only must our aesthetic power of judgment be far more cultivated, but also so must the cognitive powers on which it is based* [bei weitem grössere Cultur nicht bloss der ästhetischen Urteilskraft, sondern auch der Erkenntnissvermögen, die ihr zum Grunde liegen, erforderlich zu sein]. (§29, 5:264; my emphasis)

This means, prima facie, that judgments of the sublime are *not* really universal—the condition for the possibility of these judgments is the cultivation of taste and cognitive faculties. Furthermore, if their possibility depends on the cultivation of both taste and cognitive powers, then judgments of the sublime seem to be a bit more empirically based than we might like for our transcendental inquiry. Note here, however, two things: it is not sufficient that our taste be more cultivated—which might be an empirical, namely, a cultural or physiological matter—but Kant also insists that being able to pass judgment on the sublimity of nature depends on the further development of our cognitive powers, in this case, reason and imagination.

The idea that the sublime requires a pair of more developed cognitive capacities is elucidated by Kant in his examples of the "Savoyard peasant man" and the "savage." In both cases, these men are unable to make judgments about the sublime. When they look at the stormy ocean or the glacier mountains, they find them merely repellent, because they are "uncultured" or "unrefined people" (*rohen Menschen*), lacking in the development of moral ideas (§29, 5:265). They are not "prepared by culture," like Kant, to call that feeling that actually enlarges the mind toward its practical domain "sublime": they merely cower in the face of such terrifying experiences; they remain at the level of displeasure caused by the agitation of the mind. They find such sights "terrifying."

But is this an empirical issue, one that can be solved by an aesthetic education, so to speak, of the "peasant" and the "savage"? Would the "unrefined men," in time and after receiving this kind of an education and cultivation, be able to pass judgment on the sublimity of nature just like Kant?[6] If this is the claim, then judgments of the sublime cannot have a transcendental deduction, because then they would be empirically based and not even belong to transcendental philosophy. But if judgments of the sublime are indeed universal, Kant cannot make them dependent on such empirical contingencies as culture or cultivation. He also explicitly denies this and asserts that there is an a priori basis of these judgments (§29, 5:265–66). This is why we would need a transcendental deduction, to show its a priori basis, in order to explain how *all* human beings are entitled to this kind of a claim and feeling. Kant then needs to show that the cultivation of our cognitive capacities has an a priori basis.

Things get even more complicated at this point in the text. Kant says that no separate deduction is needed here, because we just need to note that the sublime is "attributed merely to our way of thinking, or rather, to the foundation this has in human nature" (§30, 5:280). These judgments, he notes, "contain a purposive relation of the cognitive powers, which we must lay *a priori* at the basis of the power of purposes (the will) and which is therefore itself *a priori* purposive; and that already provides their deduction, i.e., the justification of the claim of such a judgment to universally necessary validity."

This cannot be the reason why the sublime does not require a separate deduction, however, because the feeling of the beautiful *also* refers to a way of thinking, to a purposive relationship between the two faculties, of imagination and the understanding, and yet there is an official, separate deduction of the judgments of the beautiful in the text. If showing that a feeling is grounded in a purposive relationship of the human faculties is sufficient for a deduction, then it is the beautiful, not the sublime, that should not require a deduction separate from its exposition. As Henry E. Allison puts it, "since sensitivity to the sublime requires a much greater degree of mental cultivation than the capacity to appreciate the beautiful (at least in nature), the modality of judgments of sublimity seems more problematic."[7] Allison also points out that Kant's explanation here about exposition being the deduction only covers the dynamically sublime (since it relates to the

---

6. As both Spivak and Lloyd point out, the idea of just such an aesthetic education seems to be Friedrich Schiller's wager; Spivak, *Critique of Postcolonial Reason*, 15–16, 30–31; Lloyd, *Under Representation*, 59, 69–94.

7. Allison, *Kant's Theory of Taste*, 333.

will), and not the mathematical sublime.[8] Regardless, the question reemerges: What exactly in its exposition was the deduction of the sublime?

Deduction of the Judgment of the Sublime as Its Modality

Allison interprets Kant's claim that the judgments of the sublime do not require a deduction of their own as follows:

> Kant does not deny that the sublime requires a deduction, but merely that it needs one distinct from its exposition. Kant does not tell us where in this exposition, that is, in the Analytic of the Sublime, the deduction is to be found; but it seems clear that the only plausible candidate is its final section (§29), which deals with the modality of the sublime. Moreover, even though this section is officially included within the dynamically sublime, Kant speaks there of the sublime as such and evidently intended the account to cover both species.[9]

I agree with Allison that section 29 is where a supposed deduction should take place. The question about the deduction, to repeat, is the following: If "we cannot with the same readiness [as in the case of judgment of beauty] count on others to accept our judgment about the sublime in nature," then what does it mean for our aesthetic power of judgment as well as our cognitive powers on which the sublime is based to be more cultivated, and more importantly, for this cultivation to have an a priori, not empirical, basis? Let me look at how Kant elaborates on this cultivation in the remainder of section 29.

Kant makes four interrelated points here to unpack his idea of cultivation of the cognitive powers: First, he says that the mind must be "receptive to ideas." When reason exerts its power over sensibility in the feeling of the sublime, this is not domination for its own sake, but it is for the sake of expanding sensibility to a point commensurate with reason's own, that is, practical domain (§29, 5:265). Second, and relatedly, if reason's dominion over sensibility merely repels an uncultured person, this is because they are "lacking in the development of moral ideas," and thus

8. Allison, *Kant's Theory of Taste*, 334–36.

9. Allison, *Kant's Theory of Taste*, 332.

"one must be *prepared by culture to be able to judge something as sublime*" (§29, 5:265; my emphasis). This is where we have his example of the "good and otherwise sensible Savoyard peasant," who cannot judge glacier mountains as sublime, because he cannot see past the hardships associated with them. He is unable to make the leap from this hardship and agitation of his mind to the "sublime vocation" of reason; he finds it merely terrifying (§29, 5:265).[10] However, third, just because the judgment of the sublime requires culture and receptivity of the mind to ideas of reason, we cannot say that it was initially produced by culture. This would make the sublime a social convention of sorts, the result of an empirical cultivation of taste and cognitive powers, which Kant denies, as I have also mentioned above (§29, 5:265). In order to underscore that the feeling of the sublime is not empirically developed but has an a priori basis, Kant tells us that this feeling originates from something in human nature. On this fourth point, he writes that the feeling of the sublime "has its foundation in human nature: in something that, along with common sense, we may require and demand of everyone, namely, *the predisposition to the feeling for (practical) ideas, i.e., to moral feeling* [Anlage zum Gefühl für (praktische) Ideen, d.i., zu dem moralischen]" (§29, 5:265; my emphasis).

Allison argues that, despite some of the inconsistencies in the text regarding Kant's claims about culture and civilization, we can nonetheless take the judgments of the sublime to be universally grounded. He takes the statement about "the predisposition to the feeling for practical ideas, i.e., to the moral feeling," as the core of Kant's deduction, for Kant ends this thought by saying that "this is what underlies the necessity—which we include in our judgment of the sublime—of the assent of other people's judgment to our own" (§29, 5:265).[11] Allison squares Kant's claim in section 28 that " 'even the commonest judgment' can judge on the basis of the principle underlying the feeling of the sublime" with his statements about the "peasant" and the "savage" not being able to judge so by saying that Kant is arguing for the commonality of judging something as higher than life, not necessarily for a consciousness of its ground. That is, according to Allison, everyone, even the commonest judgment, is capable of judging based on "the principle" that underlies judgments of the sublime—while Kant does not tell us what this principle is, the fact that "even the savage is capable of

10. "Merely terrifying" is a sub-category of the feeling of the sublime in *Observations*; see 2:209–10.

11. Allison, *Kant's Theory of Taste*, 333–35.

an aesthetic appreciation of the sublimity of the warrior" suggests that he can make such a judgment, "albeit lacking a consciousness of its ground."[12] Thus, for Allison, the supposed ambiguity regarding the universality of the judgments of sublimity only concerns the *quid facti* (what is the case) rather than the *quid juris* (what ought to be the case).[13] We can say that everyone, including the "savage" and the "peasant" ought to make judgments of the sublime, even though they do not actually identify the feeling as sublime.

If the predisposition (*Anlage*) to moral feeling is found in everyone, then, Allison concludes, "after all, even Kant's savage and the uncultivated Savoyard peasant *supposedly* have this predisposition, and so we may assume that with the appropriate cultivation they could come to appreciate the sublime" (my emphasis). Thus, even if they do not really understand *why* they might find something sublime, they do have the potential to do so—*if*, indeed, they supposedly have this predisposition (*Anlage*) to moral ideas. This is a big "if" that is in no way justified in the text, as I will show next.

Culture and *Anlage*: A Feeling for Moral Ideas

Here we need to go back to the differences between the beautiful and the sublime, specifically to the cognitive powers involved in each kind of judgment: in judgments of beauty, a relationship is established between the understanding and the imagination, whereas in judgments of the sublime, the negative-turned-positive pleasure results from a back-and-forth between reason and imagination (§23, 5:244). If the judgment of the sublime requires that these two cognitive powers, namely, the imagination and practical reason, are more developed, then everyone must be able to develop these capacities in order for such judgments to be truly universal.

Rudolf Makkreel helpfully clarifies what Kant might have meant by the claim that the exposition of the sublime is its deduction in his seminal work *Imagination and Interpretation in Kant: The Hermeneutical Import of the "Critique of Judgment."*[14] Importantly, he argues that, "if recognition of limits

12. This seems to be an example of the "terrifying sublime," again, harkening back to *Observations*, 2:209.

13. Allison, *Kant's Theory of Taste*, 334.

14. Makkreel frames the main difference between the judgments of the beautiful and the sublime in terms of the role of imagination in each case and shows that the sublime is incorporated into transcendental philosophy due to its activation of a regress of the imagination; see *Imagination and Interpretation*, 79–84.

is made evident in the very exposition of the sublime, then it in fact needs no separate deduction."[15] Contra Paul Guyer, who argues that there is no deduction of the sublime because it refers to the formless,[16] Makkreel shows that there is a form or purpose undergirding the feeling of the sublime: it is true that we make judgments of beauty with reference to a purposiveness of the object, but "the judgments of the sublime involve *a purposiveness of the subject*."[17] The purposiveness at stake in the sublime is *a moral purposiveness*—a consciousness of the moral vocation of the mind, practical reason. This jibes well with the idea, as Makkreel also points out later, that one needs *cultural development* in order to appreciate the sublime.[18] Lastly for Makkreel, the very condition of possibility of judgments of the sublime is the recognition of the limits of one's cognitive faculties.[19] Out of this recognition we first experience an inadequacy that is nonetheless overcome by superiority.

The crux of the matter is that *neither* this recognition of limits *nor* the subsequent awareness of the moral vocation is transcendentally or universally grounded in the text. Even Allison's most charitable interpretation that "the savage and the peasant" do judge something as "higher than life" admits that they will not know *why* they judge it as such. Thus, they will not be recognizing the limits of their existence and cognitive powers without being afraid of these limits. If they cannot recognize these limits, they will also be unable to make the jump from being merely terrified to the awareness of a purpose higher than life, to their moral vocation.[20] For these "raw men," the experience of being terrified is all that there is here; the inhibition of their vital powers is not then followed by "an outpouring of them that is all the stronger," and so these men do not make the transition to a life-affirming feeling.

Kant continues to confuse us in section 29, when he contrasts this feeling of the sublime with taste itself:

> But we demand both taste and feeling of every person, and if he has any culture at all, we presuppose that he has them. But we do so with this difference: taste we demand unhesitatingly

15. Makkreel, *Imagination and Interpretation*, 81.

16. Guyer, *Claims of Taste*, 265–66.

17. Makkreel, *Imagination and Interpretation*, 83.

18. Makkreel, *Imagination and Interpretation*, 84 (my emphasis).

19. Makkreel, *Imagination and Interpretation*, 84.

20. Compare *Observations*, 2:209–10.

> from everyone, because here judgment refers the imagination merely to the understanding, our power of concepts; in the case of feeling, on the other hand, judgment refers the imagination to reason, our power of ideas, and so we demand feeling *only under a subjective presupposition* (*though we believe we are justified and permitted to require [fulfilment of] this presupposition in everyone*): *we presuppose moral feeling in man*. And so we attribute necessity to this kind of aesthetic judgment as well. (§29, 5:265–66; my emphasis)

The only possible candidate for the transcendental and a priori basis of the feeling of the sublime is this requirement of a moral feeling in man.[21] Again, we are supposed to be able to count on everyone having this moral feeling, because of the predisposition (*Anlage*) toward it. If Kant showed that everyone has this predisposition and that this is a transcendental rather than a cultural or subjective capacity, then we would indeed have a transcendental deduction of the sublime, even if it were not explicitly named as such.

However, Kant argues in the text precisely that we cannot count on everyone having this *Anlage*. If this were a warranted a priori presupposition, we would not be able to say that those *rohen Menschen* lack this capacity to judge something as sublime, or, with Allison, that they lack the consciousness of the ground of this judgment. The judgments of the sublime are not about the external world, and thus they are not objective—so they require that the subjects making this type of a judgment actually have this feeling *and* understand it as such as well. Kant's claim here that "we believe we are justified and permitted to require (fulfilment of) this presupposition" is an empirical one. Just earlier in the text he showed that we are justified in the case of cultured men, but not in the case of the "savage" and the "peasant" men, for the latter do not have this feeling.

Does this make the sublime just a more refined feeling? If this is the case, it becomes more difficult to locate the qualitative differences between the feeling of the sublime in the third *Critique* and the just more refined feeling that he describes in the *Observations on the Feeling of the Beautiful and the*

21. I follow Kant in using "man" here, and it will become clearer later in the essay that it is not necessarily interchangeable with all human beings for Kant. On the gender-neutral use of language in talking about Kant's thought, see Pauline Kleingeld, "The Philosophical Status of Gender-Neutral Language in the History of Philosophy: The Case of Kant," *Philosophical Forum* 25, no. 2 (1993): 134–50.

Sublime. The judgments of the sublime here in the *Critique* are supposed to carry with them a kind of necessity that has a priori principles as their basis, and they are in this way "lifted out of the reach of empirical psychology" and brought to transcendental philosophy (§29, 5:266). However, there is nothing in the text that warrants this supposition, especially when we look at the way in which culture operates as an empirical precondition for the ability to judge something as sublime. Thus, conditions for the possibility of judgments of the sublime, which were supposedly transcendental, turn out to be empirical conditions regarding human nature and cultural development.[22]

This feeling of moral purpose or vocation is not a priori and in fact developed empirically, through culture of skill (*Geschicklichkeit*) and of discipline (*Zucht*). Kant says this much when he claims that in the case of the sublime "the liking concerns only our ability's vocation, revealed in such cases, insofar as the predisposition [*Anlage*] to this ability is part of our nature, *whereas it remains up to us, as our obligation, to develop and exercise this ability*" (§28, 5:262; my emphasis). Later in the "Critique of Teleological Judgment," Kant writes that, together with culture of skill (*Geschicklichkeit*), culture of discipline (*Zucht*) is what we need in order to develop as moral agents. While *Geschicklichkeit* is an aptitude for setting ends in general, *Zucht* helps to free the will from the "despotism of desires" (§83, 5:282).[23] In a word, the condition for the possibility of being able to recognize the limits of one's cognitive capacities and appreciating these limits as an indicator of one's moral purpose seems to be empirically grounded, as it is a matter of what Kant will call later in the third *Critique* the culture of discipline (*Zucht*) (§83, 5:432).

Makkreel further shows that culture of skill alone is not sufficient for our full development; we need culture of discipline in order to "gain some rational control over [our natural desires] so that we are no longer tied to sensuous objects alone."[24] It is a type of aesthetic education or a process of civilization, then, that will allow us to distance ourselves from the sensible world and the sensuous objects, such as the hardships associated with the

22. The corruption of its transcendental nature here might be yet another reason why the sublime is a "mere appendix to our aesthetic judgment," which is thoroughly transcendental (§23, 5:246).

23. On the Eurocentric overdetermination of *Geschicklichkeit* in Kant's thought, see Dilek Huseyinzadegan, *Kant's Nonideal Theory of Politics* (Chicago: Northwestern University Press, 2019), 87–116.

24. Makkreel, *Imagination and Interpretation*, 139.

glacier mountains, and to come closer to appreciating the supersensible, the ideas. This is what it means to be "receptive to ideas"; one needs to be prepared by culture of discipline (*Zucht*) to be able to appreciate the sublime and judge it as such.[25]

The feeling of the sublime will "awaken the ideas of reason" in those who have a certain predisposition (*Anlage*) toward morality. Gayatri Chakravorty Spivak translates *Anlage* as a tendency as well as a blueprint or a program.[26] This is in line with Makkreel's suggestion that we need to cultivate our sensibility to rid ourselves of the despotism of the sensuous world by means of a program of morality. Judgments of the sublime require, then, a certain kind of person with the *Anlage*, the blueprint, already programmed toward being "receptive" to the appreciation of that which is larger than life. It turns out that since we cannot count on the fulfilment of this tendency or blueprint in everyone, it cannot really be presupposed a priori. Douglas Burnham points this out:

> There is an empirical factor which is required for the sublime: the mind of the experiencer must be "receptive" to rational ideas, and this can only happen in a culture that *already* understands morality as being a function of freedom or, more generally, conceives of human beings as having a dimension which in some way transcends nature. *The sublime, properly speaking, is possible only for members of such a moral culture (and, Kant sometimes suggests, may reciprocally contribute to the strengthening of that culture).* So, the sublime is subjected to an empirical contingency.[27] (my emphasis)

In the end, however, Burnham also reconciles this idea of an empirical contingency by claiming that "we are justified in demanding from everyone that they necessarily have the *transcendental conditions* for such moral culture, and thus for the sublime, because these conditions are (as in the

---

25. While I cannot develop this idea here, note that the German word for culture of discipline here, *Zucht*, can also mean "breed," "stock," and "breeding" and "rearing," suggesting a specific breed or stock of people from a known lineage who can develop their capacities according to the program of practical (moral) reason.

26. Spivak, *Critique of Postcolonial Reason*, 11.

27. Douglas Burnham, "Immanuel Kant: Aesthetics," in *Internet Encyclopedia of Philosophy*, accessed January 19, 2019, https://www.iep.utm.edu/kantaest/#SH2c.

case of the beautiful) the same as for theoretical and practical thought in general."[28]

The issue at stake, of course, is whether or not we can count on, in the Kantian schema, everyone having the same conditions for such moral culture, even if they are the same for theoretical and practical thought. If the so-called transcendental conditions of moral culture consist of being able to separate sensibility from reason and feeling the superiority of the latter over the former, then such moral culture starts to sound provincial, not universal. And if the "unrefined men" are unable to do this, then these conditions of moral purposiveness are not really transcendental: they are empirical. It is clear that the "raw men" are incapable of practical thought, practical reason, or practical ideas. Even if Thomas Moore is right that we all have the same power of imagination (transcendentally speaking),[29] it does not seem to be the case that, for Kant, we all have the same *Anlage* or blueprint for moral culture. So even if the imaginations of all the observers operate in the same way transcendentally, practical reason still needs culture to become receptive to ideas and therefore to be able to judge something as sublime as opposed to being merely terrified of it. The judgments of the sublime do not seem to be transcendentally grounded after all—unless we go ahead and posit European culture and civilization as *the* transcendental conditions for the possibility of making such judgments.

What Is in a Deduction?

A deduction is a claim of legitimacy and entitlement established through proper ancestry or lineage. In the *Critique of Pure Reason*, Kant writes that, "when speaking of entitlements and claims, jurists distinguish in a legal matter between the questions about what is lawful (*quid juris*) and that which concerns the fact (*quid facti*), they demand proof of both, they call the first, that which is to establish entitlement or the legal claim, the deduction" (A84/B116).[30] While giving a transcendental deduction of our entitlement to the a priori pure concepts of the understanding in the first *Critique*, Kant tells us here that proofs from experience are not sufficient

28. See also Clewis, *The Kantian Sublime.*

29. Moore, "Kant's Deduction of the Sublime," 351–52.

30. Immanuel Kant, *Critique of Pure Reason,* trans. and ed. Paul Guyer and Allen W. Wood (Cambridge: Cambridge University Press, 1998).

to show that these concepts are lawful for experience. And yet, proofs from experience are what Kant gives us in the third *Critique* to establish the lawfulness or the universality of the feeling of the sublime. He is not explaining the way in which this feeling can relate to its objects a priori, which would amount to a transcendental deduction. Rather, he is showing us that the sublime is acquired through being prepared by previous experience and through reflection on one's moral purpose—this is his definition of an empirical deduction (A85/B117). His exposition/deduction of the sublime in the third *Critique* is not about its universality or lawfulness, but about how certain people come to possess it, and have a right to claim it. This corrupts the transcendental nature of the judgments of the sublime and shows that the modality of these judgments is contingency: they depend on a kind of culture that understands morality to be a function of freedom, where supersensible ideas constitute the basis of the feeling of the sublime.

Grounding the judgments of the sublime in the moral *Anlage* only shows that their lineage or ancestry is that of experience of a white western European kind of culture of discipline (*Zucht*). Deriving the ancestry of the experience of the sublime not from a priori sources but from a fact of moral culture is not a transcendental deduction, but an empirical one. Thus, Kant is providing in the text an anthropological ground for the judgments of the sublime, or, what we may call an empirical or an anthropological deduction that shows that only white western European educated, upper-middle-class, refined/civilized, or urban men are entitled to make these kinds of judgments.[31] This is what many Kant interpreters take as transcendental in order to be able to make sense of his claims about the universality of the judgments of the sublime.

In conclusion, I agree that the only plausible candidate for a transcendental deduction of the sublime is located in section 29 of the *Critique of Judgment*; I disagree, however, with the impulse to make Kant's claim more consistent than warranted by the text. I suggest that we do not, by default, trust Kant that this judgment is universal, because I do not find evidence in the text that clearly shows this. A transcendental deduction has to show that the judgments in question have an a priori basis. Kant fails to show in the exposition of the sublime that the *Anlage* grounding this feeling is a priori. More importantly, he does say, again and again, that it is in fact tied to

31. On this point and how this exclusion bears on politics, public sphere, or subjecthood in general, see also Spivak, *Critique of Postcolonial Reason*, 14; David Lloyd, *Under Representation*, 59–61.

cultural development and thus a posteriori. One way to answer the question why the judgments of the sublime do not require a separate deduction then would be to say that there cannot be a transcendental deduction of these judgments because they are not universal. By Occam's razor, the simplest textual reading highlights Kant's empirical or anthropological deduction and in this way removes any ambiguity or inconsistency that we find in the text regarding the role of culture in appreciating the sublime. Kant does not give us any reason to think that culture is a transcendental construct; furthermore, he explicitly names culture and civilization as prerequisites of the feeling of the sublime.[32]

The fact that the sublime requires culture, a particular culture, brings the *Critique of Judgment* into closer relationship to the *Observations on the Feeling of the Beautiful and the Sublime*. As Meg Armstrong reminds us, there is a "prevalent association between the sublime and various, embodied, forms of difference," which points to a continuity, despite the so-called "critical turn," between the *Observations* and the *Critique of Judgment*.[33] Obviously, the third *Critique* belongs to the critical system, and as such, judgments about universal validity require transcendental deductions, not just phenomenological or "physiological" observations. Kant here cannot just get away with saying things like, "the blonde is beautiful, brunette is sublime" (2:213) or "the night is sublime, the day is beautiful" (2:209), as he did in the *Observations*. But there is an important textual continuity between his claims regarding (white) women's and non-Western, non-European, non-white people's lack of appreciation of the sublime in the *Observations* (2:228–31; 2:252–56) and the necessity of a *certain* kind of culture and predisposition here in the third *Critique*. In his *Observations*, we find a straightforward empirical and anthropological deduction of the feeling of the sublime allocated to gendered, racialized, and nationalized moral predispositions (or the lack thereof). In that previous work, the fact that culture, race, and sex/gender are the preconditions of being able to have a feeling of the sublime is clear. These so-called empirical conditions, while ostensibly not in the text of the

32. On specific European culture as the bridge between nature and freedom for Kant, see also Inder S. Marwah, "Bridging Nature and Freedom? Kant, Culture, and Cultivation," *Social Theory and Practice* 38, no. 3 (2012): 385–406.

33. Meg Armstrong, " 'The Effects of Blackness': Gender, Race, and the Sublime in Aesthetic Theories of Burke and Kant," *Journal of Aesthetics and Art Criticism* 54, no. 3 (1996): 213–36, 213.

third *Critique*, seem to have gained a transcendental ground after the critical turn. In other words, if Kant wanted to move this feeling from empirical psychology or anthropology to transcendental philosophy and to show the legitimacy of the sublime a priori in the *Critique of Judgment*, then he would need to leave this precritical conception, which is so closely tied to culture, civilization, race, nationality, and gender, behind. Instead, he put a certain kind of predisposition and its cultural development via discipline (*Zucht*) at the basis of the feeling of the sublime in the third *Critique*. This means that, if there is a deduction, a proof of lineage that legitimizes this kind of feeling, it is an empirical or anthropological one that ascribes it to a certain kind of people with a certain kind of culture and civilization.

The case that Kant's notion of culture is not universal but Eurocentric has been made in the literature for the past few decades.[34] In this essay, I simply wanted to point out that in our interpretations of the Kantian sublime, we trust him too much when he says that something is universal to actually pay attention to *how he frames and conceives of this universality*. The text is far less ambiguous on the deduction if we take seriously his examples of cultured and uncultured men and the inability of the latter to appreciate the sublime. Rather than being unfortunate and dismissible prejudices of his time, I have shown that his claims about the "raw men" frame his entire discussion of the feeling of the sublime and its legitimacy, so much so that these remarks in fact provide an anthropological exposition and deduction of the sublime. This means that cultural, ethnic, or racial judgments continue to play a central role in the formation of Kant's, and by extension, modern aesthetic theory.

In the way that Kant describes and justifies it, then, the sublime is a feeling that exclusively belongs to white, Western, educated or urban European men. Even if Allison might have a point in saying that the "savage" or the "peasant" man might have this feeling without realizing its actual ground, Makkreel reminds us that being conscious of this ground, that is, the limits of one's cognitive capacities, is part of the feeling or the *Anlage* (blueprint) itself. So, the "unrefined men" overall are barred from the domain of this life-affirming feeling. If this feeling is a temporary inhibition of vital powers, followed by a stronger outpouring of them upon consciousness of

34. See Tsenay Serequeberhan, "Eurocentrism in Philosophy: The Case of Immanuel Kant," *Philosophical Forum* 27, no. 4 (1996): 333–56; Marwah, "Bridging Nature and Freedom?"; Huseyinzadegan, *Kant's Nonideal Theory*, 87–103, among others.

its ground in the purposiveness of the will, then the "raw men," lacking the innate predisposition to moral ideas, will not achieve this second step into full humanity[35]—to them, the sublime is not life-affirming or enhancing; it is "merely terrifying" and rather deadly.

35. On the life and death of nonEuropeans in Kant's thought, see also Mark Larrimore, "The Sublime Waste: Kant on the Destiny of the Races," *Canadian Journal of Philosophy* 29, no. 1 (1999): 99–125.

Chapter 9

On the *Sensus Communis* as a Feeling of Life

Rodolphe Gasché

In a judgment that declares something to be beautiful, whether it is an object of nature or of art, the one who judges is not a subject in general, but a singular subject who by his or her judgment has submitted the object to his or her "own eyes" (§8, 5:216).[1] Furthermore, this subject in its very singularity calls from the start upon "the entire sphere *of judging persons* [*der Urteilenden*]" (§8, 5:215) for assent—not, however, to all of them in the abstract, but to each singular individual in this sphere. As Kant writes, concerning the sphere in question, "we solicit everyone else's assent [*um jedes anderen*]" (§19, 5:237); that is, from each one individually. The judging subject "expects" (*zumutet*) assent to their judgment (§8, 5:216); "*requires* [*sinnet . . . an*, ascribes, or imputes] this agreement from everyone"; "lay[s] claim [*macht Anspruch*] to the agreement [*Beitritt*] of everyone"; "expects [*erwartet*] confirmation . . . from the agreement of others"; " counts [*sich verspricht*, promises himself] on everyone's assent"; and "holds [*will*, wishes] that everyone *ought* to give their approval [*Beifall geben*] to the object at hand and that he too should declare it beautiful" (§19, 5:237). In other words, a judgment of taste *is* not simply of universal sweep—that would imply

1. All page references in the text are to Immanuel Kant, *Critique of Judgment*, trans. Werner Pluhar (Indianapolis: Hackett, 1987). Kant also says that in a judgment of taste, "I must hold the object directly up to *my* feeling of pleasure and displeasure" (§8, 5:215; emphasis mine).

exorbitant foolishness—rather, its universality (under the condition that the judgment is correctly made) is tied to its assent by all others who judge.[2] Indeed, the judging subject expects their judgment to be confirmed by each other participant in the sphere of those who judge, who do so individually. Now, the judging subject not only passively "expects" all individual others to join him or her, but as the specific verbs Kant uses demonstrate, he or she seems actively to "solicit everyone else's assent" (*wirbt um . . . Beistimmung*) (§19, 5:237), and even "demand[s] [*fordern*] universal assent" (§22, 5:239) when making such a judgment. The prefix *Bei-* in *Beistimmung*, *Beitritt*, or *Beifall* clearly emphasizes that what is demanded, or solicited, of others is to join the one who judges through assent with him or her. All these terms with the prefix *Bei-* imply that others are expected and asked to come together not only in approval of the judgment, but to enter into a relation with the judging subject intent on forming on this occasion a community of sorts. By thus calling upon the confirmation and approval of others, and "actively" soliciting it, the aesthetic judgment shows itself to be intrinsically interwoven with the web of human relations in a way that theoretical or practical judgments are not.

A judgment of taste is one in which its subject reaches out to all other subjects, imputing first of all that everyone, now and in the future, when making such a judgment, is dependent on everyone's potential consent. It is a kind of judgment that ab initio implicates all others to stand in a relation of community to its utterer.[3] Judgments that are grounded on objective concepts, or on the moral law, have a universal validity that does not need to demand that others join in. Such agreement is presupposed from the beginning. However, in aesthetic judgments the presupposition is

2. Gérard Lebrun remarks that the very universality that the judging subject claims with seemingly crazy arrogance "already limits the exorbitance of its pretention: the right to speak in the name of all others is a right that I expect to be granted to me from the outside, and through the opinions of the others." Gérard Lebrun, *Kant et la fin de la métaphysique* (Paris: Armand Colin, 1970), 555.

3. It is not insignificant that, when Kant in section 8 formulates for the first time the peculiar claim to universal validity that comes with a judgment of taste, he uses the German verb *ansinnen*. This conveys a particular privilege to this verb over all the other substitutes that he will later employ. Rendering *ansinnen* as "to require," "to impute," or "to ascribe" is certainly correct, but its meaning in Middle High German as *an einen sinnen*, in the sense of *jemanden angehen um etwas*—that is, approaching, if not going (*gehen*) to someone in view of something—gives this verb a much more active thrust than the one suggested by its English translation.

of an entirely different order. In each of its judgments, the judging subject evokes or actualizes something universal that, because it originates in the subject itself, obliges this subject and requires it to appeal to others for assent. It is a call to others that animates his relation to others, and vice versa. All the acts of solicitation of the assent of others are acts by which a community with everyone is sought and (ideally) established. The appeal to all others individually is the index that something is requested (from all others individually) that seeks and confirms a basic agreement. Kant refers to this agreement at one point as "an original contract dictated by (our) very humanity" (§42, 5:297), but this reference occurs in the context of a chapter that investigates the empirical interest in the beautiful, and hence its significance regarding the human being's natural inclination to sociability. However, in the transcendental inquiry of the third *Critique*, this contract is only of the order of an idea that at once is presupposed and initiated by every individual who judges, and who calls on all others individually to participate in this judgment as an example of the idea in question.

Yet even though a judgment on the beautiful addresses itself to all other judging subjects, and expects and solicits assent from all of them individually, it is only in society—in actual empirical life with others—and, moreover, only in one where human beings are sufficiently skilled to do so, that one "has the inclination . . . to [actually] communicate this pleasure to others . . . and is not satisfied with an object unless he can feel his liking for it in community with others" (§41, 5:297). Only under such empirical conditions can everyone expect and demand from everyone else a regard to universal communication.[4] By contrast, before all empirical interest into the beautiful can arise in conjunction with "the urge [*Trieb*] to society" (§41, 5:296) natural to human beings—that is, the anthropological, cultural, and psychological tendency toward sociability (*Geselligkeit*)—Kant's analysis of the judgment of taste shows that such a judgment, because of the absence in it of objective concepts, has the peculiarity of only imputing or ascribing a consent to all individual others without yet implying any attempt to actually talk them into an agreement. Needless to say, Kant's talk of the judging subject soliciting the consent of all others has an anthropological and empirical ring, but this demand, or expectation, must not only be held free of such connotations; it is also a first attempt to articulate the

4. Editor's note: See Dilek Huseyinzadegan's chapter for an analysis that puts pressure on precisely this kind of contingency in Kant's account—in her case, with respect to Kant's discussion of the sublime.

implications of aesthetic judgment's strange claim to universality, in short, its essential communicability in advance of what will be referred to as a *sensus communis* to be construed as the latter's condition of possibility. However, before delving deeper into these aspects of the claim made by a judgment of taste, let us not forget the complex interrelation with all others that its formation implies. By imputing universality, an aesthetic judgment made by a singular subject inaugurates a living relation to all other individual subjects, and vice versa. In other words, it is a judgment that presupposes that the singular subject shares something with all others, and that, at the same time, animates his or her intertwinement with a kind of communal life.

Contrary to Hans-Georg Gadamer's contention that Kant's "subjectivist" interpretation of the judgment of taste, abandons the moralist and political tradition of the *sensus communis* and its concern with practical life, but contrary also to Hannah Arendt's reductive interpretation of Kant's understanding of the *sensus communis* as a psychological and empirical sense for community,[5] it should already be clear from what I have so far shown about the judgment of taste that with its concern one finds oneself right in the middle of the universal conditions of sociability (*Geselligkeit*). At stake in a judgment of taste is, indeed, an activity through which the judging subject becomes a being capable of life with others. What appears as the universal condition of possibility of such togetherness is on the part of the judging subject the call on others for consent, a call that is an active expectation. The aesthetic judgment reaches out to all others, one by one, and expects of them reciprocation through consent. On the part of the other, the possibility of assent rests on the judging subject's successful freeing of their judgment of everything private, or particular. With the aesthetic judgement one touches therefor not at the core, or heart of community—these notions already presuppose its existence, or consider it to be a given—but at the problematic of community as something to be accomplished on universal grounds, in short as an idea, that is, as a task.

Notwithstanding the fact that a judgment of taste does not make its subject drum up assent for his assertion by persuading others in rhetorical or discursive fashion of its truth—indeed, if this were possible it would only convince a limited number of individuals, not all others as a judgment of taste demands, and thus such a judgment could never claim universality—it

5. Hans-Georg Gadamer, *Truth and Method*, trans. Joel Weinsheimer and Donald G. Marshall (New York: Continuum, 1995); Hannah Arendt, *Lectures on Kant's Political Philosophy*, ed. Ronald Beiner (Chicago: University of Chicago Press, 1982).

is a judgment that merely imputes universal assent. What that means, first of all, is that an aesthetic judgment of the beautiful is in essence a public judgment, even if it is made in silence or in isolation from others. Already in section 8 Kant asserts that in distinction from private judgments, judgments of taste "are put forward as having general validity (as being public)" (5:214). How are we to understand "public" in this context? It certainly does not mean that judgments of taste require a factual public, as opposed to a private space for their utterance, but only that their intrinsic claim to universality implies an appeal to all others. Their public nature consists in their intrinsic claim to a universality that is interwoven with the demand that all others should confirm their estimation.[6] In making such judgments that lay claim to the consent of everyone, the singular subject, as Kant holds, believes themself to have (*für sich zu haben*) "a universal voice"; that is, a voice common to all; a voice that is universal in that it seeks the agreement of everyone (5:216). Kant's writes:

> Nothing is postulated in a judgment of taste except such a *universal voice* about a liking unmediated by concepts. Hence all that is postulated is the *possibility* of a judgment that is aesthetic and yet can be considered valid for everyone. The judgment of taste itself does not *postulate* everyone's agreement (since only a logically universal judgment can do that, because it can adduce reasons); it merely requires [*sinnet . . . an*] this agreement from everyone, as an instance of the rule, an instance regarding which it expects confirmation not from concepts but from the agreement of others. Hence the universal voice is only an idea. (5:216)

6. When Kant remarks that what is "strange" (*befremdlich*) about the taste of reflection is that it cannot only demand "such agreement universally, and that it does in fact require this agreement from everyone for each of its judgments," but that what those who "make these judgments dispute about [*in Streite sind*] is *not* whether such a claim is possible" (§8, 5:214; emphasis mine and translation modified), even if in particular cases it remains questionable whether such a claim has been correctly made, the point is that there is an undisputed unanimity (*Einstimmung*) regarding their possibility. In other words, the universality claim of judgments of taste is one for whose principal possibility uncontested universality exists. This agreement and absence of conflict is in a way the minimal nexus of all communality. Let me also point out that what Kant says about having arguments (*Streiten*) about aesthetic judgments, which as such cannot be disputed, presupposes certainty regarding the possibility of making judgments about the beautiful that can legitimately claim universality. Arguing is possible only where the protagonists are not in conflict regarding the possibility in question.

In making a judgment such as "this is beautiful," nothing is predicated in an objective manner about the object of a representation. As a consequence, the universality that is ascribed to it must be of "a special kind" (5:215). It is a universality that concerns something regarding only the subject, but that, nonetheless, "extends" over the whole sphere of all those who judge. The universal voice postulated by the singular subject is not universal, however, in the sense that everyone else has already been bound by the voice in question (as in the case with conceptual rules, or the concept of the good). This voice's claim to universality will only be confirmed if all others consent to it. Postulating this universal voice on grounds that are subjective rather than objective, confirmation by all other individual subjects as judging subjects is the only way in which this claim to universality is validated. It is, therefore, "only" an idea because no number of actual confirmations could ever validate the claim in question. Even though Kant does not elaborate on whether it is an idea of reason, or only an analogon of it in the domain of the sensible, or whether it is constitutive or regulative, the fact that only the assent of all others, one by one, seems to be able to validate it, suggests, at first, that it is an idea in a regulative sense. One by one, the judging subject demands assent of all others, thus highlighting the universality of the subjective determining ground of the judgment in question, but also that this judgment's universality is not possible without an "active" task of seeking consent.

For the time being, I leave the issue regarding the status of this idea without a response. However, for the point that I intend to make, the fact that the claim to universality in a judgment of taste by one subject is constitutively intertwined with the plurality of all other subjects is crucial. Every plural other is solicited and expected to exemplify the rule according to which this universal voice can only be validated by everyone's individual *Beitritt*. Simply put, the universal voice is a voice that accomplishes universality only through the *Einstimmung* of all other voices; in short, by entering into a community with all the voices of the others—a community that it does not only presuppose but of which such a judgment is also exemplary, and formative, in what amounts to an infinite process of approximation. Life in community with others is the horizon with respect to which a judgment of taste is uttered, and that by appealing to communal consent of others also furthers life together. Even though the example only illustrates the empirical interest in the beautiful, Kant's assertion in section 41 that "someone abandoned on some desolate island" would not "just for himself" adorn him or herself (5:297), clearly suggests that interest in the beautiful presupposes being together with others.[7] Aesthetic judgments regarding the beautiful are made only within the horizon of an ideal social fabric, and the life characteristic of such a fabric is a life transcendentally prior to sociability (*Geselligkeit*).

At this point, the grounds on which the subject of a judgment of taste is justified to postulate a universal voice need to be spelled out. Kant broaches the issue already in section 9 under the title of the free play of the faculties, but for what interests me I will take my starting point in section 21. However, before taking up the much-discussed problematic of the free play of the faculties, let me point out that, as the subjective determining ground of a judgment of taste, the state of the mind in question is said to be one that is characterized by "universal communicability [*Mitteilbarkeit*]" (§9, 5:217). It is on the basis of the communicability of this subjectively purposive ground of a judgment of taste—its essential public nature—that its subject can claim for itself a universal voice. The one who judges an object to be beautiful can rightly assume that the pleasure associated with such a judgment will necessarily be experienced by every other judge of the object in question; in short, that it is a feeling that is universally communicable without the mediation of concepts. But what needs to be kept in mind is that it is not a question of actual communication, but only of its possibility; namely, universal communicability. Without this exigency of communicability the subject of a judgment of taste could not claim to have a universal voice, and could not impute consensus by all others who also judge. Furthermore, to get Kant's argument straight, it is also imperative to remind oneself that the term "communicability" translates the German *Mitteilbarkeit*, which literally means "shareability": the universal "ability" of being shared. In section 39, Kant says of the pleasure concerning the sublime in nature that it too lays claim to "universal participation" (*allgemeine*

7. In the case of an intellectual interest in the beautiful, someone can "all by himself (and without intention of communicating his observation to others)" indulge in the pleasure in a beautiful object of nature, but one does so by a turning away from society (and thus continuing to relate to it). See the example of someone who freely leaves a society to savor the beauties of nature (as opposed to someone abandoned on an island) (§42, 5:307–8; translation modified). See also Immanuel Kant, *Anthropology from a Pragmatic Point of View*, in *Anthropology, History, and Education*, ed. Robert B. Louden and Günter Zöller (Cambridge: Cambridge University Press, 2007), 227–429, 7:117–333; 343–44, 7:240–41.

Teilnehmung) (5:292).[8] In other words, at issue in a judgment of taste is the possibility of universally participating, or in "publicly" taking part, in the feeling of pleasure that accompanies it.

So let me turn now to the play of the faculties: the subjective powers of cognition that are the imagination and the understanding whose harmonious interrelation in the absence of concepts for a given object secures cognition in general, and that is accompanied by a subjective satisfaction that is universally communicable. As Kant makes explicit in section 9, this play consists "of a reciprocal [*wechselseitigen*] subjective harmony between [*unter einander*] the cognitive powers" (5:218). In the same paragraph, he also highlights the fact that through this reciprocal correspondence the powers of the mind are animated (*belebt*) to an activity in unison (*einhelliger Tätigkeit*). They are rendered alive through the play in question *for* "the business of the understanding in general" (5:219), a state of mind that causes the pleasure whose universal communicability is at stake in judgments of taste. In their interpretation of the play of the faculties, many Kant scholars have underlined this animation of the powers of the mind for cognition in general through their mutual correspondence. But what is it precisely that compels these powers to recognize a reciprocity among them and to enter into a relation of mutual correspondence with each other? What is the determining ground for their becoming alive for an activity to be executed in unison? And above all, what kind of life is it that is realized in this play of the faculties?

That the issue of life is a decisive topic of the *Critique of Judgment*, not only in the second part regarding organic bodies but already in the part on the aesthetic judgment, is by now firmly established.[9] Indeed, beginning

8. Paul Guyer has devoted a lengthy but inconclusive discussion to the question of whether there is a real difference between universal validity and universal communicability, and whether universal communicability is a condition of the former. If his discussion does not result in a conclusion, is it not because universal communicability is an implication of Kant's understanding of universal validity, and does it not imply empirical intersubjectivity, hence actual communication? See Paul Guyer, *Kant and the Claims of Taste* (Cambridge, MA: Harvard University Press, 1979), 282–324. Jean-François Lyotard, by contrast, insists that the communicability, or shareability, of a judgment of taste is an essential transcendental feature of the latter. See Jean-François Lyotard, *Lessons on the Analytic of the Sublime*, trans. Elizabeth Rottenberg (Stanford, CA: Stanford University Press, 1994), 191–223.

9. Rudolf A. Makkreel's work on *Imagination and Interpretation: The Hermeneutical Import of the "Critique of Judgment"* (Chicago: University of Chicago Press, 1990) has been crucial in this respect, and so has Howard Caygill's *Art of Judgment* (Cambridge:

with section 1of the third *Critique*, it is made manifest that "the feeling of pleasure and displeasure" in which "the subject feels himself, (namely) how he is affected by the presentation [*Vorstellung*]" in an aesthetic judgment, is not a feeling among others, but a "feeling of life" (5:204).[10] When throughout the "Analytic of the Beautiful" the feeling of pleasure and displeasure is characterized as the subject's feeling of life, the life that is felt, as well as the feeling that is lived, endows this feeling with a status that is incomparable to any other feeling that the subject could possibly experience. The very notion of a "feeling of life" thus calls for several remarks. First, when in *On Free Choice of the Will* Saint Augustine resorts to the Aristotelian tradition of the *sensus communis* as *koine aesthetica* in order to determine the specific nature of animal life, he points out that "it is one thing to be alive and quite another to know that one is alive."[11] This "knowledge of life" (*scientia vitae*) is what distinguishes animals from beings that are endowed with reason, even if they enjoy a prereflexive "life we call the inner sense [*sensus interior*] that excels the bodily senses" and that allows them to judge what they perceive.[12] Kant's notion of a feeling of life is, first, a clear indication that he is not speaking of the forms of organic life in general—not even animal life as the life of "inner sense"—but only of human life. The feeling of life is a feeling by which the human being "knows" that he or she is alive, a feeling thoroughly different from all other feelings. Second, since such a feeling of life in aesthetic judgments is no longer a private feeling, but essentially communicable, it also follows that the feeling of life that it represents is not the feeling of the human being as an isolated individual being. But it is not, therefore, a feeling that one experiences as a member of a species. Rather, it is a feeling of life that because it is essentially communicable, characterizes an individual subject who from the outset is in a community with other subjects. Furthermore, notwithstanding the fact that the feeling of life involved in a judgment of taste is of the order of a feeling, this feeling may have a relation to reason that according to Saint

---

Cambridge University Press, 1989). See also my *The Idea of Form: Rethinking Kant's Aesthetics* (Stanford, CA: Stanford University Press, 2003).

10. Recently, Jan Völker has even spoken of the first part of the third *Critique* as an aesthetic of life, or rather of an aesthetic of aliveness. See Jan Völker, *Ästhetik der Lebendigkeit: Kants dritte Kritik* (Munich: Wilhelm Fink, 2011).

11. Augustine, *On Free Choice of the Will*, trans. A. S. Benjamin and L. H. Hackstaff (Indianapolis: Bobbs-Merrill, 1964), 17.

12. Augustine, *On Free Choice*, 17, 43.

Augustine distinguishes the human being, since it is a feeling that only a being endowed with this power can experience. But let us also remind ourselves that reason for Kant is the faculty of ideas.

Now if this feeling of life that, however subjective, arises on the occasion of a judgment of taste is universally communicable, it is because in distinction from the other two forms of consciousness—logical and moral consciousness—in aesthetic consciousness the powers (*Kräfte*) of representation themselves, rather than their individual representations, enter into a relation. Since this relationship of the powers of representation is not to be understood in a merely abstract logical sense, but as one that fosters their animation in that each one is given a direction, we will now have to take up section 21 where Kant proceeds to a deeper elaboration of what exactly happens in the famous play of the faculties. An analysis of this paragraph will help clarify what orients the life of this play so as to become universally communicable, and thus in turn to animate through expectation, imputation, and solicitation the togetherness of "the entire sphere of *judging persons*."[13]

After having established in this paragraph that even objective cognition requires the communicability of the subjective disposition (*Stimmung*) of the powers of the mind in view of cognition generally, Kant writes that "this [attunement] does actually take place whenever a given object, by means of the senses, induces the imagination to its activity (*in Tätigkeit bringt*) of combining the manifold, the imagination in turn inducing the understanding to its activity of providing unity for this manifold in concepts" (5:238). Depending on the nature of the objects given in representations, the disposition of the cognitive powers has each time a different proportion that is suitable for making a determined cognition of the different objects in question. But Kant adds: "And yet there must be one attunement in which this inner relation is most conducive to the (mutual) quickening of the two mental powers (the one through the other [*einer durch die andere*]) with a view to cognition (of given objects) in general; and the only way this attunement can be determined is by feeling (rather than by concepts)" (5:238–39).[14] This one form of the relationship of the powers of the mind is the one that uniformly obtains when no determined concept is available for the cognition of an object of a representation, and that thus corresponds to the felt disposition of the faculties in their free play, a disposition that

13. For how the direction (*Richtung*) particular of the distinct powers that enter into the play of the faculties determine the play in question, see Hermann Cohen, *Kants Begründung der Ästhetik* (1889, repr. Saarbrücken: VDM Verlag Dr. Müller, 2007), 173–76.

14. Translation modified.

is beneficial for cognition in general. This "inner relation" between the imagination and the understanding enlivens both powers and represents a state without which no experience in general is possible. But how does this quickening or animation take place? Crucial here is Kant's claim that one power becomes animated through the other. The power of the imagination activates the power of the understanding, and vice versa. What this means is, first of all, that (unlike in determined cognition) both faculties are free, and none dominates the other. It also means not only that both forms of representation are there for one another but they are also what they are only by way of the other. Later in section 40, having recalled one more time what happens in determined cognition, Kant writes: "Only where the imagination is free when it arouses [*erweckt*] the understanding, and the understanding, without using concepts, puts the imagination into a play that is regular (i.e., manifests regularity), does the presentation communicate itself not as a thought but as the inner feeling of a purposive state of mind" (5:295–96). Here the animation of one power by the other is described as an awakening from slumber, as it were, of one by the other, to life. In other words, in the free play of the faculties, the faculties in question, by overcoming their isolation and activating each other, enter into a relationship to begin with, and this relating of the powers to one another is what endows them with life—with a life for cognition in general.[15] But there is more to this mutual enlivening in that if each one of the powers is animated only through the other, then each becomes a part of this inner relationship in which each represents a means and a purpose for the other. The pair of the powers that are involved in the free play beneficial for cognition in general thus form the mind into a whole. Yet to the extent that each part of this whole is what it is only by way and in view of the other, this whole is a living whole; an organism, as it were. As Kant remarks in the second preface of the *Critique of Pure Reason*, "in an organized body, every part exists for the sake of all the others as all the others exist for its sake" (B/23).[16] With the "inner relation" of the two faculties as faculties, their free play thus meets Kant's understanding of the organism as a living whole based on a reciprocal means and purpose relationship.[17] No wonder that the feeling of life that

15. The powers of representation become enlivened when, interrelated, they become attuned to cognition in general.

16. Immanuel Kant, *Critique of Pure Reason*, trans. and ed. Paul Guyer and Allen W. Wood (Cambridge: Cambridge University Press, 1998).

17. Reinhardt Löw, *Philosophie des Lebendigen: Der Begriff des Organischen bei Kant, sein Grund und seine Aktualität* (Frankfurt a. M.: Suhrkamp, 1980), 145–48, 154.

comes with this state of mind is also characterized by Kant as a feeling that maintains itself; that strives to strengthen and reproduce itself (§12, 5:222).

The universal voice postulated by an aesthetic judgment declares this self-maintaining feeling of life to be indicative of an inner relationship of the faculties that is uniquely communicable, hence universal. But, already beginning with section 8, Kant seems also to suggest that it is necessary to terminologically distinguish logical universality from that of the subjective quantity of a judgment. For such a universality that does not contain an objective quantity of judgment but only a subjective one, Kant uses "the expression common validity [*Gemeingültigkeit*]" (5:214).[18] The validity of such general, or common, validity, rather than deriving from the relation of a representation to the faculty of cognition, originates in a feeling of pleasure and displeasure that a representation causes in every subject. Even though it concerns only a feeling, "common validity" is a validity that is nevertheless shareable by all subjects. But despite having pointed out the need to terminologically distinguish between universality (*Allgemeingültigkeit*) and common validity (*Gemeingültigkeit*), Kant ignores this difference again when he rephrases the latter as a "subjective . . . universal validity" as opposed to a validity that is objectively valid (5:215).[19] Yet, in spite of this inconsistency, we should not lose sight of the difference in question, were it only because of the nature of the aesthetic judgment's directedness to others whose consent it solicits. After all, in speaking of *Allgemeingültigkeit*, the meaning of universality of this term is so overwhelming as to obliterate the sense of communality; of the shareability in common of the validity it designates. By directing itself to others to confirm its claim, a judgment of taste reveals that it presupposes "a basis . . . that is common to all" (§19, 5:237), which the title of section 20, "The Condition for the Necessity Alleged by a Judgment of Taste Is the Idea of a Common Sense," introduces as a *Gemeinsinn*, that is, a *sensus communis*.

In section 8, Kant held that in a judgment of taste nothing but a "universal voice" (*allgemeine Stimme*) is postulated. Yet the idea of this voice is not the same as the idea of common sense, since the universal voice presupposes the latter as a principle on the basis of which it can make claims to universality. It follows from this that all the further developments regarding common sense serve to expand on the grounds on which such a voice can

18. Translation modified.

19. For Kant's proposal to speak of *Gemeingültigkeit* in the context of judgments of taste as a "universality" that is ascribed to anyone, see Wolfgang Wieland, *Urteil und Gefühl: Kants Theorie der Urteilskraft* (Göttingen: Vandenhoeck & Ruprecht, 2001), 253.

make universal claims. Judgments of taste, Kant advances here, must have "a subjective principle, which determines only by feeling rather than by concepts, though nonetheless with universal validity, what is liked or disliked. Such a principle, however, could only be regarded as a *common sense* [*Gemeinsinn*]. This common sense is essentially distinct from the common understanding that is sometimes also called common sense (*sensus communis*); for the latter judges not by feeling but always by concepts, even though these concepts are usually only principles conceived obscurely" (§20, 5:238). By distinguishing common sense from common understanding (*gemeinen Verstande*), sometimes also referred to by the Latin expression *sensus communis*, but which is still a logical sense—a *sensus communis logicus* as opposed to taste as a *sensus communis aestheticus* (§40, 5:295)—Kant commences a reinterpretation of the notion of *sensus communis* that will culminate in section 40. Given the tradition of common sense, I propose to call this reinterpreted concept of *sensus communis*, *sensus communis* in a Kantian sense.

By invoking the notion of a *sensus communis*, Kant places himself in a double tradition, one Aristotelian regarding the interconnection of the individual senses—the *koine aesthetic*a (in which the idea of a sixth sense has also been debated)—and a Latin tradition that is above all concerned with a sense for communal life. This latter tradition of the *sensus communis* resurges in the humanistic conception of educational formation (*Bildung*), for which the ideal of *eloquentia* as a way of involvement in communal life has been instrumental. Yet, when on at least two occasions in the third *Critique* Kant insists that "common sense" (*Gemeinsinn*) (§20, 5:238) is something entirely different from "common understanding" (*gemeiner Verstand*), or "merely . . . sound [*bloss gesunden*] (not yet cultivated) understanding" (§40, 5:293), it is not simply for merely pedantic reasons. For a thinker who in the name of critical rationality has been severely critical of the notion of common sense in both the early and later stages of his work, is it not surprising to still make a positive use of this notion? Therefore, distinctions such as those between the different forms of understanding—common or merely healthy understanding—are clear indication that in the positive use he makes of the term "common sense," he has a specific conception of it in mind that is not identical with the contemporaneous understandings of it.[20] Given that "common understanding" is commonly taken to be a *sensus communis*, Kant's eventual retranslation in section 40 of the German term

20. For Kant's repeated objections to the notion of common sense, see Manfred Kuehn, *Scottish Common Sense in Germany, 1768–1800: A Contribution to the History of Critical Philosophy* (Kingston, ON: McGill-Queen's University Press, 1987), 194–98.

Gemeinsinn back into the Latin *sensus communis* is highly revealing. By this retranslation he demarcates his own use of the term from the change of meaning that *Gemeinsinn* had undergone during the eighteenth century under the influence of the naturalist English notion of common sense—at the hands, in particular, of Scottish common sense philosophy—thus reestablishing a link of this term to (perhaps) its twofold tradition: the *koine aesthetica* and its Latin, or humanist, meaning.[21] But this reestablishment does not take place without an implicit debate with both traditions. As we will see, in redefining *sensus communis*, Kant interrogates both the notion of sense—it is not a sense in any sensory understanding, and certainly not a supplementary, or sixth sense *for* communal life—and the notion of being in common.[22] As a result, a new meaning of *sensus communis* emerges with section 40 that as a subjective principle of judgments of taste grounds these judgments' universality claims in the idea of a communal consent.

Let us recall that common sense (or nonemphasized sensus communis) in the quality of common understanding is conceptual, however obscure it may be. Distinct from it, the common sense (*Gemeinsinn*) that underlies judgments of taste as their principle is of the order of a feeling that is shareable by all.[23] "Sense" in "common sense" understood as *Gemeinsinn*

---

21. Kuehn, *Scottish Common Sense*, 238. As Kuehn has shown, two conceptions of common sense dominate early Enlightenment: a theological conception in the tradition of pietism under the name of "healthy reason, or understanding" (*recta ratio*), and a more secular one of "common understanding" (*gemeiner Verstand*) (258), meaning "good judgment, or opinion of the majority in a certain society" (241). Kant rejects both these conceptions as criteria, or tools of philosophical inquiry (202).

22. In contradistinction to Gadamer's claim that "by narrowing the concept of the sense of community to a judgment of taste about what is beautiful," the full moral and political range of the humanist tradition would have been forgotten, I hold that Kant's insistence on the distinction of *Gemeinsinn* (as a sense for the communal) from *gemeiner Verstand* and his translation of the former using a term that emphasizes a sense of communal life shows that the humanist tradition (possibly including its rhetorical heritage) and its concern with the form that life takes in society remains very alive in the third *Critique*. Gadamer, *Truth and Method*, 34. The very way by which the universal communicability required by a judgment of taste includes a demand regarding one who judges not only to lay claim to the consent of others, but also to (actively) seek it, situates him or her from the beginning in the idea of communal life. Undoubtedly, the active expectation of consent by others does not take the form of rhetorical persuasion, but the demand on others to ratify my judgment is inscribed in intrinsic fashion in any judgment of the kind.

23. Kant's strategy of italicizing on specific occasions a term such as sensus communis, in order to distinguish it from its ordinary, or colloquial meaning—as "the sound and common understanding" (*gemeinen und gesunden Verstande*)—is part and parcel of the argument he is trying to make (§39, 5:293).

does not designate a sensory faculty similar to the five senses. When Kant observes that by common sense "we . . . do not mean an outer sense, but mean the effect arising from the free play of our cognitive powers" (§20, 5:238), common sense is, unmistakably, detailed as a shared feeling. Indeed, in the singular, *Sinn* names a feeling as an inner relationship to something. More precisely, this feeling is one of pleasure or displeasure that derives from the inner relationship of the powers of representation. It is not a private feeling, as has already been noted, but a feeling that from the start is public—that is, communicable—and that, because it is shareable (*gemein*), can be ascribed (*ansinnen*) to everyone. And if this feeling can be imputed to all others by the judging subject, it is precisely because of the existence of a common sense: of a feeling that is common to all—and that, as we have seen, is the feeling of a fundamental aliveness.

In its very title, section 40 indicates that the notion of common sense that is to be considered as the principle of judgments of taste is "a kind of *sensus communis*" (5:293). As a kind, this notion of *sensus communis* is thus distinct from what commonly is meant by the expression. The paragraph is remarkable in that Kant proceeds here to a wholesale reinterpretation of the two notions that make up the expression, beginning with a reflection on the notion of "sense" followed by one on how *communis* is to be taken, before returning to the meaning of "sense." After having pointed out that "when we speak of a sense of truth, a sense of decency, of justice, etc.," it is at best metaphorically, because "a sense cannot contain these concepts" since the senses have not "the slightest capacity to pronounce universal rules," Kant evokes the name attributed to "*common human understanding*"; that is, "merely sound (not yet cultivated) understanding" (5:293). Given the ambiguity of the adjective "common" (*gemein*), not only in Latin but also in German (and in many other languages), to call common human understanding "common sense" (*sensus communis*) is to make this sense into something merely vulgar (5:293). If this is so, it is ultimately because "sense" is understood here from the lower faculties, which lack the possibility of elevating themselves to the higher ones that distinguish the human being from the animal. It follows that sense in the "kind" of *sensus communis* that Kant has in mind cannot be a sense in a sensory way, nor in a figurative sense of this notion of sense, but a "sense" of a different order.[24] Yet, if the goal is to demonstrate that a *sensus communis* is the principle that instructs

24. Nor is it a supplementary sense, such as a sense *for* life in community as, indeed, common sense is understood in particular from the Earl of Shaftesbury to Giambatista Vico, up to Henri Bergson and Hannah Arendt.

judgments such as judgments of taste, "common" in "common sense" too needs to be conceived in a new way.

I draw attention to the fact that before redefining "common," Kant retranslates the term back into Latin and italicizes it: "sensus *communis*." The new translation of this Latin term into German as *gemeinschaftlich*, rather than *gemein*, signals a new interpretation. *Communis* now signifies "communal" rather than "common." But Kant does not simply reinterpret here the terms by which the expression is formed. *Sensus communis*, distinct from common sense and healthy human understanding, becomes the name of the power of judgment as it manifests itself in reflective judgments of taste. Kant avers: "We must (here) take sensus *communis* to mean the idea of a sense *shared* (by all of us) [*gemeinschaftlichen Sinnes*, i.e., a communal sense], i.e., a power to judge that in reflecting takes account (a priori), in our thought, of everyone else's way of presenting (something), in order *as it were* [*gleichsam*] to compare our own judgment with human reason in general and thus escape the illusion that arises from the ease of mistaking subjective and private conditions for objective ones, an illusion that would have a prejudicial influence on the judgment" (5:293–94). With its emphasis on the communal, the sensus *communis* shows itself not as a psychological, or empirical faculty, but as the idea of a faculty for judging that in thought (i.e., not in an empirical manner) takes into consideration everyone else's way of representing, so as to make judgments that can impute consent by all others. To this idea of a faculty of judging that takes everyone's way of thinking into account—what all universally share as thinking subjects—Kant gives the name of a *communal* sense. "Communal" here means, first, that such a judgment takes the subjective conditions of everyone else regarding their way of representing into consideration, which it does "merely by abstracting from the limitations that (may) happen to attach to our own judging," and not by some empathy with, or any sort of transfer via imagination, to others (5:294). Indeed, Kant's observation that in such judgments one "think[s] from the standpoint of everyone else," not by comparing "the actual as rather . . . the merely possible judgments of others," excludes empathy as an empirical and psychological disposition. It is only through a (negative) relation to others in which one occupies the place of others by stripping one's own judgment from everything private, hence from everything noncommunicable and nonuniversalizable, that one puts oneself in the place of others. As a result of such abstraction, one's judgment demonstrates communal sense.[25] Second, it is a communal sense insofar as

---

25. In spite of the fact that Kant explicitly qualifies the following discussion about the maxims of common human understanding (*gemeinen Menschenverstandes*) as "a

by judging in this manner, one's judgment is held up, as it were, to human reason as a whole: to reason as an idea, measuring itself against the standard of the universality this idea stands for. What follows from this is that the judgment of taste as a faculty that takes every other's way of representation into account, whose principle is thus a sensus *communis*, is a faculty that presupposes and is formative of life in togetherness, not in general but through individual participation.

Having thus recast the meaning of communis in sensus *communis*, Kant returns to the question of what is meant by *sensus* in the expression when he writes "that taste can be called a *sensus communis* more legitimately than can sound understanding, and that the aesthetic power of judgment deserves to be called a shared sense more than does the intellectual one, if indeed we wish to use the word *sense* to stand for an effect that mere reflection has on the mind, even though we then mean by sense the feeling of pleasure" (5:295). A judgment of taste regarding the representation of an object in the absence of a determining concept causes a feeling of pleasure or displeasure in response to the free play of the faculties that prove this representation to be beneficial for a cognition in general. This feeling of pleasure corresponds to the "sense" involved in the *sensus communis*, and is a feeling that, because it can be attributed to everyone in that it is testimony to the inner relationship between the faculties required universally for any determined cognition, is what is shareable by all. With this, Kant's recast notion of sensus communis should be evident: sensus *communis* in the Kantian sense is a feeling of pleasure that one has (or is expected to have) in making judgments that are made in community with others, hence a communal pleasure.[26] It is not a sense *for* community in any sensory sense, but a feeling of pleasure of being universally in a community through judgments that by their very nature imply the place of all individual others and are an invitation to them to declare their joining agreement.

---

digression" (*Episode*) (§40, 5:295) that does not belong to his transcendental inquiry, and only serves to render what has been established so far more clear through examples for readers endowed with popular wisdom, many commentators—among them Hannah Arendt—have overlooked Kant's admonition. As a result, the remarks on the second maxim, "To think from the standpoint of everyone else," have been used to psychologize his critical understanding of what, from a transcendental perspective, it means to put oneself in the position of everyone. For a detailed discussion of this interpretative error see my *Persuasion, Reflection, Judgment: Ancillae Vitae* (Bloomington: Indiana University Press, 2017), 204–11.

26. Lebrun, *Fin de la métaphysique*, 563.

To conclude, several speculative questions are warranted. But first let us not lose sight of Kant's characterization of the *sensus communis* as an idea. The response to the question left in abeyance of what it is that, when in the face of an object without a determined concept, guides the faculties to enter a relation that animates them in a way that is purposive for cognition in general, is this idea of a sensus *communis*. It is as an idea that the sensus *communis* puts both the imagination and the understanding into movement, and thus brings them to life.[27] Yet, as we have seen, the sensus *communis* is the idea of a feeling of life. Needless to say, the life in question is not animal life, but life as it senses itself in the human being; that is, spiritual life. The sensus *communis* as an idea of life is one of being alive mentally, of being together in spiritual fashion, the pleasure of which is the only one that suits human beings as human beings and is as such universally communicable. This idea is the rule that orients the faculties to enter into a relation by which they become enlivened in a subjectively purposive readiness for experience, or cognition. It is an idea necessary for them to lend themselves to forming an organized whole of the mind. But to speak of the feeling of life as an idea that guides the judgment of taste, does this not also suggest that "idea" must be taken in a specific sense? Compared to the role that ideas assume in theoretical and practical reason, is the idea in the sense of a sensus *communis* understood as a feeling of life not an entirely novel principle of reason? Can one indeed speak of an animation by way of an idea in any other context than that of Kant's inquiry into the transcendental conditions of the power of judgment? In the context of this question, Kant's hesitation regarding the status of the idea of a sensus *communis* as either constitutive or regulative might be anything but accidental. As an idea of a universally communicable pleasure of aliveness, it may be neither one nor the other. Undoubtedly, it is a specific form of idea exclusively meant for the power of judgment that serves to secure the inner relationship of the faculties by which they become alive for what is called cognition, or experience, in general, to form the minimal whole without which no such task of the mind can get off the ground. Is, then, the idea of the sensus *communis*, an idea of life, not also the idea necessary to bridge not only the distinction between the two other types of idea—constitutive and regulative—but, ultimately, also to close the gulf between the two uses of reason that are theoretical and practical reason?

27. See Löw, *Philosophie des Lebendigen*, 165.

Chapter 10

Kant, the Feeling of Life, and the Reflective Comprehension of Teleological Purposiveness

Rudolf A. Makkreel

In this chapter, I will examine how Kant defines the nature of human life in his anthropological and aesthetical writings and what bearing these explorations have for his efforts to make sense of the purposiveness of organisms at a time when the sciences aimed to conceptually *understand* (*verstehen*) and explain nature in exclusively mechanistic terms. In the final section, I will delineate a conception of reflective *comprehension* (*begreifen*, *comprehendere*) to characterize the way Kant describes and contextualizes organic processes.

The themes of life and purposiveness come together in the *Critique of Judgment* where Kant explores both the enlivening subjective purposiveness of aesthetic judgment and the objective purposiveness of teleological judgment. It will become evident that the terms "life" and "enlivenment" are much more prominent in the first aesthetic half of the *Critique of Judgment* than in the second teleological half, which raises the question whether Kant is aiming at a naturalistic definition of life at all. Since he also hesitates to define life metaphysically, I will consider to what extent the aesthetic feeling of life evoked by beauty and sublimity can orient us in comprehending the way organisms function.

The Shifting Meaning of the Term "Life" in Kant

As I showed in *Imagination and Interpretation in Kant*, the term "life" does not occur often in Kant's main writings but can be found mostly in his "Reflections" and his lectures on metaphysics and anthropology. There I used some of these comments about life to shed light on Kant's claims about aesthetic enlivenment in a chapter titled "The Life of the Imagination."[1] A more extensive account of Kant's reflections about life and aesthetics can be found in the chapter by Courtney D. Fugate in this volume, and one of the important contributions he makes there is to show the way in which Kant was influenced by Christian August Crusius. In this chapter, I will bring all this forward to better define what Kant means by the immanent purposiveness of organisms.

Perhaps Kant's earliest published definition of human life is in "Dreams of a Spirit-Seer" (1766) where it is said to be "the inner capacity to determine one's self by one's free choice" (2:327n).[2] In the *Metaphysical Foundations of Natural Science* (1786), Kant refers to life more generally in a note as "the capacity of a substance to determine itself to act from an inner principle, of a finite substance to determine itself to change" (4:544).[3] He then adds that "we are not acquainted [*kennen*] with any other inner principle of a substance to change its state other than desire and no inner activity whatever other than thought about what depends on such desire, namely, the feeling of pleasure or displeasure, and appetite or will." From this he argues that material substances are inherently lifeless. This means that the primary sense of life for Kant is mental and that here at least he is suspending any cognitive claims about what we call biological life.

In the *Critique of Practical Reason* (1788), there is another note in which Kant refines this mental sense of "life" within the moral context as "the capacity of a being to act in accordance with the laws of the faculty

1. Rudolf A. Makkreel, *Imagination and Interpretation in Kant: The Hermeneutical Import of the "Critique of Judgment"* (Chicago: University of Chicago Press, 1990), ch. 5.

2. Immanuel Kant, "Dreams of a Spirit-Seer Elucidated by Dreams of Metaphysics," in *Theoretical Philosophy, 1755–1770*, trans. David Walford, with Ralf Meerbote (Cambridge: Cambridge University Press, 2003), 301–59, 2:315–373.

3. Immanuel Kant, *Metaphysical Foundations of Natural Science*, ed. and trans. James Ellington (Indianapolis: Bobbs-Merrill, 1970).

of desire" (5:9n).[4] Pleasure is then briefly referred to as "the representation of the agreement of an object or an action with the subjective conditions of life." Since pleasure is merely considered as a gauge of how our relation to the world affects the well-being of our life, Kant considers it as only relevant to matters of prudence and of no further concern for matters of morality proper.

The *Critique of Judgment* (1790) is the first of Kant's major works to refer to the idea of life in the main text. In section 1, he writes that what is represented in an aesthetic judgment "is referred only to the subject, namely to his feeling of life, under the name of the feeling of pleasure or displeasure, and this forms the basis of a very special power of discriminating and judging . . . that holds the given representation [*Vorstellung*] in the subject up to the entire power of representation, of which the mind becomes conscious when it feels its own state" (§1, 5:204).[5]

Life is disclosed in an overall state of mind, and it is made more clear than before that feeling rather than cognition provides our access to life. The felt pleasure of aesthetic appreciation is not cognitive, yet it enlivens the overall play of our cognitive faculties and contributes to the life of the mind by expanding its scope. The feeling of life can gather our representations into coherent wholes.

Aesthetic pleasure is subjectively purposive, but it is disinterested and does not satisfy any interests of the subject. It displays a mental purposiveness that is not aimed at any specific intellectual or moral purpose. Aesthetic purposiveness serves to "preserve our representational state" as we "*linger* in our contemplation of the beautiful" (§12, 5:222). And whereas ordinary perceptual representations need synthetic acts of the understanding to be reproduced, the aesthetic representational state has the power to "strengthen and reproduce itself." This language of preservation and self-reproduction resembles that of biologists when they describe the ways organisms function. This, together with the fact that Kant speaks of the aesthetic mental state as a cooperative interplay among the faculties that produces equilibrium, raises the possibility that the first half of the *Critique of Judgment* can prepare us

4. Immanuel Kant, *Critique of Practical Reason*, in *Practical Philosophy*, trans. and ed. Mary J. Gregor (Cambridge: Cambridge University Press, 1996), 133–272, 5:1–163.

5. Immanuel Kant, *Critique of Judgment*, trans. Werner Pluhar (Indianapolis: Hackett, 1987). Here and throughout, I translate *Vorstellung* as "representation" rather than "presentation." Whenever I alter a translation, Kant's German terms will be inserted in square brackets to signal that.

for and illuminate Kant's treatment of the purposiveness of organisms in the second half.

Whereas the enlivening pleasure of pure beauty remains at the mental level of a calm play of the imagination and the understanding, the more complex sublime pleasure resulting from experiencing a powerful waterfall or storm can be initiated by the displeasure of bodily fear or fright. When discussing the dynamical sublime, Kant acknowledges an actual disruption of our vital powers, but his focus is mostly about how this convulsion can be resolved by reminding us about our power of reason and by reorienting ourselves to our supersensible moral destination. We learn nothing about our sensible life except that it can be stirred by an "emotion" (*Rührung*) such as fear. What initially "inhibits our vital forces" and does violence to the ordinary temporal flow of experience can be recontextualized by reason to release an outpouring of these forces "that is all the stronger" (§23, 5:245). The piecemeal nature of "inner [*innere*] sense" gives way to what Kant later calls a more holistic "interior [*inwendige*] sense" (*Anthropology from a Pragmatic Point of View*, 7:153)[6] through which we feel a greater vitality of mind. Most scholarly discussions of the Kantian sublime focus on the dynamical sublime because it can more readily be explored for its moral and religious import, but the mathematical sublime is just as significant because it allows us to relate the aesthetic feeling of life to the equally spiritual feeling of theoretical respect for what surpasses human measurement. We experience the mathematical sublime when we confront the incomparable magnitude of a mountain range that overwhelms the imagination. According to Kant, this produces a regress of the imagination and transforms it from a sensible power that serves the understanding to a power that bows to reason. In section 27, this regress is described as "a comprehending in one instant [*Augenblick*] of what is [normally] apprehended successively. . . . It cancels the condition of time in the imagination's [empirical] progression and makes *simultaneity* intuitable" (5:258–59). This should make us question the widely held view that the mathematical sublime represents merely the inadequacy of the imagination relative to reason. The above passage about the regress together with the later comment that "the imagination acquires an expansion and a might that surpasses the one it sacrifices," opens up

6. Immanuel Kant, *Anthropology from a Pragmatic Point of View*, in *Anthropology, History, and Education*, ed. Günter Zöller and Robert B. Louden (Cambridge: Cambridge University Press, 2007), 227–429, 7:117–333. See also Makkreel, *Imagination and Interpretation*, 94–97.

a new kind of *Augenschein* of simultaneity (§29, 5:269–70). According to the *Critique of Pure Reason*, the simultaneity of substances cannot be determinately *perceived* in the successive timeline of human apprehension. We can only *conceptually apperceive* many things being objectively simultaneous or coexisting by means of the third relational category of "the reciprocity among that which acts and that which suffers [*zwischen dem Handelnden und Leidenden*]" (A80/B106).[7] For multiple "substances in appearance" to be cognized as being simultaneous, they must be located in the "pervasive [*durchgängiger*] community of interaction with each other" (A213/B260). This overall systematic context is normally only "mediately" accessible, but in the sublime regress of the imagination, simultaneity is immediately *felt* in an instant, which is a vanishing limit point of the time-line. The displeasure of being perceptually frustrated by a great magnitude now impels our imagination to feelingly project the "*whole vocation* of the mind" (§27, 5:259). The ordinary sense-based and gathering mode of "comprehension" (*Zusammenfassung*) of the imagination is replaced with a felt flash-like "comprehension" (*Comprehension*) that opens up the supersensible potential of the life of the mind.[8] Natural reciprocity that allows for action at a distance between the earth and the moon is now internalized as the more intimate mental reciprocity of enlivenment.

Whereas the purposive aesthetic play of the beautiful gave us some formal clues about self-preservation and equilibrium that can be transferred to organisms, the sublime discloses that life coexists with an environment that can be hostile and disruptive. The sublime offers the paradoxical lesson that displeasure that seems unpurposive can be made purposive, just as pain can become a warning signal to an animal organism to protect itself from external harm. Despite the more exalting tendencies of the sublime in the direction of the supersensible, it also provides insight into the reciprocity of the acting and suffering that defines animal organisms. Whereas in the mechanistically conceived world of the first *Critique*, causal action is manifested in the surface-suffering of impact and reaction, in the third *Critique* we discern a more animated agency as well as a more deeply felt suffering that characterize creaturely responses and human creativity. While beauty celebrates the equilibrium of undisturbed harmony, sublimity can

7. Immanuel Kant, *Critique of Pure Reason*, trans. and ed. Paul Guyer and Allen W. Wood (Cambridge: Cambridge University Press, 1998).

8. See Makkreel, *Imagination and Interpretation*, ch. 4, for a more extensive treatment of the sublime in Kant.

restore a harmony that has been disturbed. These analogies are suggestive for describing organic behavior but remain vaguely formal.

It is with the discussion of music, which Kant mistakenly regards as the lowest of the fine arts, that he begins to directly bring in a more concrete sense of life, namely, our bodily feeling of well-being or health. He acknowledges that the tones of music manifest a "language of affects" that has a pervasive power that "communicates . . . aesthetic ideas" (§53, 5:328–29). Although aesthetic ideas are prized by Kant for stimulating a shared kind of attitude, he thinks that this communicative effect is transitory with music and does more to stimulate the life of the body than the life of the mind. In a long remark, we are told that music generates sensory "gratification (even if its cause happens to lie in ideas)" in that it promotes "the total life of the human being, including the furtherance of bodily well-being, i.e., of health" (§54, 5:331). Thus the benefit of music descends from the level of the head and the mental play of ideas further down the body to encompass "the feeling of health resulting from an intestinal agitation. . . . This vibration of our organs . . . helps restore their equilibrium" (§54, 5:332). Similarly, the play of thought that leads to laughter rather than cognition is said to promote the vital processes of the body. Laughter is described as "*an affect that arises if a tense expectation is transformed into nothing*" (§54, 5:333). Both music and humor can "generate [*hervorbringen*] in the body an equilibrium of the vital forces" and instruct us, as Kant writes, "that we can reach the body also through the soul and use it as the physician of the body" (§54, 5:332–33).

These discussions of life and vital processes in the "Critique of Aesthetic Judgment" could be seen as a kind of preparation for the later discussions in the "Critique of Teleological Judgment" about how organisms function, but they do not really help us to conceptually understand how organisms, especially plants that do not seem to feel, are generated and how they fit into a mechanistically conceived world. Since Kant believes that matter is inert and dead, what is it that enables material organisms to move themselves? *The Critique of Pure Reason* could only explain the movements of material bodies and changes in them as mechanically caused from without. This billiard-ball notion of change cannot account for self-initiated movements. Analogously, the *Metaphysics of Natural Science* could only account for the appearance of life in matter by seeking its cause "in another substance different from matter, although bound up with it" (4:544). This other substance is the soul. But in the "Critique of Teleological Judgment," Kant does not appeal to the life of a soul in describing how organisms function. This would be especially inappropriate in the case of organisms like plants.

This hesitation to ascribe a soul to an organism should be seen in the context of an interesting feature of Kant's philosophy, namely, that its appeal to the traditional metaphysical postulate of the soul recedes over time. We see this especially in the evolution of his lectures on anthropology, where he increasingly supplements references to the soul with references to mind and spirit when describing human life. The final published *Anthropology from a Pragmatic Point of View* (1798) replaces psychological introspection of the soul with observations that are concerned with "cognizing both the interior as well as the exterior of the human being" (7:125). The goal of correlating inner experience with our surrounding context so as to effectively interact with it, leads Kant to also reject a physiological anthropology, because that would study human beings merely in terms of their animal nature and their earthly origins. Instead, he proposes an anthropology that is worldly and cosmopolitan. It considers human beings not only in terms of what nature has made of them, but also according to what they can make of themselves as persons with practical reason. Although the nature of our humanity is at the heart of Kant's anthropology, what makes us human cannot be understood without reference to our animal nature and our moral destination. Both his writings on anthropology and religion offer three ways of explicating what life means for us on the basis of our predispositions to animality, humanity, and personality.

Soul, Mind, and Spirit as Three Levels of Life

Kant's approach in his writings on anthropology and religion is to break up the monolithic idea of a soul as a kind of substance into a more variegated consideration of three functional levels at which human life manifests itself. This could be seen as another illustration of what Ernst Cassirer considered to be one of Kant's main contributions to modern philosophy, namely, the transition from substantial to functional thinking.[9] The functions of the soul are contextualized in relation to those of mind and spirit. We see the beginnings of this new way of speaking about life in a passage from the early Collins anthropology lecture notes from 1772–1773 where Kant distinguishes between lower and higher powers of the soul. The lowest power of soul that we share with animals is "the capacity to be modified," or to have "impressions that the body suffers passively," and it is called "*anima*"

9. Ernst Cassirer, *Substance and Function* (Chicago: Dover, 1923).

(*Seele*, soul) (25:16).[10] We humans also have what Kant calls "*animus* [*Gemüth*, mind] and *mens* [*Geist*, spirit]." He then adds that soul, mind, and spirit "are not three substances, but *three ways we feel ourselves living*. In regard to the first way we are passive, in regard to the other [second] we are passive but simultaneously reactive [*reagirend*], in regard to the third way we are entirely self-active." This way of delineating the lower function of the soul related to the body would allow Kant to acknowledge that all mammals may have a soul while lacking the other aspects of soul that define human beings, namely, the higher functions assigned to mind and spirit. But even this is not certain, because most of Kant's references to animal life are contained in the lectures on anthropology and refer to it as one aspect of human nature. In the "Metaphysik L_1" of the mid-1770s, he spoke of plants as manifesting "a beginning of life" and of the animal kingdom as disclosing "small degrees of life" (28:205).[11] These remarks, and the claim that nonrational animals cannot experience the true "spontaneity" (28:249) of life, show a reluctance to fully apply the idea of life to organisms.

Kant suggests that at the initial stages of our lives when the *predisposition to animality* dominates, we rely mainly on the lower, passive power of soul to register sense impressions rather than on the consciousness related to mind (7:127).[12] Merely being alive is about coping with how we are affected. In *Religion within the Boundaries of Mere Reason* (1793), Kant writes that our predisposition to animality defines us as a mere "living being" (6:26),[13] conceived as acting on the basis of "physical or mechanical self-love, i.e., a love for which reason is not required." Even if the life of the soul is not mechanically determined from without, it is physically conditioned and mechanical in the sense of being instinctively routine. Our "predisposition to animality" is needed for "self-preservation . . . the propagation of the

---

10. Immanuel Kant, "Anthropologie Collins 1," in *Vorlesungen über Anthropologie*, Bd. 25 of *Kant's gesammelte Schriften*, ed. Berlin-Brandenburgischen Akademie der Wissenschaften (Berlin: de Gruyter, 1997), 25:7–238.

11. Immanuel Kant, "Metaphysik L_1," in *Vorlesungen über Metaphysik und Rationaltheologie*, Bd. 28 of *Kant's gesammelte Schriften*, ed. Berlin-Brandenburgische Akademie der Wissenschaften (Berlin: de Gruyter, 1970), 28:167–350.

12. Kant notes that when children begin to speak, they refer to themselves in the third person. About a year later "a light seems to dawn" and they start to "speak by means of 'I.'" Merely feeling themselves is replaced by thinking themselves.

13. Immanuel Kant, *Religion within the Boundaries of Mere Reason*, in *Religion and Rational Theology*, trans. and ed. Allen Wood and George di Giovanni (Cambridge: Cambridge University Press, 1998), 39–215, 6:1–202.

species, [and] for community with other human beings." What Kant calls mechanical self-love at the lowest level of soul is not necessarily egoistic, for it extends to one's family and local community. We could thus say that at the stage of our animality, self-love encompasses a sense of solidarity with those akin to us. As long as children are dependent on their parents, they will tend to comply with their demands. Although these demands come from others, they are consented to because of a natural family bond.

Gradually we are expected to rise above this natural life of familial love, but to the extent that it involves basic instincts of survival, it can be accepted as one of the "original predispositions to good in human nature." Kant claims that if there are vices associated with this level of animal self-love, they are grafted onto it. He has been accused by Friedrich Nietzsche and others of wanting to negate our sensuous animal nature as much as possible, but as is made clear later in the same *Religion* text, "incentives of self-love" may be "incorporated" (6:36) into the maxims of action of adults if they do not claim priority over the way respect for the moral law is incorporated as well. In this section, where Kant is concerned with moral goodness, he is still willing to acknowledge man's dependence on the incentives of "sensuous nature because of his equally innocent natural predisposition . . . (according to the subjective principle of self-love)."

It is at the level of the second *predisposition to humanity* that the more lively powers of mind manifest themselves. In elaborating what is involved in our predisposition to humanity, Kant claims that it exhibits another form of self-love. It too is physical, but not merely mechanical; it "*involves comparison* (for which reason is required); that is, only in comparison with others does one judge oneself happy or unhappy" (6:27). This mental form of self-love is more egoistic because it is concerned to gain worth in the opinion of others in society at large. We feel ourselves as being in competition with others and want to maintain our honor. To again make use of the language of the Collins anthropology lecture notes, the predisposition to humanity involves a state of mind that is reactive to threats from without. But it seems that nonrational animals like dogs and cats also react to their surroundings, which raises the question why there are passages in Kant where he does not admit that they can be conscious.[14] After all, in the "First

14. See Immanuel Kant, *Handschriftlicher Nachlaß: Logik*, Bd. 16 of *Kant's gesammelte Schriften*, ed. Königlich Preußische Akademie der Wissenschaften (Berlin: de Gruyter, 1914), R1678 (16:79); R1680 (16:80); "Reflexionen zur Metaphysik," in *Handschriftlicher Nachlaß: Metaphysik*, Bd. 17 of *Kant's gesammelte Schriften*, ed. Preußische Akademie der Wissenschaften (Berlin: de Gruyter, 1926), 17:227–745, R4230 (17:469). In the

Introduction to the *Critique of Judgment*," Kant goes so far as to say that "even animals reflect [*reflectiren*]" (20:211),[15] which is commonly regarded as a conscious activity that can compare things. But Kant seems to think that because animals such as dogs lack human reason, they compare things nonconceptually. Thus we are told that they reflect not in an attempt to attain a new concept, but "only instinctively" to determine an inclination. Nonrational animals seem to be able to reflect *that* one sense impression differs from another, but they cannot consciously hold them together with any faculty of cognition and judge *how* they differ and can be distinguished. Because they relate to things instinctively, nonhuman animals remain at the level of mechanical movement that is either activated from without or from within by an impulse or drive that is irresistible. What distinguishes the human power to reflect (*überlegen*) about things is that it can be responsive in a more lively or conscious manner, and what gives our reflecting a humanizing quality is the ability to not just differentiate things, but to also judge what those differences mean (*Die falsche Spitzfindigkeit*, 2:60).[16]

The third or *rational predisposition to the good that pertains to personality* is defined as "the susceptibility to respect for the moral law *as of itself a sufficient incentive to the power of choice*" (6:27). Here reason is self-actively alive in the sense that only spirit can be. The predisposition to animality does not make any use of reason, only of sense and instinct, and therefore can merely generate natural goods. The next level of the predisposition to humanity "is rooted in a reason which is indeed practical, but only as subservient to other incentives" (6:28). Our humanity is displayed in how we apprehend others in our social and political dealings and by the

---

"Wiener Logik" we read: "Thiere erkennen auch ihren Herrn aber sind sich dessen nicht bewußt." *Vorlesungen über Logik*, Bd. 24 of *Kant's gesammelte Schriften*, ed. Akademie der Wissenschaften (Berlin: de Gruyter, 1966), 24:790–940, 846. In these lectures *erkennen* is being used at all levels of cognition and can be either conscious or not. Because the "Jäsche Logik" distinguishes between *kennen* and *erkennen*, the above sentence would have to read "animals are also acquainted with [*kennen*] their masters, but do not consciously or explicitly recognize [*erkennen*] them." *Immanuel Kant's Logik: Ein Handbuch zu Vorlesungen*, in *Kant's gesammelte Schriften*, Bd. 9, ed. Königlich Preußische Akademie der Wissenschaften (Berlin: de Gruyter, 1923), 9:1–150.

15. Immanuel Kant, "First Introduction," in *Critique of Judgment*, 383–441, 20:193–251.

16. Immanuel Kant, *Die falsche Spitzfindigkeit der vier syllogistischen Figuren, erwiesen von M. Immanuel Kant*, in *Vorkritische Schriften II: 1757–1777*, Bd. 2 of *Kants gesammelte Schriften*, ed. Königlich Preußische Akademie der Wissenschaften (Berlin: Georg Reimer, 1912), 2:47–61.

incentive to reproductively reinforce our own standing while maintaining civil relations in our prudential affairs. Finally, our personality is "rooted in reason practical of itself, i.e., in reason legislating unconditionally." It is the spiritual source not only of our moral life, but also of everything that we productively strive for in communal life.

These three predispositions to what is good have a theoretical analogue in the *Critique of Pure Reason* where Kant sketches a progressive scale that starts with the term "representation in general" (A320/B376), which I would call a vague kind of awareness. For a representation to reach the level of "consciousness," according to Kant, it must be "perceptual," by which he means that it is either a "sensation that modifies the state of a subject" or an "objective perception" that is cognitive. Clearly, Kant thinks that only human animals have cognition. Like other animals, human beings have sense impressions at the level of the life of the soul that can provide what Kant calls "Anticipations of Perception." He speaks here of "the real of the sensation" by which "the subject is affected" (A165/B207). But a "sensation in itself is not an objective representation" (A165/B208) of the world. Sensations are not cognitive according to Kant. They are subjectively real, but not objectively actual. Sensations exist as "instantaneous" (A99) limiting points on the timeline of our consciousness. What is instantaneously given by sense affects us at the lowest level of the life of the soul, whereas cognition begins at the level of mind or representational apprehension.

A sensation is comparable to what Kant calls "*prehension* [*fassen*] in one glimpse [*Blick*]" (§26, 5:254). In the "Subjective Deduction" of the first edition of the *Critique of Pure Reason*, Kant makes it clear that for sense to be intuitable as a manifold representational content, it must be "run through" over time by a synthetic act of *apprehension* (*auffassen*). But what is distributively run through must also be taken together in a third act of "*Zusammennehmung*" (A99). This will require the perceptual imagination to reproduce what was initially run through in order to allow the understanding to gradually *comprehend* (*zusammenfassen*) the unity of the apprehended manifold over time.

We can now supplement our earlier discussion of the mathematical sublime by more fully contrasting its instantaneous regressive comprehension (*Comprehension*) with the gradually accumulated progressive account of representational comprehension (*Zusammenfassung*). Whereas our passive being *affected* by sense occurs at the lowest limit of consciousness, the sublime discloses a more "vigorous *affect*" or "agitation of the mind" (§29, 5:272) aimed at the highest limit of consciousness. Thus for us life is not only the capacity to instantaneously register how our body is affected at the sensory level of soul, but also the sublime capacity of mind to be instantaneously enlivened by the imagination. Finally, it is worth noting that Kant speaks of the sublime not as providing a cognitive representation (*Vorstellung*) of something finite, but as providing a "*negative* presentation/exhibition [*Darstellung*]" of the "infinite" (§29, 5:274). If human life is to be more *positively* represented, mind must be related to the next level of self-activating spirit.

Our thinking about life as such must ultimately have a spiritual source, as Kant makes clear in section 49 of the *Critique of Judgment*: "*Spirit* [*Geist*] in an aesthetic sense is the enlivening [*belebende*] principle in the mind [*Gemüthe*]. But what this principle uses to enliven the soul, the *material* [*Stoff*] it employs for this, is what imparts to the mental powers a purposive momentum, i.e., imparts to them a play which is such that it sustains itself on its own and even strengthens the powers for such play" (§49, 5:313).

The material alluded to here is not physical, but representational. Kant is referring to how aesthetic ideas qua representations of the imagination can "prompt much thought, but to which no determinate thought whatsoever, i.e., no [determinate] concept can be adequate" (§49, 5:314). Kant gave our capacity to conceptually understand nature a formal grounding by means of the transcendental unity of apperception. But the "imagination (as a productive cognitive faculty)" can take this formal spontaneity of the understanding a step further "in the creation [*Schaffung*], as it were, of another nature out of the material that actual nature gives it" (§49, 5:314).[17]

The human, aesthetic imagination is creative in transforming our ordinary experience of the natural world into "something wholly different" and allowing us to "feel our freedom from the law of association (which attaches to the empirical use of the imagination)." It can creatively transform mechanistic nature as we know it into something else, but as Kant makes clear in his *Anthropology*, this transformative power of our imagination must be distinguished from a divine-like creative power called "*Schöpfung*" (7:168). Our imagination can be *schaffend* in being "inventive" (*dichtend*), but it is "not exactly *schöpferisch*, for it is not capable of producing a sense representation that was *never* given to our faculty of sense" (7:168). This means that we humans cannot ex nihilo create anything and certainly not any living creature (*Geschöpf*). Yet, the transformative *Schaffung* of the aesthetic imagination can produce things that are lifelike and thus serve as a kind of model for reflecting on what life means. We already saw that the aesthetic play of the imagination at the level of mind can enhance our

17. Translation modified.

feeling of life to maintain itself, and that this is more significant than the instinctive feeling of life at the lowest level of soul, which merely provides instantaneous, ephemeral impressions. And at the level of spirit, the imagination produces aesthetic ideas that can prefigure/configure what Kant will say about organisms in the "Critique of Teleological Judgment" as systems that preserve themselves and procreate. But these intimations will only be regulative and reflective, as will be made clear later.

In one of his "Reflexionen zur Metaphysik," Kant takes a step further by defining life as movement conceived transcendentally (R4786, 17:728). And in the *Opus postumum*, we read that the a priori capacity of the subject to initiate movement involves at the same time the capacity to "anticipate the counteracting moving forces of matter" (22:506).[18] This claim makes it possible to regard life as the transcendental condition for both the power to move and be moved and frames the agency of life in communal and systematic terms. Updating what I claimed in *Imagination and Interpretation in Kant*, we can say that it is the human/mental feeling of life associated with an aesthetic reflective judgment that provides the transcendental point of unity for both the spontaneity of the understanding and the receptivity of sense.[19] And at the level of spirit, the feeling of life allows us to not just be reactive, but to be actively responsive and anticipate the kind of reciprocity Kant finds in organic nature. He is careful not to directly project our feeling of life onto the biological sphere of nature, yet the realization that this mental feeling is holistic and that its cognates of vital and interior sense pervade our whole body, provides a source of orientation to supplement our *determinate* understanding of the mechanisms of nature with what will be shown to be an *indeterminate* reflective comprehension of organic reciprocity.

Orientation serves an important function in relating our own life to the world. To the extent that living creatures have the capacity to move, they need to be able to orient themselves in the world around them to avoid danger and attain their aims. The power to orient oneself enhances the feeling of life in that it is also perceptual. Kant calls it an a priori feeling whereby on the basis of distinguishing the left and right sides of one's body one can perceptually find one's way in unfamiliar territory. Orientation is all that we can expect from what we have said about life so far as we move into the territory of organic nature.

18. Immanuel Kant, *Opus postumum*, ed. Eckart Förster, trans. Eckhart Förster and Michael Rosen (Cambridge: Cambridge University Press, 1993).

19. Makkreel, *Imagination and Interpretation*, 105–6.

A Functional Exposition of Organic Beings

We are acquainted (*kennen*) with life through feeling but cannot conceptually cognize (*erkennen*) it according to Kant. We are constituted with the power to understand the causation of mechanical motion, not of self-initiated movements. Mechanistic causes as we can understand them must have sensible confirmation, which means that they are necessarily external to what they affect. But if there is self-initiated movement, it is by nature internal and cannot receive sensible confirmation. This suggests that biology which aims to study organisms must start with provisional judgments. Categorial judgments concerning mechanical causation are determinant or explanative because they appeal to universal laws of nature from which particular cause-effect relations can be inferred. The provisional judgments that Kant calls on to move beyond the bounds of our grasp of mechanism are reflective and proceed inductively from the particular to the general. They reflect on particulars as individuals that develop a self-contextualizing identity relative to their environment. These judgments reflectively characterize particular beings whose behavior manifests changes that are not predictable from known laws and thus seem to be contingent. If those changes nevertheless further the well-being of such a particular being, we may, according to Kant, judge them to be purposive.

This ascription of purposiveness renders such a being an internally ordered system whose parts are judged to be reciprocally related. Plants and animals can be judged to be organic systems that cause changes that affect themselves in terms of their own growth. Each such organism is assumed to "generate [*erzeugt*] itself as an individual" (§64, 5:371) and be its own end.[20] Kant writes that some parts in an "animal body (such as skin, bone, or hair) could be grasped as accumulations governed by merely mechanical laws. Still the cause that procures the appropriate matter, that *modifies and forms* it in that way, and that deposits it in the pertinent locations must always be judged teleologically. Hence everything in such a body must be regarded as organized; and everything, in a certain relation to the thing itself, an organ in turn" (§66, 5:377).

Formative modification rather than *motion* becomes the appropriate way to describe how organisms behave. Organisms manifest "a self-propagating formative power [*fortplanzende bildende Kraft*], which cannot be explained

20. Pluhar translates *erzeugt* as "produces," which is problematic, as I will show in my conclusion.

through the capacity for movement alone (that is, mechanism)" (§65, 5:374). The shift from movement to formative modification is important in that it makes room for plants as organic beings. But the assignment of purposiveness to plants and nonhuman animals that lack reason must be clarified. This purposiveness is not like the conscious, and possibly rational, purposes that humans project for themselves. Organic purposiveness, however, is primarily internal. Describing an organism as internally organized is technically purposive for our way of judging. It provides a means for us to reflect and make sense of what is going on and leaves open the possibility that a true mechanistic explanation can eventually be found. Yet as long as the ideal of a universal legislative order of nature cannot be fully filled in, it is heuristically useful to explore organisms as intermediate regions of organizational order.

Although from a contemporary perspective Kant's characterization of organic systems as teleological may strike us as antiquated, it can be shown to be less anthropomorphic than it seems at first. Just as aesthetic purposiveness of the imagination of the first half of the *Critique of Judgment* is a purposiveness without a determinate purpose, so the immanent purposiveness ascribed to organisms discloses no intentional purpose and seems to be primarily self-furthering. Aesthetic purposiveness is about feeling oneself into a context of *possibilities*, whereas organic purposiveness is about being adaptive to an immediate *actual* context.[21] For Kant, the reciprocal causality of the parts of an organism is not just about its organs reciprocally affecting each other. They also "are reciprocally cause and effect of their form" (§65, 5:373). This is the "basis on which someone judging this whole cognizes the systematic unity in the form and combination of all the manifold contained in the given matter." An organism must be judged not just in terms of its causal antecedents and constituents, but as a reciprocal system in which actions and reactions are in play, including from its surrounding context. This refers back to Kant's third relational category of community that was

21. In the introduction to the *Critique of Judgment*, Kant distinguishes four topological contexts that can orient our judgments: a general field (*Feld*), a territory *(Boden)* of experience, a law bound domain (*Gebiet*), and a habitat (*Aufenthalt*) that is merely empirically ordered (5:174). An organism forms a habitat that must contend with its surrounding territory. To the extent that we can also discover laws governing its behavior, we can judge an organism to be a domain-like system. The significance of the relation between reflective judgment and these four contexts is developed in chapter 3 of Rudolf A. Makkreel, *Orientation and Judgment in Hermeneutics* (Chicago: University of Chicago Press, 2015).

mentioned earlier when explicating the simultaneity of the sublime. It is worth commenting that in a note, the idea of a contextually organized system is compared to the coordinative *organization* of the political community thought to be the United States of America (§65, 5:375). What is at stake is a reflective comprehension of what is simultaneously cogenerated. In section 59, Kant already prepared us for this kind of comparison in symbolic terms by speaking of an "animate body" (*beseelten Körper*) as a reflective analogue for his ideal of a republican state that is law-governed and resists being controlled from without. Kant acknowledges that there is no one-to-one correspondence between organisms and nation states. Yet they exhibit a functional analogy that makes them reflective counterparts. To comprehend these reflective analogues is to draw on one of the formative functions of the imagination that Kant called "*Gegen-bildung* or counter-formation."[22] *Gegenbildung* is the imaginative power to discern symbolic rather than literal counter-parts in different contexts. These comparisons lead me to suggest another counterpart pairing. Organisms for Kant are self-organizing wholes whose parts possess *systemic* internal functions, but whose overall *systematic* formation must counter what could resist it from its surrounding context.

I think that this way of contextualizing organisms by moving beyond the second relational category of causality to the third relational category of community provides a way to both acknowledge and overcome Hannah Ginsborg's carefully argued distinction about "two kinds of mechanical inexplicability" of organisms.[23] The first kind of inexplicability points to the causal limits of *matter* that cannot account for the well-structured arrangement of the parts of individual things such as artifacts and organisms. The second kind of mechanical inexplicability pertains to what makes organisms *natural* rather than *artifactual*, namely, their display of certain ongoing "regularities." Yet by dwelling on this difference at the level of causality and not adequately considering the communal level of interaction, Ginsborg comes to place undue stress on what she calls the design-like nature of organisms. For her, an organism is an object that must be regarded "as if it had been designed, yet without committing ourselves to the claim that it was designed," which "is just to judge that the object conforms to a concept of how it ought to

22. Makkreel, *Imagination and Interpretation*, 15, 123; for more details about *Gegenbildung*, see also 13–15, 19.

23. Hannah Ginsborg, *The Normativity of Nature: Essays on Kant's "Critique of Judgement"* (Oxford: Oxford University Press, 2014), 299–303.

be."[24] In explicating what she means by such "standards,"[25] Ginsborg focuses on the purposiveness of organs like the eye whose "perfection"[26] is measured by an external task. But what especially characterizes organic purposiveness for Kant is the internal purposiveness among its various organs. This involves an organizational adaptation that need not be governed by the normative oughts associated with design, for, as Kant writes, we often find "certain parts" in organisms that "on account of their deficiencies or impediments, form in an entirely new way so as to preserve what is there, and so bring forth an *anomalous* creature" (§64, 5:372). This accommodation to chance imperfections is not just accepted by Kant but embraced as "among the most marvelous properties of organized creatures."

We can provisionally agree with Ginsborg that if the heart fails to pump blood to certain parts of the body, it is not functioning as we think it ought. But this could also be explained by the calcification of the arteries. Which part of an organism is deficient is not always readily apparent. Also, what is often inadequately noted about the immanent purposiveness of an organism is that beyond the modifications or inner adaptations among its parts we also see ways in which the organism as a whole adapts itself to its context where there are no clear oughts at work. What Kant calls "the intrinsic natural perfection" (§65, 5:375) of an organism does not exhibit the design-like perfection of a projected external end. There is something pre-fixed or static about completing a design, which goes against the self-modificatory powers of an organism. Therefore, intrinsic natural perfection is at best a self-modifying and adaptive perfection in which different coexisting contextual forces converge and intersect. The justification for adding the idea of contextual adaptation to Kant's own terminology will become more evident in the next section where organic epigenesis is discussed. In sum, I think the normativity Ginsborg discerns in organisms is reducible to the question of what is normal and what is not normal or anomalous. True

24. Ginsborg, *Normativity of Nature*, 241.

25. Ginsborg, *Normativity of Nature*, 276.

26. Ginsborg, *Normativity of Nature*, 242. The passages about perfection in Kant that are alluded to here are very general. They are not specifically about the way organisms function, but about things in general and are taken from the first half of the third *Critique* and finally from the "First Introduction" where Kant conceived perfection ontologically as applicable to the "formal unity" of "something composite" whether that be a constructed "hexagon" or an "organized being" (20:228).

normativity will be discussed later when it comes to how reflective judgment relates to what Kant means by comprehension.

Just as the aesthetic purposiveness of appreciating the beauty of a flower is not a cognitive pleasure in the perfection of some artistic design, so the organizational purposiveness of an organism is not the manifestation of some self-contained design. Kant's immanent purposiveness points to an organizational functioning that is somewhat metaphorical and figurative, but so is the current genetic language about cells of organisms exchanging signals and about neurons in the brain transmitting information to each other. We must be careful not to read too much into this kind of genetic transmission and realize that it is not tantamount to the conscious communication of meaning. And when Kant says that although the composition of the bones in our bodies can be causally explained, they must also be judged teleologically, this should be read heuristically as framing further questions about how these bones can continue to function properly in our bodies. Or, to elaborate on Kant's own description, it is to make sure that the "appropriate" minerals are found to be transmitted to the "pertinent locations" in the bones. His teleological judgments about the immanent purposiveness of organisms are not themselves supplementary explanations, but merely establish the appropriate meaning framework for pursuing further inquiry and eventual explanations.[27]

In the same vein, the feeling of life and the holistic self-enhancing frame of mind that were explored in the "Critique of Aesthetic Judgment" have no explanative value for the "Critique of Teleological Judgment." All that I would claim for them is the orientational function of providing some imaginative *augenscheinliche* clues or even an instantaneous transcendental glimpse into what it means for an organism to be in a general state of equilibrium or to adapt to disturbances caused by a more encompassing context. Yet it compensates for the fact that metaphysical efforts to ground life and make organisms less causally "inscrutable" have failed according to Kant. Thus metaphysicians who determinately assign organisms "the property of life" are accused of "hylozoism" (§65, 5:374) in that they would attribute life to matter itself, which he considers to be self-contradictory.

27. To be sure, Kant had personal doubts that there would ever be a Newton who could explain a blade of grass in the way that the motions of the planets have been explained through the mere mechanism of nature. On the other hand, he thought it presumptuous to rule out eventual mechanistic explanations. See §75, 5:400.

Equally unacceptable is the "alien principle of a soul standing in communion [*Gemeinschaft*]" with matter. To appeal to the metaphysical idea of a soul is to explain the self-organizing power of matter by moving outside of nature toward theism. The formative power that is reflectively ascribed to organisms must be "imparted [*mitgetheilt*] to their material" by nature itself, not by a metaphysical principle of life. Both these metaphysical approaches acknowledge the purposive behavior of organisms but make assumptions that are either self-contradictory or speculative.

Another approach that Kant finds unacceptable is to altogether dismiss the idea that organisms are purposive. Philosophers who have done this either follow Epicurus, who starts with "lifeless matter" and regards organisms as mere contingent aggregates resulting from mechanistic laws, or they resemble Spinoza, who is accused of having posited a "lifeless God" (§72, 5:392n6). If the world is permeated by a divine order or fatalistic *architectonic*, then the contingency associated with the generation of organisms is simply explained away. What Kant proposes instead is a more limited *tectonic* of nature that acknowledges the contingency involved in organic processes, but nevertheless seeks for a lawfulness there that is not determinant but reflective. The purposiveness that Kant tries to manifest in his exposition of organic processes of formative modification is a "lawfulness of the contingent" (§76, 5:404). It is the lawfulness of coordinative order rather than subordinating order. It inserts a provisional tectonic of organic nature within the architectonic of mechanistic nature. Instead of imposing the idea of life onto organisms or skeptically denying it of them, Kant explores how much sense we can make of the way organisms function by in effect suspending the idea of life. Kant only uses the term "life" twice in the context of his extensive discussions of how organisms are generated and how they function. One of these occasions is when he claims that the explanation provided by hylozoism moves us in "a circle: we try to derive the natural purposiveness in organized beings from the life of matter, while yet we are familiar [*kennen*] with this life only in organized beings" (§73, 5:394). We should not expect to conceptually cognize what "life *in* matter" is by appealing to the "life *of* matter." The other instance is when he casually refers to beasts of prey who "feed only on what has life" (§82, 5:426). Those like Ginsborg who use the translation by James Creed Meredith may not have noticed Kant's hesitancy to directly endow organisms with life, because Kant's neutral term *Geschöpf* is not properly translated as "creature" but as "form of life." Similarly, when Kant speaks of "organized [*organisirte*] creatures," Meredith substitutes "organic life" (§64, 5:372).[28] Meredith may have felt justified in using the phrase "form of life" because Kant had just claimed that repeated defoliation of a tree could "kill it" (§64, 5:372). In response, I would say that while we are on an everyday basis acquainted (*kennen*) with trees as "living and dying," from the scientific or technical standpoint of cognizing (*erkennen*) the immanent purposiveness of organisms, we should not be looking for some special unifying natural property of "life." Even when discussing our own internal sense of life, we saw Kant speak of three ways in which we feel ourselves as "living."

Organic and Mental Epigenesis

Kant finds support for his standpoint in Johann Friedrich Blumenbach's theory of epigenesis insofar as it starts with "organized matter" (§81, 5:424) rather than with living matter. This is elaborated in a section about relating "Mechanism to the Teleological Principle in Explaining Natural Purposes as Natural Products," (§81, 5:421) in order to find a middle ground between natural epigenesis and preformationism.

Although Kant's conception of the immanent purposiveness of organisms ascribes a kind of inherent form to them, it should not be confused with the traditional preformationism rejected by epigenesists who hold that the embryo forms and differentiates itself after conception. They deny the claim, made by ovists, for example, that the embryo is preformed in the mother and that the male's semen only mechanically stimulates its growth. Similarly, Kant attempted to move beyond the traditional belief that the form of each individual is divinely preformed or designed. He replaced the theory of individual preformation with a "system of generic preformation" (§81, 5:423) that applies to a whole zoological species. This new system conceives form "virtually" (*virtualiter*) as a "predisposition imparted to the stock." This reduced mode of preformationism leaves room for the theory of epigenesis that Kant prefers scientifically. "For in considering those things whose origin can be conceived only in terms of a causality of purposes, this theory, at least as far as propagation is concerned, regards nature as itself bringing them forth [*hervorbringend*] rather than merely developing them; and so it minimizes appeal to the supernatural" (§81, 5:424).

28. Immanuel Kant, *Critique of Judgment*, ed. and rev. Nicolas Walker, trans. James Creed Meredith (Oxford: Oxford University Press, 1952).

The simplest way to conceive of the immanent purposiveness of organisms is in terms of growth and differentiation, self-preservation, and resisting external harm, all of which involves contextual adaptation. The first epigenetic manifestation of growth and differentiation of mammals occurs in the enclosed context of the mother's womb. After birth, they are usually nurtured in a protected environment and gradually learn to protect themselves in order to gain a relative independence from the larger world.

In the second edition of the *Critique of Pure Reason*, Kant speaks of the "epigenesis of pure reason" (B167). By this he means that our cognition of the world is "not all borrowed from experience," for there are elements of cognition that are "self-thought." Thus the categories of the understanding are not mere "subjective predispositions for thinking implanted in us . . . in such a way that their use would agree exactly with the laws of nature along which experience runs." These would seem to be the laws of nature that govern the processes of the human brain. The epigenesis of reason upholds the thesis that however our brain functions in providing us with the contents of experience after our release from the womb, our mind has the power to contribute a spontaneous form to them. We can thus formulate the following parallel: the immanent purposiveness of organisms points to self-organization in a mechanistic world and the spontaneous epigenesis of reason involves a "self-birth" (*Selbstgebärung*) (A765/B793) of the categories that first give meaning to the sensory givens of experience. It is thus not surprising that Kant speaks of reason as its own organic power or organ.[29] But whereas organisms adapt to contexts, reason adopts its own contexts.

Instead of determinately assigning life to organisms, Kant refers to a "self-propagating formative power" that can be reflectively ascribed to the patterns of change they exhibit in their natural context. Descriptive contextual judgments based on objective observation are interpreted as reflective judgments that are purposive from the human standpoint. Kant asserts that for an archetypal intellect that proceeds from whole to parts nothing would be contingent and no special appeal to purposiveness is necessary (§77, 5:407). But for our ectypal or discursive intellect that proceeds from part to part, a special regulative principle of overall purposive connectedness is needed for a reflective comprehension of what is observed.

29. For more on this see Jennifer Mensch, *Kant's Organicism: Epigenesis and the Development of Critical Philosophy* (Chicago: University of Chicago Press, 2013), ch. 7.

What Is Reflective Comprehension of Purposiveness?

In the "Critique of Aesthetic Judgment," we came across two modes of comprehension: the temporal *Zusammenfassung* of representations assigned to the imagination and the instantaneous *Comprehension* of a presentational *Augenschein.* In the "Critique of Teleological Judgment," we find another mode of comprehension (*Begreifen*) that is more intellectual and can be related to the "Jäsche Logic." There Kant's cognitive scale moves up from representations that count as mere acquaintance (*kennen*) to those that provide conscious recognition (*erkennen*) and conceptual cognition or understanding (*verstehen*). The highest level is rational cognition, which can either provide complete insight (*einsehen, perspicere*) or a comprehension (*begreifen, comprehendere*) (9:65)[30] of things relative to some purpose. The relativity of rational comprehension means that it is not to be confused with a divine or absolute encompassing knowing for which nothing is contingent.

An instructive explication of this rational but relative mode of comprehension (*Begreifen*) is given in the earlier "Vienna Logic" (ca. 1780) where it is defined as the possession of "sufficient insight, insofar as something serves a certain purpose" (24:846).[31] Comprehension as a mode of rational cognition is thus simultaneously theoretical and practical, that is, normative. Kant also adds that comprehension is "something requiring much delicacy" (*etwas sehr delicates*), which indicates that it requires tactfulness or reflective skill in the use of human reason.[32]

This suggests that the purposiveness of rational comprehension can be reflective, and indeed we see it applied as such in the second half of the *Critique of Judgment.* Kant first points to this kind of comprehension when discussing the purposiveness that a geometrical figure like an ellipse can have for projecting the trajectories of celestial bodies (§62, 5:364). But this is a formal and a priori purposiveness rather than a teleological a posteriori purposiveness. The former makes "comprehensible [*begreiflich*] the unity of many rules which result from the construction" (§62, 5:364)

30. Immanuel Kant, "The Jäsche Logic," in *Lectures on Logic,* trans. and ed. J. Michael Young (Cambridge: Cambridge University Press, 1992), 521–640, 9:1–150.

31. Immanuel Kant, "The Vienna Logic," in *Lectures on Logic,* 249–378, 24:790–937.

32. For a more detailed treatment of the role of comprehension, see Rudolf A. Makkreel, "Kant on Cognition, Comprehension, and Knowledge," in *Natur und Freiheit: Akten des 12. Kant-Kongresses,* ed. Violetta L. Waibel, Margit Ruffing and David Wagner (Berlin: de Gruyter, 2018), 1297–304.

of a single geometrical figure; the latter purposiveness makes empirically observed behavior "comprehensible [*begreiflich*] by analogy with a subjective basis on which we connect representations within us" (§60, 5:360). Although we cannot expect to understand the behavior of animals in any determinate manner and give causal explanations for many aspects of it, we can reflectively comprehend general patterns of their behavior by judging them normatively as organisms whose parts are functioning well together. What I have referred to as "reflective comprehension" about these organized and self-adjusting beings allows us to ascribe an internal purposiveness to them from our standpoint. Such reflective or interpretive judging can make regulative claims about animals as natural beings while suspending any appeal to a generic principle of life. Yet the fact that animals like beavers have building skills resembling human technical skills leads Kant to reject the Cartesian assumption that nonhuman animals are merely well-coordinated machines or *automata* (§90, 5:464n). This reflects a change from "Reflexion 3855," which Erich Adickes places anywhere between 1764 and 1770, where Kant referred to animals as *automata* (17:313).[33] In the "Appendix on the Methodology of Teleological Judgment," Kant writes that "we can quite correctly infer *by analogy* . . . that animals too act according to *representations* . . . and that regardless of the difference in specific kind between them and man, they are still of the same genus [*Gattung*] as human beings (namely, as living beings)" (§90, 5:464). Here animals such as beavers are called living beings to the extent that we see an analogy with the human representational skill to produce things. We saw that we are entitled to consider all organisms as purposive because they can modify themselves from within. But if a beaver can build dams and canals as the means to produce a shallow pond in which it builds its so-called lodge, then we can also ascribe to it something akin to our representational power to produce artifacts that serve our life goals. However, their representational skills are instinctive and not consciously designed. Ultimately, Kant seems to place skillful animals at the level of the life of the mere soul as distinct from the more human levels of mind and spirit that can call on the freedom and

33. For information on Erick Adickes's dating system see Paul Guyer, introduction to Immanuel Kant, *Notes and Fragments*, ed. and trans. Paul Guyer, trans. Curtis Bowman and Frederick Rauscher (Cambridge: Cambridge University Press, 2005), xiii–xxviii; Erich Adickes, "Einleitung in die Abtheilung des handschriftlichen Nachlasses," in *Kant's gesammelte Schriften*, Bd. 14, ed. Königlich Preußische Akademie der Wissenschaften (Berlin: Georg Reimer, 1911), 14:xv–lxii.

spontaneity of reason. More generally, since the inherent purposiveness of organisms is only self-organizing and self-modifying, Kant would not need to ascribe any soul-based life to plants, trees, and insects. All organisms are generative and organizationally adaptive, but not all develop representational productive skills.

We started with the metaphysical idea of the life of the soul that can determine itself from an inner principle and has the capacity to move itself. This traditional substantial notion of soul was made functional by delimiting the soul to the capacity to be modified and focusing more on how the mind reacts and spirit is self-active. The aesthetic feeling of life was then explicated as an active responsiveness that mediates between the pure spontaneity of the intellect and the passivity of sense. Finally, we supplemented the imaginative comprehension of mental life with a reflective judgmental comprehension of organic purposiveness that replaced the efficacy of self-movement with that of self-modification and the ideal of self-determination with a mode of self-organization. Although organisms are natural products, most are merely reproductive.[34] Only organisms with productive skills can be reflectively comprehended as living. The most common trait of organisms is that they are generative where self-modification is at the same time adaptive.

34. Kant speaks of trees generating (*erzeugen*) themselves and their offspring as well as of nature bringing forth (*hervorbringen*) anomalous creatures to compensate for special circumstances or injuries. Unfortunately, Pluhar translates both words as "producing."

Chapter 11

Organizing the State

Mechanism and Organism in Kant's Political Writings of the 1780s and 1790s

Susan Meld Shell

A state without the means of some change is without the means of its conservation. . . . The two principles of conservation and correction operated strongly at the two critical periods of the Restoration and Revolution, when England found itself without a king. At both those periods the nation regenerated the deficient part of the old constitution through the parts which were not impaired. They kept these old parts exactly as they were, that the part recovered might be suited to them. They acted by the ancient organized states in the shape of their old organization, and not by the organic moleculae of a disbanded people.

—Edmund Burke[1]

1. Edmund Burke, *Reflections on the Revolution in France* (New York: Oxford University Press, 1999), 30. The German translation by Friedrich von Gentz reads: "Ein Staat, dem es an allen Mitteln zu einer Veränderung fehlt, entbehrt die Mittel zu seiner Erhaltung. . . . Beyde Principien, das Erhaltungs- und das Verbesserungsprincip, wirkten mächtiglich, als sich England in den beyden critischen Perioden der *Restauration* und *Revolution*, ohne König fand. In beyden Perioden hatte die Nation den Schlußstein ihres alten Gewölbes verlohren, aber darum warf sie nicht den ganzen Bau über den Haufen. Im Gegentheil, sie richtete . . . den fehlenden Theil der alten Constitution durch Hülfe der unangefochtnen Theile wieder auf. Diese alten Theile wurden unberührt gelassen,

> An empire consisting of one nation [*Das Reich eines Volks*] is a family, a well-ordered household: it reposes on itself, for it is founded on nature, and stands and falls by time alone. An empire forcing together a hundred peoples and a hundred twenty provinces is a monstrosity and no state body.
>
> —Johann Gottfried Herder[2]

Few political metaphors are more fraught than the comparison of the political community to a living being. This is especially so in the discourse that arose in the aftermath of the French Revolution, in which warring factions competed to claim the organic mantle for their own preferred pro- or anti-revolutionary model. At a time in which the emerging biological sciences were at the forefront of scientific research, resolution of the conflict seemed critical, not only for its immediate partisan import but also for its implications for science at a time in which the limitations of Newtonianism were being felt with increasing acuteness across a range of fields, from psychology to chemistry.

Erupting onto the scene under the self-declared banner of Enlightenment, the revolution and its aftermath put reason itself on trial in the eyes of many. No one was more acutely aware of this threat than Immanuel Kant, who had absorbed Rousseau's earlier critique into his own critical defense of reason in the early 1780s. Beginning as early as the 1760s, Kant incorporated Rousseau's "organic" model of the state into his own concept of republican freedom. Less noticed, however, is the transformation that this model underwent in the 1790s, partly owing to new theoretical discoveries first given definitive form in the *Critique of Judgment* (1790), but also in response to both the death of Frederick the Great and to the French Rev-

damit der verlohrengegangene sich nach ihnen wieder bilden und ihnen wieder anpassen konnte. Sie wirkten durch die alten bereits organisirten Stände nach dem Formen ihrer alten Organisation, nicht durch die formlosen Grundstoffe eines aufgelöseten Volkes." Friedrich von Gentz, *Betrachtungen über die französische Revolution: Nach dem Englischen des Herrn Burke neu bearbeitet* (Berlin: F. Vieweg, 1793), 29. Gentz translates Burke's "states" by *Stände*, making the maintenance of traditional aristocratic privilege more explicit than in the original version.

2. Johann Gottfried Herder, *Outlines of a Philosophy of the History of Man*, trans. T. Churchill (New York: Bergman, 1966), 325.

olution and its aftermath.[3] Owing to the latter events, Kant found himself newly on the defensive both intellectually and politically. At the same time, the revolution—or, as he preferred to say, a certain unselfish response to it—opened up a morally encouraging historical prospect for which the concept of the state as a self-organizing being served as a particularly apt model, one capable of countering the competing organic metaphors both of anti-revolutionary "Burkeans" like Friederich Gentz, on the one hand, and of revolutionary champions like Johann Gottfried Herder and Johann Gottlieb Fichte,[4] on the other. The following study aims both to describe Kant's emerging conception of the state as an organized and self-organizing being and to sketch some of that conception's implications for his larger theoretical and practical project.

Kant's Prerevolutionary Political Organicism

The history of the comparison of the political community to an "organic" whole begins, for present purposes, with Thomas Hobbes. Hobbes famously likened the state to an artificial man understood as a mechanical device of which men were both the "matter" and the "makers"—one whose creation (as a mortal God) rivaled that of God himself. Hobbes's analogy was an explicit affront not only to the traditional comparison of the Christian community to the body of Christ, but also to older conceptions of the "body politic." Such conceptions, tracing back to Plato and Aristotle, identified political authority with a ruling or commanding part that aimed at a particular understanding of the human good and was analogous in

3. See, for example, Katrin Flikschuh, *Kant and Modern Political Philosophy* (Cambridge: Cambridge University Press, 2000); Elizabeth Ellis, *Kant's Politics: Provisional Theory for an Uncertain World* (New Haven, CT: Yale University Press, 2005); Arthur Ripstein, *Force and Freedom* (Cambridge, MA: Harvard University Press, 2009); Pauline Kleingeld, *Kant and Cosmopolitanism: The Philosophic Ideal of World Citizenship* (Cambridge: Cambridge University Press, 2012); Maliks Reidar, *Kant's Politics in Context* (Oxford: Oxford University Press, 2015).

4. See, for example, Johann Gottlieb Fichte, *Foundations of Natural Right*, ed. Frederick Neuhouser, trans. Michael Bauer (Cambridge: Cambridge University Press, 2000); Johann Gottlieb Fichte, *Grundlage des Naturrechts nach Prinzipien der Wissenschaftslehre*, in *Fichtes Werke*, ed. Immanuel Hermann Fichte, Bd. 3, *Zur Rechts- und Sittenlehre 1* (Berlin: de Gruyter, 1971), 1–385, 209.

this respect to the role of "reason" in the human soul. Hobbes's new "civil science" (which he claimed to be the "first" true civil science) had Aristotle specifically in its sights. No longer would political authority rest on a claim to superior rational knowledge of "the good" (knowledge of a sort that the new physics of Francis Bacon and René Descartes had largely discredited) but would instead flow from the collective wills of the governed, pledging their obedience to an overarching sovereign for no motive higher than their own preservation. Hobbes's mechanistic psychology was thus an exercise in rhetoric as a foray into metaphysics. By abstracting from men's competing ends as much as Bacon had abstracted from the diversity of natural kinds, Hobbes meant to make human behavior as predictable as the interaction of material bodies. The "end" of motion both inanimate and animate, in this new, anti-Aristotelean scheme, was not the perfection of a thing's specific nature but—in keeping with the new principle of inertia—repetition of the same, or what Hobbes calls "endeavor" or "conatus." Although the model remained hierarchical inasmuch as all power rested in the will of the sovereign, the basis of the latter's claim was no longer so: public confession of men's natural equality being, according to Hobbes, a law of nature necessary to public peace, given men's natural propensity to quarrel.

If Kant was impressed by the essentially Hobbesian model that had been widely adopted under the reign of Frederick the Great, Kant was even more deeply influenced by Jean-Jacques Rousseau's crucial defection from the party of Hobbes's Enlightenment followers. Drawing partly on the emergent chemical and biological investigations of Pierre Roussel, Comte de Buffon, and others, Rousseau eschewed the metaphysical dogmatism of both the Hobbesian materialists and their dualist or spiritualist adversaries as equally inadequate to explain many of the commonly observable phenomena with which we are most intimately familiar, beginning with the sentiment of one's own free existence.

The qualitative transformations and natural living wholes, self-conscious and not, for which mechanical science seemed unable to adequately account (despite the ingenious attempts of many) could be more helpfully approached, Rousseau suggested, in terms drawing on the new notion of "organized being" put forward by Buffon and others. Whether one opted, finally, for mechanical causation, or for one of the competing metaphysical views that proliferated in the early to mid-eighteenth century, certain observable peculiarities, both external and internal, of living beings, beginning with our own, offered the promise of a rigorous anthropology compatible with, without thereby being reducible to, a study of the natural forces that formed the subject of mathematical physics.

"Organism" and related or cognate terms for animate existence were themselves modern innovations, capturing observable features peculiar to living beings (such as the reciprocal interdependence of their parts) without reversion to neo-scholastic models of the soul and similar scientific anachronisms. Even where "soul" talk remained,[5] the principle of unity thereby implied tended to be formal and functional rather than concrete or substantive, directed more toward the preservation of the individual along with the perpetuation of its specific type than toward the achievement of a concrete, kind-specific perfection. Buffon's definition of a species as a group capable of common fertile generation is in this respect particularly instructive, abstracting as it does from the similarity in "looks" by which Carolus Linneaus, not to speak of earlier naturalists, took their classificatory bearings.[6] Human nature for Rousseau was most accessible in similar terms: in our observable beginnings rather than through the distorting lens of artificial "ideals" dependent on what society has made us. Man is born free and everywhere in chains—natural wholes unto ourselves, that is to say, and social beings only by an act of will.

Rousseau's starting point—insofar as it impressed a metaphysically disillusioned Kant first encountering him in the early 1760s—was the formal act of will by which freedom might not only be regained but also reconciled with a scientifically progressive civilization. Rousseau's peculiar conception of the (healthy) state as an organized being, united by a general will, provided the approximate model for Kant's subsequent republican "idea," along with his accompanying attempts to achieve it ever more closely.

Initially, to be sure, that inspiration yielded two seemingly discrete versions of civic union: republicanism and monarchy. The former, which yielded both unity and equality, cleaved closely to Rousseau's own republic

5. See the helpful discussion of lingering "neo-Aristotelean" views by Jean-Luc Guichet in *Rousseau, l'animal et l'homme: L'animalité dans l'horizon anthropologique des Lumières* (Paris: Le Cerf, 2006), ch. 2.

6. See also in this regard Immanuel Kant, *Von den verschiedenen Racen der Menschen*, in *Vorkritische Schriften II: 1757–1777*, Bd. 2 of *Kant's gesammelte Schriften*, ed. Königlich Preußische Akademie der Wissenschaften (Berlin: Reimer, 1912), 2:427–43, 2:429. All translations are my own; page citations are to the standard Academy edition of *Kant's gesammelte Schriften*, ed. Königlich Preußische Akademie der Wissenschaften (Berlin: Georg Reimer/Walter de Gruyter, 1902–); volume numbers are followed by page numbers.

of virtue; the other, better adapted to the moral laxity that is attendant on scientifically "progressive" times, adopted the Hobbesian strategy of grounding sovereignty in the arbitrary will of an all-powerful monarch—a scheme that offered "unity but not equality" ("Bemerkungen zu den Beobachtungen über das Gefühl des Schönen und Erhabenen," 20:166).[7]

In subsequent years Kant would combine these ideals in a model of justice in which reciprocal freedom is secured by the irresistible will of an enlightened ruler, thereby overcoming the problem that Rousseau's *First Discourse on the Arts and Sciences* had presented as (nearly) insoluble. Civic freedom and equality, Rousseau maintained, required the passionate identification of citizens with the wider community; hence his famous doubt as to the possibility of reconciling civic health with progress in the arts and sciences. For all his praise of Rousseau's genius,[8] Kant never shared in that pessimism. Even in his *Remarks* Kant had sought to reconcile progress in the arts and sciences with civic health by prioritizing the universal, and hence rational, form of the general will, over its particular content (20:161). The general will on Kant's maturer understanding "gives" the law ("by virtue of its form") rather than "making" it (by virtue of its matter). And the existence of a just community no longer depends, as with Rousseau, on passions that are both parochial and difficult to sustain, particularly under conditions of modern enlightenment. Instead, equal freedom under law can be secured, or at least approached, by an appeal to reason—either in a higher, moral sense that takes men as they ought to be, or in a lower, merely prudential sense that takes them as they are. But in neither case, in Kant's writings prior to the French Revolution, need subjects themselves participate in positive law-*making* (as with Rousseau). It suffices, from the standpoint of right, that the ruler treat them "in accordance with their dignity" as *potential* lawgiving members of a moral kingdom of ends.[9]

This development is aided, in turn, by emergent accounts of "life,"

7. Immanuel Kant, "Bemerkungen zu den Beobachtungen über das Gefühl des Schönen und Erhabenen," in *Handschriftlicher Nachlaß*, in *Kant's gesammelte Schriften*, Bd. 20, ed. Preußische Akademie der Wissenschaften (Berlin: de Gruyter, 1942), 20:1–192.

8. See, for example, "Bemerkungen," 20:43.

9. See Immanuel Kant, "Beantwortung der Frage: Was ist Aufklärung?," in *Abhandlungen nach 1781*, Bd. 8 of *Kant's gesammelte Schriften*, ed. Königlich Preußische Akademie der Wissenschaften (Berlin: Georg Reimer, 1912), 8:33–42, 8:42; "Idee zu einer allgemeinen Geschichte in weltbürgerlicher Absicht," in *Abhandlungen nach 1781*, 8:15–31, 8:22; *Kritik der reinen Vernunft*, in *Kant's gesammelte Schriften*, Bd. 4, ed. Königlich Preußische Akademie der Wissenschaften (Berlin: Georg Reimer, 1911), 4:1–252, A 316/B 372–73.

both animal and spiritual, that reach their apex in the mid-1770s,[10] a decade during which Kant was hard at work on the *Critique of Pure Reason*, and published little other than an essay on race and a review of an anatomical work of Rousseauian provenance. The initial outlines of that account first appear in *Dreams of a Spirit Seer*, a work roughly contemporary with the *Remarks*. Though relegated to the ranks of metaphysical fantasy, the intelligible world there described bears a more than passing resemblance to the moral world of Kant's later critical writings, and is endorsed, even in this early work, only for the sake of practical ends. The true world, on this early account, is a community of beings united by spiritual and organic laws, the latter specifically applying to those spiritual beings who also find themselves embodied in the material world and thereby also subject to the latter's laws of action and reaction. While Kant is dismissive of theoretical claims as to the reality of such a spirit world, he confesses practical allegiance to its moral import, along with a feeling of freedom, and accompanying susceptibility to the laws of conscience, bias toward which he cannot "and would not wish" to remove (*Träume eines Geistersehers*, 2:350).[11] His subsequent attempts to identify moral conscience with a feeling for "spirit" as the "principle of life" in his anthropological lectures of the 1770s were put definitively to rest by the theoretical breakthroughs of the late 1770s, and accompanying abandonment of any claim to theoretical cognition, via such an "inner feeling," of the soul as substance.[12] In their place, Kant adopted the two-tiered vital scheme that is given perhaps its most moving rhetorical expression in the famous conclusion of the *Critique of Practical Reason*, which juxtaposes the natural "vital force" with which "we have been for a short term provided we know not how" with a higher, "moral life" independent of animality "at least insofar as this can be inferred from the purposive determination of my existence by [the moral] law" (*Kritik der praktischen Vernunft*, 5:162).[13]

10. For a fuller discussion, see Susan Meld Shell, "Kant as 'Vitalist': The 'Principium of Life' in 'Anthropologie Friedlaender,'" in *Kant's Lectures on Anthropology: A Critical Guide*, ed. Alix Cohen (Cambridge: Cambridge University Press, 2014), 151–71.

11. Immanuel Kant, *Träume eines Geistersehers, erläutert durch Träume der Metaphysik*, in *Vorkritische Schriften II: 1757–1777*, Bd. 2 of *Kant's gesammelte Schriften*, ed. Königlich Preußische Akademie der Wissenschaften (Berlin: Reimer, 1912), 2:315–73.

12. See Corey Dyck, *Kant and Rational Psychology* (New York: Oxford University Press, 2014).

13. Immanuel Kant, *Kritik der praktischen Vernunft*, in *Kant's gesammelte Schriften*, Bd. 5, ed. Königlich Preußische Akademie der Wissenschaften (Berlin: Georg Reimer, 1913), 5:1–163.

Rousseau's *Emile*, which Kant read carefully,[14] had famously adopted three methodological premises: first, that all natural predispositions are good; but second, that in man alone these predispositions, left to develop on their own and without rational direction, put man out of harmony with himself and others—a condition that can be ameliorated, though never fully rectified, through the judicious use of reason aided by the imagination; and third, that a primary cause of social ills stemmed from the gap between the time at which human beings are physically able to generate their kind and when they are capable of forming and sustaining the stable domestic attachments necessary for any enduring social order (the conflictual span of time, as Kant will later describe it, between men's sexual and civil maturity) ("Mutmaßlicher Anfang der Menschengeschichte," 8:116n).[15] Kant adapted these methodological premises without sharing fully in Rousseau's remedies,

---

14. This is clear not only from his *Remarks* from the early 1760s, but also from his continuing return to *Emile* in later works. See, for example, "Mutmaßlicher Anfang der Menschengeschichte," in *Abhandlungen nach 1781*, 8:107–23, 8:116 and *Anthropologie*, 7:326, in which the "Profession of Faith of a Savoyard Vicar" is listed as a separate work, an indication that Kant had indeed read *Emile* very carefully. Immanuel Kant, *Anthropologie in Pragmatischer Hinsicht*, in *Kant's gesammelte Schriften*, Bd. 7, ed. Königlich Preußische Akademie der Wissenschaften (Berlin: Georg Reimer, 1917), 7:117–333. For more on the *Remarks*, see the editors' introduction to *Kant's Observations and Remarks: A Critical Guide*, ed. Susan Meld Shell and Richard Velkley (Cambridge: Cambridge University Press, 2012).

15. In his 1771 "Recension von Moscatis Schrift: Von dem körperlichen wesentlichen Unterschiede zwischen der Structur der Thiere und Menschen" (in *Vorkritische Schriften II: 1757–1777*, 2:421–25), Kant traces the physical ills arising from our upright gait to the tension between the four-legged structure best suited to our animal existence and preservation as a species and the upright posture best suited to our rational and moral development. That Kant by his own account suffered from some of these ills (e.g., "narrow-chestedness" [2:423–24]), and *Der Streit der Facultäten*, in *Kant's gesammelte Schriften*, Bd. 7, ed. Königlich Preußische Akademie der Wissenschaften (Berlin: Georg Reimer, 1917), 7:1–116, 7:104); along with an accompanying "predisposition to hypochondria" (7:104), adds a note of personal poignancy to Kant's endorsement of Moscati's claim that "the upright gait of the human being is contrived and against nature" (2:423). That punctuated model of human maturity, according to which "nature has grounded in us predispositions for two different ends," one pertaining to humanity as an animal species and one to humanity as a moral one, is also reflected in "Conjectural Beginnings of Human History," which expands on that claim in a lengthy footnote (8:116n). Immanuel Kant, "Conjectural Beginnings of Human History," in *Anthropology, History, and Education*, ed. Günter Zöller and Robert B. Louden, trans. Allen W. Wood (Cambridge: Cambridge University Press, 2007), 160–75, 8:107–23.

which he instead supplemented with an "idea" of cosmopolitan history as the progressive realization of natural predispositions destined to develop fully only in the species.

In works prior to 1789, the republican state figures in this history both as a "body" in its own right and as the matrix (*Schoss*) or husk (*Hülle*) in which alone all human predispositions can develop both freely and without mutual conflict and hence "fully." No less than the cosmological play of planetary action and reaction to which Kant's "Idea for a Universal History with a Cosmopolitan Intention" (1784) specifically compares human history, the play of human action and reaction constitutes a system, on this account, leading (it may be hoped) to the eventual emergence of a "great state body" (*Staatskörper*) with recognizably "organic" features and of which the previous world knows no example: "Although this political body exists for the present only in the roughest of outlines, it nonetheless seems as if a feeling is beginning to stir in all its members, which is laid in each for the maintenance of the whole. And this gives hope that, after many revolutions . . . the highest purpose of nature, a universal *cosmopolitan condition*, will at last come to pass as the matrix [*Schoss*] within which all the original predispositions of the human race will be developed" ("Idee zu einer allgemeinen Geschichte," 8:28).

Unlike the cosmological idea, which is merely "regulative" (*Kritik der reinen Vernunft*, A671/B699), moreover, a cosmological idea of history, newly brought to consciousness, would contribute to its own realization, as Kant explains in his ninth and final thesis:

> It is admittedly a strange and at first sight absurd proposition to write a history according to an idea of how the world course should go if it is to conform to certain rational ends; it would seem that only a novel could result from such premises. Yet if it may be assumed that nature does not work without a plan and purposeful end, even amidst the arbitrary play of human freedom, this idea might nevertheless prove useful. And although we are too short-sighted to perceive the hidden mechanism of nature's scheme, this idea may yet serve as a guide to us in exhibiting an otherwise planless aggregate of human actions at least considered in gross as a system. For if we . . . trace the influence of the Greeks upon the formation and misformation [*Bildung und Missbildung*] of the state body of the Roman people . . . and follow down to our own times the influence of Rome upon

> the Barbarians . . . [transmitted through enlightened peoples down to our own times], we shall discover a regular process of improvement in the state constitutions of our continent (which will probably give laws to all others). (8:29)

Responding, it would seem, to Rousseau's challenge (in wishing that the "novel/romance" [*roman*] of Emile and Sophie could be the "history of our species"),[16] Kant here provides the "end" that the former thinker had left open. Whereas Rousseau, in arguing for mankind's "perfectibility," had explicitly denied that its terminus was knowable, Kant offers a final end of nature as a determinate point of reference toward whose actualization we are driven, as it were, by instinct, but that can be furthered, and ultimately is to be directed, by conscious rational guidance.

Kant's introduction of the principle of autonomy with the 1785 publication of the *Groundlaying of the Metaphysics of Morals*[17] adds a refining element to this account of the formation, misformation, and transformation (*Bildung*, *Missbildung*, and *Umbildung*) of the body politic, as suggested in an unpublished reflection from the mid to late 1780s that deserves quotation in full:

> If I think to myself that there is in nature, apart from the material (not merely formal) mechanism, also life, i.e., an activity in natural things according to laws of the faculty of desire, there emerges the concept of needs and an organism, which may be automatic or grounded in pre-established harmony. Since the things outside of each living being are directed to have effect not for themselves but necessarily and originally toward the need and maintenance of living nature, it follows that the natural order can hardly be grounded in anything other than the idea of an author, hence an organism.
>
> The causality of these living beings, that is, the determination of their faculty of desire, is either autonomy or heteronomy. In the latter case grounded through instinct as organon of the

16. Jean-Jacques Rousseau, *Oeuvres complètes*, vol. 4, *Emile ou De l'education*, ed. Bernard Gagnebin and Marcel Raymond (Paris: Gallimard, 1969), book 5, 4:777.

17. Immanuel Kant, *Grundlegung zur Metaphysik der Sitten*, in *Kant's gesammelte Schriften*, Bd. 4, ed. Königlich Preußische Akademie der Wissenschaften (Berlin: Georg Reimer, 1911), 4:385–463.

> ends in the idea of another being, in the former case grounded though freedom in the idea belonging to the beings themselves. In the former it is always only a formal mechanism of nature in accordance with physical laws, in the latter a spontaneity in accordance with practical laws, and its nature is determinable not (merely) organically [struck out: but rather] and physically, but also morally. In sofar [as this is so] this being directs itself not merely in accordance with its natural needs, i.e., a foreign and impressed [*eingedrückten*] idea, but rather in accordance with their own, which can emerge [*entspringen*] a priori from themselves, and their causality is freedom.
>
> Hence all causality is either [struck out: merely] material mechanism or instinct or freedom. ("Reflexionen zur Metaphysik," R5995, 18:418–19)[18]

All causality, according to this tripartite scheme, is either physical, organic (whether "automatic" or "pre-established"), or moral, corresponding to the threefold causal grounds of material mechanism, instinct, and freedom. Material mechanism and instinct are the external and inner tools, respectively, by which a higher author (as we are constrained to think, if we would think of living beings at all) supports the existence of living nature; while freedom allows us to adopt these external and internal tools to ends that are not impressed, as it were, by an external author but "ideas" originating in one's own law-giving reason.

The implications of that threefold schema for Kant's concept of the state are difficult to map precisely, given the paucity of published material on the subject, from 1784 until the outbreak of the French Revolution, though an earlier note from the late 1770s, which contrasts an "organic" monarchy with a despotic government that is (merely) mechanistic, sheds suggestive light on the then direction of his thought: "In monarchy the state contains the organism that presupposes a life in the state body; despotic government changes it into the mechanism that always depends on a foreign hand" ("Reflexionen zur Rechtsphilosophie," R7688, 19:491).[19] The monar-

18. Immanuel Kant, "Reflexionen zur Metaphysik," in *Handschriftlicher Nachlaß: Metaphysik*, Bd. 18 of *Kant's gesammelte Schriften*, ed. Preußische Akademie der Wissenschaften (Berlin: de Gruyter, 1928), 18:3–725.

19. Immanuel Kant, "Reflexionen zur Rechtsphilosophie," in *Handschriftlicher Nachlaß: Moralphilosophie, Rechtsphilosophie und Religionsphilosophie*, Bd. 19 of *Kant's gesammelte*

chical state, on this earlier account, does not *itself* constitute an organism but instead "contains" one, here identified with the "life" that animates the "body" of the state. Such a body under despotism becomes a "mechanism" guided by a foreign hand (rather than, as Kant will put it in the late 1780s, by a "patriotic" sovereign who treats the "organization" of the "fatherland" as [if it were] the organization of his own person) (R8054, 19:595).

Kant's prerevolutionary theory of sovereignty combines a Rousseauian standard of justice[20]—namely, that the general will is the only legitimate source of externally binding legislation—with Hobbesian means of execution and enforcement absent of which the former is an idea lacking effectual existence.[21] On the one hand, the people are sovereign in the sense that the actual sovereign ought to pass no laws to which a (rational) people as a whole could not consent. On the other hand, without an actual head of state who is irresistible in practice, rights cannot be enjoyed and are without effect. Hence subjects may not actively oppose a head of state but at most passively refuse to carry out immoral actions.[22]

One reason, beyond ordinary political prudence, for Kant's public reticence as to the character of this civic "life," as well as of the "hand" capable of directing its mechanism nondespotically, may have been the publication of

Schriften, ed. Preußische Akademie der Wissenschaften (Berlin: de Gruyter, 1934), 19:442–613.

20. The general will is the sole source of legislation that cannot be unjust, given the principle that no one can do an injury to himself ("Reflexionen zur Rechtsphilosophie," R7713, 19:498). Both Hobbes and Rousseau in their respective elaborations of a theory of right in which laws in the proper sense cannot be unjust, centrally rely on the principle, common to both, that no one can do himself an injury. But whereas for Hobbes, the subject's authorizing consent is to a partial sacrifice of liberty that is supposed to save the rest, Rousseau insists that freedom, like the will itself, is either whole or nothing. Like Rousseau, Kant regards freedom from the arbitrary will of others to be a greater good than life itself. Like Hobbes, he takes the end of the state to be "security" ("Reflexionen zur Moralphilosophie," in *Handschriftlicher Nachlaß: Moralphilosophie, Rechtsphilosophie und Religionsphilosophie*, 19:92–317, R7275, 19:300), albeit in the specific sense of being unrestricted in pursuing one's private ends consistent with the equal freedom of others. For a fuller discussion, see Susan Meld Shell, "'Men as They Are and Laws as They Can Be': Legitimacy and the State of Nature in Rousseau and Hobbes," in *The Rousseauian Mind*, ed. Eve Grace and Christopher Kelly (London: Routledge, 2019), ch. 5.

21. For a somewhat different account, see Katrin Flikschuh, "Elusive Unity: The General Will in Hobbes and Kant," *Hobbes Studies* 25 (2012): 21–42.

22. "Reflexionen zur Rechtsphilosophie," R7680, 19:487. An early note puts this even more dramatically: "the people have no strict right but only an ideal because the people cannot establish rightful authority [*Gewalt*]" (R7737, 19:504).

Herder's *Outlines of a Philosophy of the History of Man* (1784–1791) whose promiscuous (as Kant saw it) appeal to "organic force" as a universal and all pervasive animating principle might well have stayed Kant's rhetorical hand, absent completion of the more thorough investigation of organic form (and related teleological principles) in which Kant was then engaged. Given his strongly worded public critique of Herder, Kant was hardly in position to use the term "organic" casually, and still less with respect to the life of states and nations on which Herder had discoursed all too freely, as Kant saw it.

Three of Kant's objections have particular relevance to his understanding at this time of the most appropriate natural analogy for the republican form: (1) the disjunction *within* nature between the structure most accommodating to our animal existence (and directed toward what we call "happiness") and that necessary to the development of our rational faculties; (2) the impossibility of accounting either rationally or historically for the temporal origin of thought and language (or of reason from unreason); (3) the necessary failure of physical theology and related efforts to base the immortality of the individual soul on an analogy with either natural "palingenesis" (as in the transformation of a caterpillar into a butterfly) or a progressive arrangement of species toward ever greater complexity. Kant's theory of race, which he first published shortly after his review of Moscati, followed the same punctuated scheme: While the human germ harbored a capacity for adaptation to different climates for the sake of animal survival and reproduction (and expressed in the emergence of distinct races) (*Von den verschiedenen Racen*, 2:436), man's predisposition to reason both was universal and presupposed a freedom irreducible to natural forces and in tension with his purely natural ends. Between nature's evident destruction of the individual and our own moral longing for immortality lay a chasm that Herder's enthusiastic conflation of reasoned argument and poetically expressed sentiment only served to confuse. Above all, Herder's attack, in the name of individuality, on what he called Kant's Averroism, or reification of universal concepts, was "incommunicable," a challenge to which Kant's later theory of taste (as both communicable and nonconceptual) would specifically respond.

Any conception of civic order along explicitly organic lines is likely to have been further complicated by Kant's own emerging understanding of organized being more generally. As recent scholars have shown, some crucial changes in Kant's theoretical philosophy during the 1780s, including certain differences between the A and B editions of the *Critique of Pure Reason*, track closely with the contemporary conflict between genetic preformationist and epigenetic accounts of generation and growth—schools of thought that were themselves both varied and undergoing rapid transformation—as researches sought to reconcile the competing claims of an ascendant natural science capable of strict quantification, traditional moral and religious views (e.g., as to human freedom and the immortality of the soul), and the most recent experimental findings, including the evident contribution of both sexes to the formation of the embryo.[23] Kant's preferred theory at the time, one he would later call "general preformation," *constrained* the vital force championed by Caspar Friedrich Wolff and Johann Friedrich Blumenbach within the limits set by preformed "seeds" and "predispositions," lest that force, in its sheer plasticity, breach all preset barriers (as with Herder). Such barriers, for Kant, were necessary no less intellectually than they were genetically, given that the possibility of organic unity could not be thought without conceptual reference to the "end" of an (unknown) author and that was seemingly at odds with the necessary homogeneity of matter. At the same time, that end, no less than its Rousseauian forebear, was a strictly functional one: namely, to survive and propagate given the peculiar niche the larger natural economy in which this or that organism finds itself (as with, e.g., the double layer of feathers that enables one species of bird to survive in different climates). Man alone, on this account, has a set of capacities that went beyond "the mechanical ordering of his animal existence," capacities whose unfolding he must "bring forth from himself" ("Idee zu einer allgemeinen Geschichte," 8:19).

Kant did leave a telling hint, at the end of his 1784 essay "What Is Enlightenment?," in envisioning a future in which rulers would at last treat their subjects as "more than a machine." Absolute rule, provided that the ruler possesses the appropriate "way of thinking," is accordingly preferable, as Kant presents matters under Frederick II's reign, to a state affording greater civic freedom, providing, as it does, the "hard husk" (*Hülle*) beneath which nature can "unwrap" a "seed" (*Keim*) consisting in the "propensity and calling to *think* freely." "Thus when nature has unwrapped, from under this hard shell, the seed for which she cares most tenderly, namely the propensity and calling to *think* freely, the latter gradually works back upon the people's way of thinking (which thereby gradually becomes capable of freedom in *acting*) and eventually even upon the principles of *government*,

23. See, for example, John H. Zammito, *The Gestation of German Biology: Philosophy and Physiology from Stahl to Schelling* (Chicago: University of Chicago Press, 2017), 215–43; Jennifer Mensch, *Kant's Organicism: Epigenesis and the Development of Critical Philosophy* (Chicago: University of Chicago Press, 2013); Phillip R. Sloan, "Preforming the Categories: Eighteenth Century Generation Theory and the Biological Roots of Kant's *A Priori*," *Journal of the History of Philosophy* 40 (2002): 229–53.

which finds it profitable to itself to treat the human being, *who is now more than a machine*, in keeping with his dignity" (8:41–42).

An unpublished note roughly dating from the early to mid-1780s, contemporary with these two essays, sheds suggestive light on what Kant means here by *Hülle*: "The yoke in the egg only contains the *matrix* or *Hülle* (the cartridge [*patrone*]. These are merely the product of the mother, not preformed, because they are not organized toward life) in which the viscera should form themselves, and is for all chicks the same" ("Reflexionen zur Anthropologie," R1378, 15:602).[24] The "husk" or "matrix" on this account is a natural product that is not itself organized for life but instead provides the necessary external support, not itself preformed, for the self-organization of a living individual.

Kant had already spoken, in his "Idea for a Universal History," of the cosmopolitan condition as the "matrix" (*Schoss*) that would enable "all the seeds" lying in our nature, including that of "enlightenment" itself, to unfold (*entwickeln*) fully (8:30). Putting these passages together yields a conception of enlightened monarchy that allows subjects to extend themselves to the extent that they can do so without mutual inhibition (as with trees growing straight and tall within the narrow confines of a forest [8:22]). Perfected domestic civil orders, on this view, are everywhere formally and functionally alike. And they guarantee a freedom whose maximum expansion is strictly horizontal, with no allowance for the active civic "membership" on which Kant would later insist. Membership is instead reserved to the states themselves as co-contributors to cosmopolitan order that Kant does not hesitate to characterize analogically in explicitly organic terms (8:28).

The individual state, so understood, is both an organ and a husk,[25] both a functionally differentiated member of an emergent cosmopolitan community

24. Immanuel Kant, "Reflexionen zur Anthropologie," in *Handschriftlicher Nachlaß: Anthropologie*, Bd. 15 of *Kant's gesammelte Schriften*, ed. Berlin-Brandenburgische Akademie der Wissenschaften (Berlin: Georg Reimer, 1913), 15:55–654.

25. On the negative connotations of *Hülle* see "Jäsche Logic," in which the "ideas" by which historical knowledge is increasingly extended without reduction of content, a process he compares to the removal of the slag or "ignoble *Hülle*" in the purification of metal. The accompanying invention of new methods will make possible a "wholesale" as distinguished from merely "retail" acquisition of knowledge, making "the multitude of books dispensable," since we will be able, thanks to these new methods and principles, "to find anything we desire without burdening memory." Immanuel Kant, *Immanuel Kant's Logik*, in *Kant's gesammelte Schriften*, Bd. 9, ed. Königlich Preußische Akademie der Wissenschaften (Berlin: de Gruyter, 1923), 9:1–150, 9:43–44. "Wit" can sometimes be the *Hülle* of reason, see *Anthropologie*, 7:192; while "enlightenment" consists in knowing the difference between true religion and its *Hülle* (7:222). On the latter point, see also *Streit der Facultäten*, 7:45.

and the container (everywhere functionally the same) of a higher, moral life into which the state enters only indirectly. Viewed from the perspective of Kant's tripartite causal distinction, the cosmopolitan order bridges the gap between instinct and freedom, or between organic automaticity and moral autonomy. The individual state, for its part, occupies the uneasy role of a "formal mechanism" that may "contain" moral life but can share in it directly only as member of a future cosmopolitan community, and that depends for the foreseeable future on the continuing existence of "enlightened" rulers such as Frederick II. Establishment of such a community is thus, as Kant properly concludes, given his implicit deployment of the distinction between "hull" and "germ," both the "greatest problem" that nature has set the human species and "the most difficult" (8:22). For it would require a conjunction of correct theory, extensive experience, and the "good will" to accept what follows from them—a serendipitous combination to be anticipated only after many years of fruitless attempts, and never perfectly, given the "crookedness" of human timber (8:23).

The Organized State in Kant's Later Thought

Two major events decisively altered Kant's understanding of the state along with the light shed on its historic role by the concept of organic life: the death of Frederick II, in 1786, and the storming of the Bastille, in the summer of 1789. These events and their aftermath—in one case, the ascendance to the throne of a king distinctly hostile to Kant's larger purposes, in the other, an increasingly radical and violent revolutionary turn in France along with the accompanying domestic reaction—forced Kant to address practical political matters more directly and thematically than previously, while also prompting him to revisit his earlier confidence in enlightened monarchy as the surest practical route to human progress.

Accompanying those changes in Kant's external situation, and equally if not more important to his theory of the state, was a new understanding on his part of the systematic role and purpose of reflective judgment (first elaborated in the *Critique of Judgment*, whose last pages were completed in the final months of 1789). The accompanying a priori teleological principles not only lent critical grounding and precision to Kant's previously freestanding historical presumption that "all natural predispositions of a creature are determined sometime to develop themselves completely and purposively"

(8:18); they also provided new conceptual tools for his emerging understanding of the state as an "organized" whole.

Two issues loom especially large in this redirection of Kant's focus toward a more direct engagement in political affairs: freedom of religion and the purported right of revolution.

As to the first: Under Frederick the Great, Kant had enjoyed wide latitude to publish what he wished—so much so that he dedicated the *Critique of Pure Reason* to Frederick's official censor, who was also a personal friend. His successor, Frederick William II, took a different, and more restrictive, view, especially in matters of religious liberty, preferring to confine the officially recognized sects to professing their official doctrines, and restricting others to near silence. Whatever justification such policies might have had from the standpoint of maintaining sectarian peace, they were devastating to Kant's then strategy for the promotion of enlightenment (in his peculiar sense), one that relied, above all else, on freedom to argue publicly, particularly on religious matters.[26]

The impact of the French Revolution was even more far-reaching. The appearance of a German translation in 1791 of Burke's *Reflections on the Revolution in France*, followed by August Wilhelm Rehburg's endorsement of Burke's work in the same year and the fuller and far more influential translation of Burke's work published by Friedrich Gentz in 1793, helped set in motion a conservative reaction even prior to the execution of Louis XVI and subsequent Terror that seemed to confirm Burke's darkest predictions. That this reaction included sometime followers of Kant such as Gentz and Rehburg was a particular blow, and culminated, in the first instance, in Kant's publication of "On the Common Saying: That May Be Correct in Theory, but It Is of No Use in Practice" (1793),[27] which can be read as a direct response to Burke's charge, reaffirmed by Gentz and Rehburg, that metaphysics had caused the revolution ("Vorarbeiten zu 'Theorie und Praxis,'" 23:127);[28] it also represents Kant's first effort to bring a priori

26. See Susan Meld Shell, *Kant and the Limits of Autonomy* (Cambridge, MA: Harvard University Press, 2009).

27. Immanuel Kant, "Über den Gemeinspruch: Das mag in der Theorie richtig sein, taugt aber nicht für die Praxis," in *Abhandlungen nach 1781*, 8:273–313.

28. Immanuel Kant, "Vorarbeiten zu 'Über den Gemeinspruch: Das mag in der Theorie richtig sein, taugt aber nicht für die Praxis,'" in *Handschriftlicher Nachlaß: Vorarbeiten und Nachträge*, Bd. 23 of *Kant's gesammelte Schriften*, ed. Deutsche Akademie der Wissenschaften

teleological principles to bear in a practical context. Kant in this and subsequent political works emphatically denies the right to revolution, while also insisting on a priori principles of right that support not just the horizontal equality of citizens (as in his earlier model) but also the right of "active" citizens to participate in positive lawgiving.[29] The accompanying revision in Kant's organic model of the state steers a narrow but consistent course, as we shall see, between the Burkean appeal to an organic ancient order and the plasticity of organic form that was embraced by Herder, who defended the revolution while also arguing for the "natural" basis of peoplehood.

Kant had already sketched out his new, more systematically integrated concept of a living organism in the essay "On the Use of Teleological Principles in Philosophy"[30] (1788), which appeared two years prior to the *Critique of Judgment*. As he there suggested, the true model for animal life to the extent that we are able to conceive its possibility is our own practical experience as makers of artificial products, whose reciprocally purposive organs (in the literal sense of "tools") are both "ends and means" to one another (8:181). These organs are in turn reciprocally dependent on a whole whose possibility is grounded in the "end" or intention of its maker. Animals and other forms of natural organic life are necessarily conceived (if their possibility is to be thinkable at all) as "natural products" analogous in this regard to products of our own making, albeit with the proviso that the actual cause or causes in which the existence of such "products" is grounded cannot be known, given the limitations of human reason (§68, 5:382).

A roughly contemporary note from the late 1780s suggests that the political implications of these newly formulated teleological principles were already on his mind. That government is "patriotic," as distinguished from "despotic," as he now puts it, in which the "sovereign" does not treat the people as his "property" but instead regards the "organization" of the "fatherland" as that of his "own person." And though democracy can rule despotically, that is, where its constitution lacks insight (as in Athens), the people can never

---

zu Berlin (Berlin: de Gruyter, 1955), 23:125–44. For a persuasive argument to this effect, see Jonathan Allen Green, "Burke's German Readers at the End of the Enlightenment, 1790–1815" (PhD thesis, University of Cambridge, 2017).

29. See "Theorie und Praxis," 8:295–96; Immanuel Kant, *Die Metaphysik der Sitten*, in *Kant's gesammelte Schriften*, Bd. 6, ed. Königlich Preußische Akademie der Wissenschaften (Berlin: Georg Reimer, 1914), 6:203–493, 6:313–15.

30. Immanuel Kant, "Über den Gebrauch teleologischer Principien in der Philosophie," in *Abhandlungen nach 1781*, 8:157–84.

consider itself property, from which Kant draws the following conclusion: "There can be despotic government but never a despotic state constitution, i.e., a constitution through the people's united will and in accordance with a formal [*förmliche*] law." To which he adds: "Only in a patriotic constitution can there be constitutive organization, i.e., organization proper [*eigentliche organisation*]" ("Reflexionen zur Rechtsphilosophie," R8054, 19:595).

It is tempting to conclude that only with the organization of a state the teleological principles presupposed by the concept of an organic whole are, or can become, "constitutive" rather than remaining merely regulative, as with so called "products of nature." This temptation gains further support from the consideration that with organization of a state, as distinguished from a natural product, both the author and the causal principle at issue are knowable, at least in principle.

Two passages from the *Critique of Judgment*, each of which compares the state to a living body, bear directly on this issue. In the first, from part 1, Kant is less concerned with that comparison per se than with illustrating the distinction between schemata, which exhibit a concept "demonstrably," and symbols, which do so only indirectly and "analogically."[31] Nevertheless, the accompanying depiction of the difference between despotic and nondespotic monarchy contrasts tellingly, and in three respects, with his characterization of that difference in the note (as earlier quoted) from the late 1770s:

> All intuitions, which one supplies for a priori concepts, are thus either *schemata* or *symbols*, of which the former contain direct, the latter indirect, exhibitions [*Darstellungen*] of the concept. The former does this demonstratively, the latter by means of an analogy (for which empirical intuition also serves), in which judgment performs a double function [*Geschäft*]: it applies the concept to the object of a sensible intuition, and then applies the mere rule by which it reflects upon that intuition of which the first is only the symbol. Thus a monarchical state is represented by an ensouled body, if it is governed by inner laws of the people [*inneren Volksgesetzen*], and by a mere machine (like a hand-mill) if governed by an individual absolute will; but in

31. On the progressive and yet holistic implications of Kant's political symbolism see Günter Zöller, "Mechanism or Organism: Kant on the Symbolic Representation of the Body Politic," in *Kant and the Metaphors of Reason*, ed. Patricia Kauark-Leite et al. (Hildesheim: Olms, 2015), 303–20.

> both cases only *symbolically.* For between a despotic state and a hand-mill there is, to be sure, no similarity; but there is a similarity in the rules according to which we reflect upon these two things and their causality. This function has been little analyzed [*auseinander gesetzt*] hitherto, for it deserves a deeper investigation; but this is not the place to pursue it. (§59, 5:352)

First, unlike his earlier identification of monarchy with a mere "husk," monarchy is now likened to a living body insofar as it is governed by "inner laws of the people," a specification missing from his earlier note. Second, the comparison is now explicitly called "indirect," there being "no [actual] similarity" between "a despotic state and a hand-mill" but only "in the rules according to which we reflect upon them and their causality." Third, Kant qualifies the entire discussion by proclaiming "this function" insufficiently examined and in need of a "deeper investigation" not here provided. Might such an analysis bear on the relation between a living body and a monarchical government in accordance with popular laws (a relation he does not here explicitly define)? Might there indeed be an additional similarity between a living being and a monarchical state governed in accordance with popular laws (as distinguished from a despotic state and a hand-mill), albeit one requiring more discussion than Kant is here prepared to offer?

The second passage, from part 2 of the *Critique of Judgment*, sheds additional light on the above questions. It appears in a footnote to section 65, entitled "Things as Natural Ends [*Naturzwecke*] Are Organized Beings," and following Kant's conclusion that "strictly speaking . . . the [self-] organization of nature has nothing analogous to any causality known to us," although to call this "inscrutable property of nature" an "analogue of life" may, as he had just allowed, "come close" to accuracy in this regard (5:375):

> On the other hand, one can elucidate a certain connection [*Verbindung*], encountered more in the idea than in reality [*Wirklichkeit*], through an analogy with the above named immediate natural purposes [*Naturzwecken*]. Thus in the recent complete transformation [*Umbildung*] of a great people into a state the word "organization" was very aptly used for the establishment of magistrates, etc., and even for the whole state body. For each member [*Glied*] should indeed/freely [*freilich*] serve in such a whole not merely as a means but also and at the same

> time as an end, co-effecting [*mitwirk(en)*] the possibility of the whole, the idea of which, in turn, determines each with respect to both place and function [*Function*]. (5:375n)[32]

In what, then, does the "elucidating" analogy between a natural end and the state, to which Kant here draws specific attention, consist? Kant offers four criteria that a being must meet if it is to be regarded as an organized product of nature (§65, 5:373–74):

1. The possibility of its parts (as to existence and to form) must depend upon its relation to the whole.
2. It must have within itself and its inner possibility reference to purpose without the causality that rational beings outside it have.
3. It must be both organized and self-organizing, i.e., possess a "formative force" not reducible to motive force alone, that allows it to maintain itself.
4. It must be self-propagating, importing its formative force to matter not already organized.

At the same time, the concept of a natural end as an organized, self-organizing being places reason in a seeming quandary; for one must either endow matter with a "life" that contradicts its essence (given the principle of inertia), or one must endow it with an alien soul, which is either redundant (if one assumes a matter already organized) or explains nothing. Hence the concept of a thing as in itself a natural end cannot be "a constitutive principle of either understanding or of reason," but is of use merely for the guidance

32. In calling this property of nature merely an "analogue" of life Kant seems to have in mind the difficulty of associating that property directly with consciousness, given the insupportable alternatives to which the latter seemingly gives rise: that is, hylozoism, on the one hand, and something like a "world soul," on the other. Kant had previously defined "life" as "the faculty of being able to act in accordance with the laws of desire." Only in the case of our own conscious action is the gap between life and material nature, or the laws of desire and those of physics, overcome, albeit merely empirically, and without providing further insight into what makes their conjunction possible, although Kant's discussion in the B edition of the *Critique of Pure Reason* of the so-called "epigenesis" of reason may be suggestive in this regard. On the latter point, see especially Mensch, *Kant's Organicism*.

of our theoretical investigation and the enhancement of our moral powers with respect to our own practical purposes (5:375).

The concept of the state as an organized and self-organizing being, on the other hand, eludes these difficulties, by transforming a seemingly insuperable conflict between the laws of motion and those of desire (to refer once again to Kant's tripartite scheme) into a practically remediable tension between "organism" and "reason." Put another way, the essential components of the body politic are not just "parts" but "members"—not just "material" but embodied rational beings who can cooperate in organizing the state because they are already organized and self-organizing in their own right. Here the location of the idea or concept of the whole is no longer a mystery (guiding the actions as it does, at least ideally, of all civic members, who reciprocally effect, whether actively or merely passively, the existence and form of each citizen as member of the whole).[33] And insofar as they depend upon the state for their material existence as human beings as well as their ideal existence as citizens, they satisfy the condition that in the case of natural products required appealing to a "formative force" whose ground remained a mystery.

Kant here for the first time publicly refers to individual subjects as coefficient "members" of the state, rather than as merely "inherent" in the latter's "substance," as he stated in a note dated from the early 1780s.[34] And for the first time he explicitly connects the state with an "idea" that determines each not merely as to place (i.e., as reciprocally limited and limiting through the sovereign's irresistible will, as in the first *Critique*), but also with respect to coefficient function.

Kant expands upon the nature of this newly formulated civic body in "Theory and Practice," which presents it as arising from a common "patriotic way of thinking" and accompanying "patriotic" (*vaterländische*; as distinguished from paternal [*väterliche*]) government, that regard the "land" (*Land*) as the "paternal soil" and the common wealth (*gemeine Wesen*) as the maternal womb (*mütterlichen Schooß*), as he now puts it, from which each citizen has arisen and that each must leave behind a sacred pledge (8:291): "In a patriotic way of thinking [*Denkungsart*] everyone in a state (not excluding its head) regards the common wealth as the maternal womb, or the land as the paternal soil, from which has arisen and which each must

33. For a suggestion to this effect, see Immanuel Kant, *Opus postumum*, *Kant's gesammelte Schriften*, Bd. 22, ed. Preußische Akademie der Wissenschaften (Berlin: de Gruyter, 1938), 22:622.

34. "Reflexionen zur Rechtsphilosophie," R8065, 19:600.

leave behind as a dear pledge [*Unterpfand*],[35] only in order to protect the latter's rights through the laws of the common will, but not to subject it to the use of his own unconditioned preference."[36]

The "hard husk" and "matrix" (*Schooß*) of Kant's prerevolutionary writings, which allowed the "predisposition to think freely" to expand so to speak mechanically, that is, by reducing external friction to a minimum, has been replaced by a "*maternal* womb" (emphasis added) from which the citizen emerges consanguineously, as it were. The state, as he will put it two years later, in *Toward Eternal Peace*, is a tribe/trunk (*Stamm*) with "its own roots [*Wurzel*]," a society whose "existence as a moral person" cannot be cancelled without contradicting the idea of an original contract that depends, in turn, on a "patriotic way of thinking" (*Zum ewigen Frieden*, 8:344).[37]

This patriotic way of thinking, moreover, now explicitly includes all parties to the original contract, who by virtue of that *Denkungsart* regard land and commonwealth, respectively, as the generative *Material* from which each is, as it were (re)born. So conceived, the state makes intelligible—or, rather, as intelligible as it *can* be, given human limitations—the otherwise mysterious process by which the two sexes generate a new living individual.[38]

Kant will expand on the analogy in distinguishing, in his later *Anthropology from a Pragmatic Point of View* (1798), among a "people" (*Volk*), a "nation" (*Nation*), and a "rabble" (*Pöbel*): "By the word *people* [Volk] (populus) is meant the number of human beings united in an extent of country [*Landstrich*] insofar as they constitute a *whole*. This number, or even a part of it that recognizes itself as united into a civic [*bürgerlichen*] whole by common descent [*Abstammung*], is called a *nation* [*Nation*] (gens); the part that exempts itself from these laws (the savage [*wilde*] portion within this people) is called the *rabble* (vulgus), whose counter-lawful association is the *mob* [Rottiren] (agere per turbas); this behavior excludes them from the quality of a citizen" (7:311).

35. As in security for holding a mortgage.

36. For a much earlier version of the analogy—one that omits all reference to a "maternal womb"—see "Reflexionen zur Rechtsphilosophie," R7686, 19:490, from sometime in the 1770s: "the despotic monarch holds the state as his inheritance (patrimony), the patriotic monarch as his fatherland. The land itself is a confraternity [*Verbrüderung*] from a common father."

37. Immanuel Kant, *Zum ewigen Frieden*, in *Abhandlungen nach 1781*, 8:341–86. See also *Anthropologie*, 7:315.

38. On this difficulty from a moral point of view, see *Streit der Facultäten*, 7:39n.

Civic nationhood, on this account, is partly natural and partly notional, a combination of factors falling under the fields of physical geography and anthropology, on the one hand, and a rational construction grounded in an idea of reason, on the other. Although the members of a civic whole will ordinarily naturally descend from common ancestors, their civic identity is overridingly bound up with how they recognize one another civically, and in implicit reference to the idea of the original contract, absent which binding civic laws would not be thinkable, inasmuch as no party could rationally regard itself as rightfully bound.

Kant's enhanced postrevolutionary conception of the state is also reflected in his new understanding of what he calls the "representative system"—one roughly modeled on that introduced by Abbé Sieyès in 1789 and subsequently adopted by French lawmakers. Where Kant had earlier assigned "representation" of the people to the actual ruler,[39] he now carves out an explicit "representative" role for an elective legislature.

Kant's later *Metaphysics of Morals* offers the following clarification: "Every true republic . . . is and can be nothing other than a *representative system* of the people, in order to procure its rights in the people's name, through all state citizens united, by means of its delegates [*Abgeordneten*] (deputies)" (6:341).[40] Accordingly, the "people" of Kant's "true republic," circa 1797, no longer need to be "represented" by a (sole) head of state in order for the concept of right to have effectual existence (as in Kant's earlier writings). Instead, "the united people" are, or can once again become, the "sovereign itself" as in the telling case of Louis XVI:

> It was thus a great misstep in judgment on the part of a mighty ruler [*Beherrschers*] of our time when to help himself out of the embarrassment of large state debts he left it to the people to take on this burden and distribute it as they deemed good; for then the lawgiving authority naturally came into the people's hands, not only with regard to the taxation of subjects but also with regard to governing [*Regierung*], namely that it not incur

39. See "Naturrecht Feyerabend," in *Vorlesungen über Moralphilosophie*, Bd. 27 of *Kant's gesammelte Schriften*, ed. Akademie der Wissenschaften der DDR (Berlin: de Gruyter, 1979), 27:1319–94, 27:1382. For a very early reference to the sovereign as "representative of the state" in his capacity as "vicar of God," see "Reflexionen zur Anthropologie," R1399, 15:610.

40. *Metaphysik der Sitten.*

> new debts through wastefulness [*Verschwendung*] or war, so that the entire power of ruling [*Herrschergewalt*] of the monarchy entirely vanished [*verschwand*] . . . and passed over [*überging*] to the people, to whose lawgiving will the mine and thine of each subject was subjected. (6:341–42)

The rulership of a "wasteful" king could "vanish" without the state thereby descending into lawless anarchy, because the people, as Kant now sees it, can be a "whole" without being "represented" by an independent head of state who wields effectual power, as on his earlier, more Hobbesian model. And it introduces a crucial exception to his general preference, as presented in the *Metaphysics of Morals*, for "metamorphosis" (or change of shape) over palingenesis (or "rebirth")[41] as the preferred exemplar of constitutional alteration (6:339–40). As Kant there writes: "It is *futile* to inquire into the *historical certification* of the mechanism of government. . . . But it is *punishable* to undertake this inquiry with the intention of changing the standing constitution by force. For this transformation [*Umänderung*] would have to happen through the people acting as a mob, not through lawgiving; but insurrection [*Meuterei*] in such a standing constitution would be its dissolution, and transition to a better constitution would not be a metamorphosis but a palingenesis, demanding a new social contract, on which the former one, now cancelled, would have no influence."

And yet in the exceptional case of France, whose revolution was singularly pivotal for a progressive human history as Kant now sees it (7:85)—"rebirth" (*Wiedergeburt*) rather than metamorphosis (as a mere change of outward shape) is apparently the appropriate mode of constitutional improvement. For France's civic renewal occurred, as Kant writes in an unpublished note, without an intervening "death," and despite all "atrocities," the state's "feverish inner movement" did not destroy "all art belonging to culture":

41. "Metaphysik Mrongovius" describes palingenesis as what happens when a soul receives an entirely new body without itself disappearing, see *Kant's Vorlesungen: Ergänzungen*, Bd. 29 of *Kant's gesammelte Schriften*, ed. Akademie der Wissenschaften der DDR (Berlin: de Gruyter, 1983), 29:743–940, 29:919; but cf. "Metaphysik Dohna," in *Vorlesungen über Metaphysik und Rationaltheologie*, Bd. 28 of *Kant's gesammelte Schriften*, ed. Deutsche Akademie der Wissenschaften (Berlin: de Gruyter, 1970), 28:615–702, 28:689. On palingenesis and metamorphosis in the *Metaphysics of Morals*, see Howard Williams, "Metamorphosis or Palingenesis: Political Change in Kant," *Review of Politics* 63 (2001): 693–722.

> In France the National Assembly was able to alter the constitution even though it was called together, to be sure, only in order to bring order to the credit system [*Creditwesen*] of the nation. For they were representatives of the entire people, whom the king had allowed to decree in accordance with indeterminate plenary power. The king otherwise represented the people; here he was thus negated [*vernichtet*]; because the people themselves were present [*gegenwärtig*]. . . . Thus the misfortune of the king comes directly from his own sovereignty, after he had once allowed the people's deputies to assemble, then he was nothing; for his entire lawgiving authority was founded only on his representing the whole people; this also illuminates the injustice of a single person as sovereign. He cannot admit that that which he represents [*repräsentirt*] presents itself [*sich selbst darstelle*]. Because he represents [*vorstellt*] the whole, he becomes nothing when this whole, of which he is not a part but merely the proxy/place holder [*Stellvertreter*], is allowed to present itself [*sich selbst stellen lässt*]. ("Reflexionen zur Rechtsphilosophie," R8055, 19:595–96)

Kant's punning plays here on the term *stellen* to bring home his current dissatisfaction with his own earlier, more strictly Hobbesian account of representation. The people's representative should not take their place in the manner of a proxy [*Stellvertreter*], but should instead belong to what it represents, as with the people's deputies once summoned by the then ruling sovereign.

An added note suggests, moreover, the importance of active citizenship in giving "substance" to a popular unity that otherwise depends on representation by proxy:

> The National Assembly was called in order to save the state by covering with their guarantee [*Guarantie*] (not merely drawing up bills/plans [*Entwürfe*]) all the debts imposed on the state by the extravagance of the government [*Regierung*]. They therefore had to freely [*freywillig*] guarantee [*verbürgen*] it with their property (they had therefore to put themselves in a condition such that they alone could dispose of their property, hence in a condition of freedom, albeit under laws, but those that they gave themselves, that is, a republican condition or condition of

> free citizens [*freybürgerlichen*], and the court had itself yielded the right to encumber them. But so that they could achieve this state of citizenry [*Bürgschaft*], they had to establish a constitution that could exercise no authority/force [*Gewaltthätigkeiten*] over them. (R8055, 19:596)[42]

Kant's verbal play on *Bürger* and *verbürgen* ("citizen" and "to back up" or "guarantee") draws attention to the integrative character of citizenship, and helps explain why, in his final estimation, "self-subsistence" (*Selbständigkeit*) (6:314)[43] replaces "dependence" (*Abhängigkeit*) upon common legislation (*Zum ewigen Frieden*, 8:349–50) as the essential characteristic of the (active) citizen. While the savage may be "independent" in the negative sense of being "his own master" (6:237), only one who is capable of sustaining himself collectively without ceasing to be self-directing, counts as "self-subsistent" in a way that makes one capable of voting or "giving voice" (*Stimmgebung*), and thereby "organizing" (*organisiren*) the state in common with others (6:315).

Kant's note also sheds light on the civic "pledge" referred to in *Toward Eternal Peace*, a pledge coincident to the generation of the state, and concomitant emergence of the citizen, out of the generative *Material* of "soil" and "womb." For each citizen makes the state effectually possible through the substance (in the sense of property) he/she provides as surety, and for which he/she is, in turn, dependent on the whole. Whereas "active" citizens can be regarded as substances in community with other substances (in accordance with the a priori concept of "relation"), passive citizens "lack civic personhood [*bürgerlichen Persönlichkeit*]" and, as Kant adds, "their existence is, as it were, merely adherence" (6:314).

Kant's comparison of the active citizen to substance metaphysically conceived contrasts revealingly with a similar, prerevolutionary analogy. According to that earlier analogy, *all* citizens exist merely as inherences in the "substance" of state, by which each is maintained, and without which none would have a future he or she could count on.[44] "Because an individual human being can achieve no other security for his future preferences, he is

42. See also R8048, 19:593.

43. See also "Theorie und Praxis," 8:290.

44. On the state's *Selbständigkeit*, see also "Reflexionen zur Rechtsphilosophie," R8023, 19:585 (from the 1780s).

juridically only *accidens*, which can only exist *inhaerendo*. A civil whole is substance" ("Reflexionen zur Rechtsphilosophie," R8065, 19:600).

It seems to be the state alone, and not individual citizens, on Kant's prerevolutionary understanding, that counts as self-subsistent, capable of existing in reciprocal community (*commercium*) with others—a *commercium* here identified not with the individual state, as in his later work, but solely with a "league of nations." Thus, according to the same unpublished reflection:

> The question is whether the end of humanity is the transformation [*Verwandlung*] of substance into accident or whether it is of accident into substance, and the duty of the state toward itself is to preserve itself as a particular state, such that this duty could not be yielded. In the latter case the unity of commercium (league of nations [*Völkerbund*]) remains the sole thing that constitutes the end of humanity, not the unity of inherence, not the unity of dependence [*dependentz*] of a highest referee [*Schiedsrichter*], but the freedom of each individual state under universal laws. Autonomy.

The restriction of *Selbstständigkeit* to the state in these comments sheds suggestive light on Kant's changing conception of the *Völkerbund*, between 1784 and 1795, from a federation that is both externally coercive and universally inclusive, in the "Idea for a Universal History" (8:26) in accordance with the principle of "autonomy" as elaborated in the *Groundlaying of the Metaphysics of Morals*, to his later noncoercive and more restrictive conception, in *Toward Eternal Peace*, of a noncoercive federation of republics (and their like), or to what the *Metaphysics of Morals* describes as a noncoercive "federation" that "can be withdrawn from at any time" (6:344). For states, as organized beings in their own right, have "outgrown" (*entwachsen*) external constraint, as he strikingly puts it (*Zum ewigen Frieden*, 8:356)—making use of an organic metaphor that recalls his earlier reference to the "trunk" (*Stamme*) and "root" that precluded the union of states through the marriage of their respective sovereigns (8:344).

In sum, revolutionary developments in France seem to have provided Kant with convenient conceptual tools for integrating his new understanding of organized being (originally formulated with respect to "natural purposes") within the framework of his longstanding republican "idea."[45] The "active"

45. See in this regard the following passage from an unpublished draft of the *Metaphysics of Morals*: "The state is a people [*Volk*] that rules itself. The fascicles of all nerves which

citizens of such a state are not just inherent parts (as with citizens as such, in Kant's prerevolutionary understanding) but substantive members, "organizing [*organisiren*] or cooperating/co-effecting [*mitzuwirken*] to introduce new laws" (6:315). Their representation is not merely personal (as in Kant's earlier model) but systematic; that is, unified by the idea of a united will whose self-organizing realization is carried out by all active citizens, and that has, as such, "outgrown" subjection to the coercive authority of others.

The state initiates and maintains itself not by imparting organization to matter not yet organized, but rather (to pursue Kant's own metaphor) through an act of civic (re)birth and accompanying "patriotic way of thinking." By virtue of that way of thinking, citizens regard themselves not only as constituting a "general will," but also as co-descended from both land and commonwealth as common parents. Territory is not only not the "patrimony" of the ruler; it is to be regarded as the paternal soil in which civic community is rooted. By the same token, the state is no longer conceived merely as an external husk but as a living commonwealth [*gemeine Wesen*] that every citizen pledges to sustain. Indeed, as we have seen, Kant goes so far as to suggest in an unpublished note that the historically decisive model of constitutional improvement is best understood not as a "metamorphosis" but as a "rebirth"—conceived as the irruption of a new life without cessation of the old one.

But Kant's organic analogy is perhaps as significant for what it doesn't claim as for what it does. Faced with the increasing encroachment of organic language into political discourse throughout the 1790s, including thinkers as diverse as Burke and Fichte, Kant was forced to walk a narrow line between implicitly endorsing revolutionary excesses that he opposed, and joining the forces of moderate reaction spearheaded by erstwhile followers and former friends like Gentz. Gentz's explanatory comment appended to his influential translation of Burke's *Reflections on the Revolution in France* are in this respect especially instructive. For Gentz appears to favor precisely the sort of gradual "metamorphosis" to which Kant later gave his public approval: "In its most wonderful metamorphoses nature allows the old husk [*Hülle*] to remain . . . so that new forces can achieve completion. When this is achieved, the supplanted garment slips away, and nothing other than a light tremor announces that a gentle transformation has been accomplished

together constitute lawgiving. The *sensorium commune* of right deriving from their agreement. 3. The *facultas locomativa* of government." Immanuel Kant, "Vorarbeiten zu *Die Metaphysik der Sitten*," in *Handschriftlicher Nachlaß: Vorarbeiten und Nachträge*, 23:207–370, 23:347.

through organic construction of members [*organischen Gliederbau*]. To imitate the course of nature is high wisdom, and only this wisdom promises lasting prosperity, security, unity and harmony: only this wisdom sustains the moral character without which the greatest operations of the state as little as the least private actions have rational and enduring value."[46]

Closer examination, however, reveals two important differences. First, whereas Gentz's comparison of the old political forms to a plant's "husk" borrows the language of Kant's earlier "What Is Enlightenment?," Kant's own understanding of metamorphosis incorporates his new conception of the state as a civic organism in its own right, animated by an ideal constitution ("anima pacti originarii") (6:340), or what he also calls the "spirit" of a "representative system" (8:352), that cannot be formally repudiated without committing "civic suicide" (6:322n).

Insurrection, including even assassination of the monarch, though it dissolves the state, does not constitute civic suicide, because the rebels can conceive their actions to be rationally self-interested, and hence rational, although still immoral—that is, an "exception" to a rule they otherwise endorse. The formal execution of a monarch, on the other hand, be it that of Charles I (6:321n), which Gentz, along with Gentz's Burke, excused, or that of Louis XVI, which Gentz inconsistently condemns, involves adoption of a principle "that would make impossible the regeneration [*Wiedererzeugung*] of the state that had been subverted" (6:322n). Such formal execution, were it indeed imputed to the people, would in principle make even palingenesis, or rebirth, of the state impossible: a second difference to Burke and Gentz. Accordingly, one must attribute the formal execution of Louis XVI to self-deceit on the people's part (and regard Cromwell's political creation as an "abortive monster" [7:92n]). Improvement in the constitution is achieved not by retaining the old husk to allow the new to generate itself as it were by natural processes (as Gentz insists), but to govern in accordance with laws that subjects can regard as rationally justified and hence obey without doing violence to their own rightful sense of honor (7:86n).

A ruler who keeps the transcendental principles of public right in view and whom subjects can reasonably regard as moving toward genuine republicanism with all deliberate speed can count on a people "satisfied with

---

46. Friedrich Gentz, *Gesammelte Schriften*, Bd. 6, *Übersetzungen, Einleitungen und Kommentare*, ed. Günther Kronenbitter (Zurich: Olms-Weidmann, 1998), 98; quoted in Jonathan Allen Green, "Friedrich Gentz's Translation of Burke's *Reflections*," *Historical Journal* 57, no. 3 (2014): 639–59, 653.

their constitution" (7:86n). At the same time, the only "constitution of a state that lasts" is one dependent on no particular person, and in which "law rules" (6:341).

But how can "law rule" when the republican way of governing is distinguished precisely through the distinction between legislation and ruling? The apparent answer, though Kant does not here spell things out explicitly, is a "representative system" in which self-subsistent citizens elect representatives who rule, either by enacting positive laws or, where necessary, through partial transfer of authority to a directorate that must still seek the approval of the people's representative council in order to go to war, as was true in contemporary France as distinguished from Britain ("Reflexionen zur Rechtsphilosophie," R8077, 19:606).[47]

Kant's "metamorphosis" is not a natural event suitable for imitation by human actors, as Gentz implies, but a "symbol" that exhibits analogically, and thereby renders intuitable, a relation that is otherwise purely intellectual. Kant picks up the point in the *Metaphysics of Morals*:

> The human beings who constitute a nation [*Volk*] may [*können*] be represented as born from the land [*Landeseingeborne*] according to the analogy of generation [*Erzeugung*] from a common ancestral trunk [*Elterstamm*] (*congeniti*), even though they are not: and yet in an intellectual and rightful meaning as born from a common mother (the republic), constituting as it were one family (*gens, natio*), whose members (citizens) are of equal birth, and who do not mix with those ignoble ones who may live near them in a state of nature, although these savages [*Wilden*] fancy themselves, in turn, more noble, owing to the lawless freedom they have chosen [*sie gewählt haben*], even though they constitute national groups [*Völkerschaften*] and not states. (6:343)

Nationhood in a juridically relevant sense is not a natural occurrence, suitable for study under the heading of physical geography, but is instead grounded in a free "choice" to be or not to be the member of a state. Kant here lays down a marker that will continue to divide "liberal" nationalism, which puts the emphasis on constitutional formation as the basis of common citizenship, and other nationalisms of the coming years that give primacy

47. Kant's argument, which involves an innovative theory of representation, cannot be developed here.

to "blood and soil." At the same time, his accompanying incorporation of sexual differentiation, on whose essential mystery Kant contemporaneously remarks (*Opus postumum*, 22:495),[48] highlights an ongoing tension between civilization and ethnicity, form and matter, that remains unresolved.

48. See also Kant's letter to Schiller of 30 March, 1795: "An Friedrich Schiller," in *Briefwechsel Band III, 1795–1803*, in *Kant's gesammelte Schriften*, Bd. 12, ed. Königlich Preußische Akademie der Wissenschaften (Berlin: Georg Reimer, 1902), 12:10–12.

Chapter 12

Kant on the Feeling of Health

Michael J. Olson

As German intellectuals at the close of the eighteenth century reflected on the most significant advances in the study of medicine and warned of the greatest threats to future progress in the field, many singled out one author in particular that modern readers might not expect: Immanuel Kant. We are familiar with Kant's contributions to the history of the life sciences, to the histories of astronomy, anthropology, and geography. Modern analyses of Kant's contributions to or impact on the history of medicine, however, remain rare. An introductory remark in one of those rare studies distills the pervasive attitude: "what Kant specifically wrote about medicine has remained, to put it roughly, of little importance."[1] This judgment could hardly be more out of step with that of Kant's contemporaries.

In many instances, those who called attention to the medical value of Kantian thought cloaked their analyses of the state of medicine at the end of the eighteenth century in rhetoric borrowed from Kant's critical philosophy. Johann Christian Reil (1759–1813), for example, invoked a Kantian conception of the limits of knowledge and wrote that "philosophy would do medicine a great service," if philosophy could "show it the limits over which human examination must never pass, and if it were to lead medicine out of the domain of metaphysics, where it happily loses its way, and back

1. Urban Wiesing, "Immanuel Kant, His Philosophy and Medicine," *Medical Health Care and Philosophy* 11, no. 2 (2008): 221–36, 221.

into the zone of physics."[2] Carl Christian Erhard Schmid (1761–1812) echoed Kant's analyses of the systematic unity of a rational knowledge when he argued that the improvement of medicine requires "an effort to use all that is rhapsodically good in old and new doctrines for the realization of the idea of a simple, interconnected system and through that to construct a philosophy of medicine."[3] Another anonymous commentator observed that philosophers have made promising contributions to the rationalization of medical investigation. They write, "what Wolffian philosophy purified of only the coarsest slag, Kantian philosophy brings the most perfect possible integrity and clarity."[4] Still another observer, the Nuremburg physician Johann Karl Osterhausen (1764–1839), played on Kant's essay "What Is Enlightenment?" when he celebrated the importance of "man's emergence from his self-imposed immaturity in things concerning his physical well-being."[5]

For every author that sought to bind the state and prospects of medicine to Kant's critical system, however, there is an unflinching attack on the deleterious effect of philosophy—and transcendental philosophy in particular—on the physician's efforts to heal his patients. Christian Gottfried Gruner (1744–1815), for example, warned that "philosophy must purify our concepts, must teach us to think properly, but philosophy cannot and must not ever become the benchmark for medicine. A medical system following Aristotle, Ramus, Descartes, etc., is and remains a building on brittle and unsustainable ground."[6] Many saw the philosophical interest in

---

2. Johann Christian Reil, "Zuschrift: An die Professoren Herrn Gren und Herrn Jakob in Halle," *Archiv für die Physiologie* 1, no. 1 (1795): 3–7, 5. Unless noted otherwise, all translations from German sources are mine. Translations of Kant's work are based on *Kant's gesammelte Schriften*, ed. Königlich Preußische Akademie der Wissenschaften (Berlin: Georg Reimer/Walter de Gruyter, 1902–).

3. Carl Christian Erhard Schmid, *Physiologie, philosophisch betrachtet* (Jena: Akademische Buchhandlung, 1798), 1:xxx.

4. "Eine Übersicht der vornehmsten Erfindungen, Theorien und Systeme in der Arzneykunde, von 1700–1790," in *Des achtzehnten Jahrhunderts Geschichte der Erfindungen, Theorien und Systeme in der Natur- und Arzneywissenschaft*, ed. August Friedrich Hecker (Gotha: Justus Perthes, 1799), xi–lxxxxi, x.

5. Johann Karl Osterhausen, *Ueber medicinische Aufklärung* (Zurich: Geßner, 1798), 8–9; quoted in Wiesing, "Immanuel Kant, His Philosophy and Medicine," 223.

6. Christian Gottfried Gruner, "Systemsucht ist unser Verderben," *Almanach für Aerzte und Nichtaerzte auf das Jahr 1792* 11 (1792): 233–50, 237. This article is in large measure a summary of Francois Thiery, *Erfahrungen in der Arzneywissenschaft* (Leipzig: Adam Friedrich Böhme, 1778).

systematicity to be at odds with the pragmatic and therapeutic ends of medical practice. In this vein, the same anonymous commentator who praised Kantian philosophy for its purifying effects, inveighed against the tendency of transcendental philosophers to drift away from the very empirical experience they enshrined as the only source of knowledge. It is, we read, not difficult to find "very unphilosophical and uncritical physicians wrapping themselves in the language of the critical philosophy while . . . dreaming of an *a priori* medicine and striding on the stilts of transcendental philosophy out of the limited realm of experience and into the limitless field of oneiric transcendental medicine."[7]

It is true that advocates of Kant's contributions to medicine pointed to epistemological elements of the critical philosophy rather than to any specifically medical ideas and that authors dismissive of the medical value of transcendental philosophy took aim at Friedrich Schelling more directly than they did at Kant himself.[8] The degree to which Kant figured in polemics surrounding efforts to take stock of the state of the discipline at the end of the century is nonetheless suggestive. Maybe Kant has more to say about medicine and health than it initially appears. This chapter will thus investigate Kant's understanding of human health, what causes it to decline, and what we might do to ward off such decline. As we unpack Kant's remarks on these issues, we consider the degree to which published texts, unpublished notes, early drafts, and student lecture notes that address questions of health and medicine might justify the idea that Kant in fact had a considered and durable view about the nature of human health. This latter consideration opens the related question of how Kant's published comments about human health and how we ought to safeguard it stand with respect to the system of transcendental philosophy in general. Despite the snickers Kant's recommendations in this domain elicit among modern readers, we will show that his thinking about medicine and health is more intimately related to his central interest in the a priori structures of human experience and with the systematic unity of knowledge in general than one might expect.

---

7. "Übersicht," xi. See also Kurt Sprengel, *Kritische Übersicht des Zustandes der Arzneykunde in dem letzten Jahrzehend* (Halle: Johann Jacob Gebauer, 1801), §§10, 13.

8. See Guenter B. Risse, "Schelling, 'Naturphilosophie' and John Brown's System of Medicine," *Bulletin of the History of Medicine* 50, no. 3 (1976): 321–34; Urban Wiesing, "Der Tod der Auguste Böhmer: Chronik eines medizinischen Skandals, seine Hintergründe und seine historische Bedeutung," *History and Philosophy of the Life Sciences* 11, no. 2 (1989): 275–95.

For those interested in the systematic implications of Kant's views on human health, there is no more appropriate place to start than with the *Critique of Judgment*, which famously appeals to life as a means of securing the unity of Kant's critical project. Sandwiched between Kant's analysis of the relative aesthetic values of the fine arts and the "Dialectic of Aesthetic Judgment," we find in Kant's "Comment" (i.e., §54) a curious section devoted to a specific form of bodily gratification (*Vergnügen*) and its relation to the free play of the faculties, on the one hand, and health, on the other. The main thrust of section 54 appears to be to distinguish a form of gratification caused by listening to music from the universal and disinterested pleasure characteristic of judgments of beauty.

Games of chance, music, and witty conversation, Kant observes, each engender a free play of sensations reminiscent of the free play of the imagination and the understanding in judgments of beauty. The variation of notes in a piece of music triggers certain affects in us, which in turn arouse ideas of the objects of those affects. Just as quickly as the music invokes an object of fear or anticipation, however, we are returned to the fact that the music does not actually represent that object, which means that "in the end nothing is thought" (§54, 5:332).[9] The stimulating alternation between the invocation and collapse of ideas "quicken[s] the mind" (5:331), but "consists [merely] in the feeling of health that is produced by an intestinal agitation corresponding to such play" (5:332). The gratification characteristic of our enjoyment of music, in other words, is a function of the music's effects on our bodies and not a consequence of a disinterested judgment of the formal characteristics of the piece itself. Though there is a parallel between the free play of the faculties in a judgment of beauty and the agitation of the intestines and diaphragm, both of which are occasioned by the harmony of musical tones, we must distinguish the bodily gratification, that is, the feeling of health, for which the beauty of the music "merely serves as a necessary vehicle," from the disinterested pleasure of aesthetic judgment.

Kant's comments about the feeling of health can thus be read as a return to a central topic of the "Analytic of the Beautiful." In section 5, Kant differentiates three kinds of objects whose presentation elicits a feeling of pleasure: the agreeable, the good, and the beautiful. Section 54 adds the gratifying to this list. It makes sense that Kant would leave a discussion of gratification out of the early stages of his analysis of aesthetic judgment

9. Quotations of the *Critique of Judgment* use the Werner Pluhar translation (Indianapolis: Hackett, 1987).

since the similarity between the bodily gratification of wit and music and the aesthetic pleasure of beauty only comes into view following his analysis of the free play of the faculties. So one can read section 54 as a simple comment that circles back to an earlier distinction to clarify how it relates to a topic Kant regularly discussed in his anthropology lectures, namely, the salutary effects of convivial socialization.

This interpretation clarifies the relationship between Kant's comments about the feeling of health, for which certain kinds of beauty are said to be a necessary vehicle, within the context of the "Analytic of Aesthetic Judgement." There are readers, however, who argue that section 54 has broader ramifications. Perhaps the most prominent example appears in Rudolf Makkreel's *Imagination and Interpretation in Kant* (1990). Makkreel argues that "the idea of life can . . . be used to point to the fundamental coherence of the two parts of the *Critique of Judgment*."[10] More specifically, the progressively unfolding idea of life at the heart of that text, according to Makkreel, appeals at a crucial moment to Kant's conception of health. It is only after "having brought life to the level of bodily health," Makkreel claims, that "we are now ready to observe the transition in the *Critique of Judgment* from the aesthetical to the teleological."[11] Kant's explanation of the mental pleasure connected to subjective aesthetic judgments moves into an analysis of the regulative teleology of objective judgments about living organisms by first commenting in section 54 on "a feeling that a person's life is being furthered generally, and [this feeling] thus includes furtherance of his bodily well-being, i.e., his health" (5:331). The tertium quid that connects aesthetic judgment's promotion of a mental feeling of life to Kant's later analysis of the self-organization of living things is, in other words, the subjective feeling of bodily life in moments of gratification. On Makkreel's reading, the subjective feeling of an objective state of bodily health is the logical hinge connecting the subjective and objective purposiveness discussed in the two halves of the *Critique of Judgment.*

Other readers have also found Kant's discussions of health to be significant, and not simply for articulating the conceptual unity of the third *Critique*. Patrick Giomario argues, for example, that laughter occupies a more central place in Kant's aesthetics than we (or indeed Kant) have acknowledged. On Giomario's reading, the connection laughter establishes

10. Rudolf A. Makkreel, *Imagination and Interpretation in Kant: The Hermeneutical Import of the "Critique of Judgment"* (Chicago: University of Chicago Press, 1990), 88.

11. Makkreel, *Imagination and Interpretation*, 99.

between aesthetic ideas, the promotion of our vitality, and a movement of the mind recommends the conclusion that "laughter constitutes the most basic aesthetic judgment in Kant" such that judgments of the beautiful and the sublime "both presuppose laughter as their condition of possibility."[12]

John H. Zammito also acknowledges that Kant's discussion of the feeling of health in section 54 of the third *Critique* concerns transcendental and not merely empirical matters. He explores the broader stakes of this section by connecting it with Kant's practical philosophy. The gratification we glean from the feeling of health experienced while laughing or listening to music, Zammito notes, bears on "the whole life of the person," not merely the physiological dimensions of that life. Thus, he writes, "*Lebensgefühl* . . . is involved in that complex dualism of human experiences as between pure reason and mere matter. It can be read simply physiologically. . . . But it can also be read mentally, in accordance with the technical sense of Kant's term life. In the latter sense, both *Lebensgefühl* and *Willkür* offer the possibility of a transcendental significance."[13] Where Giomario seeks to elevate laughter to a transcendental dignity, Zammito aims to distinguish the merely empirical and physiological dimension of Kant's treatment of laughter's attendant feeling of the promotion of health from its practical and transcendental dimension, namely, "a feeling of autonomous spirituality (*Geistesgefühl*)."[14] On this interpretation, the true import of the feeling of health is as a way of inducing a distinctly nonphysiological awareness. Zammito concludes, "reflection, through *Lebensgefühl*, becomes aware of a relation to its own immanent rationality, and of the authority of that rationality in the subject."[15] On this view, Kant's remarks on the bodily effects of wit, music, and games of chance have no transcendental significance of their own, though they are useful in alerting us to the related feeling of our own rational freedom.

Yvonne Unna too is interested in how Kant's reflections on health bear on the transcendental elements of his practical philosophy. She points

12. Patrick Giomario, "'Making Reason Think More': Laughter in Kant's Aesthetic Philosophy," *Angelaki* 22, no. 4 (2017): 161–76, 162 (emphasis in original). See also Annie Hounsokou, "'Exposing the Rogue in Us': An Exploration of Laughter in the *Critique of Judgment*," *Epoché* 16, no. 2 (2012): 317–36.

13. John H. Zammito, *The Genesis of Kant's "Critique of Judgment"* (Chicago: University of Chicago Press, 1992), 296.

14. Zammito, *Genesis*, 297. Rachel Zuckert makes a similar point in *Kant on Beauty and Biology: An Interpretation of the "Critique of Judgment"* (Cambridge: Cambridge University Press, 2007), 266n58.

15. Zammito, *Genesis*, 299.

to a passage in Kant's preparatory notes for the *Metaphysics of Morals* that indicates he may think of physiological health as more proximate to our rational freedom than Zammito's reading of the third *Critique* allows. Kant writes: "The *summa* of all duties to oneself is: *mens sana in corpore sano*" ("Vorarbeiten zu *Die Metaphysik der Sitten*," 23:400).[16] When our health is compromised and we are in pain, it is simply more difficult to achieve the moral apathy that is necessary for genuinely moral action. Thus Kant takes us to have perfect moral duties to ourselves to ward off illness and preserve health by adopting an appropriate dietetic regimen, which "serves to safeguard the ability of the embodied rational being for moral action."[17] Kant's writings on dietetics and the importance of attending to subjective feelings of health and illness are thus, according to Unna, linked to core aspects of Kant's pure practical philosophy. Nonetheless, she argues, these concerns belong more properly to the domain of technique or skill than to pure practical reason itself.

Divergences in scholarly estimation of the meaning and significance of Kant's remarks on the feeling of health in the third *Critique* echo variations in the way Kant himself thought about the nature of health and its relevance to transcendental or metaphysical investigations of human life. It is telling that after noting that the highest duty to oneself involves cultivating a healthy mind in a health body, Kant immediately adds, "it is only necessary to determine what health [*Sanität*] is" (23:400). Though he rarely dedicates substantial portions of his published writings to the topic, reflections on the nature of health, the varieties and causes of illness, and dietetic regimens designed to preserve health are scattered across nearly the full length of his professional life. In 1767, Kant published the "Essay on the Maladies of the Head," which offered a taxonomy of mental illness and a brief commentary on the behavioral causes of some such illnesses. His continued interest in health and disease during the critical period is in evidence in the short "Note to Physicians," which concerns the flu epidemic of 1782, his 1786 rectoral address, "On the Philosophers' Medicine of the Body," his discussions of health in the *Metaphysics of Morals* (1797), which include an explicit endorsement of John Brown's theory of health and illness, the *Anthropology from a Pragmatic Point of View* (1798), as well

16. Immanuel Kant, "Vorarbeiten zu *Die Metaphysik der Sitten*," quoted in Yvonne Unna, "A Draft of Kant's Reply to Hufeland: Key Questions in Kant's Dietetics and the Problem of Its Systematic Place in His Philosophy," *Kant-Studien* 103, no. 3 (2012): 271–91, 285.

17. Unna, "A Draft," 285–86.

as the comments in the *Critique of Judgment*.[18] We also find notes about health and disease right through to the last notes that make up the *Opus postumum*.[19] Despite never addressing the issue systematically, then, it is clear that Kant thought about the nature of health and disease throughout his career. Reconstructing how Kant thought about health and disease gives us some insight into his estimation of the philosophical stakes of those concepts, which in turn sheds light on the question of how to interpret the role that the feeling of health that interests us here plays in his system of transcendental idealism more generally.

Despite the regularity with which Kant discussed health, his published remarks on the topic are spare. We will thus glean a more comprehensive picture of Kant's thoughts on what health is and what it means to feel one's health if we also consider his unpublished notes and the student notes from relevant lectures. Each of these sources is saddled with hermeneutic challenges. Student lecture notes might of course mispresent Kant's views; unpublished ideas might have remained unpublished because he never fully endorsed them. On the topic of health and the feeling of health, however, Kant's published comments, unpublished notes, and his students' lecture notes all approach the matter from a similar angle, namely, by defining health with respect to a balance or equilibrium of the vital forces (*Lebenskräfte*), the feeling of health in terms of returning to or approaching that balance, and illness as falling away from it. This convergence suggests that the unpublished sources accurately reflect Kant's thinking, so we will draw on them as we reconstruct his views, sketchy as they may be, of health.

Kant's lectures on anthropology offer a wealth of information about health and how his views changed over time. The structure of the anthropology lectures changed over the years. From the first time he offered the course in 1772–1773, however, Kant began by discussing our three basic mental capacities: knowing, feeling, and desiring. Kant adapted this feature from

18. Immanuel Kant, "Essay on the Maladies of the Head," in *Anthropology, History, and Education*, ed. Günter Zöller and Robert B. Louden (Cambridge: Cambridge University Press, 2007), 63–77, 2:259–65; "A Note to Physicians," in *Anthropology, History, and Education*, 105–6, 8:6; "On the Philosophers' Medicine of the Body," in *Anthropology, History, and Education*, 182–91, 15:939–53; *Anthropology from a Pragmatic Point of View*, in *Anthropology, History, and Education*, 227–429, 7:117–333; *The Metaphysics of Morals*, in *Practical Philosophy*, ed. and trans. Mary Gregor (Cambridge: Cambridge University Press, 1999), 353–603, 6:203–493.

19. Immanuel Kant, *Opus postumum*, ed. Eckart Förster, trans. Eckhart Förster and Michael Rosen (Cambridge: Cambridge University Press, 1993).

Alexander Baumgarten's discussion of empirical psychology in the *Metaphysics* (fourth edition, 1759), which was the textbook for the course. As part of his discussions of the feelings of pleasure and pain, Kant regularly noted a specific pleasure associated with the feeling of one's own vitality, health, or recovery from illness. Baumgarten does not touch on the issue other than to note that we are typically acutely aware of our own states so that the pleasures and pains associated with the perfections and imperfections of our own lives are greater than those of external objects.[20] Kant's consistent interest in the gratification of feeling one's own health thus complements Baumgarten's analysis without being reducible to it. As we will see, his views on the structure of the gratification arising from feeling one's vitality or health changed over time, sometimes describing one's health as readily accessible through feelings of pleasure or pain, sometimes denying that it is really felt at all.

Kant's first anthropology lectures set the parameters for his thinking about how one experiences one's own health and how one is aware of the underlying order or disorder of the vital forces over the succeeding decades. According to the notes from 1772–1773, Kant says: "We have a certain gratification [*Vergnügen*] that arises from the feeling of life in an individual organ. One who feels his whole life is content. One can feel the sum of all impressions without reflecting on it. Thus after eating, when one can be calm, one feels one's life. It is curious that human beings almost never feel their health because we sense only what drains it. For this reason many young people are not content, since they are healthy" ("Anthropologie Parow," 25:368–69)."[21]

When we feel our organs at work—as in quiet moments of satisfied digestion—our subtle awareness of the smooth functioning of the vital processes whirring along in our bodies gratifies us.[22] Even if we do not recognize it as such, the notes suggest, we regularly or even constantly feel our own vitality as a form of background pleasure. In contrast to the

20. Alexander Baumgarten, *Metaphysics: A Critical Translation with Kant's Elucidations, Selected Notes, and Related Materials*, ed. and trans. Courtney D. Fugate and John Hymers (London: Bloomsbury, 2013), §660.

21. Immanuel Kant, "Anthropologie Parow," in *Vorlesungen über Anthropologie*, Bd. 25 of *Kant's gesammelte Schriften*, ed. Berlin-Brandenburgische Akademie der Wissenschaften (Berlin: de Gruyter, 1997), 25:243–463.

22. It is worth noting that Kant's understanding of gratification (*Vergnügen*) departs from Baumgarten's use of the term (*gratum*), which takes it to be the feeling of a reduction in displeasure (Baumgarten, *Metaphysics*, §658).

regularity of the feeling of life, however, health is not an ordinary object of corporeal awareness. We feel the diminution of health or the onset of illness, the notes say, but we almost never feel ourselves to be healthy. In subsequent years, Kant alters his position on this point.

The anthropology lecture notes from the late 1770s and early 1780s indicate that Kant drew on a number of philosophical and scientific sources as he thought about life, health, and the pleasure they bring us. He offers a definition of health, for example, that tracks the position of Herman Boerhaave (1668–1738) almost exactly: "Health is the possession of all the powers of life, also of the strength and might which accompanies the complete life" ("Anthropology Friedländer," 25:583).[23] The 1777–1778 notes show Kant developing his ideas about gratification by distinguishing his views from those of Christian Wolff (1679–1754) and Pietro Verri (1728–1797), whose *Discourse on Pleasure and Pain* (1774) was translated into German in 1777.[24] Wolff, like Baumgarten, linked pleasure to the perception of perfection, which, Kant argues, fails to account for the variety of pleasures we experience. Verri, by contrast, incorrectly argues that since pleasure is subjective its cause or object cannot be specifically determined. In the 1772–1773 lectures, Kant had already claimed that gratification was caused by an awareness of our own bodily vitality. In the later lectures, Kant looks to hone that idea, which leads him to move away from the understanding of health he initially adopted from Boerhaave.

According to the lecture notes, Kant introduced a new approach to thinking about the feeling of life and health in his 1777–1778 course. Whereas the earlier notes describe gratification as the feeling of life in individual organs or in the body as a whole, Kant now explicitly rejects that idea. Life is felt just as much through pain and struggle as it is through gratification, so his explanation of how our awareness of our bodies gives rise to pleasurable feelings needs to be refined. Thus, we read in the notes, "not that the feeling of life is gratification; we feel also through pain that

23. Immanuel Kant, "Anthropology Friedländer," in *Lectures on Anthropology*, ed. Allen W. Wood and Robert B. Louden (Cambridge: Cambridge University Press, 2012), 37–256, 25:469–728. See Herman Boerhaave, *Phisiologie*, trans. Johann Peter Eberhard (Halle: Renger, 1754), §2.

24. See Christian Wolff, *Psychologia empirica* (Frankfurt and Leipzig, 1738), §511; Pietro Verri, *Idee sull'indole del piacere* (Livorno: Giuseppe Galeazzi, 1774); Pietro Verri, *Gedanken über die Natur des Vergnügens*, trans. Christoph Meiners (Leipzig: Weygand, 1777).

we are living, and even far more" ("Anthropology Pillau," 25:786).[25] Gratification is now said to be the feeling of the *promotion* of life rather than the feeling of life *simpliciter*. Understanding what exactly the promotion of life is requires a discussion of health.

On the model introduced in the late 1770s and articulated more fully in the lecture notes of the mid-1780s, the body is thought to be healthy when it is in a state of equilibrium. Excessive as well as deficient degrees of vitality compromise the body's integrity. According to the 1784–1785 notes: "Life has a certain measure beyond which it does not go, that is, health. But now a continuous enjoyment would intensify life to infinity, and thus when it went beyond the measure it would again weaken [us]; hence pain, which cancels health, must always precede, and gratification consists in the cancellation of the hindrance and the promotion of life towards health" ("Anthropology Mrongovius," 25:1318–19).[26]

This idea weaves Baumgarten's definition of gratification as the cessation of pain into Kant's interest in our affective awareness of our bodies.[27] We feel pain when the body's healthy equilibrium is disturbed or compromised and gratification when at least some of that pain is eliminated by moving the body closer to its own measure, that is, when we become healthier. Just as we do not feel our lives as such on this view, the genuinely healthy person "is he who feels nothing" (25:1319).[28] Bodily feelings of pleasure and displeasure are indices of our departures from and returns to our body's healthy equilibrium, that is, indices of changes of state rather than of states themselves.

Precisely what kind of equilibrium health is remains unknown, according to these notes, not just to Kant, but in general: "The doctors cannot define the state of a healthy person, for, it is true, they say it is when all the animal functions operate regularly, but we do not know whether any human being has ever been so healthy that he does not lack the least thing"

---

25. Immanuel Kant, "Anthropology Pillau," in *Lectures on Anthropology*, 257–80, 25:733–847. See also "Blomberg Logic," in *Lectures on Logic*, trans. and ed. J. Michael Young (Cambridge: Cambridge University Press, 1992), 5–246, 185, 24:16–301, 24:233; "Anthropologie Busholt," in *Vorlesungen über Anthropologie*, 25:1435–531, 25:1500.

26. Immanuel Kant, "Anthropology Mrongovius," in Kant, *Lectures on Anthropology*, 335–510, 25:1207–1429 (translation modified).

27. Baumgarten, *Metaphysics*, §660.

28. See also "Anthropology Mrongovius," 25:1219.

(25:1303). Indeed, if any human being ever had been fully healthy, on Kant's view, she would not have been alerted to her blessed state by any feeling of health and would have likely not noticed how fortunate she was. So from the mid-1770s through the 1780s, the notes from Kant's anthropology lectures indicate that he thought of health as an unknown state of bodily equilibrium that allowed a person to make use of all of her natural faculties. We are aware of our falling away from this equilibrium through illness or injury by virtue of the pain occasioned by the hindrance of life. The gratification characteristic of the promotion of life similarly alerts us when we are on the mend and returning to health.

If the lecture notes are an accurate guide, this is more or less Kant's view when he writes the third *Critique*. Given the consistency of the discussions of our feelings of health and life across more than ten years of notes and five different note takers, we have little reason for doubt on that score. This raises a question, however, for our interpretation of section 54 of the third *Critique*. If Kant maintained in his anthropology lectures from 1777 through 1789 that strictly speaking we feel neither our lives nor our health but only the promotion or hindrance of health, what should we make of the claim that the play of sensations and ideas occasioned by music, games of chance, and dinner parties arouses a feeling of health analogous to the quickening of the mind that accompanies judgments of beauty? One explanation would be to say that Kant simply changed his mind between the time he discussed the issue in the 1788–1789 lectures and the completion of the manuscript of the *Critique of Judgment* in September or October of 1789. There is debate about when exactly Kant completed drafts of specific sections of that text, but the timing could fit.[29]

If Kant's comments on the feeling of health generated by music and dinner parties in the third *Critique* represent a departure from the position of the anthropology lectures, then it is only a temporary one. By the time of the publication of the *Anthropology from a Pragmatic Point of View* (1796) and the *Metaphysics of Morals* (1797), Kant once again claims in print that health is not a state of which we have direct affective awareness. We read in the *Anthropology*: "Small inhibitions of the vital force [*Lebenskraft*] mixed in with advancements of it constitute the state of health that we erroneously consider to be a continuously felt well-being; when in fact it consists only of intermittent pleasant feelings that follow one another (with pain always

29. See Zammito, *Genesis*, 3–8. One might also think that the views presented in the lecture notes reflect the textbook Kant used for the course rather than his own views. Since Baumgarten does not discuss health in the *Metaphysics*, this is not a compelling explanation.

intervening between them). Pain is the incentive of activity, and in this, above all, we feel our life" (7:231).

Just as in the lectures from the 1780s, the *Anthropology* holds that we do not feel healthy as such. Instead, we feel the intermittent pain and pleasure characteristic of falling away from and approaching the dynamic equilibrium of health. He reiterates this point in the *Metaphysics of Morals*: "Health is only a negative kind of well-being: it cannot itself be felt" (6:484). Indeed, his unpublished notes repeat this point until at least 1800.[30] If section 54 departs from this position, which Kant appears to hold for a quarter century that spans the writing of the *Critique of Judgment*, then we have little reason to suspect that the comments in that section of the text can bear much systematic weight. If we revisit Kant's descriptions of the feeling of health that accompanies the range of agreeable activities surveyed in section 54 with the forgoing discussion of his other comments on health, we will see that this is not the case.

An initial interpretation of the claim that gratification "consists [merely] in the feeling of health that is produced by an intestinal agitation corresponding" to a play of ideas and affects clearly contradicts the claim that health "cannot itself be felt" (§54, 5:332). If we presume, however, that the *Critique of Judgment* is not an aberration in Kant's otherwise fairly stable view on this matter, then a more nuanced understanding of what the feeling of health consists in is required. Fortunately, such an understanding is also supported by the text. When Kant claims that "any changing free play of sensations . . . gratifies us, because it furthers our feeling of health" (5:331), we can draw on our analysis of the anthropology lectures to conclude that this means that the feeling of gratification stems from an improvement in our health through a promotion of our vital forces in the direction of a state of healthy equilibrium. This makes some sense out of his interest in section 54 in "the slackening in the body by the vibration of the organs" (5:332), the "alternating tension and relaxation of the elastic parts of our intestines that is communicated to the diaphragm," and the way that during a hearty laugh our lungs "rapidly and intermittently expel air, and so give rise to an agitation that is conducive to our health" (5:334). The feeling of health Kant associates with agreeable experiences like lively conversation

30. See Immanuel Kant, "Reflexionen zur Anthropologie," in *Handschriftlicher Nachlaß: Anthropologie*, Bd. 15 of *Kant's gesammelte Schriften*, ed. Berlin-Brandenburgische Akademie der Wissenschaften (Berlin: de Gruyter, 1923), 15:55–654, R290, 15:109; see also "Zweiter Anhang: Medicin," *Handschriftlicher Nachlaß: Anthropologie*, 15:937–80, R1539, 15:964; and Kant, *Opus postumum*, 22:99.

and hearing a good joke is not a feeling of a stable state of health. It is rather the gratification that results from promoting life by agitating the organs, which brings us closer to the ideal equilibrium of health. In other words, what he glosses with the phrase "feeling of health" in the *Critique of Judgment* is actually a kind of shorthand for "feeling of the promotion of life and a return to health." This reading has the virtue of making section 54 consistent with his broader published and unpublished remarks on the matter. This reading also raises a new question. If section 54 represents Kant's considered view, what makes him think that agitating the intestines, diaphragm, and lungs is conducive to health in the sense that these motions bring the body closer to its ideal internal equilibrium?

A brief investigation of the historical sources of Kant's idea that the agitation of the organs caused by enjoyable social interactions and laughter fleshes out Kant's elliptical remarks on the topic. As we shall soon see, appreciating the origins of Kant's view also sheds some light on the larger question of whether his interest in how and when we feel our own health and life bears any systematic significance.

The ideas that bodily health consists in a kind of equilibrium of the vital forces and that we can feel ourselves approaching or falling away from that equilibrium through our affective awareness of the promotion and hindrance of life in our organs or body appeared first, as we saw above, in the lecture notes emerging from the 1784–1785 anthropology course. The Scottish physician John Brown (1735–1788) defended a very similar view in his *Elementa medicinae* (1780). Brown writes:

> Excitement, the effect of the exciting powers, the true cause of life, is, within certain boundaries, produced in a degree proportioned to the degree of stimulus. The degree of stimulus, when moderate, produces health; in a higher degree it gives occasion to diseases of excessive stimulus; in a lower degree, or ultimately low, it induces those that depend upon a deficiency of stimulus, or debility. And, as what has been mentioned, is the cause both of diseases and perfect health; so that which restores the morbid to the healthy state, is a diminution of excitement in *the cases of* diseases of excessive stimulus, and an encrease *of the same excitement* for the removal of diseases of debility. (emphasis original)[31]

31. John Brown, *The Elements of Medicine; or a Translation of the Elementa Medicinae Brunonis* (London: J. Johnson, 1788), 1:§23.

Kant explains how gratification that intensifies life beyond its proper measure results in a weakening of life in a way that echoes Brown's claim here that health amounts to an appropriate degree or measure of excitation. Kant's interest is in the feeling of health, so he emphasizes pleasure and pain where Brown discusses excitation. The *Elementa medicinae* is, however, dense with examples of pain caused by excessive or deficient degrees of excitement: gout, peripneumony, gastritis. Moreover, Brown argues that the use of opium as a stimulant to correct deficiencies in excitement results in the cessation of these pains, which feeling Kant calls gratification. There are, then, suggestive parallels between Kant's conception of health from the mid-1780s and the theory laid out in the *Elementa medicinae*.

The idea that Brown's ideas might have informed Kant's thinking on this score gains further traction when we consider the salutary effects Kant associates with the agitation of the intestines and the lungs. The agitation of the organs, we recall, is at the root of Kant's claims that we don't just feel ourselves to be alive in moments of convivial excitement but that we can feel the promotion of our health. Brown also associates the intermittent contraction and relaxation of the organs to be characteristic of health. He claims, "the healthy and vigorous state of motion consists not in the degree of contraction, but, with a certain degree of that, in the well proportioned alternation between contraction and relaxation."[32] Brown associates contraction with excitement and relaxation with lassitude. The alternation of contraction and relaxation of a muscle, organ, or blood vessel is thus linked to a balanced state of excitement, whereas persistent contraction or relaxation indicate illness. To feel the intermittent contraction and relaxation of the organs of the body, then, is to feel oneself in a state of good health. Though initially puzzling to us, the connection Kant saw between the agitation of the organs and a state of good health reflects new medical ideas that would come to dominate German debates at the turn of the nineteenth century.

The parallel between the Brown's *Elementa medicinae* and Kant's anthropology lectures suggests that Kant may have read and begun to incorporate Brown's new medical ideas sometime between the winter semesters of 1781–1782 (the anthropology lecture notes of that year do not touch on this theory of health) and 1784–1785. There is not, to my knowledge, unambiguous evidence of when Kant first encountered Brown's ideas. Brunonian medicine was well-known and very controversial in German intellectual

32. Brown, *Elements of Medicine*, 1:§229n(p).

life from the 1790s into the first decades of the nineteenth century.[33] We know Kant was aware of Brown during that time. He expressed his support for Brown's ideas in 1797 in a brief passage in the *Metaphysics of Morals*, where he explains that there is "only one principle for systematically classifying diseases (Brown's)" (6:207). In his early biography, Ehregott Andreas Christoph Wasianski (1755–1831) reports Kant's keen interest in theories of health and medicine, which he links to Kant's obsessive attention to his own health. Kant's interest in these matters is exemplified, on Wasianski's telling, by his early adoption of Brown's ideas, which Kant embraced "as soon as Weikard adopted them and made them known."[34] Adam Melchior Weikard (1742–1803) published the first German translation of *Elementa medicinae* in 1795.[35] Samantha Matherne has argued more recently that Brown's influence on Kant is legible in the *Critique of Judgment*, which, if she is correct, means Kant was familiar with the ideas already in 1789.[36] Mary Gregor gives us reason to think that Kant may have known about Brown even earlier, in 1786.[37] The notes for Kant's rectoral address in October of that year, "On the Philosophers' Medicine of the Body," echo Brown's ideas along lines similar to those we have just sketched, when Kant notes, for example, "although [affects], too, agitate the body by a certain assault on it, they can be healthful, provided they do not reach the point of enervating it" (15:940). Those notes also speculatively link Felix Mendelssohn's death to an unbalanced dietetic regimen (not enough food, too much thinking) that eventually exhausted his vital forces. There is evidence, then, to support the claim that Kant was aware of Brown's ideas before Weikard's translation was published. Our analysis of Kant's conception of health based on the anthropology lecture notes builds on Matherne's and Gregor's claims that

---

33. Nelly Tsouyopoulos, "The Influence of John Brown's Ideas in Germany," *Medical History*, suppl. 8 (1988): 63–74.

34. E. A. C. Wasianski, *Immanuel Kant in seinen letzten Lebensjahren* (Königsberg: Friedrich Nicolovius, 1804), 42.

35. Adam Melchior Weikard, *Johann Browns Grundsätze der Arzneilehre aus dem Lateinischen übersetzt* (Frankfurt a. M.: Andreä, 1795).

36. Samantha Matherne, "Kant's Expressive Theory of Music," *Journal of Aesthetics and Art Criticism* 72, no. 2 (2014): 129–45, 142n47. Reinhard Löw makes a similar claim in *Philosophie des Lebendigen: Der Begriff des Organischen bei Kant, sein Grund und seine Aktualität* (Frankfurt a. M.: Suhrkamp, 1980), 96–97.

37. Mary J. Gregor, introduction to "On the Philosophers' Medicine of the Body," in *Kant's Latin Writings*, ed. Lewis White Beck (New York: Peter Lang, 1986), 195–203, 191–92.

textual parallels suggest Kant encountered Brunonian medicine in the mid-1780s, likely before the end of 1784.[38]

If it is true that Kant was engaging with Brunonian medical ideas already in 1784 and that these ideas illuminate Kant's remarks in section 54 of the *Critique of Judgment*, then we can draw some interesting conclusions about the systematic significance of those comments. The connection between our historical claim and the systematic role of Kant's investigations of the feeling of health hinges on Kant's notes about the strengths of Brown's theory of excitement. We have already seen that Kant's introductory remarks about the systematic unity of knowledge in the *Metaphysics of Morals* endorse Brown's as the only true theory of medicine. What precisely leads Kant to this conclusion remains unspecified there. If we turn to Kant's notes from the period, however, we get a clearer sense of what attracted Kant to the view. After a brief sketch of Brown's theory of excitability (*Erregbarkeit*), Kant writes:

> One can admit that Brown has presented impeccably the concept of the system of the moving forces of human life as far as its form is concerned, since it is an *a priori* and merely theoretical concept. *Materially* and practically (hygiene, treatment, as well as dietetics as a therapy), he has offered what are certainly terrible remedies, both in regard to quality and quantity. But apart from these, which are merely empirical principles of his medical teachings, one cannot deny that his taxonomy, which he connects only with reason, contains the right guide and that in

38. William Cullen (1710–1790), Brown's teacher and rival, is another potential source of Kant's thinking about health as a balance within the vital forces. Though Brown's ideas more closely resemble the ideas in Kant's anthropology lectures, Cullen's texts were discussed in German intellectual circles more broadly in the 1780s, around the time the notes first show Kant discussing health as a balance of forces. Cullen's *First Lines of the Practice of Physic*, was published in four volumes between 1777 and 1784 and was translated into German beginning in 1778 (*Grundriss der ärztlichen Praxis für Studenten*, 1784). The third volume of that work, which was translated into German in 1784, describes the dynamics of excitement (*Erregung*) and collapse (*Zusammenfall*) as determinative of a wide range of the body's states. Kant's notes include two references to Cullen ("Zweiter Anhang: Medicin," *Handschriftlicher Nachlaß: Anthropologie*, R1544, 15:967; *Opus postumum*, 22:407). In each case, however, Cullen's name is immediately linked with Brown's, while Kant mentions Brown without naming Cullen on many occasions. This suggests that Brown was the more salient influence on Kant's thinking on this issue.

> respect to the practice of purification it is capable and worthy. ("Zweiter Anhang: Medicin," R1539, 15:963; emphasis original)

The terrible remedies Kant has in mind are primarily whiskey and opium, which Brown prescribed liberally to both himself and others as a means of stimulating the moving forces of the body and combatting ill health caused by laxity.[39] Though Brown mistook how his theory ought to be applied in practice, Kant claims, the principles of the theory possess the certainty of theoretical concepts derived from reason alone. Kant's support for Brown's ideas rests not on their therapeutic or diagnostic success, in other words, but on their a priori character.

In another note from this period, Kant positively contrasts the systematic nature of Brunonian medicine with Boerhaave's, which lacks the unity characteristic of science (15:961–62). In the preparatory notes to his response to Christoph Wilhelm Hufeland's *The Art of Prolonging Human Life* (1797),[40] which would eventually become the third part of the *Conflict of the Faculties*,[41] Kant again grants medicine an a priori foundation. Kant writes that dietetics, the branch of medicine focused on preventing rather than curing disease, "is really a *philosophy*, that is a rational knowledge from concepts, and Stoic principles based on it; to be more precise [it] is a (technically-) practical philosophy hence with regard to its matter, the sensations, empirical, but with regard to form [of the use and] arrangement of the same for the preservation of health a knowledge *a priori* (not that of an empiricist)."[42] Dietetics, in other words, has an a priori core. Kant's unpublished notes as well as the brief comment at the opening of the *Metaphysics of Morals* show that he had come to think Brown's theory of excitability provided an a priori foundation for the systematically unified philosophy of medicine by the late 1790s.[43]

---

39. Kant recommends against the ingestion of opium and strong spirits at *Anthropology*, 7:170 and *Metaphysics of Morals*, 6:428.

40. Christoph Wilhelm Hufeland, *Die Kunst das menschliche Leben zu verlängern* (Vienna and Prague: Franz Haas, 1797).

41. Immanuel Kant, *The Conflict of the Faculties*, in *Religion and Rational Theology*, ed. Allen W. Wood and George di Giovanni (Cambridge: Cambridge University Press, 1996), 233–328, 7:5–116.

42. Yvonne Unna, "A Draft of Kant's Reply to Hufeland: Autograph, Transcription (Wolfgang G. Beyerer), and English Translation (Yvonne Unna)," *Kant-Studien* 103, no. 1 (2012): 1–24, 17 (emphasis original).

43. See also *Opus postumum*, 21:89.

Against the backdrop of the third *Critique*'s generally negative conclusion about the possibility of a genuinely systematic knowledge of organic life, this is surprising. When examined in the light of the so-called Transition Project that formed the heart of the *Opus postumum*, less so. Kant's goal in the never-completed Transition Project was to establish a bridge between the a priori structures of transcendental philosophy and the metaphysical foundations of Newtonian mechanics, on the one hand, and the profusion of empirical natural laws described by natural philosophers, on the other.[44] No less than the systematic unity of experience was on the line and Kant turned over a great many leaves in his efforts to explain the unity of the sciences. The attraction of Brunonian medicine in this context is that it represents the healthy body as an equilibrium of the moving forces—sthenic and asthenic affects, as Kant calls them, following Brown, in the *Anthropology* (7:255). In the *Metaphysical Foundations of Natural Science*, Kant argues that characterizing impenetrable matter as the product of the equilibrium of the basic attractive and repulsive forces governing all physical existence allows for an a priori dynamic matter theory on the basis of Newtonian laws.[45] It is easy enough to see how one might think of the living forces that determine the relative health of a human body in analogy to the attractive and repulsive forces of matter in general in an effort to sketch an a priori account of human health or well-being. Perhaps this is what Kant had in mind in 1797.

Regardless of what exactly Kant had in mind when he wrote about the systematic quality and a priori validity of a philosophy of medicine rooted in Brunonian principles, it is clear that Kant saw no space for an a priori science of human life when he published the third *Critique* in 1790. If there is no hope "that perhaps some day another Newton might arise who could explain to us, in terms of natural laws unordered by any intention, how even a mere blade of grass is produced" (§75, 5:400), then certainly we cannot reasonably take Brown to be the Newton of human health.[46] If

44. The details of the Transition Project are of course an object of considerable debate. For an excellent overview of the debates and an explanation of the relation of the Transition Project to the critical philosophy, see Eckart Förster, *Kant's Final Synthesis: An Essay on the "Opus postumum"* (Cambridge, MA: Harvard University Press, 2000).

45. Immanuel Kant, *Metaphysical Foundations of Natural Science*, in *Theoretical Philosophy after 1781*, ed. Henry E. Allison and Peter Heath (Cambridge: Cambridge University Press, 2002), 171–270, 4:467–565.

46. Kant himself draws precisely this comparison approximately nine years later. See *Opus postumum*, 21:612.

it is in principle impossible to marry the mechanical explanations produced by experience with a teleological explanation of the organic unity of living things in general, then it is similarly impossible to do so in the case of a specific living thing, namely, the human being. The smooth functioning of a healthy human body epitomizes its organic unity: the healthy functioning of one organ both contributes to and relies on the healthy functioning of every other organ and the body as a whole. Mechanical explanations of health, on this model, can only ever be partial and incomplete. We must not, then, read Kant's later interests in exploring the prospect for an a priori philosophy or science of human health back into section 54 of the *Critique of Judgment*. That is not to say, however, that Kant's later gestures in that direction are entirely foreign to the *Critique*.

The purpose of section 54 is to acknowledge a similarity between the pleasure of the free play of the mental faculties occasioned by judgments of beauty and the gratification of the body triggered by the free play of ideas in music and convivial socialization. Though these types of pleasure are similar, there is, Kant is clear, "an essential difference between *what we like when we merely judge it*, and what *gratifies* us (i.e., what we like in sensation). The second, unlike the first, we cannot require of everyone" (5:330; emphasis original). Whereas the formal characteristics of a judgment of beauty license an expectation that others will concur, what gratifies is idiosyncratic and personal. The strikingly unfunny jokes that Kant reports elicited uproarious laughter are testament enough to this.[47] But we should not let this difference obscure the similarity that leads Kant to explore gratification at the end of the "Analytic of Aesthetic Judgment."

What gratification shares with the pleasure elicited by beauty that the latter does not share with the pleasure characteristic of agreeable things is that gratification is produced through a free play of representations. Gratification is, in other words, a corporeal analog of the pleasure of beauty insofar as they both arise from a harmonious effect of mental free play. In beauty, the free play of the understanding and the imagination pleases as it demonstrates the harmony of the cognitive faculties. In lively dinner conversation, the quickening of the mind as it moves from one idea, affect, or intuition to the next gives rise to a parallel excitation of the vital forces of the body, agitation of the organs, and a consequent feeling of health. In some cases, beautiful objects are the triggers for gratification: "It is not our

47. Kant underlines this point with his criticism of Burke's "physiological" exposition of aesthetic judgment. See *Critique of Judgment*, "General Comment," 5:277–78.

judging of the harmony we find in tones or in flashes of wit—this harmony, with its beauty, merely serves as a necessary vehicle . . . which constitutes the gratification we find in the fact that we can reach the body through the soul as well, and use the soul as the physician of the body" (§54, 5:332). There are at least some occasions when pure judgments of beauty act as a vehicle for an excitation of the body that engenders a feeling of health that corresponds to the quickening of the mind and the feeling of life aroused by the aesthetic judgment itself.[48] These occasions are doubly gratifying, Kant says, in that the harmony of the body and mind they exemplify provides still another layer of pleasure.

While Kant undermines the prospect for a true a priori science of life, and a fortiori of human health, in the "Critique of Teleological Judgment," he suggestively comments on a parallel between the a priori structures of aesthetic judgment and the empirical constitution of the body in a way that links long-running topics covered in his anthropology courses and the later Transition Project. That the body is agitated in a way that produces a feeling of health by at least some of the same objects that also enliven the mind through a disinterested free play of the mental faculties suggests that the transcendental conditions of aesthetic judgment and the purposiveness of beauty find a meaningful analog in the body. Makkreel's gloss on aesthetic judgment establishes clearly the terms of this parallel: "The feeling of pleasure in beauty . . . provide[s] an interior sense of an overall equilibrium in the mental life of the subject, an equilibrium which has a restorative function."[49] This echoes precisely the salutary equilibrium felt in the gratifying agitation of the organs in hearty laughter, listening to certain music, and so on. Certain instances of beauty give rise to pleasures that promote both mental and physical well-being.

Makkreel is right to conclude that section 54 of the *Critique* has a broader significance than many readers have acknowledged. His sensitivity to the role that Kant's comments about the feeling of health play in linking the subjective purposiveness of aesthetic judgment to the objective purposiveness of teleological judgment sheds valuable light on the conceptual unity of the

48. Though Kant refers to beauty as a necessary vehicle for gratification in the passage just cited, the fact that he lists, in addition to music, conversation and games of chance as objects of gratification (here and in the anthropology lectures) certainly indicates that he means to say that it is not the beauty that gratifies when beautiful things gratify. Non-beautiful things can also gratify.

49. Makkreel, *Imagination and Interpretation*, 96.

Critique of Judgment. In this chapter we have tried to expand Makkreel's insight by focusing more narrowly on Kant's conception of health and how it changed through the 1770s, 1780s, and 1790s. What our investigation has shown is that the suggestive parallel elaborated in section 54 between the transcendental structure of judgments of beauty, on the one hand, and the empirical constitution of the human body and the salutary effects of a free play of ideas in the mind, on the other, is not a wayward aside at the end of the "Analytic of Aesthetic Judgment." It is one node in a complex of explorations of the possibility of constructing an a priori, systematic knowledge of the structure of embodied human life. During the critical period in particular, he investigated connections between the spiritual and corporeal dimensions of human life. Zammito is right that Kant highlights the way that the bodily feeling of life might trigger an awareness of our rational spontaneity and orient us toward our spiritual nature. What we hope to have shown here is that the related feeling of health returns us to our corporeal nature and Kant's persistent interest in establishing points of contact between the transcendental structures of mental life and the systematic study of embodied human nature.

Published and unpublished writings indicate Kant's sympathy for the idea that a systematic a priori theory of human health could be constructed on the basis of John Brown's concept of excitability. His attraction to this line of thinking never leads him unambiguously to mount an argument for any a priori knowledge of the healthy structures and functions of the body to match those of the healthy use of reason. He was wary, to echo the anonymous critic of 1799, of "strid[ing] on the stilts of transcendental philosophy out of the limited realm of experience."[50] The "limitless field of oneiric transcendental medicine" was certainly a dream for Kant in the 1790s, but no more than that. In this regard, section 54 of the *Critique of Judgment* reflects Kant's broader position: It suggests an a priori harmony of the mind and body and opens the possibility that transcendental philosophy might incorporate material or bodily conditions into its a priori explanation of human life; it provides arguments against the possibility of producing a true science of embodied human life while at the same time remaining keenly interested in new ways of exploring the possibility of such a project.

50. "Übersicht," xi (see note 7).

Chapter 13

Kant and Organic Life

Joan Steigerwald

> The perception of the organism as a product, in which what it is *it is through itself*—which is simultaneously cause and effect of itself, means and end—will be justified as in accordance with nature.
>
> —Friedrich Wilhelm Joseph Schelling[1]

> Each of the organs is in alterations, which it experiences in each moment, the alterations so adjusted to all other organs, and it is so united in a system of simultaneous and successive alterations, that, according to our way of talking, each becomes reciprocally cause and effect of the others.
>
> —Carl Friedrich Kielmeyer[2]

At the turn of the nineteenth century there was a growing preoccupation with the distinct characteristics of organic life. In part this preoccupation emerged in response to a range of inquiries across natural history and physiology

1. Friedrich Wilhelm Joseph Schelling, *First Outline of a System of the Philosophy of Nature, trans. Keith R. Peterson* (Albany: State University of New York Press, 2004), 51; *Erster Entwurf eines Systems der Naturphilosophie*, in *Sämmtliche Werke*, Bd. 3, ed. Karl Friedrich August Schelling (Stuttgart: Cotta, 1858), 1–268, 66.

2. Carl Friedrich Kielmeyer, *Über die Verhältnisse der organischen Kräfte untereinander in der Reihe der verschiedenen Organisationen*, in *Gesammelte Schriften*, ed. Fritz-Heinz Holler (Berlin: W. Keiper, 1938), 59–102, 62.

that drew attention to the capacities of living beings to develop gradually, to regenerate themselves when injured, to vary under changed physical environments, and to be responsive to external stimuli while maintaining their individuality. Although the study of such capacities was not wholly new, by the end of the eighteenth century the range and the extent of inquiries into vital phenomena posed with unprecedented intensity questions regarding what constitutes organic life and what are the appropriate methods for its study. These questions were compounded by rapidly developing inquiries into chemical and physical processes in both inorganic and organic bodies. In the face of the apparent blurring of boundaries between the living and the nonliving, organic life became a problem rather than a self-evident starting point for investigation. Moreover, these issues were raised in the context of naturalists, physicians, and physiologists as well as chemists and physicists forging new identities for themselves through the formation of new societies, new periodicals, and new university and teaching positions, complicating the disciplinary loci from which such inquiries were undertaken. In German settings, the constitution of the sciences or *Wissenschaften* was also the concern of critical philosophy, which highlighted the epistemic challenges of proposals for a science of life or biology.[3]

Kant intervened into these debates. As he was writing before the development of evolutionary and genetic theories, Kant's conception of organisms is often regarded as necessarily dated, in contrast to his more enduring legacies within epistemology, aesthetics, and moral philosophy. Yet the settlement with the Darwinian synthesis has been increasingly called into question through new concerns in both biology and philosophy with emergence, epigenetics, ecology, individuation, organization, and agency.[4] As we rethink what organic life might be in the present, we are also led to

---

3. See Joan Steigerwald, *Experimenting at the Boundaries of Life: Organic Vitality in Germany around 1800* (Pittsburgh: University of Pittsburgh Press, 2019).

4. See, for example, Matteo Mossio, ed., *Organization in Biology* (Berlin: Springer, 2023); Jan Baedke, *Above the Gene, Beyond Biology: Toward a Philosophy of Epigenetics* (Pittsburgh: University of Pittsburgh Press, 2018); Denis Walsh, *Organisms, Agency, and Evolution* (Cambridge: Cambridge University Press, 2015); Frédéric Bouchard and Philippe Huneman, eds., *From Groups to Individuals: Evolution and Emerging Individuality* (Cambridge, MA: MIT Press, 2013); Catherine Malabou, *Before Tomorrow: Epigenesis and Rationality*, trans. Carolyn Shread (Cambridge, UK: Polity, 2016); Arne de Boever, Shirley S. Y. Murray, and Jon Roffe, eds., *Gilbert Simondon: Being and Technology* (Edinburgh: Edinburgh University Press, 2013); Elizabeth Grosz, "Matter, Life, and Other Variations," *Philosophy Today* 55 (2011): 17–27.

reconsider how it has been rendered in the past, when a science of life was first articulated and the boundaries between the organic and inorganic were first being explored. Kant's contributions to the historical development of biology might be recast in light of such reconsiderations of the importance of organic individuation and generation to that development. Kant sought a conception of organisms adequate to the emerging inquiries in natural history and physiology into their organization and self-organization. In the *Critique of Judgment*, he addressed these issues as part of a larger critical examination of teleological judgment as a mode of reflective judgment. Scholarship on Kant's account of teleology often focuses on the ends of nature as a whole or the destiny of human beings. But much of Kant's discussion of teleological judgment in the third *Critique* was concerned with organisms, and the question of how we are to comprehend these distinctive natural products as bounded and self-forming beings. It is argued in this chapter that although Kant did not solve these problems, he did articulate them in a compelling fashion, which opened up, rather than settled, the question of what organic life is or might be conceived to be.

It is important to situate Kant's contributions to understandings of organized and self-organizing beings within eighteenth-century concerns in natural history. He addressed the unique capacities of organisms across several texts that contributed to contemporary debates on the generation, propagation, and variation of organic kinds. In his 1755 *Universal Natural History and Theory of the Heavens*, he raised the problem of the place of organisms within the historical formation of our world, arguing that their first appearance cannot be explicated through the mechanical laws of matter and its forces.[5] But even in his precritical works he rejected supernatural explanations of the immediate generation of individual plants and animals as untenable. In his 1770s essays on race, Kant advocated a history of nature modeled on Georges-Louis Leclerc de Buffon's approach to natural history, which was concerned with the genealogical lineage or propagation of organic kinds as well as with the variations of species through changes to the physical earth and natural migrations. Kant's essays on race have become notorious for their discussion of different races of humankind and linking differences of intellectual and moral development to racial difference.[6] As

5. Immanuel Kant, *Universal Natural History and Theory of the Heavens*, in *Natural Science*, ed. Eric Watkins (Cambridge: Cambridge University Press, 2012), 182–308.

6. Kant's contributions to the racialization of human beings have been receiving increased attention. See, for example, Robert Bernasconi, ed., *Race* (Oxford: Blackwell, 2001); Sara

contributions to natural history, these essays raised the problem of how variations in organic kinds might be propagated or inherited. Kant speculated on the existence of germs (*Keime*) and predispositions (*Anlagen*) that have the potential to unfold variously depending on particular conditions, ensuring organized beings were suited to their environment. Once specific capacities are unfolded, they preclude others, and are invariably propagated as hereditary traits of race.[7] During the latter half of the eighteenth century, compelling empirical demonstrations of the gradual or epigenetic formation of organisms were presented by Caspar Friedrich Wolff and Johann Friedrich Blumenbach. In the *Critique of Judgment*, Kant praised Blumenbach's account of the formative capacities of organisms, for explaining as much as possible through mechanical forces, while also recognizing a formative drive (*Bildungstrieb*) acting in reproductive matter to propagate and gradually form organized beings. Kant now explicitly distinguished his account from contemporary theories in which organisms were regarded as developing from preformed germs. Instead, he termed his account "generic preformation," ascribing the productive capacity to the "purposive predispositions" of its propagated reproductive matter (§81, 5:423).[8] Kant's interventions into these concerns in natural history were noteworthy and discussed by many contemporary naturalists and philosophers.[9]

Eigen and Mark Joseph Larrimore, eds., *The German Invention of Race* (Albany: State University of New York Press, 2012); Justin E. H. Smith, *Nature, Human Nature, and Human Difference: Race in Early Modern Philosophy* (Princeton, NJ: Princeton University Press, 2016).

7. Immanuel Kant, "Of the Different Human Races," in *Kant and the Concept of Race: Late Eighteenth-Century Writings*, ed. Jon H. Mikkelsen (Albany: State University of New York Press, 2013), 41–54.

8. Immanuel Kant, *Critique of Judgment*, trans. Werner Pluhar (Indianapolis: Hackett, 1987). All citations of Kant's *Critique of Judgment* are to paragraph number, then Academy edition volume and page number.

9. Considerable attention has been given to these contributions. See, for example, Peter McLaughlin, "Blumenbach und der Bildungstrieb: Zum Verhältnis von epigenetischer Embryologie und typologischem Artbegriff," *Medizinhistorisches Journal* 17, no. 4 (1982): 357–72; Phillip R. Sloan, "Preforming the Categories: Eighteenth-Century Generation Theory and the Biological Roots of Kant's *A Priori*," *Journal of the History of Philosophy* 40, no. 2 (2002): 229–53; Robert J. Richards, *The Romantic Conception of Life: Science in the Age of Goethe* (Chicago: Chicago University Press, 2002), 329–37; John H. Zammito, "'This Inscrutable *Principle* of an Original *Organization*': Epigenesis and 'Looseness of Fit' in Kant's Philosophy of Science," *Studies in History and Philosophy of Science* 34, no. 1

Kant's most important contributions to the development of understandings of organic life did not lie in his specific theories of generation or propagation but in his conception of the self-organizing capacities of organized beings and his reflections on the judgments productive of that conception in the *Critique of Judgment*. He contended that "*an organized product of nature is one in which everything is* [*an end* (Zweck)] *and reciprocally also a means*" (§66, 5:376).[10] A natural product, yet comprehended as possible only as a natural purpose, "it must relate to itself in such a way that it is both cause and effect of itself" (§65, 5:372). It was this conception of the reciprocity of means and ends, of cause and effect, as characteristic of organisms that was cited repeatedly by naturalists, physiologists, and philosophers attempting to develop a science of life at the turn of the nineteenth century. Even figures like Carl Friedrich Kielmeyer and Friedrich Wilhelm Joseph Schelling, whose projects for a history of nature or philosophy of nature departed from Kant's in significant ways, enlisted this formulation and found it productive. It is thus important to examine Kant's conception closely.

Kant did not use the expression "organic life." In discussing organisms, he used the expressions "organized beings" or "an *organized* and a *self-organizing* being" (*organisirtes und sich selbst organisirendes Wesen*) (§65, 5:372, 374). He denied life could be attributed to organic beings, reserving the attribution of life to beings with intelligence and will, to human beings and the life of the mind (*Gemüth*). In the *Critique of Judgment*, Kant explored "the feeling of life, under the name of the feeling of pleasure or displeasure," as the basis for judgments of taste (§1, 5:204). Rudolf Makkreel offers expansive analyses of this feeling of life. He presents the feeling of pleasure or displeasure as a mode of interior sense that designates a responsive mode of consciousness; it is a sensitivity to the overall state of the mind and a

(2003): 73–109; Robert Bernasconi, "Kant and Blumenbach's Polyps: A Neglected Chapter in the History of the Concept of Race," in Eigen and Larrimore, *German Invention of Race*, 73–89; Philippe Huneman, "Reflexive Judgement and Wolffian Embryology: Kant's Shift between the First and the Third Critiques," in *Understanding Purpose? Kant and the Philosophy of Biology*, ed. Philippe Huneman (Rochester: University of Rochester Press, 2007), 75–100; Smith, *Nature and Human Difference*, 231–63; Catherine Wilson, "The Building Forces of Nature and Kant's Teleology of the Living," in *Kant and the Laws of Nature*, ed. Michela Massimi and Angela Breitenbach (Cambridge: Cambridge University Press, 2016), 256–74; Ina Goy, *Kants Theorie der Biologie: Ein Kommentar, eine Lesart, eine historische Einordnung* (Berlin: de Gruyter, 2017).

10. My amendment to the Pluhar translation.

responsiveness of either affirming or rejecting that state. The life of the mind is the inner capacity to act and determine oneself as well as the consciousness of being acted upon and a capacity to respond to that consciousness.[11] In his contribution to this volume, Makkreel shows how Kant included in the aesthetic affects, for example, of music and humor the stimulus of the vital processes and well-being of the body as well as the mind. If animal life is one aspect of human life, so too is spirit as the enlivening principle of the mind and of the free spontaneity that orientates human beings to their moral destiny. Kant's depiction of aesthetic consciousness as involving the "animation" or "quickening" (*Belebung*) of mental powers is one of several striking vital metaphors in the "Critique of Aesthetic Judgment." The pleasure in the reciprocal harmony of cognitive powers serves to "*preserve*" or "keep" (*erhalten*) and "reproduce" (*reproducirt*) this state (§12, 5:222).

When Kant turned to organized bodies in the "Critique of Teleological Judgment," it is their capacity to self-organize, to generate, preserve, and reproduce their form that concerned him. These are the predominate capacities of the simplest organic bodies, of plants and polyps, capacities found in all organisms, in contrast to the capacities of mobility or sensibility found only in more developed organisms. Despite new investigations of these capacities, they remained contested, poorly understood, and difficult to explain. The remarkable generative capacities of organisms are natural processes, yet they elude the determinative concepts of mechanical explanations. These phenomena encountered in empirical inquiry also cannot be grasped through the subjective feeling of life of the mind. Kant's "Critique of Teleological Judgment" is significant for recognizing a new area of empirical inquiry and the problems it posed for cognition. His analysis of teleological judgments and concept of natural purpose, situated between mechanical causality and human purposes, offered generative reflections for developing studies of the unique capacities of organic beings.

Organisms as Reciprocal Means and Ends of Themselves

It is posited here that Kant's conception of organisms as reciprocal means and ends, or causes and effects, of themselves is derived from his critical reflections on the mode of judgment enlisted to grasp their capacities to

11. Rudolf A. Makkreel, *Imagination and Interpretation in Kant: The Hermeneutical Import of the "Critique of Judgment"* (Chicago: University of Chicago Press, 1990), 88–107.

generate, maintain, and propagate their organization. This argument makes sense of Kant's placement of his most extensive analysis of our understandings of organisms in the *Critique of Judgment* rather than in a treatise on natural history or the metaphysical principles of natural science, devoting its second part to the "Critique of Teleological Judgment." His analysis began from the inadequacy of explanations of organic capacities in terms of the mechanisms of nature or ideas of designed wholes or final ends. He extended this analysis by exploring a series of (dis)analogies to our judgments of organic self-organization as ways of thinking through how we might make sense of these unique natural products. As a mode of reflective judgment, teleological judgments of the self-formation of organized beings are not only different than determinative judgments, but also have both analogies and disanalogies to aesthetic judgments and teleological judgments of nature as a whole. Through the process of exploring the similarities and differences of reflective judgments of organized bodies to other modes of judgment, Kant arrived at the conception of organisms as reciprocal means and ends of themselves.

In the third *Critique*, Kant echoed the assertion made repeatedly since his first writings on natural history—the inadequacy of mechanical laws and efficient causality to account for the possibility of organized beings. "For when we point, for example, to the structure of birds, regarding how their bones are hollow, how their wings are positioned to produce motion and tails to permit steering, and so on, we are saying all of this is utterly contingent if we go by the mere *nexus effectivus* in nature," or "nature, considered as mere mechanism" (§61, 5:360). As his 1786 *Metaphysical Foundations of Natural Science* had already made explicit, by mechanism Kant meant Newtonian mechanical laws and forces of matter.[12] Indeed, in the third *Critique*, he concluded that it is absurd for human beings "to hope that perhaps some day another Newton might arise who could explain to us . . . how even a mere blade of grass is produced" (§75, 5:400). Kant thus was clear that this inadequacy of mechanical explanations is not merely temporary, the contingency merely a gap to be filled in gradually through the further development of mechanical explanations, but rather an inadequacy projected into any possible future of natural science. Kant was writing these words at a historical juncture in which the physical sciences were undergoing a radical transformation through new investigations in

12. Immanuel Kant, *Kant: Metaphysical Foundations of Natural Science*, trans. Michael Friedman (Cambridge: Cambridge University Press, 2004).

chemistry, electricity, and magnetism. Kant nevertheless boldly claimed that a closer study of physical phenomena is not going to help us grasp what is distinctive about organisms.

A repeated refrain across Kant's works is also the inadequacy of final causality to provide an explanation of organized beings. "It would also be too presumptuous for us to judge that, supposing we could penetrate to the principle in terms of which nature made the familiar universal laws of nature specific, there simply *could* not be in nature a hidden basis adequate to make organized beings possible without an underlying intention [*Absicht*]" (§75, 5:400). His example of a bird suggests the need for "a principle of purposes" beyond natural mechanisms to provide an account of its unity and its structure so well-suited for flight (§61, 5:360). Yet Kant complicated this argument by examining how an organized body, as a natural product, organizes itself. Taking the example of a tree, he highlighted how "with regard to its *species*," it "produces itself [*erzeugt sich selbst*] . . . both generating [*hervorbringend*] itself and being generated by itself ceaselessly" (§64, 5:371). A tree also produces or generates itself as an individual, able to grow and "develop itself" (*bildet sich selbst*) by assimilating matter into its composition or its own product. Moreover, the parts of the tree are able reciprocally to produce or generate themselves, "as there is a mutual [*wechselsweise*] dependence between the preservation of one part and that of the others" (§64, 5:371). The tree is thus enabled to preserve itself and its internal functioning in the face of varied external influences or injuries. Through this example Kant demonstrated his familiarity with recent investigations of naturalists and physiologists regarding the singular characteristics of organisms. A tree, he proposed, is "*both cause and effect of itself*" (§64, 5:370).

Kant clarified this formulation through examining the differences between the production or generation of organized beings and the production of art or artifacts. In the production of artifacts, "the concept or idea must determine a priori everything that the thing is to contain" (§65, 5:373). In contrast to efficient causality, which is conceived in terms of a linear series of causes and effects, in final causality, the concept of the end result or effect acts as a cause. Kant offered two distinct examples of causality in terms of final causes or concepts of reason. The first example is a house, in which the concept of possible income through rent "caused the house to be constructed" (§65, 5:372). The second example is a watch, in which the conceptual design is the cause of the arrangements of its parts. The production of organisms is clearly different from both, although it is the latter example that offers the most significant disanalogy for Kant's analysis. In the production of an artifact, the rational concept or cause "lies outside nature and in a being who can act according to the ideas of a whole that he can produce through his own causality." The extrinsic idea of the end or whole determines the combination of the parts. It is "the reason why one gear in the watch does not produce another; still less does one watch produce other watches" (§65, 5:374). In organic production, however, the organized being forms itself, so what is needed is not only that "the possibility of its parts (as concerns both their existence and their form) must depend on their relation to the whole," but also that "all its parts, through their own causality, produce one another as regards both their form and combination, and . . . in this way produce a whole" (§65, 5:373). The parts of a watch are present for the sake of one another and make the others move; they are not the result of one another and do not form one another.[13] In contrast to artifacts, then, as a natural product, an organized and self-organizing being is reciprocally cause and effect of itself, or what Kant termed a "natural purpose."

It is important to remark that the examples Kant enlisted to explore the disanalogy between artistic and organic production are artifacts, such as watches, and not fine art works. In the first part of the *Critique of Judgment*—"Critique of Aesthetic Judgment"—he distinguished artistic production from natural operations in order to make evident the character of fine art as a free doing and as a practical ability rather than a theoretical science based on concepts. Beautiful art seems spontaneous and the result of natural genius, as if it is not designed, although we know it is a product of an artist. Organic productivity seems to mirror artistic productivity, in that an organism is only conceivable through the idea of a purpose, as if it is designed, although we know it is a product of nature.[14] Nevertheless, the analogy between artistic and organic productivity breaks down because artists, for all their natural talent, remain extrinsic creators of the art product. Kant's appeal to artifacts in the "Critique of Teleological Judgment" made

13. For a detailed discussion of these distinctions, compare Peter McLaughlin, *Kant's Critique of Teleology in Biological Explanation: Antinomy and Teleology* (Lewiston, NY: E. Mellen Press, 1990), 38–50, and Hannah Ginsborg, "Two Kinds of Mechanical Inexplicability in Kant and Aristotle," *Journal of the History of Philosophy* 42, no. 1 (2004): 33–65.

14. Henry E. Allison, *Kant's Theory of Taste: A Reading of the "Critique of Aesthetic Judgment"* (Cambridge: Cambridge University Press, 2001), 278–79.

this point explicit, when he pointed out that "we say far too little" if we regard organic productivity as an analogue of art, "for in that case we think of an artist (a rational being) apart from nature" (§65, 5:374).

In organizing themselves, organized beings not only follow the same overall pattern of the species, but also allow for "deviations that might be useful for self-preservation as required by circumstances." Kant thus considered whether it might be closer to "call this inscrutable property of nature an *analogue of life*," rather than "an *analogue of art*" (§65, 5:374). By life Kant meant intentional or rational agency—the mental life of human beings. Angela Breitenbach suggests that Kant's concept of natural purpose can be read productively through this analogy to human life. She contends that the ways in which organic beings appear directed toward structural and functional ends can be regarded as similar to how human reason sets ends and strives toward their realization. The ways in which the acting parts of an organism are related to preserving the organism as a whole can be regarded as similar to how humans' rational capacities are purposively related to realizing and maintaining their rational agency as a whole.[15] Kant cautioned that conceiving natural products as an analogue of life requires we endow "matter, as mere matter," with the property of life (hylozoism) "that conflicts with its nature [*Wesen*]," or "supplement matter with an alien principle (a soul) *conjoined* to it" (§65, 5:374). Breitenbach does not attribute the metaphysical positions of hylozoism or animate souls to Kant and instead uses the analogy to life as a means to make sense of natural purposes. But in foregrounding this analogy to life she loses sight of Kant's insistence that natural purposes have only a "remote analogy with our own causality in terms of purposes" (§65, 5:375) and does not focus on what he regarded as their natural capacities to be causes and effects of themselves. Hannah Ginsborg also implicitly enlists an analogue to life or practical reason in her analysis of Kant's arguments. She cites a passage in the unpublished "First Introduction" to the *Critique of Judgment*, where Kant stated that in considering organized natural products, such as an eye, we "make the judgment that it [*ought* (*sollen*) to have been] suitable for sight" (20:240).[16] Ginsborg contends this appeal to what ought to or should occur means organic structures are subject to normative constraints or standards.

15. Angela Breitenbach, "Laws in Biology and the Unity of Nature," in *Kant and the Laws of Nature*, ed. Michela Massimi and Angela Breitenbach (Cambridge: Cambridge University Press, 2017), 237–55.

16. My amendment to the Pluhar translation.

She does not suggest that these norms play a causal role in the production of organisms, as they would if they were designed or intentional. But they allow us to regard organic structure and function as lawlike, while distinguishing organic regularities, as what should occur in proper functioning, from mechanical necessity, as what must occur.[17] But this bare appeal to a norm, as what ought to occur, does not elaborate Kant's conception of organized bodies as natural purposes able to generate and preserve themselves under variable circumstances.

In introducing the concept of natural purposes, Kant emphasized that it is "not a constitutive concept either of the understanding or of reason. But it can still be a regulative concept for reflective judgment . . . to guide our investigation of organized objects" (§65, 5:375). In the *Critique of Judgment*, Kant drew a distinction between the determining and reflecting powers of judgment. "When judgment *determines* . . . it only *subsumes* under laws or concepts that are given it as principles" (§69, 5:385), the a priori laws of the understanding that are the conditions of objective cognition of an object. "When judgment *reflects*, on the other hand, it has to subsume under a law that is not yet given" (§65, 5:385). Reflective judgment, then, must serve itself as a principle, but merely as a subjective principle for our reflection on certain kinds of objects. The contrast presented in these passages is striking—a contrast between determinative, constitutive, objective understanding, on the one hand, and regulative, subjective reflections, on the other. This sharp contrast elides the mediating processes that Kant detailed as aiding the activity of determinative judgment in the *Critique of Pure Reason*, enabling the general laws of the understanding to be applied to the particulars of sensory intuitions.[18] For example, imagination plays a role in judgment, empirically synthesizing the manifold of sensory perceptions into appearances and producing schemata of intuitions that can be recognized by the understanding. The understanding provides a priori principles

17. Hannah Ginsborg, "Kant on Understanding Organisms as Natural Purposes," in *Kant and the Sciences*, ed. Eric Watkins (Oxford: Oxford University Press, 2001), 231–58.

18. Immanuel Kant, *Critique of Pure Reason*, trans. Werner S. Pluhar (Indianapolis: Hackett, 1996). See Béatrice Longuenesse, *Kant and the Capacity to Judge: Sensibility and Discursivity in the Transcendental Analytic of the "Critique of Pure Reason,"* trans. Charles T. Wolfe (Princeton, NJ: Princeton University Press, 1998); Joan Steigerwald, "Natural Purposes and the Reflecting Power of Judgment: The Problem of the Organism in Kant's Critical Philosophy," in *Romanticism and Modernity*, ed. Thomas Pfau and Robert Mitchell (New York: Routledge, 2011), 29–46.

as well as concepts to enable cognition of appearances. Nevertheless, in the "Transcendental Deduction" of the first *Critique*, Kant claimed the epistemic warrant for the universality and objectivity of the a priori concepts of the understanding is grounded in the transcendental unity of apperception. In the third *Critique*, Kant argued that in reflective judgment in contrast, judgment is thrown back on itself, generating its own principles and concepts, rather than applying principles or concepts already determined through understanding or reason. The structuring analogy of the two parts of the *Critique of Judgment* is between judgments of taste and judgments of organisms as modes of the reflecting power of judgment, and the contrast of both to determinative judgments and rational purposive action.

Kant depicted aesthetic appraisal as concerned with the state of mind of a subject in apprehending an object. Judgments of taste are based on the feeling of pleasure or displeasure produced in a subject because of the harmony or disharmony of cognitive powers, a free play of the imagination and the understanding that does not involve a concept. Judgments of taste are aesthetic, as the relation is felt rather than grasped cognitively. To decide whether or not something is beautiful, its representation is related "only to the subject, namely to his feeling of life, under the name feeling of pleasure and displeasure." This forms the basis of a "special power of discriminating and judging," which "does not contribute anything to cognition, but merely compares the given [representation (*Vorstellung*)] in the subject with the entire [representational] power, of which the mind becomes conscious when it feels its own state" (§1, 5:204).[19] In contrast to determinative judgments of experience, judgments of taste are without a conceptual representation of the form of an object. In contrast to practical reason, judgments of taste are not based on a concept of the purpose of their object and are independent of the subject's desire for or interest in the object. In judgments of beauty the consciousness of a "subjective purposiveness" or "merely formal purposiveness in the play of the subject's cognitive powers" is the feeling of pleasure and contains the determining basis for the subject's activity with regard to the "quickening" of cognitive powers, namely, to preserve or "keep" this state of mind (§12, 5:222).

Judgments of taste are subjective, but nevertheless claim common validity and the assent of other judging subjects. In judgments of taste, the reflecting power of judgment acts as its own principle and provides its own condition of validity. Judgment "is, subjectively, object to itself as well as

19. My amendment to the Pluhar translation.

law to itself" (§36, 5:288). The epistemic warrant of judgments of taste is thus subjective. The judgment of taste is grounded only in "the subjective formal condition of a judgment," yet these are the subjective conditions of all judgments or "the employment of the power of judgment as such" (§35, 5:287, 290). All judgments rest on the harmony of the two representational powers—imagination and understanding. In judgments of beauty, the singular, subjective feeling of the pleasure felt from the reciprocal animation of the imagination and understanding is assumed of all judging subjects. It is "*the universal validity of this pleasure*, perceived as connected in the mind with our mere judging of an object, that we [represent] a priori as [a] universal rule for the power of judgment, valid for everyone" (§37, 5:289).[20] Kant appealed to a "*sensus communis*" or sense shared by all, that is a "power to judge that in reflecting takes account (a priori), in our thought, of everyone else's way of [representing], in order *as it were* to compare our own judgment with human reason in general" (§40, 5:293).[21] As Rodolphe Gasché argues in his contribution to this volume, this expectation of agreement, of communication with all human subjects, of the connection and community of judging subjects, remains a possibility or task, a regulative idea.

Kant presented the teleological judgments through which we attempt to make sense of organized beings as modes of reflective judgment. As is the case in all reflective judgments, the understanding provides no concepts or principles through which we can judge these unique natural objects. In analogy to judgments of taste, the reflective judgment of organisms must seek a principle for itself through which to make sense of them. In contrast to judgments of taste, however, because organisms are objects of natural inquiry, more than an appraisal of the subjective state of our cognitive powers or the consciousness of the "subjective purposiveness" or "formal purposiveness in the play of the subject's cognitive powers" (§12, 5:222) is required from this reflective activity. Judgments of organized beings are concerned with something "we cognize . . . as a natural product [*Naturproduct erkennt*]" (§64, 5:370). The cognition of a natural product is possible only with a conceptual representation of the form of its object. Kant introduced the concept of "natural purpose" (*Naturzweck*) as a "regulative concept for reflective judgment" (§65, 5:375). If "a thing is a natural product but yet we are to cognize it as possible only as a natural purpose [*nur als Naturzweck möglich erkannt werden soll*], then . . . it must relate to itself in such a way

20. My amendment to the Pluhar translation.

21. My amendment to the Pluhar translation.

that it is [reciprocally (*wechselseitig*)] cause and effect of itself" (§65, 5:372).[22] Although the concept of natural purpose is regulative, not determinative, Kant argued it makes possible the cognition of organized and self-organizing beings as natural objects.

The principle that judgment gives itself to guide its reflection on organisms is "*an organized product of nature is one in which everything is [an end (Zweck)] and reciprocally also a means*" (§66, 5:376).[23] This principle is "derived from experience," prompted by the empirical investigations of organized beings, yet also has a generality that "cannot rest on merely empirical bases but must be based on some a priori principle" (§66, 5:376). Recognizing the insufficiency of mechanical explanations of their capacity for self-organization and reflecting on "a remote analogy with our own causality in terms of purposes," reflective judgment gives itself this principle as "a *maxim* for judging the intrinsic purposiveness [*innern Zweckmäßigkeit*] of organized beings" (§65, 5:375, 376). This principle is thus a product of the reflective judgment of organized beings. This principle, the end product of the activity of reflective judgment, is reciprocally also the means by which judgment reflects. The circularity of reflective judgment is expressed in its principle; reflective judgment and its principle act as means and ends of one another. The circular and reciprocal form of reflective judgment and its principle provides not only the means for judging organisms but also the concept of natural purposes produced as the end product of this reflective process. This concept in turn enfolds the reciprocal logic of its formation.[24]

As an "a priori principle," this maxim has "universality and necessity," even if it is "merely regulative" (§65, 5:376). Arising through the reflective activity of judgment, this teleological principle and the concept of natural purpose lack the objective validity of the principles and concepts of the understanding. Yet concerned with natural products, the reflective judgment of organized beings requires more than the subjective validity of aesthetic judgments. Kant acknowledged that, unlike in his considerations of a priori concepts applied in determinative judgments of experience and the reflective judgments of taste, he could not provide a deduction for our judgment of organized beings as natural purposes. These judgments, accordingly, had a special status in his critical philosophy:

---

22. My amendment to the Pluhar translation.

23. My amendment to the Pluhar translation.

24. See also Steigerwald, *Experimenting at the Boundaries of Life*, 111–12, 117–19.

> Teleological judgment is not a special power, but is only reflective judgment as such proceeding according to concepts (as it always does in theoretical cognition), but proceeding, in the case of certain natural objects, according to special principles, namely of a power of judgment that merely reflects upon but does not determine objects. Hence, as regards its application, teleological judgment belongs to the theoretical part of philosophy; because of its special principles, which are not determinative (as would be required in a doctrine), it must also form a special part of the critique. ("Introduction," 5:194)

Although the teleological judgment of organized beings requires critical examination and is properly part of the *Critique of Judgment*, it remains distinct from the theoretical cognition that objectively determines natural objects as well as distinct from the aesthetic assessment of natural or artistic objects that is subjectively accorded on the basis of the condition of our cognitive powers.

Teleological judgments have radically different scopes and scales in the text, from the modest concern with organized beings as objects of experience to grand visions of the ends of nature and the ends of humanity. Kant argued that organized beings, which must be thought of possible only as natural purposes, "first give objective reality to the concept of a *purpose* that is a purpose *of nature* rather than a practical one, and which hence give natural science the basis for a teleology" (§65, 5:375–76). He distinguished the concept of the intrinsic purposiveness of organized beings from concepts of extrinsic purposiveness or what he termed the "relative purposiveness of nature" (§63, 5:366). In cold lands, for example, the sea offers a rich supply of animals that provide peoples with nourishment, clothing, and fuel for heating their huts, and washes up timber as building material for their homes. Kant cautioned that there is no reason for human beings to live in these regions. It would thus be "arbitrary" to judge these processes to be purposes of nature, since they are useful to human beings (§63, 5:369). Similarly, that the sandy soil deposited by the sea is favorable to the growth of pine trees "is not an objective purposiveness of the things themselves," as if the sand as an effect of the sea cannot be understood without ascribing a purpose to the latter; it is a relative purposiveness, which the thing has "merely contingently" (§63, 5:368). The "*extrinsic* purposiveness of natural things does not give us adequate justification for also considering them to be purposes of nature" (§67, 5:377). To judge a thing to be a purpose of nature, "we need more than the concept of a possible purpose; we would have to cognize the final purpose (*scopus*) of nature." But that would require the relation of nature to the "supersensible," which "far surpasses all our teleological cognition of nature" (§67, 5:378).

In the introduction to the third *Critique*, Kant presented a principle of the "*purposiveness of nature*" to guide our reflection on the unity of nature despite the diversity of its particular laws (5:180). This principle of purposiveness presupposes the "harmony of nature with our cognitive power . . . as an aid in its reflection on nature in terms of empirical laws" (5:185). It might lead us to regard nature as favoring human beings in the presenting of intelligible and beautiful forms for our judgment, and as supporting the realization of the moral purpose of humankind. This principle of purposiveness might seem to suggest that we can regard nature as if it is designed with our needs in mind. Kant allowed that the concept of natural purpose leads to "the idea of all of nature as a system in terms of the rule of purposes" (§67, 5:379). Such reflections take us beyond the concepts of natural products and into the terrain of reason. As Rachel Zuckert cautions, Kant regarded the principle of purposiveness of nature as playing an epistemic function in our reflective judgments. Such purposive judging aims at an indeterminate end. It is future orientated, enabling us to anticipate what we do not yet know and to project a systematically unified whole onto the diverse and empirically given.[25] It is not nature but our judgments that are purposive, and purposiveness remains a subjective principle of reflective judgment.

The teleological judgment of the projected unity of nature for the ends of reason is distinct from the teleological judgment of organisms as reciprocally means and ends of themselves. While the former "is useful when applied to the whole of nature, it is not indispensable, since the whole of nature is not given to us," the latter is essential "if we are to acquire so much as an empirical cognition of the intrinsic character of these products" and "to even think them as organized beings" (§75, 5:398).

The principle of purposiveness leads us to assume that nature in the diversity of its empirical laws can be united into a single system of knowledge. It does not prepare us for the cognition of particular natural objects that defy our understanding and elude mechanical explanations.

---

25. Rachel Zuckert, *Kant on Beauty and Biology: An Interpretation of the "Critique of Judgment"* (Cambridge: Cambridge University Press, 2007). See also Breitenbach, "Laws in Biology and the Unity of Nature."

Kant identified an antinomy within the reflecting power of judgment, due to conflicting maxims that it can give itself to guide its investigation of the appearances of nature in its pursuit of a systematic unity. The first maxim specifies all natural products must be "judged to be possible in terms of merely mechanical laws." The second maxim specifies that some natural products "cannot be judged to be possible in terms of merely mechanical laws" and require recourse to "final causes." If taken as "objective principles for determinative judgment, the two propositions would contradict each other" and become "a conflict in the legislation of reason" between competing dogmatic systems (§70, 5:387). Kant claimedhis critical analysis removes this contradiction by considering each maxim "as a merely subjective principle governing the purposive use of our cognitive powers," and thus as but a regulative guide for our investigation of the empirical laws of nature (§69, 5:385). Kant advised that we should pursue the maxim of mechanism as far as possible in our investigation of nature, for only thus do we obtain a determinative cognition of natural phenomena. But our investigation of the distinct capacities of organisms requires the maxim of teleology. Yet, if the contradiction is removed by agreeing to use both maxims as regulative principles, the dissonance between them is not thus resolved and it is not clear how to decide between the two in particular instances. Kant acknowledged that "our reason is incapable of reconciling" the two maxims in a single principle (§70, 5:388). The different possible maxims or methods for the study of nature disrupt the ideal of systematic unity of the empirical laws of nature. Indeed, organisms seem to confound the promise of a purposive harmony between nature and our cognitive powers.

The teleological judgment of organized beings at times seems to become swept up into larger visions of the ends of nature. In the "Dialectic of Teleological Judgment," Kant argued that a principle that makes possible the unity between conflicting mechanical and teleological maxims for judging organized beings must be posited "in something that lies beyond both (and hence also beyond any possible empirical [re]presentation of nature) but that nevertheless contains the basis of nature, namely, we posit it in the supersensible" (§78, 5:412).[26] He gestured to the possibility of an intuitive understanding that could grasp the relation between the parts and whole in organisms. Following a review of varied metaphysical accounts of organisms, these suggestions might be read as presenting the specter of a divine cause

26. My amendment to the Pluhar translation.

of organisms. But it is important to read Kant's arguments here against the appendix "Methodology of the Teleological Judgment," which explicitly critiques the movement from apparent purposiveness in nature to theology. Indeed, these speculations were used by Kant for critical purposes—to highlight the limits of our understanding of organisms and the larger purposive order of nature. The contrast to an intuitive intellect is used for a critical analysis of the discursivity of human understanding, "that it must indeed be contingent for it as to what the character and all the variety of the particular may be that can be given to it in nature and that can be brought under its concepts" (§77, 5:406). The supersensible plays a similar epistemic function, with Kant insisting that a possible unity for the different approaches to the study of nature is indeterminate, beyond our cognition. An intelligent cause of organisms, like a Newton of the grass blades, turns regulative principles of reflective judgment into constitutive principles of determinative judgment. Moreover, as his prior analysis made clear, organisms, whatever their first origins, as natural products are self-organizing.

The teleological judgment of organized and self-organizing beings as natural purposes is thus a distinct mode of judgment. As organized beings are natural products, we must conceive of their organization as the effect of the forming and combining of material parts. Yet their complex organization requires that we conceive of their final form as the cause of that forming and combining of parts. An apparent product of both efficient and final causality, organized beings are conceived to be both causes and effects of themselves. A dichotomy between mechanical laws of nature and the rational concept of purpose both framed and constrained Kant's analysis. He attempted to move beyond this strict dichotomy by thinking through our conception of organisms as a product of reflective judgment. He argued that we arrive at the concept of natural purpose only through the activity of judgment, as it reflects on our empirical investigations of organisms and their possible conceptualization. Moving between theoretical cognition and practical reason, yet unable to settle in either, critically reflecting on the concepts of natural mechanism and the concepts of rational purpose, neither of which provides a determinative grasp of organisms, we arrive at the indeterminate concept of natural purposes. The amphibious nature of the concept of natural purposes—natural, yet purposive—is a product of the reflective activity of judgment as it moves between these domains. The concept enfolds and holds in tension the dichotomy Kant attempted to overcome.

As Jennifer Mensch has argued, the formative capacities of organisms seem to have been suggestive to Kant in his analysis of the form and activity of our cognitive capacities more generally.[27] Analogies between different modes of judgment trouble some of the strong distinctions he made between determinative and reflective powers of judgment and between the objectivity and subjectivity of judgments. Nevertheless, in the *Critique of Judgment*, Kant provided a nuanced analysis of judgment in which he distinguished the reflective judgment of organized beings from other modes of judgment—determinative judgments that provide objective cognition of the phenomena of experience and the mechanisms of nature; aesthetic judgments of beauty that are based on the subjective purposiveness in the relation of our cognitive powers; and teleological judgments of the unity of empirical laws guided by the subjective principle of the purposiveness of nature for our cognitive projects. He also distinguished teleological judgments of natural purposes from the purposes of reason in its practical activities and artistic productions. In closely considering the self-organizing capacities of organized beings and reflecting on the modes of judgment through which we attempt to make sense of these capacities, Kant concluded that both are guided by thinking in terms of reciprocal means and ends or causes and effects. He thus suggested a reciprocal relationship between the formative activity of organisms and the teleological judgment of natural purposes. He also distinguished both as unique processes.

A number of tensions remain unresolved in Kant's conception of organized beings as natural purposes and as reciprocal causes and effects of themselves. Kant conceded that "the concept of natural purposes is a concept solely of reflective judgment, a concept [it must use] solely for its own sake" ("First Introduction," 20:236). But the concept is indispensable in our cognition of particular objects of experience in contrast to the principle of subjective purposiveness in judgments of taste or judgments of the unity of nature. It draws on and attempts to make sense of contemporary research on the self-organizing capacities of organized beings. It is thus purely neither an objective nor a subjective concept. Moreover, the concept of natural purposes does not resolve the dialectic between different possible maxims for the study of nature. If we can reconcile the two maxims to an extent by agreeing to use both, the dissonance between them is not thus removed and it is left undecided which to use in particular instances. But

27. Jennifer Mensch, *Kant's Organicism: Epigenesis and the Development of Critical Philosophy* (Chicago: University of Chicago Press, 2013). See also Susan Meld Shell, *The Embodiment of Reason: Kant on Spirit, Generation, and Community* (Chicago: University of Chicago Press, 1996).

this conclusion seems at odds with the larger project of the *Critique of Judgment* and principle of the purposiveness that assumes "the harmony of nature with our cognitive powers" ("Introduction," 5:185). Not only do organisms defy attempts to develop a unified method for the study of natural phenomena; they appear to resist our clear conceptual grasp. The tensions enfolded within the concept of natural purposes highlight an irreducible indeterminate element in the relationship of our cognition to the world. Indeed, the disanalogy between the reflective judgment of organized beings and the other modes of judgment Kant analyzed—determinative, aesthetic, practical—leaves it without a clear place in his system of philosophy. Unlike these other modes of judgment, Kant provided no deduction for the teleological judgment of natural purposes, even as he highlighted their significance in the third *Critique*.

Yet these tensions were productive. When Kant wrote the *Critique of Judgment* in 1790, a new understanding of organic vitality was in the process of emerging. That Kant did not present a determinative conception of organisms allowed his contributions to participate in that emergence. His characterization of the processes of self-organization—the generation, growth, and maintenance of organized beings—drew attention to central puzzles of organisms. His rendering of an organized product of nature as cause and effect of itself, as a product in which everything is an end and reciprocally also a means, offered a principle for reflecting on those processes of self-organization. As will be seen in the next section, naturalists and physiologists as well as philosophers found Kant's formulation offered a starting point for thinking through how organisms form themselves as self-contained entities that nevertheless stand in relationship to the larger physical world. Kant's conception of how an organism circulates back on itself, its reciprocal formation of parts and whole, the tension within it between material processes and organization, and its internal dynamic and interaction with its environment, suggested ways of thinking about the complex involution and evolution of organic beings. That Kant provided reflective rather determinate judgments about such processes opened up rather than shut down possibilities for thinking further about the capacities of organisms.

A Science of Life

At the turn of the nineteenth century, biology was a science in the making. Naturalists and physiologists attempted to delineate the living from the nonliving, and to understand how organisms individuated themselves from the processes of nature, while retaining the capacity to be responsive to their environments. Moving well beyond Kant's analysis, their investigations explored the intersections of chemical, electrical, and magnetic phenomena with organic processes, the possibility of spontaneous generation, and how organic kinds varied as a result of their physical conditions. Yet Kant's position that organized beings were nevertheless unique natural products remained widespread. Moreover, his conception of organisms as reciprocal means and ends, causes and effect, of themselves was important to attempts to make sense of the distinctive capacities of organisms. Perhaps most strikingly, Schelling appealed to Kant's conception repeatedly across his works on the philosophy of nature, despite the radical difference of his philosophical projects from Kant's.

Kielmeyer is an example of a prominent naturalist who directly drew on Kant's analysis. In a widely-cited 1793 address, "On the Relationship of Organic Powers," he set out the relationships of organic powers in individual organisms, and comparatively in different kinds of organisms, indicating how the existence and course of the species of the living world are based in these relationships. His address opened with a reference to Kant's conception of organized bodies, a conception, he noted, that was rapidly becoming the rhetorical refrain of his generation's "way of talking." Each organ of organized bodies, suited to the others and united in a system of simultaneous and successive alterations, "becomes reciprocally cause and effect of the others." In discussing organic powers, he cautioned that he was not claiming to know what these organic powers are in a determinate sense, but rather used what he termed "the helping word [*Behelfswort*] of powers" to name groups of similar effects perceived in individual organizations. He emphasized that he was concerned not with specifying the nature of vital powers, but with the relationships of organic vitality in the series of different organizations or kinds of living beings.[28]

Kielmeyer developed these ideas in widely circulated and discussed lectures and unpublished sketches. In these notes he also alluded to Kant, highlighting the importance of general laws or concepts of alterations recognized through the faculty of representation, as opposed to simply "the piling up of a great number of facts." Kielmeyer nevertheless went beyond Kant in claiming to discern the laws of organic vitality as the foundation for a science of living organisms. Kielmeyer contended that the "circle of

28. Kielmeyer, *Verhältnisse der organischen Kräfte*, 62, 63, 69.

investigation becomes widened through the nature of the object itself," the life expressed in various material alterations. Only by tracing the temporal relationships of development can "dead description" become a "living history" and its object obtain life. Yet he also argued that the investigation of development should not be held "within boundaries that determine observations," as our mind does not yet know where the history of appearances will lead it. To uncover the general laws of the life it is necessary to take a leap, to foster a "faculty of anticipation or a feeling for the truth developed through practice." Kielmeyer presented the investigations and reflections on organic life as experimental and open-ended.[29]

Kielmeyer argued that the expressions of life are the result of the interplay between the inner powers of the individual organism and the external world, through which each organic being maintains the material conditions of life by accepting and incorporating materials into its body, and is stimulated into the activities of moving, sensing, and reproducing. The altering interplay of powers, the reciprocal relationships of causes and effects, the balance of powers expressed variously in the series of organized bodies, accounts for the continued existence and history of organic kinds.[30] In extending the expressions of life from the individual organism to the series of organizations, to the differential relationships of organic powers in different species, he set out a project for a comparative physiology. Such a characterization of the individuation of organisms through the reciprocal interaction of internal processes and the external world, varying across organic kinds and their diverse environments, became widespread in projects for a science of life in the years around 1800. Gottfried Reinhold Treviranus presented such a vision in his *Biologie*, combining physiology and natural history to offer a comparative study of how the dynamic relationships of the functions of life gave rise to different organic kinds across the regions of the earth and throughout the history of the earth.[31] The emphasis on organic functions and comparative physiology that was found in Treviranus's

---

29. Carl Friedrich Kielmeyer, "Ideen zu einer allgemeineren Geschichte und Theorie der Entwicklungserscheinungen der Organisationen," in *Gesammelte Schriften*, 102–194, 112, 114, 115. See also Steigerwald, *Experimenting at the Boundaries of Life*, 195–202.

30. Carl Friedrich Kielmeyer, "Entwurf zu einer vergleichenden Zoologie," in *Gesammelte Schriften*, 13–29, 17–27; *Verhältnisse der organischen Kräfte*, 94–95.

31. Gottfried Reinhold Treviranus, *Biologie: oder, Philosophie der lebenden Natur für Naturforscher und Aerzte*, 6 vols. (Göttingen: Johann Friedrich Röwer, 1802–1822).

Biologie can also be seen in physiological textbooks in the early nineteenth century. Like Kielmeyer, these works depicted nature as making varied attempts at viable forms of life, trying out what functions as a dynamic and reciprocal balance between inner and outer powers, and enabling the continued existence of organic kinds.

Schelling gave a philosophical articulation to these developing projects for a science of life, drawing on recent studies of naturalists and physiologists as well as Kant's *Critique of Judgment.* In a series of texts on the philosophy of nature that appeared between 1797 and 1799, he identified the central concern for studies of organic life to be the question of how organic products are able to maintain their characteristic organization and activities in distinction from and yet in relationship to the world around them. Schelling's analysis of this question began from the argument that it is a mistake to look for a singular principle or cause of life. Although he allowed that specific functions of the organism are only possible because of their adaptation to the specific conditions of their external world, like Kant, he rejected the postulate of a divine design to explain this apparent purposiveness, regarding it as the "demise of all sound philosophy." He acknowledged that material substances and powers are active in unique ways in organic bodies, yet he contended that the "fiction" of a special vital power to account for this complex dynamic is a contrivance of "lazy reason."[32] He also rejected, however, that the living body could be understood "as an accidental aggregate of organized particles, or as a hydraulic machine, or a chemical laboratory."[33] Schelling instead tried to comprehend the boundary between living and nonliving processes by exploring how such a boundary is enacted.

To conceptualize the individuation of organic life, Schelling enlisted the terms of Kant's *Critique of Judgment.* He introduced his first work on *Naturphilosophie*, his 1797 *Ideas towards a Philosophy of Nature*, by drawing on Kant's representation of organized beings, arguing that "no organization progresses *forward*, but is forever turning back always into *itself*. . . . Every organic product carries the reason of its existence in *itself*, for it is cause

32. Schelling, *First Outline*, 69, 64, 61n; *Erster Entwurf*, 92, 84. 80n.

33. Friedrich Wilhelm Joseph Schelling, *Ideas for a Philosophy of Nature*, trans. Errol E. Harris and Peter Heath (Cambridge: Cambridge University Press, 1988), 37; *Ideen zu einer Philosophie der Natur*, in *Sämmtliche Werke*, Bd. 2, ed. Karl Friedrich August Schelling (Stuttgart: Cotta, 1857), 1–343, 49.

and effect of itself."[34] He developed this idea in his 1798 *On the World Soul:*

> *Life*, however, consists in a *circulation*, a *succession of processes*, which *continually turn back into themselves*, so that it is impossible to state, which process actually life is *initially*, which is the *earlier*, which is the *later*. Each organization is a whole enclosed in itself, in which all is *simultaneous*, and where mechanical kinds of explanation desert us entirely, because in such a whole there is no *before* and no *after*. We can thus not do better than to claim that *none of these opposed processes determine the other*, but that *they both mutually determine themselves*, both mutually keep the balance.[35]

Like Kant, Schelling also drew an analogy between the organic body as a self-reverting succession that is cause and effect of itself and the reflective activity of intelligence. He developed this analogy in his *System of Transcendental Idealism* (1800). Schelling argued that for a concept to be constructed intelligence must reflect on its own activity. A succession of intuitions of appearances must be enclosed within boundaries for intelligence to grasp them synthetically. Intelligence can grasp a bounded synthesis in which intuited elements persist in a succession of changes and in which the succession turns back into itself within a finite limit in a reciprocal relation. Intelligence constructs a distinct and synthetic concept through reflection on this bounded, reciprocal relation of appearances. Schelling concluded that concepts, like organisms, are organized through an involvement with and individuation of themselves within the succession of phenomena that is generative of synthesis and difference.[36]

Schelling, however, went beyond Kant in conceiving the individuation and dynamic vitality of living organisms through his philosophical reflections on recent projects for a science of life. Kielmeyer, Treviranus,

---

34. Schelling, *Ideas for a Philosophy of Nature*, 30–31; *Ideen zu einer Philosophie der Natur*, 40.

35. Friedrich Wilhelm Joseph Schelling, *Von der Weltseele*, in *Sämmtliche Werke*, Bd. 2, ed. Karl Friedrich August Schelling (Stuttgart: Cotta, 1857), 345–583, 549.

36. Friedrich Wilhelm Joseph Schelling, *System of Transcendental Idealism*, trans. Peter Heath (Charlottesville: University Press of West Virginia, 1978), 120–27; *System des transscendentalen Idealismus*, in *Sämmtliche Werke*, Bd. 3, ed. Karl Friedrich August Schelling (Stuttgart: Cotta, 1858), 327–634, 489–98.

and others contended that an individual organism must maintain its own sphere of activity against the activities of its physical environment. Yet it must also prevent itself from falling into a condition of complete stasis if it is to preserve its vitality, and accordingly needs continual stimulus from its surroundings. Schelling depicted the processes of individuation as chemical processes that depend on inorganic materials and chemical reactions, but also as vital processes that depend on organic organization and functions. The materials incorporated are formed into specific organs and kinds of organisms, with the form and composition of the resulting organic body dependent on both the chemical qualities of the materials and the organic parts and processes participant in these processes. Whereas dead matter is receptive to every impression and is identical with its external world, living matter distinguishes itself from the external world by its receptivity to impressions being antecedently conditioned by its character as a special sphere of activity. To ensure the activities of life, the incorporation of materials must be vitalized by the "restless activity" marking the distinct character of living bodies.[37]

In his 1799 *First Outline of a System of Natural Philosophy*, Schelling elaborated this conception of how organic products distinguish themselves from other natural products within the ongoing activity of nature. Each individuated natural product, he contended, is constituted through a reciprocal interaction of productive and retarding activities, of outward evolution and inward involution. Living bodies, however, are constituted through a double involution, with the capacity of the organism to respond to, and yet to distinguish itself from, the external world dependent on a reciprocal receptivity and activity within itself. This internal dynamic forms the inner sphere and medium of living beings. The organism constitutes itself through producing an internal sphere of vitality. Accordingly, "*the organism* (taken as a whole) *must* ITSELF *be the medium through which external influences act upon it.*"[38] It is this doubled involution that enables organic products to maintain their form and vitality in distinction from their surrounds, while also enabling them to develop and transform in relation to changed environmental conditions. Schelling's philosophical analysis of contemporary life sciences shows the ways in which they opened up understandings of the internal milieu and evolution of living organisms in nineteenth-century biology. He thus revitalized and extended Kant's conception of reciprocal

37. Schelling, *Von der Weltseele*, 546.

38. Schelling, *First Outline*, 107; *Erster Entwurf*, 146.

means and ends, reciprocal causes and effects, to help make sense of these processes of the individuation and vitality of organic life.

Writing in the context of rapid developments in both the physical and life sciences at the turn of the nineteenth century, Kielmeyer, Schelling, and others exploring the boundaries of life had moved well beyond Kant's dichotomy between mechanism and purposiveness. Indeed, they drew on new studies in chemistry, physics, physiology, and natural history to complicate the notion of a clear division between the living and nonliving. Yet they accepted Kant's argument that organized and self-organizing beings are distinct. They also explicitly enlisted Kant's conception of reciprocal means and ends, causes and effects, as a way of comprehending the unique capacities of organic life. More implicitly, they found the reflective aspects of Kant's judgments of organisms productive. Rather than claiming a determinative conception of what organic life is, based on past studies that might already be outdated, reflective judgments offer an opening toward future inquiries and new possible understandings of what life might be. Indeed, the reflections on the individuation, involution, and evolution of organic life by Kielmeyer, Schelling, and others at the turn of the nineteenth century introduced new ways of thinking about a science of life that were taken up variously in nineteenth-century biology.

Chapter 14

Personality

The Life of the Finite, Moral-Rational Being

G. Felicitas Munzel

The venerability of duty has nothing to do with the enjoyment of life.

—Immanuel Kant, *Kritik der praktischen Vernunft* (5:89)[1]

In order for a sensibly affected rational being to will that which reason alone prescribes as the ought, of course requires a capacity of reason *to instill a feeling of pleasure* or of being pleased in the fulfillment of duty.

—Immanuel Kant, *Grundlegung zur Metaphysik der Sitten* (4:460)[2]

Pleasure is the representation of the agreement of an object or of an action with the subjective conditions of life, i.e., with the faculty of the causality of a representation with respect to the reality of its object

1. Immanuel Kant, *Kritik der praktischen Vernunft*, in *Kant's gesammelte Schriften*, Bd. 5, ed. Königlich Preußische Akademie der Wissenschaften (Berlin: Georg Reimer, 1913), 5:1–163. The translations in this essay are my own; citations of Kant's works are to *Kant's gesammelte Schriften*, ed. Königlich Preußische Akademie der Wissenschaften (Berlin: Georg Reimer/Walter de Gruyter, 1902–); volume numbers are followed by page numbers.

2. Immanuel Kant, *Grundlegung zur Metaphysik der Sitten*, in *Kant's gesammelte Schriften*, Bd. 4, ed. Königlich Preußische Akademie der Wissenschaften (Berlin: Georg Reimer, 1911), 4:385–463.

(or with respect to the determination of the powers of the subject to action in order to produce the object).

—Immanuel Kant, *Kritik der praktischen Vernunft* (5:9n; emphasis added)

The feeling of the promotion of life is enjoyment or pleasure. Life is the consciousness of a free and regular play of all the powers and faculties of the human being [25:559]. Freedom is the greatest life of the human being . . . no freedom can please us, except for freedom subject to the rule of the understanding. This is intellectual pleasure, which is concerned with morality [25:560]. The first source of life, however, lies in the mind [25:604]. The enlivening of the mind penetrates to the principle of life [25:605].

—Immanuel Kant, "Anthropologie Friedländer"[3]

The mind taken by itself is wholly life (the very principle of life).

—Immanuel Kant, *Kritik der Urteilskraft* (§29, 5:278)[4]

Kant's formal, objective account of morality with its heteronomy and autonomy distinction has lent itself to the perception of a sharp division between the realm of feeling and the moral law. Indeed, the first citation above from the *Critique of Practical Reason* seems to put a full stop to any discussion of the role of pleasure or feeling in Kant's vision of the human moral life—his identification of respect for the moral law as moral feeling notwithstanding. Yet the second citation, from his *Groundwork of the Metaphysics of Morals*, affirms not just the role, but the necessity for a feeling of pleasure, of being pleased in the fulfillment of duty. In the preface of the second *Critique*, we find the definition of pleasure entailing a relation between a capacity to act and the subjective conditions of life (cited in the third quotation above). The explicit association of pleasure as the promotion of life with freedom and with morality is made by Kant as early as 1776 in the "Anthropology Friedländer" (as we read in the fourth citation

3. Immanuel Kant, "Anthropologie Friedländer," in *Vorlesungen über Anthropologie*, Bd. 25 of *Kant's gesammelte Schriften*, ed. Berlin-Brandenburgische Akademie der Wissenschaften (Berlin: de Gruyter, 1997), 25:469–728.

4. Immanuel Kant, *Kritik der Urtheilskraft*, in *Kant's gesammelte Schriften*, Bd. 5, ed. Königlich Preußische Akademie der Wissenschaften (Berlin: Georg Reimer, 1913), 5:165–485.

above). The further identification of mind (*Gemüt*) with life that we find in the *Critique of Judgment* is also already made in those early anthropology lectures. The importance of Kant's conception of the faculty of mind for human moral life is clearly stated in the doctrine of method of the second *Critique* where he explains that its purpose is to show "how we can secure access to the human mind (*Gemüt*) and an influence on its maxims by the laws of pure practical reason; that is, how objectively practical reason can also be made subjectively practical" (5:51). Earlier in the text we see Kant affirming that moral feeling or "respect for the law" is "morality itself, subjectively regarded as incentive" (5:76). We thus have ample reason to inquire into how Kant's concepts of pleasure, feeling of life, life, and mind fit into his vision of human moral life.

Kant himself emphasizes the need for taking anthropology and morality into account together. As he cryptically states in the *Groundwork*, "morality requires anthropology for its application to human beings" (4:412). For his own students, unlike many modern readers, the experience and comprehension of Kant's moral teachings were always holistic, including both the objective and subjective dimensions, which he tells us (in each of his major published writings on moral philosophy) belong to the complete subject. His lectures on morality were always given in conjunction with his lectures on anthropology in the same semester, and in the Mrongovius transcripts of his lectures on morality, Kant is reported to have asserted that the two sciences of practical philosophy and anthropology "cannot subsist as one without the other," for "one must know human beings in order to know whether they are capable of performing all that is demanded of them. The consideration of a rule is useless, if one cannot make people prepared to fulfill it" ("Moral Mrongovius," 27:1398).[5] The account of morality as the relation of its objective and subjective sides is ultimately the account of the relation of practical reason and mind.[6] When one reads the *Critique of*

5. Immanuel Kant, "Moral Mrongovius," in *Vorlesungen über Moralphilosophie*, Bd. 27 of *Kant's gesammelte Schriften*, ed. Akademie der Wissenschaften (Berlin: de Gruyter, 1979), 27:1397–581.

6. My initial interpretation of Kant's complete account of morality as this relation of practical reason and mind is found in "Moral Education," in *The Kantian Mind*, ed. Sorin Baiasu and Mark Timmons (Abingdon, UK: Routledge, 2021), ch. 33. In that essay I analyze Kant's four states of mind that fulfill the feeling of pleasure in response to reason's moral imperative. It is in the section "Metaphysical Principles of Virtue" that he identifies four specific "aesthetic preliminary concepts of the mind's responsiveness to concepts of duty in general": moral feeling (as respect for the law), conscience, love of humanity, and respect for oneself (self-esteem) (6:399). Immanuel Kant, *Die Metaphysik*

Practical Reason in this light, one can recognize Kant's concept of mind as the avenue to understand the further connection that pleasure, feeling of life, and the concept of life have to human moral life.

In his scholarship, Rudolf Makkreel has long drawn attention to the importance of Kant's concept of life, arguing that "aesthetic feeling" involves the "responsiveness of life itself" and that it is "central to Kant's theory of mind."[7] "Life," he writes, "must involve not only the capacity to act, but also the consciousness of being acted upon."[8] This characterizes well the relation of practical reason and mind (as I hope to show in the ensuing discussion). Taking Makkreel's insight as a point of departure, I will ultimately argue that Kant's sense of life is most fully realized in the third and highest level of his three-part hierarchy of the human aptitudes, the level of personality or the rational, morally accountable being. The effort to show this will proceed in terms of the following steps: (1) the relation of mind and practical reason in the *Critique of Practical Reason*; (2) the further elucidation of the faculty of mind in Kant's anthropology lectures, in his *Metaphysics of Morals*, and other writings; (3) the account of moral feeling as an aesthetic concept and of the kind of pleasure or promotion of life that moral feeling entails; (4) the discernible levels in Kant's account of the feeling of life as the path to recognizing personality as its most fully realized form.

Relation of Mind and Practical Reason

To begin, we will address the apparent contradiction between the initial passage cited from the *Critique of Practical Reason* and Kant's affirmation of the role of pleasure in human moral life. The context for the negative statements about enjoyment and pleasure is Kant's concern about the basis, the cause, the ground of morality and his rejection of such empirical, moral

---

der Sitten, in *Kant's gesammelte Schriften*, Bd. 6, ed. Königlich Preußische Akademie der Wissenschaften (Berlin: Georg Reimer, 1914, 6:203–493. I go on to correlate these four aesthetically felt responses with (1) Kant's fourfold articulation of the categorical imperative, (2) his fourfold logical structure of judgment per se, and (3) the categories of freedom. In this essay I will focus on moral feeling as an aesthetic preliminary concept of the mind's responsiveness to concepts of duty.

7. Rudolf A. Makkreel, *Imagination and Interpretation in Kant: The Hermeneutical Import of the "Critique of Judgment"* (Chicago: University of Chicago Press, 1990), 106.

8. Makkreel, *Imagination and Interpretation*, 91.

sense theories as are developed by Lord Shaftesbury and David Hume. Nonetheless, insofar as moral feeling is morality subjectively regarded, the human capacity of sensible feeling is explicitly identified by Kant, even within this context, as playing an indispensable role. There is no antecedent feeling in the subject that would be attuned to morality (as moral sense theory would have it) (5:75). However, "the sensible feeling [*sinnliche Gefühl*] that lies at the basis of all our inclinations is indeed the *condition of that sensation* [*Empfindung*] that we call respect, but its determining cause lies in pure practical reason and therefore, because of its origin, this sensation cannot be called pathologically effected, but must be called practically effected" (5:75; my emphasis). The faculty in which this feeling is effected is mind (*Gemüt*), and so, interwoven into his discussion, Kant is signaling both the role of feeling and the relation of mind and practical reason. His worry is a confusion, a mistake that is all too easily made, precisely because this effect in the mind is a sensible feeling. As he underscores at length later in the text, "here there always exists the basis of an error of subreption (*vitium subreptionis*) and, as it were, an optical illusion in the self-consciousness of what one does, as distinguished from what one senses [or feels, *empfindet*], [an illusion] that even the most practiced cannot wholly avoid" (5:116). He goes on using the language of pleasure (*Lust*) and being pleased (*Wohlgefallen*) that is pervasive in the *Critique of Judgment*:

> The consciousness of the determination of the faculty of desire is always the basis of being pleased with the action that is thereby brought about; but this pleasure, this being pleased in and of itself, is not the determining ground of the action, rather, the direct determination of the will solely by reason is the basis of the feeling of pleasure, and the latter remains a purely practical, not aesthetic determination of the faculty of desire. Since this determination has inwardly exactly the same effect [of serving] as an impulse to activity, that a feeling of agreeableness [*Annehmlichkeit*] expected from the desired action would have produced, we easily view what we ourselves do to be something which we merely passively feel, and take the moral incentive for a sensible impulse, just as always happens in the so-called illusion of the senses (here of inner [sense]). (5:116–17)

Or as Kant puts it in the section on the "aesthetic preliminary concepts of the mind's responsiveness to concepts of duty in general" (in the "Metaphysical Principles of Virtue"), it is not fitting to call moral feeling a "moral sense" precisely because "by the word sense one usually means a theoretical faculty of perception directed to an object," while in this case the moral feeling is only "subjective" and "yields no cognition" (6:400). Kant devotes many pages in the second *Critique* to this misperception of the origin and so mistaken relation of cause (the agency of practical reason) and effect (the sensibly felt moral feeling in the mind)—a mistake from which the "virtuous Epicurus" too was not immune (5:116).

This context also sheds light on the apparent denial of enjoyment in the performance of duty. In the distinction Kant makes between weal and woe in contrast to good and evil, the issue of the order of the relation and so of the source of pleasure or displeasure, of enjoyment or pain, is again central. The state of one's well-being presupposes the object of pleasure or displeasure, of enjoyment or pain, whereas reason reflects on what is good and evil in itself and makes the latter the condition for taking into consideration the desired objects of well-being (5:61–62). Where one is clear about the moral order, about the source of agency bringing about the felt effect, not only are pleasure, enjoyment, or being pleased not rejected, but they are the very material (so to speak) of felt moral consciousness. True, the determination of the will (or faculty of desire) by reason is a "purely practical" and "not an aesthetic" determination, but this specifies the kind of judgment entailed in moral judging and does not preclude the role of the aesthetic in moral life (5:116). As Kant observes at the beginning of the *Critique of Judgment*, a judgment of taste differs from a cognitive and hence logical judgment in that the determining ground of an aesthetic judgment "cannot be other than subjective" (§1, 5:203). Again it is an issue of the order; in moral judging, the aesthetic cannot be the determining ground, but the aesthetic can and is a result of the moral determination. Moreover, the aesthetic has a positive role to play. The moral law is both the "material" and "objective determining ground of the objects of an action under the name of good and evil," as well as the "subjective determining ground—that is, the incentive—to this action, in that it has an influence on the sensibility [*Sinnlichkeit*] of the subject and effects a feeling that promotes the influence of the law on the will" (5:75). Exactly how this influence is effected is the question of securing access to the human mind (*Gemüt*) and an influence on its maxims by the laws of pure practical reason.

Kant's anthropology, his conception of what it is to be a finite rational being, is the backdrop to his whole discussion in the second *Critique* and in various places he explicitly invokes it. Consonant with his point that sensible feeling is the condition for the sensation of respect, he underscores that respect for the law presupposes both the "sensibility" and "finitude" of the rational beings in whom it operates (5:76). "All three concepts, of an incentive, an interest, and a maxim, can only be employed in regard to finite beings" in whom the "subjective constitution of their faculty of choice does not of itself agree with the objective laws of practical reason"; thus their nature "presupposes a need to be somehow impelled to activity" (5:79). Speculative reason cannot find any grounds for the influence of a merely intellectual idea on feeling, but one is able to see a priori that "such a feeling is inseparably bound up with the conception of a moral law in every finite rational being" (5:80). While the passages cited in this discussion are familiar to the readers of Kant, at stake here is drawing attention to the central importance of the nature and role of the *relation* of the objective and subjective sides of the moral life of this finite rational being. A complete account of Kant's vision requires the articulation and analysis of this relation that is realized between practical reason and mind.

In the doctrine of method (or "way of instruction") of the second *Critique*, Kant develops the question of influence on the mind by practical reason in terms of a two-stage process of the cultivation of moral judgment, steps that Kant explicitly relates to the beautiful and the sublime. He treats aesthetic pleasure in the beautiful as a propaedeutic stage to moral judgment proper, which is accompanied by the feeling of the sublime. In the first step of arousing consciousness of the moral law in his students' minds, Kant speaks of an "employment of judgment" that is "not yet an interest in actions and their morality"; it does, however, "give to virtue or *Denkungsart* [conduct of thought] in accordance with moral laws a form of beauty" that gives rise to "admiration," without yet therefore inspiring an effort "to seek it"; it is the "same as for everything whose contemplation produces subjectively a consciousness of the harmony of our powers of representation and whereby we feel our entire cognitive faculty (understanding and imagination) strengthened" (5:160).[9]

The second exercise resulting in the consciousness of our own inner freedom is accompanied by the two-stage experience of the sublime, the "initial sensation of pain" followed by the satisfaction ensuing from the recognition of the elevation of the soul, from the "independence from

9. Kant's formal, critical concept of moral character is defined in the *Critique of Practical Reason* as "practical resolute *Denkungsart* [conduct of thought] in accordance with invariable maxims" (5:152).

inclinations and the circumstances of fortune, and the possibility of being self-sufficient" (5:160–61). Earlier in the text Kant had observed that the moral law, in its subjectively practical form as the "true motivation" that has its source in pure practical reason, "allows us to perceive [*spüren*, literally "sense," "feel," or "get a taste of"] the "sublimity of our own supersensible existence" and "effects" (*wirkt*) within us, subjectively speaking, "respect for our higher vocation" (5:88). Once we have "set aside our self-conceit and have permitted the practical influence of this respect, one can never, in turn, have enough of contemplating the splendor of this law, and the soul believes itself to be elevated to the same extent as it sees the holy law elevated [*erhaben*] over it and its frail nature" (5:77).

Kant continues this connection of the sublime with our moral character and vocation in the *Critique of Judgment*. He notes that the reference to the "sublime in nature" is misplaced. Truly speaking, the "sublime must always have reference to our *Denkungsart*; that is, to maxims which secure supremacy over sensibility for the intellectual and for the ideas of reason" ("Anmerkungen," 5:274).[10] Or, in words that virtually echo the second *Critique*, "the feeling of the sublime in nature" is actually "respect for our own vocation" (§27, 5:257). He draws the further explicit connection with the faculty of mind. The "attunement of mind [*Gemüt*]" in the case of the "sublime in nature" is "similar" to its attunement in its "moral" use ("Anmerkungen," 5:268). In the feeling of the sublime, we find that which "repels sensibility" to be something that "at once attracts" us, because reason here "exercises its dominance solely in order to enlarge" the domain of sensibility "commensurate with its own practical domain" (§29, 5:265).

We thus have the two sides entailed in life: the actor (practical reason) and the consciousness of being acted upon (the felt perception of reason's law in and by the mind). We can map Kant's definition of pleasure (from his early footnote in the second *Critique*) on to this: the representation of the agreement of an action (on the part of practical reason) with the subjective conditions of life (faculty of mind). The harmony of the faculties here is not that of the understanding and the imagination, but of practical reason and mind. And the role of the mind is essential for the realization of the moral life of the finite rational being. As Kant writes, if "human nature were not so constituted" that "even subjectively, the exhibition of pure virtue can have more power over the human mind [*Gemüt*] and can provide far greater motivation" not only to effectuate the "legality of actions," but "to produce firmer resolve to prefer the law to everything else

10. See also §23, 5:245, 246; §29, 5:264, 265.

purely out of respect for it," than could ever be generated by appeals to the "attractions . . . of all that may be counted as happiness or even by all threats of pain and harm," if this were not so, then there would be no means of "ever bringing about the morality of the *Gesinnung* [of one's moral mindedness]" (5:151–52). He goes on to say that his intent is to "establish that this attribute of our mind, this responsiveness [*Empfänglichkeit*] to a pure moral interest, and with that the motive force [*bewegende Kraft*] of the pure representation of virtue . . . is the most powerful and . . . when it is a matter of the enduring and meticulous observance of moral maxims, the sole incentive to the good" (5:152–53). Having thus brought the nature and importance of the faculty of mind to the fore, we will turn to Kant's account of it in his other writings.

Faculty of Mind (*Gemüt*)

As with many of Kant's terms, *Gemüt* is not consistently translated. Often (with good reason) it is rendered as "heart," "soul," or "feeling soul," and in this sense it remains a prevalent concept in German language and culture. The English term "mind" is also used in a wide range of meanings, but its most prevalent use in contemporary analytical epistemological discussion takes its cue from the modern mind/body distinction, and so it connotes logical, cognitive processes. In this sense "mind" does not render the meaning of *Gemüt* in Kant's use of it. In the "Anthropology Friedländer" in his discussion of the human sense of self, Kant distinguishes two aspects of the "soul": *Geist* (intellect) and *Gemüt*.[11] "*Gemüt* is the way in which the soul is affected [*afficirt*] by things. It is the power to reflect upon one's state and to relate one's state to oneself and one's personality. . . . *Gemüt* is thus a power of being sensitive to [*empfinden*] what one feels [*empfinden*]. . . . Thus in the soul, *Gemüt* is something different from what we otherwise call heart [*Gemüt*] or feeling [*Gefühl*]" (25:474). So already in this early text, Kant's anthropology includes an account of the mind as a principle of life that is a consciousness of being affected, as well as a reflective power in relation to this

11. The translation of *Geist* as intellect (rather than its frequent translation as "spirit") expresses Kant's definition of it as the "subject which is thinking." He goes on to express his distinction in terms of the Latin *animus* and *anima*. The latter means the soul as the principle of life, while *animus* refers to soul as the principle of intellection and sensation. Its range of meaning includes intellect, understanding, mind, thought, reason, and spirit (25:474).

consciousness. It is further the power that allows us to identify ourselves with this conscious state. Several pages later in the text, Kant makes a statement that fairly resonates with his later critical moral philosophy: "The greatest perfection of the powers of the mind [*Gemüt*] is based on our subordinating them to our power of choice [*Willkür*], and the more they are subjugated to the free power of choice, all the greater perfection of the powers of the mind do we possess. If we do not have them under the control of the free power of choice, all provisions for such perfection are thus in vain, if we cannot do what we want with the powers of the mind" (25:488). Later in the text Kant spells out the implications of his distinction between nature and freedom with regard to any ensuing pleasure or displeasure:

> With the human being, we divide everything into nature and freedom. We count natural aptitude, talent, and temperament as nature, but mind, heart, and character as freedom. Something can displease me about a human being due to nature, but I cannot impute guilt to him [for it]. If all is well in regard to nature, then we call it fortunate. Guilt is imputed to the human being for what displeases in regard to freedom. . . . What appertains to freedom, appertains immediately to the inner goodness of the human being and is good or evil in itself. However what appertains to nature does not please directly, but as an instrument, which can still be applied to whatever [end]. (25:625–26)

"Natural aptitude, talent, and temperament," in turn, are the "principles of activity" with "regard to the mind," and to have spoken of these is to have "examined the source of the feelings and inclinations of human beings and the principle of life" (25:626, 628). "To examine the principle of activity to make use of these feelings and inclinations, thus the practical with human beings," Kant goes on, requires distinguishing "heart, mind, and character" (25:628). Kant discusses all these terms at length, but most germane for the present discussion is the notion of natural aptitude as underlying the distinction and relation of agency and being acted upon. In general, natural aptitude signifies the ground inherent in a living being's nature itself that is the basis for what can be made out of a given being, for what it can develop into.[12] Perhaps the most succinct statement may be found in the

12. For an overview of Kant's use of the notion of natural aptitude throughout his writings, see my entry "Natural aptitude (*Naturell, Naturanlage*)," in the *Cambridge Kant*

Anthropology from a Pragmatic Point of View where Kant identifies natural aptitude ("*Naturell* or *Naturanlage*") as the first of a threefold division of what is "characteristic" of the human being, with "temperament or conduct of the sensibilities [*Sinnesart*]" and "character in an absolute sense or conduct of thought [*Denkungsart*]" being the other two. "The first two aptitudes [*Anlagen*] indicate what may be made of the human being," while the "moral" aptitude indicates what human beings "are prepared to make of themselves" (7:285).[13] In the earlier "Anthropology Friedländer" Kant notes that "natural aptitude is the capacity of receptivity to receive certain objects. Therefore natural aptitude appertains to capacity. Talent is a faculty of producing products. . . . Temperament is the union of both" (25:625–26). "In the practical [sphere], the heart [*Herz*] is that which is a principle of activity in accordance with good impulses" (25:628)[14] and "character is the employment of our power of choice to act according to rules and principles. . . . Character constitutes the worth of a human being in and for itself, and is the origin of free actions from principles" (25:630).

It is in these lectures, then, that we find the underlying anthropology to the statements Kant makes in his critical writings; for example, to his claim in the *Critique of Practical Reason* that if "human nature were not so constituted" that "even subjectively, the exhibition of pure virtue can have more power over the human mind [*Gemüt*]," then there would be no means

Lexicon, ed. Julian Wuerth (New York: Cambridge University Press, 2021), 305–307. My entry on "Character (*Charakter*)" (102–5) is also helpful for the elucidation of all these terms. The translation of *Anlagen* as "aptitudes" emphasizes these as active, formative, and structuring principles (not as passive dispositions). See the "Note on Translation" at the beginning of my *Kant's Conception of Moral Character: The "Critical" Link of Morality, Anthropology, and Reflective Judgment* (Chicago: University of Chicago Press, 1999).

13. Immanuel Kant, *Anthropologie in pragmatischer Hinsicht*, in *Kant's gesammelte Schriften*, Bd. 7, ed. Königlich Preußische Akademie der Wissenschaften (Berlin: Georg Reimer, 1917), 7:117–333.

14. The implicit reference in this passage to the power of choice is born out by Kant's explicit association of "heart" with the "power of choice" in his *Religion within the Limits of Reason Alone* (a text in which he draws on much of his anthropological conception of human nature). For example, in speaking of the propensity for evil as the subjective ground of the possibility of maxims deviating from the moral law, Kant notes that "one can also add to this that the ability or inability of the power of choice [*Willkür*] to adopt the moral law in its maxims, that arises out of this natural propensity, may be called the good or evil heart [*Herz*]" (6:29). Immanuel Kant, *Die Religion innerhalb der Grenzen der bloßen Vernunft*, in *Kant's gesammelte Schriften*, Bd. 6, ed. Königlich Preußische Akademie der Wissenschaften (Berlin: Georg Reimer, 1914), 6:1–202.

of "ever bringing about the morality of the *Gesinnung*" (of one's moral mindedness) (5:151–52). This essential agency and the capacity both to be acted upon and to be conscious of such action requires the further point that is central to Kant's discussion in both the second and third *Critiques*, namely, that concepts give rise to feeling. Here again we find this notion in Kant's early anthropology lectures. For example, we read there that

> although, as it is, the concepts of good and evil are not objects of feeling, yet they can still serve to rouse feeling to act in accordance with these concepts; then one acts in accordance with principles and maxims. True, one cannot have insight into how the concept, for example of an injustice which has been done to someone, should rouse feeling, and [how] it can motivate [one] to stand by this individual, but still it happens. For providence has only given us instinct for [when] concepts and principles are lacking. Thus concepts are to become incentives in us, they are to rouse feeling, and to motivate us to act in accordance with such concepts, and thus according to principles. Human beings who do not have such a feeling which can be roused through a concept, have no moral feeling. This is the sensitiveness, sensitivity, or the feeling through all concepts of the understanding. (25:649–50)

The subjective condition of the possibility of concepts having power over the human mind entails, in turn, aesthetic concepts on the side of the mind itself. While reason's moral concepts are the source of moral motivation, in order for the mind to be formed, to achieve a moral attunement and responsiveness to the moral imperative and thereby raise human nature to the concrete fulfillment of its moral vocation, these aesthetic concepts allow the mind to be responsive to reason's imperative. In section 12 of the second part of his "Metaphysical Principles of Virtue," entitled "Aesthetic Preliminary Concepts of the Mind's Responsiveness to Concepts of Duty in General," Kant identifies four such specific concepts; they are natural aptitudes of mind (*Gemütsanlagen*; *praedispositio*) to be affected (*afficirt*) by concepts of duty and make us capable, from the human, subjective side of our nature, of fulfilling our moral vocation:

> There are such moral properties, that, if one does not possess them, there can also not be any duty to acquire them. These

> are moral feeling, conscience, love of neighbor, and respect for oneself (self-esteem). There is no obligation to have these, because they are subjective conditions of responsiveness to the concept of duty [and] do not serve as the basis of the objective conditions of morality. All told, they are aesthetic and preliminary, but natural aptitudes of mind [*Gemütsanlagen*] (*praedispositio*) to be affected [*afficirt*] by concepts of duty. It cannot be regarded as a duty to have these aptitudes; rather every human being has them and by means of them [every person] can be obligated. The consciousness of them is not empirical in origin, but can only follow upon [the consciousness] of a moral law, upon its effect on the mind. (6:399)[15]

With moral feeling explicitly identified, then, as an aesthetic concept of the mind's responsiveness to reason's moral concepts, and with mind identified with the principle of life, we will return to this central notion of Kant's moral philosophy to draw the connection of moral feeling to the feeling of life. Even to this point, the discussion bears out Makkreel's claim that the "idea of life" is more than "an abstract notion of spontaneity" and is instead a "more inclusive idea of responsiveness which would make aesthetic feeling truly central to Kant's theory of mind."[16] What we have seen is that this is not a belated development in Kant's philosophy, but that it is part of his anthropological account of human nature.

Moral Feeling as an Aesthetic Concept

To speak of a consciousness of the moral law is not new to the "Metaphysical Principles of Virtue." In the *Critique of Practical Reason*, in addition to the passages cited above, Kant notes that "the acknowledgment of the moral law" is "the consciousness of an activity of practical reason. . . . Respect for the moral law must be regarded . . . as a subjective ground of activity, that is as an incentive to comply with the law, and as the ground for maxims

15. For a detailed discussion of these four aesthetic concepts, see my article "Moral Education." Also see my discussion "Cultivating Moral Consciousness: The Quintessential Relation of Practical Reason and Mind (*Gemüt*) as a Bulwark against the Propensity for Radical Evil," *Educational Philosophy and Theory* 51, no. 13 (2019): 1351–60.

16. Makkreel, *Imagination and Interpretation*, 106.

of a course of life in conformity with it" (5:79). In light of these passages and of Kant's conception of mind, the explicit identification of moral feeling as one of four aesthetic concepts in the 1797 text is arguably Kant's own succinct statement of what the foregoing discussions in the various texts entail. He begins with what is most familiar, defining "moral feeling" as the "receptivity [*Empfänglichkeit*[17]] for pleasure or displeasure" arising "solely from the consciousness of the agreement or disagreement of our action with the law of duty" (6:399). He goes on to identify moral feeling as the "aesthetic state [*Zustand*]," the "affecting of inner sense" (*Afficirung des inneren Sinnes*) that follows upon the "representation of the law." This characterization is in accord with the general way in which Kant speaks (at the beginning of the *Critique of Judgment*) of the "feeling of pleasure and displeasure" as the way in which subjects feel themselves "affected by a representation" (§1, 5:204). Next in the *Metaphysics of Morals* Kant repeats that "all consciousness of obligation has this [moral] feeling as its ground, in order to become conscious of the necessitation inherent to the concept of duty" and that, as moral beings, we are originally endowed with this moral feeling and so any obligation in regard to it can only consist in "cultivating" it and "even strengthening it through admiration for its inscrutable origin" (6:399–400). He follows this observation by drawing an explicit connection to the distinctiveness of human moral life in contrast with other living natural beings. "No human being is devoid of all moral feeling; for to be totally unresponsive to this sensation is to be morally dead, and if (to speak in the language of physicians) the moral vital force [*sittliche Lebenskraft*] could no longer rouse [*Reiz bewirken*] this feeling, then [such a person's] humanity would dissolve (so to speak, as if by laws of chemistry) into mere animality and would be irretrievably blended together with the mass of other natural beings" (6:400). In short, the life that is proper to humanity would be lost. Kant's point in the *Critique of Practical Reason* about the consequence of an external constraint to prevent transgression of the law (such as God and eternity clearly seen and standing before us), instead of the internal, active exercise of freedom, draws a similar conclusion. "Thus most actions conforming to the law would be done from fear, few would be done from hope, none from duty. The moral worth of actions, on which alone the worth of the person and even of the world depends in the eyes

17. The alternate translations of receptivity and responsiveness are made with regard to the context in which Kant uses the term. The receptivity to pleasure allows the mind to be responsive to practical reason.

of supreme wisdom, would not exist at all. The conduct of human beings, so long as their nature remained as it is now, would be changed into mere mechanism, where, as in a puppet show, everything would gesticulate well but no life would be found in the figures" (5:147). We are reminded here of Kant's statement in his early 1775–1776 anthropology lectures: "Freedom is the greatest life of the human being" (25:560).

The aesthetic consciousness of this freedom is, as we have seen, the feeling of the sublime: "The feeling of the sublime in nature" is actually "respect for our own vocation" and the "sublime must always have reference to our *Denkungsart*" (§27, 5:257; "Anmerkungen," 5:274). This aesthetic state is a pleasurable consciousness of being alive: "The feeling of the promotion of life is enjoyment or pleasure," as Kant stated early on (25:559). As Makkreel has also emphasized, "the pleasure of the sublime" has the "effect of intensifying the feeling of the life of the subject."[18] "The enlivening harmony" of which he speaks, that "constitutes the pleasure in the overall vitality of our mental life and which encompasses more than the relation between the imagination and the understanding" corresponds, on my view, with the aesthetic pleasure in the beautiful as a propaedeutic stage to moral judgment proper (that Kant lays out in the *Critique of Practical Reason*).[19] "Being pleased with the beautiful directly carries with it," Kant tells us, "a feeling of the promotion of life" (§23, 5:244). In the second exercise of cultivating moral judgment that results in the consciousness of our own inner freedom, the aesthetic state is that of the double movement of the sublime: "the feeling of a momentary inhibition of the vital forces followed immediately by an outpouring of them that is all the stronger" (§23, 5:245).

Kant's own explicit connections with moral judgment are made in the *Critique of Judgment*. Practical or moral being pleased is combined with interest (i.e., it entails being pleased with the very existence, not only the purposive form, of its object) (§4, 5:207). When we "judge it aesthetically," we must "represent the intellectual, in itself intrinsically purposive moral good, not so much as beautiful, but rather as sublime, so that it will arouse more a feeling of respect (which disdains charm), than one of love and familiar affection" ("Anmerkungen," 5:271). "The object of a pure and unconditioned intellectual being pleased is the moral law in its might, [a might] that it exerts in us over any and all of those incentives of the mind [*Gemüt*] that precede it; . . . this might actually reveals itself aesthetically

18. Makkreel, *Imagination and Interpretation*, 96.

19. Makkreel, *Imagination and Interpretation*, 92.

only through sacrifice (which is a deprivation, though one that serves our inner freedom, in return for which it reveals in us an unfathomable depth of this supersensible power, whose consequences extend beyond what we can foresee)." This service on behalf of inner freedom is noted by Kant in the *Critique of Practical Reason*: well established respect for the moral law is the best, even sole guard against ignoble and corrupting impulses entering the mind (5:161). Earlier in the text he also states that the greatness of soul for which human beings, as a result of the moral motivational grounds, recognize they are destined, provides "abundant compensation" for the sacrifices that the independence from inclinations entails (5:152).

Understanding moral feeling as an aesthetic concept that is of a piece with the feeling of the sublime that, in turn, yields an intense feeling of the promotion of life, allows one to better comprehend the full import of Kant's identification of moral feeling as "morality itself, subjectively regarded" (5:76). It is morality as the existence that is proper to the human subject. So too, the famous lines that already in his lifetime became synonymous with the life of Kant himself may be better appreciated. "Two things fulfill the mind [*Gemüt*] with ever new and increasing admiration and reverence, the more often and the more steadily we reflect on them: the starry heavens above me and the moral law within me" (5:161). "I see them before me," Kant goes on, "and connect them directly with the consciousness of my existence. The first begins from that place that I occupy in the external world of sense. . . . The second begins with my invisible self, my personality, and presents me in a world that has true infinity" (5:62). Personality (*Persönlichkeit*) fundamentally means that quality that makes a person a being distinct from an animal or a thing—distinct, in other words, from either the mere animal existence or the puppetry that we have seen is all that is left for Kant where the moral life as the life of inner freedom is not cultivated. Hence, as Kant had already stated in the very context of his warning against the illusion of taking moral feeling to be a motivating sensible impulse that is the ground of morality, instead of recognizing it as an effect of reason's agency, "it is of great importance to draw attention to this attribute of our personality and to cultivate as best as one can, the effect of reason on this feeling" (5:117). What we have seen in the discussion here is what this importance consists in: our felt, conscious existence as a moral being that is so pleasing that sensible inclinations luring us to transgress the moral law are denied their efficacy and influence. To get a better sense of one's life as personality that would accomplish that, as well as its relation to the human rational being and the human animal, both of which remain intrinsic to the finite, moral rational being, we will now further explore Kant's concept of life.

Kant's Conception of Life

As we have seen, from the very outset Kant locates "the first source of life . . . in the mind" (25:604). When he reiterates this in the *Critique of Judgment,* he does so in the context of engaging Epicurus's assertion that "enjoyments and pain are always ultimately bodily" even if they "start with the imagination or even representations of the understanding" ("Anmerkungen," 5:277). Thus when Kant affirms that "the mind taken by itself is wholly life (the principle of life itself)," the question of the connection with the body and of different modes of life is in play ("Anmerkungen," 5:278). We will explore this question by starting from the general definition of life that Kant gives in the "Anthropology Friedländer": "Life is the consciousness of a free and regular play of all the powers and faculties of the human being" (25:559). Here Kant begins by speaking of the "feeling of the promotion of life" as "enjoyment or pleasure" at the level of our physical well-being, and he immediately raises the issue of a possible confusion; namely, that the degree of the feeling of the promotion or hindrance of life can be very misleading. "There can be an enjoyment which diminishes life, but increases the feeling. The feeling of animation is enjoyment." On the other hand, "the hindrance of life" could be "slight" (as in the case of a "fine cut" such as a paper cut), while the "pain is great," or alternatively, "damage to the lung is a slight pain, but a great hindrance of life." Moreover, there is even such a thing as "delight merely in the enjoyment of life, without being sensible of the cause which promotes life." Further, "enjoyments are not uniform in accordance with the objects" of enjoyment, but "they can still be added together" and then "constitute the whole of well-being" since "all delights relate to life" (25:561). The unreliability of the nature of and actual connection between felt enjoyments and the promotion of life notwithstanding, Kant goes on to say that it is "easy to gain insight" into "sensual enjoyments," while "ideal enjoyments" that are "based on the feeling of the free play of the powers of the mind require more clarification" (25:559–60).

Part of such "clarification" is a need to attend carefully to the sense in which Kant uses the various terms, including enjoyment, delight, and pleasure, but not limited to these. For example, we have seen that "natural aptitude, talent, and temperament" are the "principles of activity" with "regard to the mind," but earlier in the text in his discussion of "temperament concern[ing] the principle of life," Kant indicates that he is using this term too in different ways: "The principle of life in regard to the body [consists in] the nerves, muscles, and fibres. . . . Temperament is the unified principle of life from the constitution and the complexion. Here temperament is taken in the physical sense, and not in the psychological, [and so] where the mind does not come into consideration at all" (25:625). The "psychological considerations" are threefold: the faculties of cognition, of the feeling of pleasure and displeasure, and of desire (25:558). "The effect which things have on the whole of the mind is the faculty of pleasure and displeasure" (25:559). Insofar as we think objects, an "inner motion" may result in the mind and this is what we call "ideal enjoyments" (25:560). The confusion to be avoided in this regard is spelled out by Kant in the *Critique of Judgment*. "As we have often shown," he writes,

> there is a fundamental difference between that which pleases solely in [one's] judgment and that which one enjoys (what pleases in [one's] sensation). . . . Enjoyment (even if its cause happens to lie in ideas) seems at all times to consist in a feeling of the promotion of the overall life of the human being, and with that also of bodily well-being, that is, of health; so that Epicurus, who claimed that all enjoyment was basically bodily sensation, was perhaps to this extent not mistaken and only misunderstood himself when he included the intellectual and even practical being pleased in enjoyments. If one keeps this latter distinction in view, one is able to explain how an enjoyment could even displease someone who feels [*empfindet*] it . . . or how an intense pain could yet please someone who suffers it . . . or how an enjoyment may in addition also please . . . or how a pain could in addition be displeasing. Being pleased or displeased in these cases is due to reason and is one and the same as approval or disapproval; enjoyment and pain however can only be due to feeling or the prospect of possible weal or woe (whatever the cause might be). (§54, 5:330–31)

Life, then, as "the consciousness of a free and regular play of all the powers and faculties of the human being" encompasses this full range of feelings of weal and woe, of delight, of enjoyment, of pleasure and displeasure on the physical, intellectual, and moral planes. Equally pervasive in Kant's writings are his caveats about the illusions and mistakes to which we are inherently subject—mistaking the agency or source and so mistaking the cause and effect relation, mistaking the import of a particular enjoyment or pain, or allowing sensual pleasures to override rational direction of our choices. Implicit to Kant's caveats is a warning against failing to be self-aware, against failing to discern the nature and source of a given feeling. His caveats are serious and warranted. They reveal Kant's attention to human nature, to what it is to be a finite, embodied, and yet rational, moral being. Yet the caveats can distract his readers from what is a further pervasive theme in his writings: Kant's abiding, real appreciation for the faculty of pleasure and the importance of its role in human life. More broadly, as Makkreel has shown, for Kant, "our access to life is through feeling."[20] All of Kant's distinctions and caveats require ascertaining both the sense in which Kant is using his terms and the particular plane of human life that is the focus in a given passage. Perhaps most importantly for discerning Kant's meaning, it is essential to attend to the relation between these planes as Kant conceives of them. Again, as Makkreel has argued, "life is not a mere biological phenomenon to be set apart from spirit. In conceiving life, Kant does not think in terms of a dualism; organic life and the life of the mind constitute a continuum allowing a scale of positive and negative values."

What has emerged from the present discussion is the importance and centrality also of the faculty of mind. As we saw in Kant's early anthropology lectures: "*Gemüt* is the way in which the soul is affected [*afficirt*] by things. It is the power to reflect upon one's state and to relate one's state to oneself and one's personality" (25:474). In his published anthropology lectures, Kant distinguishes outer and inner sense as two ways in which the "human body is affected"; in outer sense, it is affected by "bodily" (or physical) "things," while inner sense is how the body is "affected by the mind" (7:153). The mind is the seat of responsiveness to reason, the seat of moral feeling as the "aesthetic state [*Zustand*]," the "affecting of inner sense" (*Afficirung des inneren Sinnes*) that follows upon the "representation of the law" (6:99). In turn, Kant is affirming that the mind affects the body. One place to see how this occurs is the overriding of those passions and inclinations that oppose the moral law; that is, Kant's point in the *Critique of Practical Reason* where he asserts that well established respect for the moral law is the best, even sole guard against ignoble and corrupting impulses entering the mind (5:161).

20. Makkreel, *Imagination and Interpretation*, 103.

In his early anthropology lectures, Kant describes the state of mind in which ignoble and corrupting impulses hold sway as an agitated mind lacking the requisite composure needed for the realization of inner freedom. It is here that he introduces his notion of affect that is found in later texts such as the *Critique of Judgment* and the *Religion within the Limits of Reason Alone*. As he articulates it in the "Anthropology Friedländer": "The agitations of the mind are twofold, affects and passions. . . . Affect is a feeling through which we lose our composure, but passion is a desire which takes away our composure. . . . When the mind loses its composure, then it is taken with affect or passion, but if it does not lose its composure, then one could call this temperate sensations and desires" (25:589–90; see also "Anmerkungen," 5:272n).[21] With his notion of the aesthetic attunement of mind, Kant effectively seeks to articulate a temperate state of mind that is at once a feeling of being "pleased in the fulfillment of duty" (4:460), a feeling that is powerful enough to prevent the mind from succumbing to human passions and inclinations. Aesthetic attunement promotes inner freedom, while other states impede it. Passions and inclinations are temptations for the power of choice to be swayed by them; in the aesthetic attunement of mind, its own capacities are governed by the free power of choice. The aesthetic attunement enables us to feel, not only understand, our vocation (*Bestimmung*) as moral beings and hence as capable of being free from subjugation to the passions and inclinations. Hence, as we saw in the *Critique of Practical Reason*, "it is of great importance to draw attention to this attribute of our personality and to cultivate as best as one can, the effect of reason on this feeling" (5:117). Or as Kant puts it in his "Metaphysical Principles of Virtue," our "obligation" in regard to moral feeling consists in "cultivating" it and "even strengthening it through admiration for its inscrutable origin" (6:399–400). This cultivation is essential for realizing the highest plane of the feeling of life: "Intellectual pleasure consists in the consciousness of the use of freedom in accordance with rules. Freedom is the greatest life of the human being. . . . Intellectual pleasure . . . is concerned with morality" (25:560).

21. It is possible for the mind to lose its composure even in the case of the moral good, for to combine the "idea of the good with affect" is to be in a state of "enthusiasm" ("Anmerkungen," 5:271–72). In his *Anthropologie*, in the section "The Inclination of Freedom as Passion," Kant writes about the role of the empirical concept of freedom in awakening an "enthusiasm" for freedom: "Thus the concept of freedom under moral laws not only awakens an affect which is called enthusiasm, but the mere sensible representation of outer freedom gives rise to the inclination to persevere therein or to enlarge [this outer freedom] . . . to the point of a fierce passion" (7:269).

Mind is thus effectively a middle term between the moral and empirical human self. Kant's account of it helps one to better understand not only his point about the elevation of the soul, about our "consciousness of independence from inclinations and the circumstances of fortune, and the possibility of being self-sufficient" (5:161), but also his point about the elevation of nature, the imparting of the form of the moral and intelligible to the natural and sensible. "In fact, in [its] idea, the moral law transfers us into a nature in which pure reason, if it were accompanied with commensurate physical capacities, would bring about the highest good; and [the moral law] determines our will to confer on the form of the sensible world, [the form] of a totality [*Ganzen*] of rational beings" (to which Kant refers elsewhere as a totality of a realm of ends) (5:43). Or as he puts it later in the text, the root of this elevation of the human being as a part of the sensible world to a totality of ends, is "nothing else than *personality*, the freedom and independence from the mechanism of nature regarded as a capacity of a being subject to special laws (pure practical laws given by its own reason), so that the person belonging to the world of sense is subject to his own personality so far as he belongs to the intelligible world" (5:86–87). We can also better appreciate Kant's observation that in the recognition of a capacity within us that is superior to nature's might, we "discover at the same time a capacity" that is the basis of "a self-preservation of an entirely different kind than the one threatened by nature outside of us" (§28, 5:261).

It is the moral form of life as a whole, so the realization of personality and its imbuing its form and life to the whole of human life, that is at stake. How personality achieves this involves Kant's conception of the natural aptitudes. We have seen that in its most general sense natural aptitude is the inherent basis for what a given being can develop into. This emphasis on the development of what lies in the inner nature of an organic being is central to Kant's earliest uses of the terminology of natural aptitudes and it is sustained in the pervasive use of his concept of aptitudes throughout his writings from the early biological, physical, and anthropological discussions to the later moral and pedagogical writings. The shift from the character of the human race to the character of the species morally conceived entails the consideration of a different set of relations informing the response and development of the original aptitudes of human nature. The crucial environment is now not so much physical but the proximity of others in society, the political forms of organization, more precisely, the civil constitution, and arguably, above all, the awakening of reason—its active assumption of its role as initiator or first principle of these further changes in the human condition. By 1797, what over thirty years earlier had been conceived as a natural process of the organic body provided for in its structuring principle is explicitly formulated as a maxim for action that we (as moral beings) are obligated to adopt: "Cultivate the powers of your mind and body such that they are adequate for fulfilling [literally, are in a condition of fitness for, *Tauglichkeit*] all purposes which you may have to face" (6:392). It is a matter of duty to "cultivate the crude aptitudes of our nature," indeed to "cultivate all our capacities in general" (both "physical" and "moral") for the sake of "promoting the purposes set before us by reason"; through such "cultivation we make ourselves worthy of the humanity" that is our calling (6:391, 392). In his 1793 *Religion within the Limits of Reason Alone*, Kant describes the "entire determination of the human being" or entire set of purposes making up the whole purpose of human existence, as a three-part hierarchy under the rubric of the "original aptitude for good in human nature": our aptitudes (*Anlagen*) as (1) living, animal beings (our animality), (2) living, rational beings (our humanity), and (3) rational, morally accountable beings (our personality) (6:26).[22] With regard to the conditions of the possibility of these aptitudes, Kant writes further that the "*first* does not have reason at its root at all; that the *second* is rooted in a reason which is indeed practical, but only as subservient to other incentives; and that the *third* alone is rooted in reason practical of itself, i.e., in reason legislating unconditionally. All these aptitudes in the human being are not only (negatively) *good* (they do not resist the moral law) but they are also predispositions *to the good* (they demand compliance with it). They are *original*," meaning that they "belong with necessity to the possibility of this being," to the "possibility of human nature" (6:28). Mind as the middle term is the faculty of the living, rational being that connects the legislation of the rational, morally accountable being with the living, animal being. The cultivation of the aptitude of personality realizes freedom as the greatest life

22. In the *Anthropologie*, Kant also names these levels as our (1) "technical" aptitude, or our conscious, mechanical abilities to work with things, (2) "pragmatic" aptitude, or skill in dealing with others in regard to attaining our goals, and (3) "moral" aptitude, or ability to "act toward oneself and others according to the principle of freedom under laws" (7:322–24). Pedagogically speaking, the cultivation of these aptitudes consists in developing "skillfulness" in relation to our talents, developing "prudence" or skillfulness in relations with others (which involves our temperament), and, thirdly, attaining moral character in its absolute sense as *Denkungsart* (9:486–87). Immanuel Kant, *Pädagogik*, in *Kant's gesammelte Schriften*, Bd. 9, ed. Königlich Preußische Akademie der Wissenschaften (Berlin: de Gruyter, 1923), 9:437–99.

of the human being. As Kant reiterates in the *Critique of Judgment*, "reason can never be persuaded that there is any intrinsic worth in the existence of a human being who lives only for enjoyment. . . . Only by what the human being does without concern for enjoyment, in complete freedom and independent of what could also be received passively from nature, does the individual procure an absolute worth for his being [*Dasein*] as the existence [*Existenz*] of a person" (§4, 5:208–9). Again, the order in which things take place is of the essence. Reason's determination of the purpose of human life orders the whole of life in accord with the plane of personality. To achieve this level of existence is to realize, *as a consequence*, the highest form of the feeling of the promotion of life.

List of Contributors

Robert R. Clewis is professor of philosophy at Gwynedd Mercy University and was a visiting scholar at the Ludwig-Maximilians-Universität Munich and the University of Pennsylvania. A recipient of an Alexander von Humboldt fellowship, he has written numerous articles and chapters on Kant's philosophy and is the author of *The Kantian Sublime and the Revelation of Freedom* (2009). He is the translator of the 1784–1785 Mrongovius lecture in Kant's *Lectures on Anthropology* (2012) and the editor of *Reading Kant's Lectures* (2015) and *The Sublime Reader* (2019). His most recent works are *Kant's Humorous Writings* (2020) and *The Origins of Kant's Aesthetics* (2023).

Courtney D. Fugate is associate professor of philosophy at Florida State University. He received his PhD in 2010 from Catholic University of Leuven, Belgium, and specializes in Kant and early modern German philosophy. He is author of *The Teleology of Reason: A Study of the Structure of Kant's Critical Philosophy* (2014), coeditor and cotranslator (with John Hymers) of Alexander Baumgarten's *Metaphysics: A Critical Translation with Kant's Elucidations, Selected Notes and Related Materials* (2013) and Johann August Eberhard's *Preparation for Natural Theology: With Kant's Notes and Danzig Rational Theology Transcript* (2016), and coeditor of *Baumgarten and Kant on Metaphysics* (2017). He is the coeditor and cotranslator (with Curtis Sommerlatte and Scott Stapleford) of Johan Nicolaus *Tetens's Writings on Method, Language, and Anthropology* (2022) and the editor of *Kant's Lectures on Metaphysics: A Critical Guide* (2019). He is currently preparing a commentary on Kant's *Critique of Practical Reason.*

Rodolphe Gasché is SUNY Distinguished Professor and Eugenio Donato Professor of Comparative Literature at the State University of New York at

Buffalo. He is the author of seventeen books, including *The Idea of Form: Rethinking Kant's Aesthetic* (2003), *The Honor of Thinking: Critique, Theory, Philosophy* (2007), *Europe, or The Infinite Task. A Study of a Philosophical Concept* (2009), *Georges Bataille: Phenomenology and Phantasmatology* (2012), *Geophilosophy: On Gilles Deleuze and Félix Guattari's What Is Philosophy?* (2014), *Deconstruction, Its Force, Its Violence* (SUNY Press, 2016), *Persuasion, Reflection, Judgment: Ancillae Vitae* (2017), and *Storytelling and the Destruction of the Inalienable in the Age of the Holocaust* (SUNY Press, 2018).

Dilek Huseyinzadegan is associate professor of philosophy at Emory University. She was educated at Boğaziçi University (Istanbul) and DePaul University (Chicago). Their primary areas of research are eighteenth-century Atlantic thought, Kant, political philosophy, critical race theory, and feminism. She is the author of *Kant's Nonideal Theory of Politics* (2019) and numerous articles on anti-racist and feminist engagements with the Western canon. Her publications have appeared in *Kantian Review*, *Hegel-Jahrbuch*, *Feminist Philosophy Quarterly*, *Cogito*, *Radical Philosophy Review*, and *Epoché*. She also helped to translate Charles Mills's book *The Racial Contract* into Turkish (2021).

Rudolf A. Makkreel (1939–2021) was the Charles Howard Candler Professor Emeritus of Philosophy at Emory University. His works include *Dilthey, Philosopher of the Human Studies* (1975; second expanded edition 1992), *Imagination and Interpretation in Kant: The Hermeneutical Import of the "Critique of Judgment"* (1990), and *Orientation and Judgment in Hermeneutics* (2015). He was the coeditor and translator (with Frithjof Rodi) of Dilthey's *Selected Works* (vol. 1, *Introduction to the Human Sciences*; vol. 2, *Understanding the Human World*; vol. 3, *The Formation of the Historical World in the Human Sciences*; vol. 4, *Hermeneutics and the Study of History*; vol. 5, *Poetry and Experience*; vol. 6, *Ethical and World-View Philosophy*). He also coedited (with David Carr and Thomas R. Flynn) *The Ethics of History* (2004), (with Sebastian Luft) *Neo-Kantianism in Contemporary Philosophy* (2010), and (with Hans-Ulrich Lessing and Riccardo Pozzo) *Recent Contributions to Dilthey's Philosophy of the Human Sciences* (2011). An Alexander von Humboldt Fellow from 1978 to 1979, he also received grants from the NEH, DAAD, Thyssen Foundation, Volkswagen Foundation, and the Heilbrun Fund. From 1983 to 1998 he served as editor of the *Journal of the History of Philosophy*. His *Kant's Worldview: How Judgement Shapes Human Comprehension* was published posthumously in 2021.

J. Colin McQuillan is professor of philosophy at St. Mary's University in San Antonio, Texas and the recipient of a Humboldt Research Fellowship for Experienced Researchers from the Alexander von Humboldt Foundation (2018–2019). He is the author of *Early Modern Aesthetics* (2015), *Immanuel Kant: The Very Idea of a Critique of Pure Reason* (2016), and the editor of *Baumgarten's Aesthetics: Historical and Philosophical Perspectives* (2021). He is also the coeditor (with Joseph Tanke) of *The Bloomsbury Anthology of Aesthetics* (2012) and (with María del Rosario Acosta López) of *Critique in German Philosophy: From Kant to Critical Theory* (SUNY Press, 2020). His current research concerns the relationship between aesthetics and logic in eighteenth-century German philosophy.

Jennifer Mensch is associate professor of philosophy at Western Sydney University, Australia. Her research is focused on the figures and debates of the long eighteenth century with a special focus on the intersection of philosophy and science during the German Enlightenment. In addition to numerous articles and book chapters, she is the author of *Kant's Organicism: Epigenesis and the Development of Critical Philosophy* (2013) and the coeditor, with Michael Olson, of *Generation, Heredity, Race: Key Texts in the History and Philosophy of the German Life Sciences, 1745–1845* (forthcoming).

G. Felicitas Munzel is Professor in the Program of Liberal Studies and the Department of Philosophy at the University of Notre Dame. She is author of *Kant's Conception of Moral Character: The "Critical" Link of Morality, Anthropology, and Reflective Judgment* (1999), *Kant's Conception of Pedagogy: Toward Education for Freedom* (2012), and articles on Kant's moral philosophy, conception of mind, critical conception of education, anthropology, aesthetics, and religion, and she is translator of "Anthropology Friedländer (1775–1776)" in *Lectures on Anthropology* (Cambridge Edition of the Works of Immanuel Kant, 2012).

Michael Olson is teaching associate professor in philosophy at Marquette University in Milwaukee. His research focuses on Kantian theoretical philosophy and its relation to the broader intellectual and social contexts in which Kant lived and wrote. He has published in *Studies in History and Philosophy of Science*, *Intellectual History Review*, and *Kant-Studien*.

James Risser is professor of philosophy at Seattle University. He has published extensively in the area of aesthetics as well as in the areas of German idealism and ancient Greek philosophy, with monographs on *Hermeneutics and the Voice of the Other: Re-reading Gadamer's Philosophical Hermeneutics* (SUNY Press, 1997), and *The Life of Understanding* (2012). He is the editor of *Philosophy, Art and the Imagination: Essays on the Work of John Sallis* (2022).

Dennis J. Schmidt is professor and chair of the Philosophy Research Initiative at Western Sydney University, Australia. He is the author of *The Ubiquity of the Finite: Hegel, Heidegger and the Entitlements of Philosophy* (1980), *On Germans and Other Greeks: Tragedy and Ethical Life* (2001), *Lyrical and Ethical Subjects: Essays on the Periphery of the Word, Freedom, and History* (SUNY Press, 2005), *Between Word and Image: Heidegger, Gadamer, and Klee on Gesture and Genesis* (2013), and *Idiome der Wahrheit* (2014). He is also editor and translator of *Natural Law and Human Dignity*, by Ernst Bloch (1986), and of *Being and Time*, by Martin Heidegger (SUNY Press, 2010), and coeditor (with Günter Figal) of *Hermeneutische Wege: Hans-Georg Gadamer zum Hundertsten* (2000) and (with Shannon Sullivan) of *The Difficulties of Ethical Life* (2008).

Susan Shell is professor of political science at Boston College. She is the author of *The Rights of Reason: A Study of Kant's Philosophy and Politics* (1980), *The Embodiment of Reason: Kant on Spirit, Generation and Community* (1996), and *Kant and the Limits of Autonomy* (2009), and coeditor (with Richard Velkley) of *Kant and the Limits of Autonomy* (2009) and (with Robert Faulkner) of *America at Risk: Challenges to Liberal Self-government in an Age of Uncertainty* (2009). She is also the editor of *The Strauss-Krüger Correspondence: Translation with Introduction and Critical Essays* (2018).

Joan Steigerwald is professor in the Department of Humanities and the graduate programs in humanities, science and technology studies, and social and political thought at York University. She is the author of *Experimenting at the Boundaries of Life: Organic Vitality in Germany around 1800* (2019). She has edited a special issue of *Kabiri*, "Schelling and Philosophies of Life," in 2024, as well as two special issues for *Studies in History and Philosophy of Science*, "Entanglements of Instruments and Media in Exploring Organic Worlds," in 2016, and "Kantian Teleology and the Biological Sciences," in 2006. She has published numerous articles on Kant, Schelling, and the German life sciences. Her new project is "A Romantic Natural History."

Kristi Sweet is associate professor of philosophy at Texas A&M University. She works principally on Kant's practical philosophy and his aesthetics. She is the author of two books on Kant: *Kant on Freedom, Nature, and Judgment: The Territory of the third* Critique (2023) and *Kant on Practical Life: From Duty to History* (2013). She has published articles on Kant's philosophy in *Kantian Review*, *Epoché*, and *Idealistic Studies*, among other venues.

Rachel Zuckert is professor in the Departments of Philosophy and German at Northwestern University. Zuckert received BA degrees from Williams College and Oxford University, and her PhD from the University of Chicago. Previous to Northwestern, she taught at Rice University and Bucknell University. She is author of numerous articles on eighteenth- and nineteenth-century philosophy, and of *Kant on Beauty and Biology: An Interpretation of Kant's Critique of Judgment* (2007) and *Herder's Naturalist Aesthetics* (2019).

Works by Kant

"An Friedrich Schiller." In Bd. 12 of *Kant's gesammelte Schriften*, edited by Königlich Preußische Akademie der Wissenschaften, 10–12. Berlin: Georg Reimer, 1902. Translated in *Correspondence*, translated and edited by Arnulf Zweig (Cambridge: Cambridge University Press, 1999), 497–99.

"Anthropologie Busholt." In *Vorlesungen über Anthropologie*, Bd. 25 of *Kant's gesammelte Schriften*, edited by Akademie der Wissenschaften, 1435–531. Berlin: de Gruyter, 1997.

"Anthropologie Collins." In *Vorlesungen über Anthropologie*, Bd. 25 of *Kant's gesammelte Schriften*, edited by Akademie der Wissenschaften, 7–238. Berlin: de Gruyter, 1997.

"Anthropologie Friedländer." In *Vorlesungen über Anthropologie*, Bd. 25 of *Kant's gesammelte Schriften*, edited by Akademie der Wissenschaften, 469–728. Berlin: de Gruyter, 1997. Translated by G. Felicitas Munzel as "Anthropology Friedländer," in *Lectures on Anthropology*, edited by Allen W. Wood and Robert B. Louden (Cambridge: Cambridge University Press, 2012), 37–255.

Anthropologie in pragmatischer Hinsicht. In *Kant's gesammelte Schriften*, Bd. 7, edited by Königlich Preußische Akademie der Wissenschaften, 117–333. Berlin: Georg Reimer, 1917. Translated as *Anthropology from a Pragmatic Point of View*, in *Anthropology, History, and Education*, edited by Günter Zöller and Robert B. Louden (Cambridge: Cambridge University Press, 2007), 227–429.

"Anthropologie Mrongovius." In *Vorlesungen über Anthropologie*, Bd. 25 of *Kant's gesammelte Schriften*, edited by Akademie der Wissenschaften, 1209–429. Berlin: de Gruyter, 1997. Translated by Robert R. Clewis as "Anthropology Mrongovius," in *Lectures on Anthropology*, edited by Allen W. Wood and Robert B. Louden (Cambridge: Cambridge University Press, 2012), 335–510.

"Anthropologie Parow." In *Vorlesungen über Anthropologie*, Bd. 25 of *Kant's gesammelte Schriften*, edited by Akademie der Wissenschaften, 243–464. Berlin: de Gruyter, 1997.

"Anthropology Pillau." In *Lectures on Anthropology*, edited by Allen W. Wood and Robert B. Louden, translated by Allen W. Wood, 257–80. Cambridge: Cambridge University Press, 2012.

"Beantwortung der Frage: Was ist Aufklärung?" In *Abhandlungen nach 1781*, Bd. 8 of *Kant's gesammelte Schriften*, edited by Königlich Preußische Akademie der Wissenschaften, 33–42. Berlin: Georg Reimer, 1912.

"Bemerkungen zu den Beobachtungen über das Gefühl des Schönen und Erhabenen." In *Handschriftlicher Nachlaß*, Bd. 20 of *Kant's gesammelte Schriften*, edited by Preußische Akademie der Wissenschaften, 1–192. Berlin: de Gruyter, 1942. Translated as "Remarks in the *Observations on the Feeling of the Beautiful and Sublime*," in *Observations on the Feeling of the Beautiful and Sublime and Other Writings*, edited by Patrick Frierson and Paul Guyer (Cambridge: Cambridge University Press, 2011), 63–202.

"Blomberg Logic." In *Lectures on Logic*, translated and edited by J. Michael Young, 5–246. Cambridge: Cambridge University Press, 1992.

Der Streit der Fakultäten. In *Kant's gesammelte Schriften*, Bd. 7, edited by Königlich Preußische Akademie der Wissenschaften, 1–116. Berlin: Georg Reimer, 1917. Translated by Mary J. Gregor and Robert Anchor as *The Conflict of the Faculties*, in *Religion and Rational Theology*, edited by Allen W. Wood and George di Giovanni (Cambridge: Cambridge University Press, 1996), 233–328.

Die falsche Spitzfindigkeit der vier syllogistischen Figuren erwiesen von M. Immanuel Kant. In *Vorkritische Schriften II: 1757–1777*, Bd. 2 of *Kant's gesammelte Schriften*, edited by Königlich Preußische Akademie der Wissenschaften, 47–61. Berlin: Georg Reimer, 1912.

Die Metaphysik der Sitten. In *Kant's gesammelte Schriften*, Bd. 6, edited by Königlich Preußische Akademie der Wissenschaften, 203–493. Berlin: Georg Reimer, 1914. Translated by Mary Gregor as *The Metaphysics of Morals*, in *Practical Philosophy*, edited and translated by Mary Gregor (Cambridge: Cambridge University Press, 1996), 353–603.

Die philosophischen Hauptvorlesungen Immanuel Kants: Nach den neu aufgefundenen Kollegheften des Grafen Heinrich zu Dohna-Wundlacken. Edited by Arnold Kowalewski. Munich: Rösl, 1924.

Die Religion innerhalb der Grenzen der bloßen Vernunft. In *Kant's gesammelte Schriften*, Bd. 6, edited by Königlich Preußische Akademie der Wissenschaften, 1–202. Berlin: Georg Reimer, 1914.

"Entwürfe zu dem Colleg über Anthropologie aus den 70er und 80er Jahren." In *Kant's Handschriftlicher Nachlaß: Anthropologie*, Bd. 15 of *Kant's gesammelte Schriften*, edited by Berlin-Brandenburgische Akademie der Wissenschaften, 655–899. Berlin: Georg Reimer, 1913.

"Erläuterungen Kants zu A. G. Baumgartens *Initia philosophiae practicae primae*." In *Handschriftlicher Nachlaß: Moralphilosophie, Rechtsphilosophie und Religionsphilosophie*, Bd. 19 of *Kant's gesammelte Schriften*, edited by Preußische Akademie der Wissenschaften, 5–91. Berlin: de Gruyter, 1934.

"Erläuterungen zu A. G. Baumgartens Metaphysica." In *Kant's Handschriftlicher Nachlaß: Metaphysik*, Bd. 17 of *Kant's gesammelte Schriften*, edited by Preußische Akademie der Wissenschaften, 5–226. Berlin: de Gruyter, 1926.

"Erläuterungen zur Psychologia empirica in A. G. Baumgartens Metaphysica." In *Kant's Handschriftlicher Nachlaß: Anthropologie*, Bd. 15 of *Kant's gesammelte Schriften*, edited by Berlin-Brandenburgische Akademie der Wissenschaften, 3–54. Berlin: Georg Reimer, 1913.

"Essay on the Maladies of the Head." In *Anthropology, History, and Education*, edited by Günter Zöller and Robert B. Louden, translated by Holly Wilson, 63–77. Cambridge: Cambridge University Press, 2007.

Grundlegung zur Metaphysik der Sitten. In *Kant's gesammelte Schriften*, Bd. 4, edited by Königlich Preußische Akademie der Wissenschaften, 385–463. Berlin: Georg Reimer, 1911.

Handschriftlicher Nachlaß: Logik. Bd. 16 of *Kant's gesammelte Schriften*, edited by Königlich Preußische Akademie der Wissenschaften. Berlin: Georg Reimer, 1914.

"Idee zu einer allgemeinen Geschichte in weltbürgerlicher Absicht." In *Abhandlungen nach 1781*, Bd. 8 of *Kant's gesammelte Schriften*, edited by Königlich Preußische Akademie der Wissenschaften, 15–31. Berlin: Georg Reimer, 1912.

Immanuel Kant's Logik: Ein Handbuch zu Vorlesungen. In *Kant's gesammelte Schriften*, Bd. 9, edited by Königlich Preußische Akademie der Wissenschaften, 1–150. Berlin: de Gruyter, 1923. Translated by J. Michael Young as "The Jäsche Logic," in *Lectures on Logic*, translated and edited by J. Michael Young (Cambridge: Cambridge University Press, 1992), 521–640.

Immanuel Kants physische Geographie. In *Kant's gesammelte Schriften*, Bd. 9, edited by Königlich Preußische Akademie der Wissenschaften, 151–436. Berlin: de Gruyter, 1923.

Kritik der praktischen Vernunft. In *Kant's gesammelte Schriften*, Bd. 5, edited by Königlich Preußische Akademie der Wissenschaften, 1–163. Berlin: Georg Reimer, 1913. Translated by Mary J. Gregor as *Critique of Practical Reason*, in *Practical Philosophy*, translated and edited by Mary J. Gregor (Cambridge: Cambridge University Press, 1996), 133–272. Another translation used in this volume is *Critique of Practical Reason*, translated by Werner S. Pluhar (Indianapolis: Hackett, 1987).

Kritik der reinen Vernunft (1. Auflage). In *Kant's gesammelte Schriften*, Bd. 4, edited by Königlich Preußische Akademie der Wissenschaften, 1–252. Berlin: Georg Reimer, 1911. Translated by Paul Guyer and Allen W. Wood as *Critique of Pure Reason*, edited by Paul Guyer and Allen W. Wood (Cambridge: Cambridge University Press, 1998). Also translated by Werner S. Pluhar as *Critique of Pure Reason* (Indianapolis: Hackett, 1996).

Kritik der Urtheilskraft. In *Kant's gesammelte Schriften*, Bd. 5, edited by Königlich Preußische Akademie der Wissenschaften, 165–485. Berlin: Georg Reimer, 1913. Translated by Werner Pluhar as *Critique of Judgment* (Indianapolis:

Hackett, 1987). Translated by James Creed Meredith as *Critique of Judgment*, edited and revised by Nicolas Walker (Oxford: Oxford University Press, 1952). Translated by Paul Guyer and Eric Matthews as *Critique of the Power of Judgment*, edited by Paul Guyer (Cambridge: Cambridge University Press, 2000).

Lectures on Ethics. Translated by Louis Infield. London: Methuen, 1930.

Lectures on the Philosophical Doctrine of Religion. In *Religion and Rational Theology*, translated and edited by Allen W. Wood and George di Giovanni, 335–451. Cambridge: Cambridge University Press, 1996.

Lectures on Philosophical Theology. Translated by Alan W. Wood and Gertrude M. Clark. Ithaca, NY: Cornell University Press, 1978.

Metaphysical Foundations of Natural Science. Edited and translated by Michael Friedman. Cambridge: Cambridge University Press, 2004.

Metaphysical Foundations of Natural Science. In *Theoretical Philosophy after 1781*, edited by Henry E. Allison and Peter Heath, 171–270. Cambridge: Cambridge University Press, 2002.

Metaphysical Foundations of Natural Science. Translated by James Ellington. Indianapolis: Bobbs-Merrill, 1970.

"Metaphysik Dohna." In *Vorlesungen über Metaphysik und Rationaltheologie*, Bd. 28 of *Kant's gesammelte Schriften*, edited by Deutsche Akademie der Wissenschaften zu Berlin, 615–702. Berlin: de Gruyter, 1970.

"Metaphysik L_1." In *Vorlesungen über Metaphysik und Rationaltheologie*, Bd. 28 of *Kant's gesammelte Schriften*, edited by Deutsche Akademie der Wissenschaften zu Berlin, 167–350. Berlin: de Gruyter, 1968. Translated by Karl Ameriks and Steve Naragon as "Metaphysics L_1," in *Lectures on Metaphysics*, edited by Karl Ameriks and Steve Naragon (Cambridge: Cambridge University Press, 1997), 17–106.

"Metaphysik L_2." In *Lectures on Metaphysics*, translated and edited by Karl Ameriks and Steve Naragon, 297–354. Cambridge: Cambridge University Press, 1997.

"Metaphysik Mrongovius." In *Kant's Vorlesungen: Ergänzungen*, Bd. 29 of *Kant's gesammelte Schriften*, edited by Akademie der Wissenschaften der DDR, 743–940. Berlin: de Gruyter, 1983.

"Metaphysik Volckmann." In *Lectures on Metaphysics*, trans. and ed. Karl Ameriks and Steve Naragon, 287–96. Cambridge: Cambridge University Press, 1997.

"Moral Mrongovius." In *Vorlesungen über Moralphilosophie*, Bd. 27 of *Kant's gesammelte Schriften*, edited by Akademie der Wissenschaften der DDR, 1395–581. Berlin: de Gruyter, 1979.

"Moralphilosophie Collins." In *Vorlesungen über Moralphilosophie*, Bd. 27 of *Kant's gesammelte Schriften*, edited by Akademie der Wissenschaften der DDR, 237–471. Berlin: de Gruyter, 1974.

"Mutmaßlicher Anfang der Menschengeschichte." In *Abhandlungen nach 1781*, Bd. 8 of *Kant's gesammelte Schriften*, edited by Königlich Preußische Akademie der Wissenschaften, 107–23. Berlin: Georg Reimer, 1912. Translated by Allen W.

Wood as "Conjectural Beginnings of Human History," in *Anthropology, History, and Education*, edited by Günter Zöller and Robert B. Louden (Cambridge: Cambridge University Press, 2007), 160–75.

"Naturrecht Feyerabend." In *Vorlesungen über Moralphilosophie*, Bd. 27 of *Kant's gesammelte Schriften*, edited by Akademie der Wissenschaften der DDR, 1319–94. Berlin: de Gruyter, 1979.

"A Note to Physicians." In *Anthropology, History, and Education*, edited by Robert B. Louden and Günter Zöller, translated by Günter Zöller, 105–6. Cambridge: Cambridge University Press, 2007.

"Notes on Moral Philosophy." In *Notes and Fragments*, edited and translated by Paul Guyer, translated by Curtis Bowman and Frederick Rauscher, 405–78. Cambridge: Cambridge University Press, 2005.

Observations on the Feeling of the Beautiful and Sublime. In *Observations on the Feeling of the Beautiful and Sublime and Other Writings*, edited by Patrick Frierson and Paul Guyer, 9–62. Cambridge: Cambridge University Press, 2011.

"On the Philosophers' Medicine of the Body." In *Anthropology, History, and Education*, edited by Robert B. Louden and Günter Zöller, translated by Mary Gregor, 182–91. Cambridge: Cambridge University Press, 2007.

Opus postumum. Bd. 22 of *Kant's gesammelte Schriften*, edited by Preußische Akademie der Wissenschaften. Berlin: de Gruyter, 1938. Translated by Eckhart Förster and Michael Rosen as *Opus postumum*, edited by Eckart Förster (Cambridge: Cambridge University Press, 1993).

Pädagogik. In *Kant's gesammelte Schriften*, Bd. 9, edited by Königlich Preußische Akademie der Wissenschaften, 437–99. Berlin: Walter de Gruyter, 1923.

Practical Philosophy. Translated and edited by Mary J. Gregor. Cambridge: Cambridge University Press, 1996.

"Proclamation of the Imminent Conclusion of a Treaty of Perpetual Peace in Philosophy." In *Theoretical Philosophy after 1781*, edited by Henry E. Allison and Peter Heath, 451–60. Cambridge: Cambridge University Press, 2002.

"Recension von Moscatis Schrift: Von dem körperlichen wesentlichen Unterschiede zwischen der Structur der Thiere und Menschen." In *Vorkritische Schriften II: 1757–1777*, Bd. 2 of *Kant's gesammelte Schriften*, edited by Königlich Preußische Akademie der Wissenschaften, 421–25. Berlin: Georg Reimer, 1912.

"Reflexionen zur Anthropologie." In *Kant's Handschriftlicher Nachlaß: Anthropologie*, Bd. 15 of *Kant's gesammelte Schriften*, edited by Berlin-Brandenburgische Akademie der Wissenschaften, 55–654. Berlin: Georg Reimer, 1913.

"Reflexionen zur Metaphysik." In *Handschriftlicher Nachlaß: Metaphysik Erster Teil*, Bd. 17 of *Kant's gesammelte Schriften*, edited by Preußische Akademie der Wissenschaften, 227–745. Berlin: de Gruyter, 1926.

"Reflexionen zur Metaphysik." In *Handschriftlicher Nachlaß: Metaphysik Zweiter Teil*, Bd. 18 of *Kant's gesammelte Schriften*, edited by Preußische Akademie der Wissenschaften, 3–725. Berlin: de Gruyter, 1928.

"Reflexionen zur Moralphilosophie." In *Handschriftlicher Nachlaß: Moralphilosophie, Rechtsphilosophie und Religionsphilosophie*, Bd. 19 of *Kant's gesammelte Schriften*, edited by Preußische Akademie der Wissenschaften, 92–317. Berlin: de Gruyter, 1934.

"Reflexionen zur Rechtsphilosophie." In *Handschriftlicher Nachlaß: Moralphilosophie, Rechtsphilosophie und Religionsphilosophie*, Bd. 19 of *Kant's gesammelte Schriften*, edited by Preußische Akademie der Wissenschaften, 442–613. Berlin: de Gruyter, 1934.

"Reflexionen zur Religionsphilosophie." In *Handschriftlicher Nachlaß: Moralphilosophie, Rechtsphilosophie und Religionsphilosophie*, Bd. 19 of *Kant's gesammelte Schriften*, edited by Preußische Akademie der Wissenschaften, 616–54. Berlin: de Gruyter, 1934.

Religion Within the Boundaries of Mere Reason. In *Religion and Rational Theology*, translated and edited by Allen Wood and George di Giovanni, 39–215. Cambridge: Cambridge University Press, 1996.

"Thoughts on the True Estimation of Living Forces and Assessment of the Demonstrations That Leibniz and Other Scholars of Mechanics Have Made Use of in This Controversial Subject, Together with Some Prefatory Considerations Pertaining to the Force of Bodies in General." In *Natural Science*, edited by Eric Watsons, translated by Jeffrey B. Edwards and Martin Schönfeld, 1–155. Cambridge: Cambridge University Press, 2012.

Träume eines Geistersehers, erläutert durch Träume der Metaphysik. In *Vorkritische Schriften II: 1757–1777*, Bd. 2 of *Kant's gesammelte Schriften*, edited by Königlich Preußische Akademie der Wissenschaften, 315–72. Berlin: Georg Reimer, 1912. Translated as "Dreams of a Spirit-Seer Elucidated by Dreams of Metaphysics," in *Theoretical Philosophy, 1755–1770*, translated and edited by David Walford, with Ralf Meerbote (Cambridge: Cambridge University Press, 2002), 301–59.

"Über den Gebrauch teleologischer Principien in der Philosophie." In *Abhandlungen nach 1781*, Bd. 8 of *Kant's gesammelte Schriften*, edited by Königlich Preußische Akademie der Wissenschaften, 157–84. Berlin: Georg Reimer, 1912.

"Über den Gemeinspruch: Das mag in der Theorie richtig sein, taugt aber nicht für die Praxis." In *Abhandlungen nach 1781*, Bd. 8 of *Kant's gesammelte Schriften*, edited by Königlich Preußische Akademie der Wissenschaften, 273–313. Berlin: Georg Reimer, 1912.

Universal Natural History and Theory of the Heavens. In *Natural Science*, edited by Eric Watkins, translated by Olaf Reinhardt, 182–308. Cambridge: Cambridge University Press, 2012.

"The Vienna Logic." In *Lectures on Logic*, translated and edited by J. Michael Young, 249–378. Cambridge: Cambridge University Press, 1992.

Von den verschiedenen Racen der Menschen. In *Vorkritische Schriften II: 1757–1777*, Bd. 2 of *Kant's gesammelte Schriften*, edited by Königlich Preußische Akademie der Wissenschaften, 427–43. Berlin: Georg Reimer, 1912. Translated as "Of the Different Human Races: An Announcement for Lectures in Physical Geography in the Summer Semester 1775," in *Kant and the Concept of Race: Late Eighteenth-Century Writings*, edited by Jon H. Mikkelsen (Albany: State University of New York Press, 2013), 41–54.

"Vorarbeiten zu *Die Metaphysik der Sitten*." In *Handschriftlicher Nachlaß: Vorarbeiten und Nachträge*, Bd. 23 of *Kant's gesammelte Schriften*, edited by Deutsche Akademie der Wissenschaften zu Berlin, 207–370. Berlin: de Gruyter, 1955.

"Vorarbeiten zu 'Über den Gemeinspruch: Das mag in der Theorie richtig sein, taugt aber nicht für die Praxis.'" In *Handschriftlicher Nachlaß: Vorarbeiten und Nachträge*, Bd. 23 of *Kant's gesammelte Schriften*, edited by Deutsche Akademie der Wissenschaften zu Berlin, 125–44. Berlin: de Gruyter, 1955.

"Wiener Logik." In *Vorlesungen über Logik*, Bd. 24 of *Kant's gesammelte Schriften*, edited by Akademie der Wissenschaften, 790–940. Berlin: de Gruyter, 1966. Translated by J. Michael Young as "The Vienna Logic," in *Lectures on Logic*, translated and edited by J. Michael Young (Cambridge: Cambridge University Press, 199), 249–378.

Zum Ewigen Frieden. In *Abhandlungen nach 1781*, Bd. 8 of *Kant's gesammelte Schriften*, edited by Königlich Preußische Akademie der Wissenschaften, 341–86. Berlin: Georg Reimer, 1912.

"Zweiter Anhang: Medicin." In *Handschriftlicher Nachlaß: Anthropologie*, Bd. 15 of *Kant's gesammelte Schriften*, edited by Berlin-Brandenburgische Akademie der Wissenschaften, 937–80. Berlin: Georg Reimer, 1913.

Bibliography

Addison, Joseph, and Richard Steele. *Addison and Steele: Selections from "The Tatler" and "The Spectator."* Edited by Robert J. Allen. New York: Holt, Rinehart, and Winston, 1970.

Adickes, Erich. "Einleitung in die Abtheilung des handschriftlichen Nachlasses." In Bd. 4 of *Kant's gesammelte Schriften*, edited by Königlich Preußische Akademie der Wissenschaften, xv–lxii. Berlin: Georg Reimer, 1911.

Adorno, Theodor W. *Gesammelte Schriften*. Vol. 7, *Ästhetische Theorie*, edited by Rolf Tiedemann. Frankfurt a. M.: Suhrkamp, 1972.

Allison, Henry E. *Kant's Theory of Taste: A Reading of the "Critique of Aesthetic Judgment."* Cambridge: Cambridge University Press, 2001.

Aquinas, St. Thomas. *The Disputed Questions on Truth*. Vol. 1, *Questions I–IX*, translated by Robert W. Mulligan. Chicago: Henry Regnery, 1952.

———. *Summa contra gentiles*. Book 4, *Salvation*, translated with an introduction and notes by Charles J. O'Neil. Notre Dame, IN: University of Notre Dame Press, 1975.

———. *Summa theologiae*. Vol. 4, *Knowledge in God (1a. 14–18)*, edited by Thomas Gornall. Cambridge, UK: Blackfriars, 1964.

Arendt, Hannah. *Lectures on Kant's Political Philosophy*. Edited by Ronald Beiner. Chicago: University of Chicago Press, 1982.

Armstrong, Meg. " 'The Effects of Blackness': Gender, Race, and the Sublime in Aesthetic Theories of Burke and Kant." *Journal of Aesthetics and Art Criticism* 54, no. 3 (1996): 213–36.

Arnoldt, Daniel Heinrich. *Versuch einer systematischen Anleitung zur Deutschen Poesie überhaupt*. Königsberg: Johann Stelter, 1732.

Augustine. *On Free Choice of the Will*. Translated by A. S. Benjamin and L. H. Hackstaff. Indianapolis: Bobbs-Merrill, 1964.

Baedke, Jan. *Above the Gene, Beyond Biology: Toward a Philosophy of Epigenetics*. Pittsburgh: University of Pittsburgh Press, 2018.

Baumgarten, Alexander. *Aesthetica*. 2 vols. Frankfurt a. d. Oder: Johannis Christian Kleyb, 1750/1758.

———. *Ästhetik*. Translated by Dagmar Mirbach. Hamburg: Felix Meiner Verlag, 2007.

———. *Metaphysik*. Edited by Dagmar Mirbach. Translated by Georg Friedrich Meier. Jena: Dietrich Scheglmann Reprints, 2004.

———. *Metaphysics: A Critical Translation with Kant's Elucidations, Selected Notes, and Related Materials*. Edited and translated by Courtney D. Fugate and John Hymers. London: Bloomsbury, 2013.

———. *Reflections on Poetry*. Translated by Karl Aschenbrenner and William B. Holther. Berkeley: University of California Press, 1954.

Beiser, Frederick. *Diotima's Children: German Aesthetic Rationalism from Leibniz to Lessing*. Oxford: Oxford University Press, 2009.

———. *Schiller as Philosopher: A Re-examination*. Oxford: Oxford University Press, 2005.

Bernasconi, Robert. "Kant and Blumenbach's Polyps: A Neglected Chapter in the History of the Concept of Race." In *German Invention of Race*, edited by Sara Eigen and Mark Joseph Larrimore, 73–89. Albany: State University of New York Press, 2012.

———, ed. *Race*. Oxford: Blackwell, 2001.

Boerhaave, Herman. *Phisiologie*. Translated by Johann Peter Eberhard. Halle: Renger, 1754.

Bouchard, Frédéric, and Philippe Huneman, eds. *From Groups to Individuals: Evolution and Emerging Individuality*. Cambridge, MA: MIT Press, 2013.

Brady, Emily. "The Environmental Sublime." In *The Sublime: From Antiquity to the Present*, edited by Timothy Costelloe, 171–82. Cambridge: Cambridge University Press, 2012.

Breitenbach, Angela. "Kant on Biology and the Experience of Life." In *Kant und die Philosophie in weltbürgerlicher Absicht: Akten des XI. Kant-Kongresses 2010*, edited by Margit Ruffing, Claudio La Rocca, Alfredo Ferrarin, and Stefano Bacin, 19–29. Berlin: de Gruyter, 2013.

———. "Laws in Biology and the Unity of Nature." In *Kant and the Laws of Nature*, edited by Michela Massimi and Angela Breitenbach, 237–55. Cambridge: Cambridge University Press, 2017.

Brown, John. *The Elements of Medicine; or, A Translation of the Elementa Medicinae Brunonis*. Vol. 1. London: J. Johnson, 1788.

Buchenau, Stefanie. *The Founding of Aesthetics in the German Enlightenment*. Cambridge: Cambridge University Press, 2013.

Budd, Malcolm. "Delight in the Natural World: Kant on the Aesthetic Appreciation of Nature, Part III, The Sublime in Nature." *British Journal of Aesthetics* 38, no. 3 (1998): 233–51.

Burke, Edmund. *A Philosophical Enquiry into the Origin of Our Ideas of the Sublime and Beautiful*. London: R. and J. Dodsley, 1757.

———. *A Philosophical Enquiry into the Origins of Our Ideas of the Sublime and Beautiful*. Edited by Adam Philips. Oxford: Oxford University Press, 1990.

———. *Reflections on the Revolution in France*. New York: Oxford University Press, 1999.

Burnham, Douglas. "Immanuel Kant: Aesthetics." *Internet Encyclopedia of Philosophy*. Accessed January 19, 2019. https://www.iep.utm.edu/kantaest/#SH2c.

Cassirer, Ernst. *Kant's Life and Thought*. Translated by James Haden. New Haven, CT: Yale University Press, 1981.

———. *Substance and Function*. Chicago: Dover, 1923.

Caygill, Howard. *Art of Judgment*. Cambridge: Cambridge University Press, 1989.

———. "Life and Aesthetic Pleasure." In *The Matter of Critique: Readings in Kant's Philosophy*, edited by Andrea Rehberg and Rachel Jones, 79–92. Manchester: Clinamen, 2000.

Chaouli, Michel. "A Surfeit in Thinking: Kant's Aesthetic Ideas." *Yearbook of Comparative Literature* 57 (2011): 55–77.

Choi, Yoon H., and Alix Cohen. "Feeling and Life in Kant's Account of the Beautiful and the Sublime." In *The Concept of Drive in Classical German Philosophy: Between Biology, Anthropology, and Metaphysics*, edited by Manja Kisner and Jörg Noller, 169–89. London: Palgrave Macmillan, 2021.

Clewis, Robert R. *The Kantian Sublime and the Revelation of Freedom*. Cambridge: Cambridge University Press, 2009.

———, ed. *The Sublime Reader*. London: Bloomsbury, 2019.

Cohen, Hermann. *Kants Begründung der Aesthetik*. Saarbrücken: VDM Verlag Dr. Müller, 2007. First published 1889 by Ferdinand Dümmlers (Berlin).

Crowther, Paul. *The Kantian Sublime: From Morality to Art*. Oxford: Clarendon Press, 1989.

Crusius, Christian August. *Entwurf der nothwendigen Vernunft-Wahrheiten*. Leipzig: Gleditschens Buchhandlung, 1766.

Cullen, William. *First Lines of the Practice of Physic*. 4 vols. Edinburgh, 1777–1784.

———. *Grundriss der ärztlichen Praxis für Studenten*. N.p.:1784.

De Boever, Arne, Shirley S. Y. Murray, and Jon Roffe, eds. *Gilbert Simondon: Being and Technology*. Edinburgh: Edinburgh University Press, 2013.

Deleuze, Gilles. *La philosophie critique de Kant*. Paris: Presses Universitaires de France, 2004.

Deligiorgi, Katerina. "How to Feel a Judgment: The Sublime and Its Architectonic Significance." In *Kant and the Faculty of Feeling*, edited by Kelly Sorenson and Diane Williamson, 166–83. Cambridge: Cambridge University Press, 2018.

———. "The Pleasures of Contra-purposiveness: Kant, the Sublime and Being Human." *Journal of Aesthetics and Art Criticism* 72, no. 1 (2014): 25–35.

Doran, Robert. *The Theory of the Sublime from Longinus to Kant*. Cambridge: Cambridge University Press, 2015.

Dyck, Corey. *Kant and Rational Psychology*. New York: Oxford University Press, 2014.

Eigen, Sara, and Mark Joseph Larrimore, eds. *The German Invention of Race*. Albany: State University of New York Press, 2012.

"Eine Übersicht der vornehmsten Erfindungen, Theorien und Systeme in der Arzneykunde, von 1700–1790." In *Des achtzehnten Jahrhunderts Geschichte der Erfindungen, Theorien und Systeme in der Natur- und Arzneywissenschaft*, edited by August Friedrich Hecker, xi–lxxxxi. Gotha: Justus Perthes, 1799.

Ellis, Elizabeth. *Kant's Politics: Provisional Theory for an Uncertain World*. New Haven, CT: Yale University Press, 2005.

Fichte, Johann Gottlieb. *Foundations of Natural Right*. Edited by Frederick Neuhouser. Translated by Michael Bauer. Cambridge: Cambridge University Press, 2000.

———. *Grundlage des Naturrechts nach Prinzipien der Wissenschaftslehre*. In *Fichtes Werke*, vol. 3, *Zur Rechts- und Sittenlehre 1*, edited by Immanuel Hermann Fichte, 1–385. Berlin: de Gruyter, 1971.

———. "Ueber Geist und Buchstab in der Philosophie." In *Fichtes Werke*, vol. 8, *Vermischte Schriften und Aufsätze*, edited by Immanuel Hermann Fichte, 270–300. Berlin: de Gruyter, 1971.

Figal, Günter. *Aesthetics as Phenomenology: The Appearance of Things*. Bloomington: Indiana University Press, 2015.

Flikschuh, Katrin. "Elusive Unity: The General Will in Hobbes and Kant." *Hobbes Studies* 25, no. 1 (2012): 21–42.

———. *Kant and Modern Political Philosophy*. Cambridge: Cambridge University Press, 2000.

Forsey, Jane. "Is a Theory of the Sublime Possible?" *Journal of Aesthetics and Art Criticism* 56, no. 4 (2007): 381–89.

Förster, Eckart. *Kant's Final Synthesis: An Essay on the "Opus postumum."* Cambridge, MA: Harvard University Press, 2000.

Foucault, Michel. *Essential Works, 1954–1984*. Vol. 1, *Ethics, Subjectivity and Truth*, edited by Paul Rabinow. New York: New Press, 1997.

Frierson, Patrick. *Kant's Empirical Psychology*. Cambridge: Cambridge University Press, 2014.

———. "A New Sort of *A Priori* Principles: Psychological Taxonomies and the Origin of the Third *Critique*." In *Kant and the Faculty of Feeling*, edited by Kelly Sorensen and Diane Williamson, 107–29. Cambridge: Cambridge University Press, 2018.

Fugate, Courtney. D. "Life and Kant's 'Critique of Aesthetic Judgment.'" In *Recht und Frieden in der Philosophie Kants: Akten des X. Internationalen Kant-Kongresses*, edited by Valerio Rohden, Ricardo R. Terra, Guido Antonio de Almeida, and Margit Ruffing, 609–21. Berlin: de Gruyter, 2008.

———. *The Teleology of Reason*. Berlin: de Gruyter, 2014.

Gadamer, Hans-Georg. "Artworks in Word and Image." *Theory, Culture and Society* 23, no. 1 (1992): 57–83.

———. *Truth and Method.* Translated by Joel Weinsheimer and Donald G. Marshall. New York: Continuum, 1995.

———. *Wahrheit und Methode: Grundzüge einer philosophischen Hermeneutik.* Bd. 1 of *Gesammelte Werke.* Tübingen: Mohr Siebeck, 1986.

Gasché, Rodolphe. *The Idea of Form: Rethinking Kant's Aesthetics.* Stanford, CA: Stanford University Press, 2003.

———. *Persuasion, Reflection, Judgment: Ancillae Vitae.* Bloomington: Indiana University Press, 2017.

Gentz, Friedrich von. *Betrachtungen über die französische Revolution: Nach dem Englischen des Herrn Burke neu bearbeitet.* Berlin: F. Vieweg, 1793.

———. *Gesammelte Schriften.* Bd. 6 of *Übersetzungen, Einleitungen und Kommentare,* edited by Günther Kronenbitter. Zurich: Olms-Weidmann, 1998.

Ginsborg, Hannah. "Kant on Understanding Organisms as Natural Purposes." In *Kant and the Sciences,* edited by Eric Watkins, 231–58. Oxford: Oxford University Press, 2001.

———. *The Normativity of Nature: Essays on Kant's "Critique of Judgement."* Oxford: Oxford University Press, 2014.

———. "Primitive Normativity and Skepticism about Rules." *Journal of Philosophy* 108, no. 5 (2011): 227–54.

———. "Two Kinds of Mechanical Inexplicability in Kant and Aristotle." *Journal of the History of Philosophy* 42, no. 1 (2004): 33–65.

Giomario, Patrick. "'Making Reason Think More': Laughter in Kant's Aesthetic Philosophy." *Angelaki* 22, no. 4 (2017): 161–76.

Goethe, Johann Wolfgang von. "The Influence of Modern Philosophy." In *Goethe: Scientific Studies,* edited and translated by Douglas Miller, 28–30. New York: Suhrkamp, 1988.

Goy, Ina. *Kants Theorie der Biologie: Ein Kommentar, eine Lesart, eine historische Einordnung.* Berlin: de Gruyter, 2017.

Goy, Ina, and Eric Watkins, eds. *Kant's Theory of Biology.* Berlin: de Gruyter, 2014.

Green, Jonathan Allen. "Burke's German Readers at the End of the Enlightenment, 1790–1815." PhD diss., University of Cambridge, 2017.

———. "Friedrich Gentz's Translation of Burke's *Reflections.*" *Historical Journal* 57, no. 3 (2014): 639–59.

Gregor, Mary J. Introduction to "On the Philosophers' Medicine of the Body." In *Kant's Latin Writings,* edited by Lewis White Beck, 195–203. New York: Peter Lang, 1986.

Grier, Michelle. "Kant and the Feeling of Sublimity." In *Kant on Emotion and Value,* edited by Alix Cohen, 245–64. London: Palgrave Macmillan, 2014.

Grosz, Elizabeth. "Matter, Life, and Other Variations." *Philosophy Today* 55 (2011): 17–27.

Gruner, Christian Gottfried. "Systemsucht ist unser Verderben." *Almanach für Aerzte und Nichtaerzte auf das Jahr 1792* 11 (1792): 233–50.

Guichet, Jean-Luc. *Rousseau, l'animal et l'homme: L'animalité dans l'horizon anthropologique des Lumières*. Paris: Le Cerf, 2006.

Guyer, Paul. "Beauty, Freedom, and Morality: Kant's *Lectures on Anthropology* and the Development of his Aesthetic Theory." In *Essays on Kant's Anthropology*, edited by Brian Jacobs and Patrick Kain, 135–63. Cambridge: Cambridge University Press, 2003.

———. "Feeling and Freedom: Kant on Aesthetics and Morality." *Journal of Aesthetics and Art Criticism* 48, no. 2 (1990): 137–46.

———. "From Nature to Morality: Kant's New Argument in the 'Critique of Teleological Judgment.'" In *Kant's System of Nature and Freedom*, 314–42. Oxford: Oxford University Press, 2005.

———. *A History of Modern Aesthetics*. Vol. 1, *The Eighteenth Century*. Cambridge: Cambridge University Press, 2014.

———. Introduction to *Notes and Fragments*, by Immanuel Kant, xiii–xxviii. Edited and translated by Paul Guyer. Translated by Curtis Bowman and Frederick Rauscher. Cambridge: Cambridge University Press, 2005.

———. *Kant and the Claims of Taste*. Cambridge, MA: Harvard University Press, 1979.

———. *Kant and the Experience of Freedom*. Cambridge: Cambridge University Press, 1996.

———. "Kant's Aesthetics in His Lectures on Metaphysics." In *Kant's "Lectures on Metaphysics": A Critical Guide*, edited by Courtney D. Fugate, 156–78. Cambridge: Cambridge University Press, 2018.

———, ed. *Kant's Critique of the Power of Judgment: Critical Essays*. Lanham, MD: Rowman and Littlefield, 2003.

———. *Kant's System of Nature and Freedom*. Oxford: Oxford University Press, 2005.

Hadot, Pierre. *Philosophy as a Way of Life: Spiritual Exercises from Socrates to Foucault*. Edited by Arnold Davidson. Malden, MA: Wiley-Blackwell, 1995.

Hamawaki, Arata. "Kant on Beauty and the Normative Force of Feeling." *Philosophical Topics* 34, nos. 1/2 (2006): 107–44.

Hegel, Georg Wilhelm Friedrich. "Das älteste Systemprogramm des deutschen Idealismus." In *Jenaer Schriften*, Bd. 1 of *Werke in zwanzig Bänden*, edited by Eva Moldenhauer and Karl Markus Michel, 234–36. Frankfurt a. M.: Suhrkamp, 1971.

———. *The Encyclopaedia Logic*. Translated by Theodore F. Geraets, W. A. Suchting, and H. S. Harris. Indianapolis: Hackett, 1991.

———. *Faith and Knowledge*. Translated and edited by Walter Cerf and H. S. Harris. Albany: State University of New York Press, 1977.

———. "Systemfragment von 1800." In *Jenaer Schriften*, Bd. 1 of *Werke in zwanzig Bänden*, edited by Eva Moldenhauer and Karl Markus Michel, 419–27. Frankfurt a. M.: Suhrkamp, 1971.

———. *Vorlesungen über die Ästhetik 1*. Bd. 13 of *Werke in zwanzig Bänden*, edited by Eva Moldenhauer and Karl Markus Michel. Frankfurt a. M.: Suhrkamp, 1986.

———. *Vorlesungen über die Ästhetik 1*. Bd. 12 of *Sämtliche Werke*, edited by Hermann Glockner. Stuttgart: Frommann-Holzboog, 1988.

Herder, Johann Gottfried. *Outlines of a Philosophy of the History of Man*. Translated by T. Churchill. New York: Bergman, 1966.

Höffe, Otfried, ed. *Immanuel Kant: Kritik der Urteilskraft*. Berlin: de Gruyter, 2018.

Hölderlin, Friedrich. "An den Bruder, Homburg, 31 Dezember 1798." In *Sämtliche Werke und Briefe in drei Bänden*, Bd. 2, edited by Michael Knaupp, 723–30. Munich: Hanser Verlag, 1992.

———. "To Karl Christoph Friedrich Gok, January 1799," 1. In *Sämtliche Werke und Briefe in drei Bänden*, Bd. 2, edited by Michael Knaupp, 726. Munich: Hanser Verlag, 1992.

———. "Wenn der Dichter einmal des Geistes mächtig ist." In *Sämtliche Werke und Briefe in drei Bänden*, Bd. 2, edited by Michael Knaupp, 77–78. Munich: Hanser Verlag, 1992.

Hounsokou, Annie. " 'Exposing the Rogue in Us': An Exploration of Laughter in the *Critique of Judgment*." *Epoché* 16, no. 2 (2012): 317–36.

Hufeland, Christoph Wilhelm. *Die Kunst das menschliche Leben zu verlängern*. Vienna: Franz Haas, 1797.

Huneman, Philippe. "Reflexive Judgement and Wolffian Embryology: Kant's Shift between the First and the Third *Critiques*." In *Understanding Purpose? Kant and the Philosophy of Biology*, edited by Philippe Huneman, 75–100. Rochester, NY: University of Rochester Press, 2007.

Huseyinzadegan, Dilek. *Kant's Nonideal Theory of Politics*. Chicago: Northwestern University Press, 2019.

Iltis, Carolyn. "Leibniz and the *Vis Viva* Controversy." *Isis* 62, no. 1 (1971): 21–35.

Kielmeyer, Carl Friedrich. "Entwurf zu einer vergleichenden Zoologie." In *Gesammelte Schriften*, edited by Fritz-Heinz Holler, 13–29. Berlin: W. Keiper, 1938.

————. "Ideen zu einer allgemeineren Geschichte und Theorie der Entwicklungserscheinungen der Organisationen." In *Gesammelte Schriften*, edited by Fritz-Heinz Holler, 102–94. Berlin: W. Keiper, 1938.

———. *Über die Verhältnisse der organischen Kräfte untereinander in der Reihe der verschiedenen Organisationen*. In *Gesammelte Schriften*, edited by Fritz-Heinz Holler, 59–102. Berlin: W. Keiper, 1938.

Kleingeld, Pauline. *Kant and Cosmopolitanism: The Philosophic Ideal of World Citizenship*. Cambridge: Cambridge University Press, 2012.

———. "The Philosophical Status of Gender-Neutral Language in the History of Philosophy: The Case of Kant." *Philosophical Forum* 25, no. 2 (1993): 134–50.

Kuehn, Manfred. *Scottish Common Sense in Germany, 1768–1800: A Contribution to the History of Critical Philosophy*. Kingston, ON: McGill-Queen's University Press, 1987.

Kukla, Rebecca. "Introduction: Placing the Aesthetic in Kant's Critical Epistemology." In *Aesthetics and Cognition in Kant's Critical Philosophy*, edited by Rebekka Kukla, 1–32. Cambridge: Cambridge University Press, 2010.

Laertius, Diogenes. *Lives of Eminent Philosophers*. Vol. 2, edited by Robert D. Hicks. Cambridge: Harvard University Press, 1925.

Larrimore, Mark. "The Sublime Waste: Kant on the Destiny of the Races." *Canadian Journal of Philosophy* 29, no. 1 (1999): 99–125.

Lebrun, Gérard. *Kant et la fin de la métaphysique*. Paris: Armand Colin, 1970.

Leibniz, Gottfried Wilhelm. "A Brief Demonstration of a Notable Error of Descartes and Others Concerning a Natural Law." In *Philosophical Papers and Letters*, edited by Leroy E. Loemker, 296–302. Dodrecht: Kluwer, 1989.

Lloyd, David. *Under Representation: The Racial Regime of Aesthetics*. New York: Fordham University Press, 2019.

Löw, Reinhardt. *Philosophie des Lebendigen: Der Begriff des Organischen bei Kant, sein Grund und seine Aktualität*. Frankfurt a. M.: Suhrkamp, 1980.

Longuenesse, Béatrice. *Kant and the Capacity to Judge: Sensibility and Discursivity in the Transcendental Analytic of the "Critique of Pure Reason."* Translated by Charles T. Wolfe. Princeton, NJ: Princeton University Press, 1998.

López, María del Rosario Acosta. "Beauty as an Encounter between Freedom and Nature: A Romantic Interpretation of Kant's *Critique of Judgment*." *Epoché* 12, no. 1 (2007): 63–92.

Lüthe, Rudolf. "Kants Lehre von den ästhetische Ideen." *Kant-Studien* 75, no. 1 (1984): 58–77.

Lyotard, Jean-François. "Answering the Question: What Is Postmodernism?" In *The Postmodern Condition*, translated by Regis Durand, 71–82. Minneapolis: University of Minnesota Press, 1984.

———. *Enthusiasm: The Kantian Critique of History*. Translated by Georges Van den Abbeele. Stanford, CA: Stanford University Press, 2009.

———. *Leçons sur l'analytique du sublime*. Paris: Galilée, 1991.

———. *Lessons on the Analytic of the Sublime*. Translated by Elizabeth Rottenberg. Stanford, CA: Stanford University Press, 1994.

Makkai, Katalin. *Kant's Critique of Taste: The Feeling of Life*. Cambridge: Cambridge University Press, 2021.

Makkreel, Rudolf A. "Baumgarten and Kant on Clarity, Distinctness, and the Differentiation of Our Mental Powers." In *Baumgarten and Kant on Metaphysics*, edited by Courtney D. Fugate and John Hymers, 94–109. Oxford: Oxford University Press, 2018.

———. *Imagination and Interpretation in Kant: The Hermeneutical Import of the "Critique of Judgment."* Chicago: University of Chicago Press, 1990.

———. "Kant on Cognition, Comprehension, and Knowledge." In *Natur und Freiheit: Akten des 12. Kant-Kongresses*, edited by Violetta L. Waibel, Margit Ruffing, and David Wagner, 1297–304. Berlin: de Gruyter, 2018.

———. "Kant on the Scientific Status of Psychology, Anthropology, and History." In *Kant and the Sciences*, edited by Eric Watkins, 185–201. Oxford: Oxford University Press, 2001.

———. *Orientation and Judgment in Hermeneutics*. Chicago: University of Chicago Press, 2015.

———. "Sublimity, Genius and the Explication of Aesthetic Ideas." In *Kants Ästhetik/Kant's Aesthetics/L'esthétique de Kant*, edited by Herman Parret, 615–29. Berlin: de Gruyter, 1998.

Malabou, Catherine. *Before Tomorrow: Epigenesis and Rationality*. Translated by Carolyn Shread. Cambridge, UK: Polity, 2016.

Marwah, Inder S. "Bridging Nature and Freedom? Kant, Culture, and Cultivation." *Social Theory and Practice* 38, no. 3 (2012): 385–406.

Matherne, Samantha. "Imagining Freedom: Kant on Symbols of Sublimity." In *The Idea of Freedom: New Essays on the Kantian Theory of Freedom*, edited by Dai Heide and Evan Tiffany. Oxford: Oxford University Press, 2023.

———. "Kant's Expressive Theory of Music." *Journal of Aesthetics and Art Criticism* 72, no. 2 (2014): 129–45.

McLaughlin, Peter. "Blumenbach und der Bildungstrieb: Zum Verhältnis von epigenetischer Embryologie und typologischem Artbegriff." *Medizinhistorisches Journal* 17, no. 4 (1982): 357–72.

———. *Kant's Critique of Teleology in Biological Explanation: Antinomy and Teleology*. Lewiston, NY: E. Mellen Press, 1990.

McQuillan, J. Colin. "A Merely Logical Distinction: Kant's Objection to Leibniz and Wolff." *Epoché* 20, no. 2 (2016): 387–405.

———. "Baumgarten, Meier, and Kant on Aesthetic Perfection." In *Kant and His German Contemporaries*. Vol. 2, *Aesthetics, History, Politics, and Religion*, edited by Daniel O. Dahlstrom, 13–27. Cambridge: Cambridge University Press, 2018.

———. "Clarity and Distinctness in Eighteenth-Century Germany: Metaphysics, Logic, Aesthetics." In *Leibniz en dialogo*, edited by Manuel Sanchez and Miguel Escribano, 149–59. Seville: Themata, 2017.

———. *Early Modern Aesthetics*. New York: Rowman and Littlefield, 2015.

———. "Kant, the Science of Aesthetics, and the Critique of Taste." *Kant Yearbook* 9 (2017): 113–32.

———. "Outer Sense, Inner Sense, and Feeling: Hutcheson and Kant on Aesthetic Pleasure." In *Kant and the Scottish Enlightenment*, edited by Elizabeth Robinson and Chris W. Suprenant, 90–107. New York: Routledge, 2017.

Meier, Georg Friedrich. *Anfangsgründe aller schönen Künste und Wissenschaften*. 3 vols. Halle: Carl Hermann Hemmerde, 1748–50.

———. *Georg Friedrich Meiers . . . Vernunftlehre*. Halle: Johann Justinus Gebauer, 1752.

Mendelssohn, Moses. "From 'On the Sublime and Naive in the Fine Sciences.'" In *The Sublime Reader*, edited by Robert R. Clewis, 91–101. London: Bloomsbury, 2019.

Mensch, Jennifer. *Kant's Organicism: Epigenisis and the Development of Critical Philosophy*. Chicago: University of Chicago Press, 2013.

———. "The Poem as Plant: Archetype and Metamorphosis in Goethe and Schlegel." *International Yearbook for Hermeneutics* 13 (2014): 85–106.

Merleau-Ponty, Maurice. *L'oeil et l'esprit*. Paris: Gallimard, 1964.

Moran, Richard. "Kant, Proust, and the Appeal of Beauty." *Critical Inquiry* 38, no. 2 (2012): 298–329.

Moore, Thomas. "Kant's Deduction of the Sublime." *Kantian Review* 23, no. 3 (2018): 349–72.

Mossio, Matteo, ed. *Organization in Biology*. Berlin: Springer, 2023.

Munzel, G. Felicitas. "Character (*Charakter*)." In *The Cambridge Kant Lexicon*, edited by Julian Wuerth, 102–5. Cambridge: Cambridge University Press, 2021.

———. "Cultivating Moral Consciousness: The Quintessential Relation of Practical Reason and Mind (*Gemüt*) as a Bulwark against the Propensity for Radical Evil." *Educational Philosophy and Theory* 51, no. 13 (2019): 1351–60.

———. *Kant's Conception of Moral Character: The "Critical" Link of Morality, Anthropology, and Reflective Judgment*. Chicago: University of Chicago Press, 1999.

———. "Moral Education." In *The Kantian Mind*, edited by Sorin Baiasu and Mark Timmons, ch. 33. Oxfordshire: Routledge, 2021.

———. "Natural Aptitude (*Naturell, Naturanlage*)." In *The Cambridge Kant Lexicon*, edited by Julian Wuerth, 305–307. Cambridge: Cambridge University Press, 2021.

Nehamas, Alexander. *The Art of Living: Socratic Reflections from Plato to Foucault*. Berkeley: University of California Press, 2000.

Nietzsche, Friedrich. *The Gay Science*. Translated by Walter Kaufmann. New York: Vintage, 1974.

Nuzzo, Angelica. *Ideal Embodiment: Kant's Theory of Sensibility*. Bloomington: Indiana University Press, 2008.

———. *Kant and the Unity of Reason*. West Lafayette, IN: Purdue University Press, 2005.

———. "Leben and Leib in Kant and Hegel." *Hegel-Jahrbuch* 2 (2007): 97–101.

Owens, Joseph. *The Doctrine of Being in the Aristotelian "Metaphysics."* Toronto: Pontifical Institute of Mediaeval Studies, 1963.

Oyama, Susan. "Boundaries and (Constructive) Interaction." In *Genes in Development: Re-reading the Molecular Paradigm*, edited by Eva M. Neumann-Held and Christoph Rehmann-Sutter, 272–89. Durham, NC: Duke University Press, 2006.

Papineau, David. "The *Vis Viva* Controversy: Do Meanings Matter?" *Studies in History and Philosophy of Science* 8, no. 2 (1977): 111–42.

Petrarca, Francesco. "The Ascent of Mont Ventoux." In *The Sublime Reader*, edited by Robert R. Clewis, 49–54. London: Bloomsbury, 2019.

Poppe, Bernhard. *Alexander Baumgarten: Seine Bedeutung und Stellung in der Leibniz-Wolffschen Philosophie und seine Beziehungen zu Kant*. Borna-Leipzig: Robert Noske, 1907.

Reidar, Maliks. *Kant's Politics in Context*. Oxford: Oxford University Press, 2015.

Reil, Johann Christian. "Zuschrift: An die Professoren Herrn Gren und Herrn Jakob in Halle." *Archiv für die Physiologie* 1, no. 1 (1795): 3–7.

Richards, Robert. J. *The Romantic Conception of Life: Science in the Age of Goethe*. Chicago: University of Chicago Press, 2002.

Ripstein, Arthur. *Force and Freedom*. Cambridge, MA: Harvard University Press, 2009.

Risse, Guenter B. "Schelling, 'Naturphilosophie' and John Brown's System of Medicine." *Bulletin of the History of Medicine* 50, no. 3 (1976): 321–34.

Ritter, Joachim, and Karlfried Gründer, eds. *Historisches Wörterbuch der Philosophie*. Bd. 5, *L–Mn*. Basel: Schwabe, 1980.

Roosth, Sophia. *Synthetic: How Life Got Made*. Chicago: University of Chicago Press, 2017.

Rousseau, Jean-Jacques. *Oeuvres completes*. Vol. 4, *Emile ou de l'Education*, edited by Bernard Gagnebin and Marcel Raymond. Paris: Gallimard, 1969.

Ryan, Vanessa. "The Physiological Sublime: Burke's Critique of Reason." *Journal of the History of Ideas* 62, no. 2 (2001): 265–79.

Sallis, John. *Kant and the Spirit of Critique*. Bloomington: Indiana University Press, 2020.

———. *Spacings—of Reason and Imagination in Texts of Kant, Fichte, Hegel*. Chicago: University of Chicago Press, 1987.

Schelling, Friedrich Wilhelm Joseph. *Erster Entwurf eines Systems der Naturphilosophie*. In Bd. 3 of *Sämmtliche Werke*, edited by Karl Friedrich August Schelling, 1–268. Stuttgart: Cotta, 1858.

———. *First Outline of a System of the Philosophy of Nature*. Translated by Keith R. Peterson. Albany: State University of New York Press, 2004.

———. *Ideas for a Philosophy of Nature*. Translated by Errol E. Harris and Peter Heath. Cambridge: Cambridge University Press, 1988.

———. *Ideen zu einer Philosophie der Natur*. In *Sämmtliche Werke*, Bd. 2, edited by Karl Friedrich August Schelling, 1–343. Stuttgart: Cotta, 1857.

———. *System des transscendentalen Idealismus*. In *Sämmtliche Werke*, Bd. 3, edited by Karl Friedrich August Schelling, 327–634. Stuttgart: Cotta, 1858.

———. *System of Transcendental Idealism*. Translated by Peter Heath. Charlottesville: University Press of West Virginia, 1978.

———. *Von der Weltseele*. In *Sämmtliche Werke*, Bd. 2, edited by Karl Friedrich August Schelling, 345–583. Stuttgart: Cotta, 1857.

Schmid, Carl Christian Erhard. *Physiologie, philosophisch betrachtet*. Vol. 1. Jena: Akademische Buchhandlung, 1798.

Schmid, Nicolaus Ehrenreich Anton. *Von den Weltkörpern: Zur gemeinnützigen Kenntnis der großen Werke Gottes*. Hannover: Schlüter, 1766.

Schmidt, Dennis J. "Aesthetics and Subjectivity: Subjektivierung der Ästhetik durch die Kantische Kritik." In *Hans-Georg Gadamer: Wahrheit und Methode*, edited by Günter Figal, 29–43. Klassiker Auslegen 30. Berlin: Akademie Verlag, 2007.

———. *Between Word and Image.* Bloomington: Indiana University Press, 2013.

———. "Einige Betrachtungen zu Sprache und Freiheit aus einem hermeneutischen Blickwinkel." In *"Dimensionen des Hermeneutischen": Heidegger und Gadamer*, edited by Günter Figal and Hans-Helmuth Gander, 59–73. Frankfurt a. M.: Klostermann Verlag, 2005.

———. *Idiome der Wahrheit.* Frankfurt a. M.: Klostermann, 2014.

———. *Lyrical and Ethical Subjects.* Albany: State University of New York Press, 2005.

———. "On the Incalculable: Language and Freedom from a Hermeneutic Point of View." *Research in Phenomenology* 34 (2004): 31–44.

———. "Thank Goodness for the Atmosphere." *Research in Phenomenology* 50, no. 3 (2020): 370–85.

Schneewind, Jerome B. *The Invention of Autonomy: A History of Modern Moral Philosophy.* Cambridge: Cambridge University Press, 1998.

Schrader, Astrid. "Responding to *Pfiesteria piscicida* (the Fish Killer): Phantomatic Ontologies, Indeterminacy, and Responsibility in Toxic Microbiology." *Social Studies of Science* 40, no. 2 (2010): 275–306.

Schwaiger, Clemens. *Alexander Gottlieb Baumgarten: Ein intellektuelles Porträt.* Stuttgart: Frommann-Holzboog, 2011.

Schweizer, Hans Rudolf. *Ästhetik als Philosophie der sinnlichen Erkenntnis.* Basel: Schwabe, 1973.

Serequeberhan, Tsenay. "Eurocentrism in Philosophy: The Case of Immanuel Kant." *Philosophical Forum* 27, no. 4 (1996): 333–56.

Shapshay, Sandra. "Contemporary Environmental Aesthetics and the Neglect of the Sublime." *British Journal of Aesthetics* 53, no. 2 (2013): 181–98.

———. "A Theory of Sublime Responses, the Thin and the Thick." In *The Sublime Reader*, edited by Robert R. Clewis, 329–39. London: Bloomsbury, 2019.

Shell, Susan Meld. *The Embodiment of Reason: Kant on Spirit, Generation, and Community.* Chicago: University of Chicago Press, 1996.

———. *Kant and the Limits of Autonomy.* Cambridge, MA: Harvard University Press, 2009.

———. "Kant as 'Vitalist': The 'Principium of Life' in 'Anthropologie Friedländer.' " In *Kant's Lectures on Anthropology: A Critical Guide*, edited by Alix Cohen, 151–71. Cambridge: Cambridge University Press, 2014.

———. " 'Men as They Are and Laws as They Can Be': Legitimacy and the State of Nature in Rousseau and Hobbes." In *The Rousseauian Mind*, edited by Eve Grace and Christopher Kelly, ch. 5. London: Routledge, 2019.

Shell, Susan Meld, and Richard Velkley. "Introduction: Kant as Youthful Observer and Legislator." In *Kant's Observations and Remarks: A Critical Guide*, edited by Susan Meld Shell and Richard Velkley, 1–10. Cambridge: Cambridge University Press, 2012.

Sircello, Guy. "How Is a Theory of the Sublime Possible?" *Journal of Aesthetics and Art Criticism* 51, no. 4 (1993): 541–50.

Sloan, Phillip R. "Preforming the Categories: Eighteenth-Century Generation Theory and the Biological Roots of Kant's *A Priori*." *Journal of the History of Philosophy* 40, no. 2 (2002): 229–53.

Smith, Justin E. H. *Nature, Human Nature, and Human Difference: Race in Early Modern Philosophy*. Princeton, NJ: Princeton University Press, 2016.

Spivak, Gayatri Chakravorty. *A Critique of Postcolonial Reason: Toward a History of the Vanishing Present*. Cambridge, MA: Harvard University Press, 1999.

Sprengel, Kurt. *Kritische Übersicht des Zustandes der Arzneykunde in dem letzten Jahrzehend*. Halle: Johann Jacob Gebauer, 1801.

Steigerwald, Joan. *Experimenting at the Boundaries of Life: Organic Vitality in Germany Around 1800*. Pittsburgh: University of Pittsburgh Press, 2019.

———. "Natural Purposes and the Reflecting Power of Judgment: The Problem of the Organism in Kant's Critical Philosophy." In *Romanticism and Modernity*, edited by Thomas Pfau and Robert Mitchell, 29–46. New York: Routledge, 2011.

Sturm, Thomas. "Kant on Empirical Psychology: How Not to Investigate the Human Mind." In *Kant and the Sciences*, edited by Eric Watkins, 163–84. Oxford: Oxford University Press, 2001.

———. *Kant und die Wissenschaft vom Menschen*. Paderborn: Mentis, 2009.

Sweet, Kristi. *Kant on Freedom, Nature, and Judgment: The Territory of the "Third Critique."* Cambridge: Cambridge University Press, 2023.

———. "Kant and the Culture of Discipline: Rethinking the Nature of Nature." *Epoché* 15, no. 1 (2010): 121–38.

Taminiaux, Jacques. *La nostalgie de la Grèce à l'aube de l'idéalisme allemand: Kant et les Grecs dans l'itinéraire de Schiller, de Hölderlin et de Hegel*. La Haye: Martinus Nijhoff, 1967.

Terrall, Mary. "*Vis Viva* Revisited." *History of Science* 42 (2004): 189–209.

Thiery, Francois. *Erfahrungen in der Arzneywissenschaft*. Leipzig: Adam Friedrich Böhme, 1778.

Todorov, Tzvetan. *Theories of the Symbol*. Translated by Catherine Porter. Ithaca, NY: Cornell University Press, 1982.

Tonnelli, Giorgio. "La formazione del testo della *Kritik der Urteilskraft*." *Revue internationale de philosophie* 8, no. 30 (1954): 423–48.

Treviranus, Gottfried Reinhold. *Biologie: oder, Philosophie der lebenden Natur für Naturforscher und Aerzte*. 6 vols. Göttingen: Johann Friedrich Röwer, 1802–1822.

Tsouyopoulos, Nelly. "The Influence of John Brown's Ideas in Germany." *Medical History*, supplement 8 (1988): 63–74.

Unna, Yvonne. "A Draft of Kant's Reply to Hufeland: Autograph, Transcription (Wolfgang G. Beyerer), and English Translation (Yvonne Unna)." *Kant-Studien* 103, no. 1 (2012): 1–24.

———. "A Draft of Kant's Reply to Hufeland: Key Questions in Kant's Dietetics and the Problem of Its Systematic Place in His Philosophy." *Kant-Studien* 103, no. 3 (2012): 271–91.

Vaihinger, Hans. *The Philosophy of the "As If."* Translated by C. K. Ogden. London: Routledge & Kegan Paul, 1935.

Vanzo, Alberto. "Christian Wolff and Experimental Philosophy." *Oxford Studies in Early Modern Philosophy* 7 (2015): 225–55.

Verri, Pietro. *Gedanken über die Natur des Vergnügens.* Translated by Christoph Meiners. Leipzig: Weygand, 1777.

———. *Idee sull'indole del piacere.* Livorno: Giuseppe Galeazzi, 1774.

Vignemont, Frédérique de. *Mind the Body: An Exploration of Bodily Self-awareness.* Oxford: Oxford University Press, 2018.

Völker, Jan. *Ästhetik der Lebendigkeit: Kants dritte Kritik.* Munich: Wilhelm Fink, 2011.

Walsh, Denis. *Organisms, Agency, and Evolution.* Cambridge: Cambridge University Press, 2015.

Wasianski, E. A. C. *Immanuel Kant in seinen letzten Lebensjahren.* Königsberg: Friedrich Nicolovius, 1804.

Weikard, Adam Melchior. *Johann Browns Grundsätze der Arzneilehre aus dem Lateinischen übersetzt.* Frankfurt a. M.: Andreä, 1795.

Weiskel, Thomas. *The Romantic Sublime: Studies in the Structure and Psychology of Transcendence.* Baltimore: Johns Hopkins University Press, 1976.

White, Stephen K. "Burke on Politics, Aesthetics, and the Dangers of Modernity." *Political Theory* 21, no. 3 (1993): 507–27.

Wieland, Wolfgang. *Urteil und Gefühl: Kants Theorie der Urteilskraft.* Göttingen: Vandenhoeck & Ruprecht, 2001.

Wiesing, Urban. "Der Tod der Auguste Böhmer: Chronik eines medizinischen Skandals, seine Hintergründe and seine historische Bedeutung." *History and Philosophy of the Life Sciences* 11, no. 2 (1989): 275–95.

———. "Immanuel Kant, His Philosophy and Medicine." *Medical Health Care and Philosophy* 11 (2008): 221–36.

Williams, Howard. "Metamorphosis or Palingenesis: Political Change in Kant." *Review of Politics* 63, no. 4 (2001): 693–722.

Wilson, Catherine. "The Building Forces of Nature and Kant's Teleology of the Living." In *Kant and the Laws of Nature*, edited by Michela Massimi and Angela Breitenbach, 256–74. Cambridge: Cambridge University Press, 2016.

Wilson, Holly. *Kant's Pragmatic Anthropology.* Albany: State University of New York Press, 2006.

Wolff, Christian. *Psychologia empirica.* Frankfurt, 1738.

Wordsworth, William. " 'The Sublime and the Beautiful.' " In *The Sublime Reader*, edited by Robert R. Clewis, 177–83. London: Bloomsbury, 2019.

Zammito, John H. *The Genesis of Kant's "Critique of Judgment."* Chicago: University of Chicago Press, 1992.

———. *The Gestation of German Biology: Philosophy and Physiology from Stahl to Schelling.* Chicago: University of Chicago Press, 2017.

———. “Kant and the Medical Faculty: One ‘Conflict of the Faculties.’ ” *Epoché* 22, no. 2 (2018): 429–51.

———. “ ‘This Inscrutable *Principle* of an Original *Organization*’: Epigenesis and ‘Looseness of Fit’ in Kant’s Philosophy of Science.” *Studies in History and Philosophy of Science* 34, no. 1 (2003): 73–109.

Zöller, Günter. “Mechanism or Organism: Kant on the Symbolic Representation of the Body Politic.” In *Kant and the Metaphors of Reason*, edited by Patricia Kauark-Leite, Giorgia Cecchinato, Virginia de Araujo Figueiredo, Margit Ruffing, and Alice Serra, 303–20. Hildesheim: Olms, 2015.

Zuckert, Rachel. “Boring Beauty and Universal Morality: Kant on the Ideal of Beauty.” *Inquiry* 48, no. 2 (2005): 107–30.

———. *Kant on Beauty and Biology: An Interpretation of the “Critique of Judgment.”* Cambridge: Cambridge University Press, 2007.

Index

Persons

Addison, Joseph, 159, 168
Allison, Henry E., 23, 71, 118, 124, 146, 176–177, 182, 184–187, 189, 195, 289, 301
Aquinas, Thomas, 8, 28, 59–64, 67
Arendt, Hannah, 28, 30, 200, 211, 213
Aristotle, 28, 38, 59–61, 70, 115, 241–242, 271, 301
Arnoldt, Daniel Heinrich, 86
Augustine, 205–206

Baumgarten, Alexander, 8, 34, 83–92, 94–101, 103–105, 159, 168–169, 279–282
Beiser, Frederick, 23, 91
Bergson, Henri, 211
Blumenbach, Johann Friedrich, 252, 296
Brady, Emily, 160, 171–172, 177
Brandom, Robert, 177
Brown, John, 284–289
Buchenau, Stefanie, 90, 95
Budd, Malcolm, 171
Buffon, Georges-Louis Leclerc de, 242
Burke, Edmund, 14, 20, 25, 130, 136, 140–142, 145, 159, 162–168, 173, 194, 239–240, 267–268
Burnham, Douglas, 191

Cassirer, Ernst, 3, 5, 37, 47, 221
Clewis, Robert R., 10–11, 145, 180, 192
Crowther, Paul, 132, 149, 171, 180
Crusius, Christian August, 8, 62–68, 71, 85, 216

Deligiorgi, Katerina, 145, 170, 173, 177
Descartes, René, 114, 242, 272
Doran, Robert, 146

Epicurus, 167, 233, 324, 336

Fichte, Johann Gottlieb, 28, 35, 241, 267
Figal, Günter, 26, 36, 113
Forsey, Jane, 171
Foucault, Michel, 83, 171
Frederick the Great, 240, 242, 255
Frederick, William II, 252, 254–255
Fugate, Courtney D., 7–8, 13, 57, 85, 216

Gadamer, Hans-Georg, 5, 6, 21, 26–28, 36, 200, 210
Gasché, Rodolphe, 12, 22, 24, 305
Gentz, Friedrich, 239–241, 255, 267–269

Ginsborg, Hannah, 176, 230–231, 233, 301–303
Guyer, Paul, 27–28, 78, 91, 103, 110, 118, 156–157, 169, 175, 178, 188, 204, 237

Hadot, Pierre, 83
Hegel, Georg Wilhelm Friedrich, 1, 21–22, 26, 28, 33, 58, 125, 158
Herder, Johann Gottfried, 14, 240–241, 251–252, 256
Herz, Marcus, 46
Hobbes, Thomas, 14, 241–242, 250
Hölderlin, Friedrich, 1–2, 21–22, 35
Huseyinzadegan, Dilek, 11–12, 133, 139, 176, 190, 199

Kielmeyer, Carl Friedrich, 16, 293, 297, 313–316, 318

Lebrun, Gérard, 198, 213
Leibniz, Gottfried Wilhelm, 62, 85, 97, 114–115, 159
Lloyd, David, 180, 184, 193
Lyotard, Jean-François, 24, 130, 158, 160, 204

Makkreel, Rudolf A., 3, 10, 13, 15, 25–26, 34, 57, 87, 98, 102, 104, 112, 135, 139, 147, 160–161, 167, 182, 187–188, 190, 195, 216, 218–219, 227, 229–230, 236, 275, 291, 297–298, 322, 331, 333, 337
Marwah, Inder, 194–195
McQuillan, J. Colin, 8–9, 84, 86, 97, 99–100
Meier, Georg Friedrich, 8–9, 84, 89, 91–100, 104–105
Mensch, Jennifer, 6, 29, 62, 102, 116, 235, 252, 259, 310–311
Meredith, James Creed, 233–234
Moore, Thomas, 180, 192
Munzel, G. Felicitas, 16–17

Nehamas, Alexander, 83
Nietzsche, Friedrich, 21, 83, 223
Nuzzo, Angelica, 3, 125

Olson, Michael, 15

Plato, 25, 28, 58, 241
Pyrrho of Elis, 153–154

Rehburg, August Wilhelm, 255
Risser, James, 6–7
Rousseau, Jean-Jacques, 14, 242–244, 248, 250

Schelling, Friedrich Wilhelm Joseph, 1, 16, 21–22, 28, 273, 293, 297, 313, 315–318
Schiller, Friedrich, 1, 21, 23, 26, 158, 270
Schmidt, Dennis J., 6
Schwaiger, Clemens, 94
Schweizer, Hans Rudolf, 91
Shaftesbury, Anthony Ashley-Cooper, 211, 323
Shapshay, Sandra, 142, 171
Shell, Susan, 14, 245–246, 250, 255, 311
Spivak, Gayatri Chakravorty, 180, 184, 191, 193
Steigerwald, Joan, 15–16, 294, 303, 306, 314
Sweet, Kristi, 9, 151

Treviranus, Gottfried Reinhold, 314, 316

Vaihinger, Hans, 45
Vico, Giambatista, 170, 211
Völker, Jan, 205

Weiskel, Thomas, 140
Wilson, Holly, 98
Wolff, Caspar Friedrich, 252, 296
Wolff, Christian, 62, 91, 94, 96–97, 159, 280

Zammito, John H., 5, 22, 29, 46, 48, 57, 124, 126, 252, 276, 282, 292, 296
Zuckert, Rachel, 10–11, 20, 102, 118–119, 134, 168, 173, 276, 308

Terms

Abstraction, 12, 92, 212
Adaptation, 7, 13, 47, 58, 107, 231, 235, 251, 315
Aesthetic affect, 94–95, 248
Aesthetic ideas, 2, 10, 33–35, 122, 139, 120, 126–127, 276, 359
Aesthetic perfection, 8, 83–85, 89–93, 96, 98, 100, 101–105
Agreeable, 76–77, 79, 89, 97, 99, 118, 176, 274, 283, 290, 323
Agreeableness, 103, 161, 100, 104, 133, 177, 197–199, 201, 213, 217, 267, 305, 319
Agreement, 53–54, 68, 70, 73, 77, 89–90, 93–94, 97–98, 326, 332
Amazement, 53, 160, 177
Analogon rationis, 69, 202
Analogy, 7–8, 38, 42, 44, 69, 74, 135, 142, 147, 230, 237, 241, 251, 257–259, 261, 265, 267, 269, 289, 301–302, 304–306, 312, 316
Analytic of the Beautiful, 75–76, 104, 119, 182, 205, 274
Animal, 8, 28, 31, 38, 59–60, 63
Anlage, 29, 180, 186–187, 189–193, 195, 296, 329–331, 340
Anthropology, 11, 15, 17, 28, 31, 48, 50, 84, 96, 98–101, 103, 105–106, 130, 162, 164–166, 169, 195, 216, 218, 221–223, 226, 242, 261–262, 271, 275, 277–289, 291, 320–322, 324, 327, 329–330, 333, 335, 337–338
Anticipation, 88, 92, 95, 138, 225, 274, 314
Apperception, 173, 177, 226, 304
Aptitude, 17, 190, 322, 328–331, 335, 339–340
Art
  Artifacts, 230, 237, 300, 301
  Fine, 3–5, 72, 122, 220, 274, 301
  Philosophy, 83–85
Assent, 12, 52, 134, 186, 197–202, 304
Attunement, 206, 326, 330, 338
Autonomy, 14, 16, 23–24, 80, 168, 248, 254, 266, 320

Beautiful, 3–4, 8–11, 15, 19–20, 22–23, 25–32, 36–40, 47, 49, 51–53, 55, 58, 74–77, 79, 82, 84, 89–95, 97–98, 101–102, 104, 109, 112, 118–127, 131, 133–134, 149–150, 155–156, 162, 164, 166, 173, 181–182, 184, 187, 192, 194, 197, 199, 201–203, 205, 210, 217, 219, 274, 276, 290–291, 301, 304, 308, 325, 33
Beauty
  Accessory, 9, 51, 52
  Free, 51
Begreifen, 227, 236
Biology, 16, 102, 228, 294–295, 312, 317–318

Causality, 13, 20, 44, 48, 68, 70, 77–79, 110, 117, 121, 147–148,

Causality *(continued)*
229–230, 234, 248–249, 258–259, 298–302, 306, 310, 319
Chemistry, 240, 300, 316, 332
Citizen, 244, 256, 260–262, 264–267, 269
Clarity
Extensive, 86, 89, 93–94
Intensive, 86, 88
Cognition
A Posteriori, 96
A Priori, 42, 96
Clear, 88
Empirical, 308
In General, 26, 78, 84, 92, 105, 204, 207, 213–214
Intellectual, 8, 84, 89, 97–98
Life of, 94, 105
Liveliness, 8, 63, 65, 68, 71, 84–90, 92–95, 99, 124
Obscure, 88, 93, 209
Sensible, 8, 84, 87–93, 97–98, 100–103, 105
Color, 85, 93–94
Common Sense, 12, 31, 186, 208–212
Communicability, 12, 25–26, 30, 32, 35, 80, 200, 203–204, 206
Community, 12–14, 110, 198–200, 202, 205, 210–211, 213, 219, 223, 229–230, 240–241, 244–245, 253–254, 265–267, 305
Comprehension, 13–14, 86, 138, 215, 219, 225, 227, 230, 232, 235–238
Consciousness, 99–100, 105, 150, 168, 172, 177, 186–189, 195, 206, 222, 225, 247, 259, 297–298, 304–305, 320, 322–328, 331–336, 338–339
Critique of Taste, 25, 46, 75, 81, 84
Culture, 10–12, 20, 54, 108, 133, 143–144, 149, 176, 180–181, 183–195, 263, 327
Death, 28, 66, 69, 140, 162, 168, 196, 240, 254, 263, 286
Deduction, 11–12, 23, 26, 58, 74, 79–80, 134, 170, 176, 179–181, 184–189, 192–195, 225, 301, 306, 312
Delight, 140–141, 159, 163, 167, 335–336
Design, 13–14, 29, 42, 47–48, 230–232, 234, 237, 290–301, 303, 308
Desire, 9, 25, 39, 42, 45–46, 49, 52, 66–69, 72, 92, 94–95, 101–105, 113, 126, 143, 148, 150, 190, 216–217, 248, 243, 259–260, 304, 323–324, 336, 338
Despotism, 190–191, 250
Dialectic of Aesthetic Judgment, 80–81, 109, 143, 274, 309, 311
Duty, 39, 107, 110, 266, 277, 319–324, 330–332, 338, 340

Emotion, 87, 91, 95, 140, 142, 155, 161, 164, 218
Empirical Psychology, 50, 85, 88, 96, 98, 105, 175, 190, 195, 279
Enliven, 6, 54, 63–65, 72–73, 78–79, 85, 105–106, 114, 141, 144, 148, 178, 207, 214–219, 226, 291, 298, 320, 333
Epigenesis, 231, 234–235, 252, 259
Equilibrium, 15, 71, 217, 219–220, 232, 278, 281–285, 289, 291
Examples, 3, 5, 69, 86, 93, 130, 183, 193, 213, 285, 300–301

Feeling
Aesthetic, 73, 149, 215, 218, 238, 322, 331
Fear, 11, 107, 135–137, 139–141, 144, 146, 160, 162–163, 166, 168, 170, 218, 274, 332

Feeling *(continued)*
Health, 15, 69, 71–72, 137, 158–159, 164, 168, 209–210, 212, 220, 243–244, 271, 273–292, 336
Horror, 163, 165, 167
Moral, 6, 17, 30, 39–40, 52, 73, 80, 122, 133, 139, 148–150, 186–187, 189, 320–324, 330–332, 334, 337–338
Pain, 9, 11, 15, 50, 55, 69, 73, 85–87, 94–95, 98–106, 129, 132, 140, 149, 153, 155, 165, 167, 175, 219, 277, 279–283, 285, 324–325, 327, 335–337
Pleasure, 5, 9, 13, 15, 19–20, 22–27, 29–31, 36, 39–40, 46–53, 66–70, 72–76, 79–80, 86–87, 94–95, 97–106, 119, 129, 132, 134, 136–138, 140–141, 145, 147, 149, 153, 155–167, 169, 173, 175, 178–179, 181–183, 187, 197, 199, 203–208, 211, 213–214, 216–219, 232, 274–275, 279–281, 283, 285, 290–291, 297–298, 304–305, 319–326, 328, 332–333, 335–338
Respect, 133, 150, 333
Terror, 11, 15, 160, 162, 164–165, 179
Foresight, 88, 92, 95
Freedom, 1–2, 4–7, 10, 12, 20, 27–28, 36, 38, 41–47, 50–55, 64, 70–74, 76–77, 103, 108–113, 118–119, 121–127, 147, 158, 160, 168, 172, 177, 191, 193–194, 226, 237, 240, 243–245, 247, 249–255, 264, 266, 269, 276–277, 320, 322, 325, 328, 333–334, 338–341
Free Play, 5–13, 15, 25–27, 29, 31–32, 39, 46, 49–50, 78, 99–100, 102, 105–106, 122, 155, 162, 173, 203–207, 211, 213, 217–220, 224, 226, 229, 247, 274–275, 282–283, 290–292, 304–305, 308, 320, 335–336
French Revolution, 15, 240, 244, 249, 255

Gemüt(h), 24–27, 29–30, 33, 39, 43, 46, 48, 50, 65, 222, 226, 297, 321, 323–324, 326–331, 333–334, 337
Generation, 16, 143, 163, 233, 243, 251, 265, 268–269, 295, 297, 300, 312–313
Genius, 2–6, 29, 33–34, 39, 72, 121, 123, 244, 301

Ideas of Reason, 122–123, 132, 147, 154–155, 186, 191, 326
Ideal of Beauty, 9, 52, 107–109, 111, 113, 118–124, 126–127
Illusion, 110, 162, 174, 212, 323, 334, 337
Imagination, 5, 9, 11, 13, 15, 33–34, 50, 78, 88, 92, 102, 105, 122–123, 126, 132–133, 135–140, 142, 145, 147, 150, 153, 155–156, 158–163, 165, 169–171, 173–176, 179, 181–184, 187, 189, 192, 204, 206–207, 212, 214, 216, 218–219, 225–227, 229–230, 236, 246, 274, 290, 303–305, 325–326, 333, 335
Individuation, 294–295, 315–318
Inertia, 66, 242, 259
Inner sense, 48, 159, 173, 205, 232, 337
Invention, 88, 92, 94–95

Judgment
Aesthetic, 3, 7–9, 12–13, 23, 25, 30, 32, 34, 36, 46–47, 50, 53,

Judgment, Aesthetic *(continued)* 58, 74–76, 80–81, 85, 102–103, 166, 173–175, 177, 181, 189–190, 198, 200–201, 203–205, 208, 215, 217, 220, 232, 236, 274–276, 290–292, 298–299, 301, 306, 311, 324
  Reflective, 2, 22–23, 25–26, 31, 44–51, 55, 108, 112, 116, 118, 181, 212, 227, 229, 232, 235, 238, 254, 295, 299, 303–308, 310–312, 318
  Teleological, 3, 7, 47, 54, 57, 102, 109, 215, 220, 227, 232, 236–237, 291, 295, 298–299, 301, 305, 307–312

Life
  Animal, 70–74, 76–79, 82, 205, 214, 222, 256, 298
  Definition of, 66–67, 77–78, 215, 335
  Ethical, 47–54
  Feeling of, 6, 8, 17, 19–20, 22, 24–27, 29–32, 34–40, 50, 73, 75, 80, 85, 104, 106, 108, 126, 145, 151, 153, 155, 161, 166, 182, 205–208, 214–215, 217–218, 227, 232, 238, 275, 279–281, 291–292, 297–298, 304, 321–322, 331, 338
  Furtherance of, 6, 15, 45, 50–51, 53–55, 68
  Hindrance of, 68–69, 73, 99, 164, 282, 284, 335
  Human, 17, 47, 53, 58, 72–80, 109–110, 118, 121, 124, 151, 205, 215–216, 221, 226, 277, 287–289, 292, 298, 302, 337, 339, 341
  Organic, 2–3, 7, 13, 15–16, 116, 205, 234, 254, 256, 289, 293–295, 297, 314–315, 318
  Principle of, 6, 24, 61, 64, 66, 70–71, 78, 98, 104, 125, 233, 237, 241, 320, 327–328, 331, 335–336
  Promotion of, 15, 17, 99, 118, 161–162, 164, 167, 282–283 284, 320, 322, 333–335, 341
  Sciences, 7, 116, 271, 317–318
  Spiritual, 70–74, 76, 78, 214
Language, 5, 14, 24, 30, 32–37, 45, 64–65, 133, 144, 163, 179, 189, 211, 217, 220, 223, 232, 251, 267–268, 273, 323, 327, 332
Liveliness, 8, 63, 65, 68, 71, 84–90, 92–94, 99, 124
Living, 9–10, 20, 50, 54, 59–60, 62–67, 74, 78, 83, 94, 97, 104–105, 114–117, 124–125, 131, 149–150, 200, 207, 222, 226–227, 234, 237–238, 240, 242–243, 248–249, 253, 256–258, 261, 267, 275, 281, 289–290, 294, 312–318, 328, 332, 340

Mechanism, 13, 16, 65, 124, 140–142, 145, 227–229, 232, 234, 247–250, 254, 263, 299–300, 309–311, 318, 333, 339
Mental, 9–10, 13–15, 25, 31, 43–44, 48, 64, 75, 78–80, 111, 125, 150, 156, 159, 173, 184, 206, 214, 216–220, 223, 226–227, 234, 238, 275–278, 290–292, 298, 302, 314, 333
Metamorphosis, 263, 267–269
Metaphor, 37, 93, 111, 148, 159, 211, 232, 240–241, 266–267, 298

Metaphysics, 21, 62, 64, 88, 96, 98, 101, 104, 106, 164, 216, 242, 255, 271
Mind, 3–9, 11, 13, 15, 23–24, 26–30, 32–33, 35–39, 43, 48, 50, 52–55, 61, 65, 76, 79, 95–97, 99, 103, 110–111, 124–125, 133, 137, 145, 149–150, 154–155, 159–161, 166, 170, 173, 182–183, 185–186, 188, 191, 203–204, 206–209, 211, 213–214, 217–223, 225–226, 232, 235, 237–238, 274, 276–277, 282, 288–292, 297–298, 304–305, 308, 314, 320–340
Modality, 12, 175, 180–185, 193
Monarchy, 243, 249, 253–254, 257–258, 263
Moral Character, 52, 268, 325–326, 329, 340
Moral destination, 53, 218, 221
Morality, 12, 17, 34, 52, 73, 134, 138–139, 143, 145–150, 168, 169, 171, 175, 191, 193, 217, 320–323, 325, 327, 330–331, 334, 338
Music, 15, 220, 274–276, 282, 290–291, 298

Natural history, 293, 295–296, 299, 314, 318
Normativity, 176–178, 231–232

Organism, 4, 7–8, 13–14, 16, 57, 102, 110, 112, 116–118, 207, 215–222, 227–235, 237–239, 243, 248–250, 252, 256, 260, 268, 275, 293–306, 308, 318
Organization, 13, 54, 117, 229–232, 235, 238–239, 250, 253, 256–258, 267, 275, 294–295, 299, 306, 310, 312–317, 339
Organized beings, 16, 233, 258, 266, 296–297, 299–300, 302, 305–313, 315
Orientation, 2, 13, 23, 47, 116, 227, 232

Pain, 9, 11, 15, 50, 55, 69, 73, 85–87, 94–95, 98–106, 129, 132, 140, 149, 153, 155, 165, 167, 175, 219, 277, 279–283, 285, 324–325, 327, 335–337
Palingenesis, 251, 263, 268
Peasant, 133, 183, 186–187, 195
Personality, 17, 221, 224–225, 322, 334, 337–341
Pleasure, 5, 9, 13, 15, 19–20, 22–27, 29–32, 36, 29–40, 46–53, 66–70, 72–76, 79–80, 86–87, 94–95, 97–106, 119, 129, 132, 134, 136–138, 140–141, 145, 147, 149, 153, 155–167, 169, 173, 175, 178–179, 181–183, 187, 197, 199, 203–208, 211, 213–214, 216–219, 232, 274–275, 279–281, 283, 285, 290–291, 297–298, 304–305, 319–326, 328, 332–333, 335–338
Poetry, 1, 5, 35, 84–87, 89
Power(s)
  Choice, 224, 328–329, 338
  Organic, 235, 313–314
  Vital, 129, 141–142, 144–146, 148, 150, 153, 156, 188, 195, 218, 313, 315
Practical reason, 2, 16, 108–109, 118, 131, 134, 137, 142–144, 148–150, 169, 187–188, 192, 214, 277, 302, 304, 310, 321–326, 331–332

Predisposition, 29, 180, 186–187, 189–191, 194–196, 221–225, 234–235, 246–247, 251–252, 254, 261, 296, 340
Purposive (-ity, -ness), 4, 13, 26, 29, 45, 47–55, 58, 78–79, 102–103, 113, 116, 118–120, 159, 170, 173, 175, 182–184, 188, 192, 196, 203, 207, 214–219, 226, 228–229, 231–238, 245, 254, 256, 275, 291, 296, 302, 304–312, 315, 318, 333

Quantity, 60, 88, 90, 91, 93, 135, 182, 208, 287
Quickening, 5–9, 15, 25, 27–29, 36–37, 39, 206–207, 282, 290–291, 298, 304

Reciprocity, 8, 13, 16, 204, 219, 227, 297
Regress, 139, 187, 218–219, 225
Regulative, 118, 202, 214, 227, 235, 237, 247, 257, 275, 303, 305–306, 309–310
Republicanism, 243, 268
Responsiveness, 238, 298, 321–323, 327, 330–332, 337
Rhetoric, 85, 88, 89, 200, 210, 242, 245, 251, 271, 313
Rule
  Cognitive, 4, 23, 26–27, 45–46, 65, 77, 79, 89, 92–95, 100–102, 104–105, 119–120, 147–148, 162, 201–202, 211, 214, 232, 236, 257–258, 305, 308, 320–321, 329, 338
  Political, 244, 252, 254, 256–258, 262–263, 266–269

Savage, 133, 183, 186–189, 195, 261, 265, 269
Self-awareness, 117, 153, 157, 169–174, 177, 323
Sensation, 11, 15, 27, 50, 64–64, 72, 96, 116, 118, 161, 166–167, 173, 225, 274, 282–283, 288, 290, 323, 325, 332, 336, 338
Sensus communis, 12–13, 30–32, 73, 175, 200, 205, 208–214, 305
Simultaneity, 218–219, 230
Soul, 8, 14, 29, 35, 59, 61–63, 65–66, 86, 88, 92, 94–95, 101, 115, 117, 123–124, 220–223, 225–227, 233, 237–238, 242–243, 245, 251–252, 257, 259, 263, 291, 302, 316, 325–327, 334, 337, 339
Spirit, 3, 5–6, 13, 20, 26, 29, 31, 33–35, 62–65, 69, 74–76, 78, 82, 92, 95, 116, 124, 126, 145, 149, 151, 214, 216, 218, 221–222, 224–227, 237–238, 242, 245, 268, 276, 288, 292, 298, 327, 337
Spontaneity, 69–70, 72, 76, 79, 124, 222, 226–227, 238, 249, 292, 298, 331
Subreption, 132–133, 168, 171, 174, 323
Symbol, 6, 13, 33–34, 36–37, 52, 131, 145, 147–150, 230, 257–258, 269
Synopsis, 89–90, 93

Taste, 4, 8, 12, 22–25, 27, 31–34, 36–37, 46–47, 49–50, 52, 57, 72–82, 84, 92, 100, 102–104, 108–109, 118–120, 122, 126–127, 161, 177, 183, 186, 188, 197–206, 208–214, 251, 304–306, 311, 324, 326
Tragedy, 158, 162
Trope, 63, 93–94
Truth, 8, 21, 71, 81, 84, 87, 89, 93, 99, 109, 112, 200, 211, 314

Validity, 25, 79, 82, 131, 170, 174, 179, 181–182, 184, 194, 198, 201, 204, 208–209, 289, 304–306